CIVIL WAR VETERANS
IN THE
20TH CENTURY

EXTRACTED
FROM

THE
ELIZABETH DAILY JOURNAL

ELIZABETH
NEW JERSEY

Harry George Woodworth

HERITAGE BOOKS
2012

HERITAGE BOOKS
AN IMPRINT OF HERITAGE BOOKS, INC.

Books, CDs, and more—Worldwide

For our listing of thousands of titles see our website at
www.HeritageBooks.com

Published 2012 by
HERITAGE BOOKS, INC.
Publishing Division
100 Railroad Ave. #104
Westminster, Maryland 21157

Copyright © 2003 Harry George Woodworth

Other Heritage Books by the author:
Civil War Veterans in the 20th Century: Extracted from the Elizabeth Daily Journal, Elizabeth, New Jersey
Vital Statistics of Bridgewater, Massachusetts
Vital Statistics of Easton, Massachusetts, 1864 to 1910

All rights reserved. No part of this book may be reproduced or transmitted in any form or by any means, electronic or mechanical, including photocopying, recording or by any information storage and retrieval system without written permission from the author, except for the inclusion of brief quotations in a review.

International Standard Book Numbers
Paperbound: 978-0-7884-1894-5
Clothbound: 978-0-7884-9133-7

DEDICATION

I wish to dedicate this book to two of my great great grandfathers who served in the Civil War, and, according to family legend, a great great great grandfather, as well as one of my CW Vet's brother.

Norman G Makepeace was born in Taunton, MA, the son of George Washington and Hannah (Smith) Makepeace. He enlisted as a Private in Taunton on August 6, 1862, Co F, 39th Reg MA Vol Inf. He was wounded in action at the Battle of the Wilderness on May 4, 1864, and taken ill at Petersburg, VA, February, 1865. He was sent to the Regiment hospital then honorably discharged on May 19, 1865, Mower Hospital, near Philadelphia, PA. He died November 27, 1914, Brockton, MA.

Ebenezer J Packard was born in either West Bridgewater, or North Bridgewater now Brockton, MA, the son of Hosea and Roxanna (Holmes) Packard. He enlisted as a Private in Roxbury, MA, on August 29, 1864, Co M, 3rd Reg MA Hvy Art, wounded at Fort Bunker Hill, MD, April, 1865, and honorably discharged June 17, 1865, Washington, DC. He died October 15, 1909, Avon, MA.

Hosea S Packard, brother of Ebenezer, enlisted in the 8th Bat MA Vol, Captain Asa H Cook, and killed on Wednesday June 25, 1862, between Trenton and Bordentown, NJ, along with soldier George Smith, in a troop train wreck. Workmen had begun taking out track for repairs after President Lincoln's train had just passed. This was the custom of the time, and workmen usually knew if another train would be coming or not. They did not know Hosea's train was approaching, and the train could not stop in time. Six cars fell into the canal next to the Camden and Amboy railroad, and the two men drowned. Hosea was taken back to Easton, MA.

My family legend CW Vet was Navy Vet **Peter Groden**. An immigrant, he might have been a substitute sailor. I have asked different military agencies about him, but have never been able to obtain definitive proof on this family legend.

TABLE OF CONTENTS

DEDICATION	iii
PREFACE	vii
INTRODUCTION	ix
MILITARY DEFINITIONS	xiii
MILITARY TITLES	xv
ABBREVIATIONS	
Genealogical	xvii
General	xviii
Grand Army of the Republic Posts	xxi
Military	xxii
Religious	xxiii
CHAPTER 1 - Obituaries of CW Vets	1
CHAPTER 2 - CW Vets From Obituaries and Articles Of Family Members	170
CHAPTER 3 - Obituaries of Black CW Vets	182
CHAPTER 4 - Living CW Vets	188
CHAPTER 5 - Living Black CW Vets	210
CHAPTER 6 - Experiences Of:	212

    Francis A Bishop   Chaplains
    Isaac S Connett   William T Goggins
    John Jackson   Benjamin Lawrence
    Robert McCandless   Washington Mills
    Nurses   Rev A J Palmer
    George H Sanborn   Clark Snow
    Theodore E Squier   G Dwight Stone
    Henry H Todd   Jarvis W Williams

CHAPTER 7 - Monitor Controversy	234
CHAPTER 8 - 75th B&G Reunions	250
INDEX	267

PREFACE

This book is about Civil War Veterans (CW Vets) obtained from obituaries (obits) and articles taken primarily from the Elizabeth Daily Journal (EDJ) newspaper of Elizabeth, New Jersey. This newpaper was established as the New Jersey Journal at Chatham, NJ, in 1779 during the War of the Revolution by Capt Sheppard Kollack, an officer in the army of Washington. (1) The newspaper folded after an existence of over 200 years. I originally began using the EDJ searching for obits and articles on the Lithuanian community, especially for those who immigrated before WWI, and mailing the material to Jessie Ecker Daraska, Department of Immigration History, Balzekas Museum of Lithuanian Culture, Chicago, IL. She was preparing her now published book *The Lithuanian Pioneers*, which includes my maternal great grandparents. (2) Beginning with the mid 1950s EDJ, and working backwards in time, it was not long before I noticed obits on CW Vets, usually with a notation such as "last CW Vet of the county." I decided to begin copying these obits, as well as any article I came across. I thought this information might prove useful, since I was always searching for any and all information on the CW Vets of my family.

By the time I reached 1900 in the EDJ, I had a wealth of information, and knew that the information should be shared. Some obits were very brief, whereas some were long, listing almost, if not all, battles the Vet participated in. Many Vets were immigrants, with some being Vets of foreign wars previous to the CW. Sometimes no place of birth is mentioned, while others give the exact date of birth as well as place. People were already mobile inside the United States. Some Vets were born and died in one area of NJ, but others resided in different towns, perhaps moving in with a relative when they became aged. Some Vets born in other states died in the Elizabeth area, whereas some born in the Elizabeth region had "gone West." Some died away from their home visiting an out of state relative for the holidays, or perhaps at the shore trying to regain their health. This mobility for whatever reason has always been a problem for descendants and researchers obtaining genealogical information.

The year 1900 seemed to be the proper year to stop gathering information and begin compiling it. It is about the half-way point between the CW years and the year when the last Vet died. These Vets saw a tremendous advancement in technology, which we now take for granted. They celebrated the arrival of the 20th Century as we celebrated the arrival of the 21st Century, and the beginning of a new Millenium. They went from trying to prod recalcitrant battlefield mules to driving automobiles, with some taking control of the aircraft during the flight they received as a birthday present. There were wars before the CW. CW Vets saw the Spanish American War, WWI, and others, after. We saw WWII, the Korean War, Vietnam and others. Yet, their war was unique, where, at the end, Americans won and Americans lost. The CW seems far away now for most people, but it really is not. My possible Navy CW Vet was a German and married as her second husband an Irish woman. They had one daughter, born in 1856 in Clifden, County Galway, Ireland. She was 9 years old when the CW ended. He immigrated to Boston, MA, in 1863, and sent for his daughter Annie G. Groden, in 1875. She lived to the end of 1954, when I was 11 years old. I knew this lady who was born before the CW began. As of 2002, I have a 146 year connection through five generations of living people extending to before the CW, so the CW is not that far away for me.

I wish to thank my co-worker Dean Iovino for proof reading the material in this book. We both graduated from Kean College now University in 1985 with a BA in Earth Science, and now work together at the National Weather Service Warning and Forecast Office in Mt Holly, NJ. His tackling of my heavy usage of abbreviations to find possible errors in content was remarkable to behold. Also, Mt Holly forecasters Art Kraus and Joe "O E" Hasko, computer experts who more than once saved the Vets from taking a one way trip into cyberspace. Finally, my good friend Ray Dougherty, who kept things under control on the home front.

(1) Obit of Sheppard Kollack, 93, died Friday October 26, 1906, Red Bank. Grandson of the Captain.

(2) Daraska, Jessie Ecker. *The Lithuanian Pioneers, A Study of Lithuanian Immigration to the United States Before World War I*. Chicago, Illinois: John R. Daraska, 2000.

INTRODUCTION

The major section of this book consists of obits and some articles on CW Vets, Black CW Vets, and family members of CW Vets. Black CW Vets is a separate category only for the convenience of black readers and researchers. The family members obits contain references to Vets not listed in the obit section, with the Vet information underlined. Any family member obit that did reference a listed Vet was put with that Vet. Obit information is formatted into 8 sections, with abbreviations heavily used. Vets are listed alphabetically. Conflicting information such as two different middle initials given in the same obit is shown, for example, as B/D. A ? following a word signifies that the word was hard to read. If some of the letters of a word are not readable, ( ) with the readable letters is used, such as ( )nd. The obit of Charles William Maxfield is used here to show this format and usage of abbreviations. Section 1 discusses vital statistics. The obit states that he was born on Monday January 14, 1839, in East Chester, New York, and was the eldest son of the late John Gillen and Mary Elizabeth Maxfield. He died on Sunday August 21, 1910, at his home, 548 Westminster Avenue, Elizabeth, New Jersey. This is shown as: MAXFIELD, CHARLES WILLIAM, b Mon Jan 14, 1839, eldest s/o late John Gillen and Mary Elizabeth Maxfield, E Chester, NY, d Sun Aug 21, 1910, at home, 548 Westminster Ave, Eliz. If a date of birth was not given, but the age was, the age would follow the name. Eliz is used for Elizabeth, NJ. Other towns, cities and places are spelled out, with some exceptions being NYC for New York City, when specifically stated as such, SI for Staten Island, LI for Long Island, and PHL for Philadelphia. If the Vet was an immigrant, the country, if given, is spelled out in full.

Section 2 pertains to Vet survivors. Mr M was survived by four sons, Charles E Evans of Newark, John Guion of Springfield, Massachusetts, Edwin Rogers of Elizabeth, Howard Hoyt of Trenton, and one daughter, Mrs Mary Guion Rollinson of

Elizabeth. Also surviving were two brothers, John F and Joseph B, and three sisters, Mrs Thomas Oakes, Mrs Joseph Hague and Mrs John A Lawrence, all living in Bloomfield, NJ. His wife predeceased him. She was the former Ellen Scriven Evans, and they had married in April 1862. This is shown as: **SURV**: ch Charles Evans, Newark, John Guion, Springfield, MA, Edwin Rogers and Mrs Mary Guion Rollinson, E, and Howard Hoyt, Trenton. sib John F, Joseph B, Mrs Thomas Oakes, Mrs Joseph Hague and Mrs John A Lawrence, all Bloomfield. Late w was frmr Ellen Scriven Evans, m Apr 1862. The last name for ch and sib is not repeated when the same, unless to prevent possible confusion. If the Vet had named any grandchild(ren), the entire name is used. Names of generations beyond grandchildren were usually not given in the obits. When towns and cities are in New Jersey, NJ is not usually used. States outside of NJ are usually given in an obit. If not, it is mostly understood where the city is, such as PA when Philadelphia is mentioned by itself. If the place of birth and/or death is repeated inside the obit, just the first initial of that place is used, such as the above E for Elizabeth.

    Section 3 contains general information on the Vet. On his maternal side, Mr M was a direct descendant of the Guion family, among the first Huguenots to arrive. He was born in the old Guion homestead, a house dating back to Revolutionary times. He worked first with the Central bank in Brooklyn, rising to teller. He resigned to go into the wholesale fruit and produce business in New York. He resided in Bloomfield when young. He resided for 10 years in Metuchen before removing to Elizabeth twenty five years ago. This would be given as: On mo side, desc of the Guion fam, among the first Hugenots to arrive. b in the old Guion homestead, a house dating back to Rev times. First biz was with Central bank, Brooklyn, rising to teller. Resigned to go into the wholesale fruit and produce biz in NY. Res Bloomfield when yng. Res Metuchen 10 yrs bfr rem to E 25 yrs ago.

    Section 4 is on the membership of the Vet in any organization.

Mr B was a member of the Grand Army of the Republic, Ulric Dahlgren Post 25, Elizabeth. He belonged to the Veterans' Association of the Twenty Third Regiment. He was a mason, with the Washington Lodge in Elizabeth. This would be given as: **MEM:** UD25. VA of the 23rd Reg. A Mason, WL, E.

Section 5 shows the religious affiliation of the Vet. Mr M belonged to the Washington Avenue Baptist Church in Brooklyn when 18 years old. Next, the First Baptist Church in Metuchen, and then Eliz, where he was a Deacon, Trustee and Supervisor of the Sunday School. When he died he was teacher of the Baraca class, begun in 1899, and the only teacher the class ever had. This would be given as: **CHH:** Washington Ave Bapt, Brooklyn, ae 18. 1st Bapt in Metuchen, then E, a Deacon, Trustee and Super of the SS. At dod teacher of the Baraca class, begun 1899, only teacher class ever had.

Section 6 shows the CW military service of the Vet. Mr M joined the Twenty Third Regiment of Brooklyn. He was put on the hospital staff to treat the Gettysburg wounded. Regiment recalled to do riot duty in New York, and he was discharged shortly after as a Sargeant. This would be given as: **SERV:** Joined 23rd Reg of Brooklyn. Put on H staff to treat Gettysburg WIA. Reg recalled to do riot duty in NY. Disc shortly aft, as Sgt.

Section 7 shows any funeral and interment information. Mr M's funeral was Tuesday afternoon at his home, the Reverent Doctor Thomas Vassar officiating. This would be shown as: **F:** Tue aft at home, Rev Dr Thomas Vassar.

Section 8 is the reference to the obit. Mr M's obit appeared in the EDJ on Monday August 22, 1910. The reference would appear as Mon Aug 22. The year has already been given in Section 1. Should the obit have be gotten from another newspaper, the name of that paper will be given. In Mr M's example, the funeral info appeared two days after the obit, so the obit ref is given after the **SERV** section, and the funeral reference after the **F** information.

If one or more sections are not given, that information was not in the obit. If there is no mention of any CW service, the obit would have had a headline similar to "Civil War Veteran." With exceptions, no specific cause of death is mentioned in this book, nor are obit accolades and praisings of the deceased.

Chapter 4 is on Living CW Vets, with Chapter 5 on Living Black CW Vets. As in Chapter 2, any information gathered on a living Vet is put after an obit of that Vet, if there is one, for reader convenience. If enough information is available, the obit sections' format, such as **MEM, CHH,** and **SERV,** are used for consistency. The EDJ occasionally ran articles on what a Vet went through during a particular battle, and these important first-hand reports compile Chapter 6, and are primarily a quote of the newspaper article. As the newspaper years went by, a controversy seemed to develop about who was actually the last Monitor survivor of the famous Monitor and Merrimac battle. Chapter 7 is about this controversy (with the last survivor being found?). The book ends with the 75th Blue and Gray reunion, the final Reunion, at Gettysburg. The remaining Vets were now in their 90s and 100s, with time not on their side. This event more than any signified the end of the CW era, and is the proper place to end this book.

MILITARY DEFINITIONS

ARTILLERY - (1) Large-caliber firing weapons, such as howitzers and cannons, that are mounted and manned by crews. (2) Troops armed with artillery. (3) The branch of an armed force that specializes in the use of artillery. (4) The science of the use of guns; gunnery.

ARTILLERYMAN - A soldier in the artillery; artillerist.

AUXILIARY - Held in or used as a reserve; auxiliary troops.

BATTALION - (1) A tactical military unit typically consisting of a headquarters company and four infantry companies or a headquarters battery and four artillery batteries.(2) A large body of military troops.

BATTERY - (1) The basic tactical artillery unit, corresponding to the company in the infantry. (2) An emplacement for one or more pieces of artillery. (3) A set of guns or other heavy artillery, as on a warship.

BRIGADE - (1) A military unit consisting of a variable number of combat battalions. (2) A former unit of the U.S. Army composed of two or more regiments commanded by a Brigadier General.

COMPANY - A subdivision of a regiment or battalion, the lowest administrative unit, usually under the command of a Captain.

CORP - (1) A separate branch or department of the armed forces having a specialized function.(2) A tactical unit of ground combat forces between a division and an army commanded by a Lieutenant General and composed of two or more divisions and auxiliary service troops.

DIVISION (1) An administrative and tactical military unit that is smaller than a Corps but is self-contained and equipped for prolonged combat activity. (2) A group of several ships of similar type forming a tactical unit under a single command of the U.S. Navy.

HEADQUARTERS - The offices of a Commander as of a military unit from which official orders are issued.

INFANTRY - The branch of an army made up of units trained to fight on foot.

INFANTRYMAN - A soldier in the Infantry.

REGIMENT - A military unit of ground troops consisting of at least two battalions.

VOLUNTEER - (1) A person who performs or gives his services of his own free will. (2) Pertaining to or consisting of volunteers; a volunteer militia.

MILITARY TITLES

ADJUTANT - A staff officer who helps a commanding officer with administrative affairs.
ADMIRAL - In the U.S. Navy, U.S. Coast Guard, and Royal Canadian Navy, an officer of the next-to-the-highest rank.
ADMIRAL OF THE FLEET - The highest rank in the U.S. Navy and Royal Canadian Navy, equivalent to General of the Army or Field Marshall.
BRIGADIER GENERAL - An officer ranking between a Colonel and a Major General in the U.S. Army, Air Force, and Marine Corps.
CAPTAIN - (1) A commissioned officer in the Army, Air Force, or Marine Corps who ranks below a Major and above a First Lieutenant. (2) A commissioned officer in the Navy who ranks below a Commodore or Rear Admiral and above a Commander. **COLONEL** - A commissioned officer in the U.S. Army, Air Force of Marine Corps ranking above a Lieutenant Colonel and below a Brigadier General.
COMMANDANT - A commanding officer of a military organization.
COMMANDER - (1) An officer in the U.S. Navy who ranks next above a Lieutenant Commander and next below a Captain. (2) The chief commissioned officer of a military unit regardless of his rank.
COMMANDER-IN-CHIEF - (1) The supreme of all the armed forces of a nation. (2) The officer commanding a major armed force.
COMMANDING OFFICER - A U.S. Army officer in charge of a unit from company to regiment or of a post, camp, or station.
COMMODORE - An officer in the U.S. Navy ranking below Rear Admiral and above Captain. This rank was abolished in 1899 but temporarily restored during WWII.
CORPORAL - A noncommissioned officer ranking below Sergeant and above Private First Class in the U.S. Army, Air Force or Marine Corps.
ENSIGN - A commissioned officer of the lowest rank in the U.S. Navy or Coast Guard.
FIRST LIEUTENANT - A commissioned officer in the U.S. Army, Air Force or Marine Corps ranking above a Second Lieutenant.
GENERAL - An officer in the U.S. Army, Air Force or Marine Corps holding a rank above Colonel.
GENERAL OF THE ARMY - A General having the highest rank in the U.S. Army and having the insignia of 5 stars.
LIEUTENANT COLONEL - An officer in the U.S. Army, Air Force, or Marine Corps ranking above a Major and below a Colonel.

LIEUTENANT COMMANDER - An officer in the U.S. Navy or Coast Guard ranking above a Lieutenant and below a Commander.
LIEUTENANT GENERAL - An officer in the U.S. Army, Air Force, or Marine Corps ranking above a Major General and below a General.
MAJOR - An officer in the U.S. Army, Air Force, or Marine Corps ranking above a Captain and below a Lieutenant Colonel.
PETTY OFFICER - A naval noncommissioned officer.
PRIVATE - An enlisted man ranking below Private First Class in the Army or Marine Corps.
PRIVATE FIRST CLASS - An enlisted man ranking below Corporal and above Private in the Army or Marine Corps.
QUARTERMASTER - (1) A military officer responsible for the food, clothing, and equipment of troops. (2) A Petty Officer responsible for the navigation of a ship.
REAR ADMIRAL - A naval officer ranking below a Vice Admiral and above a Captain.
SECOND LIEUTENANT - An officer in the U.S. Army, Air Force or Maine Corps of the lowest commissioned grade, ranking below a First Lieutenant.
SERGEANT - (1) Any of several ranks of noncommissioned officers in the U.S. Army, Air Force or Marine Corps. (2) One that hold any of these ranks.
SERGEANT MAJOR - A noncommissioned officer serving as chief administrative assistant of a headquarters unit of the U.S. Army, Air Force, or Marine Corps.
VICE ADMIRAL - An officer in the U.S. Navy or Coast Guard ranking next below an Admiral.

ABBREVIATIONS

Genealogical

1/h, 2/h, etc - first husband, second husband, etc
1/w, 2/w, etc - first wife, second wive, etc
gch, ggch, etc - grandchildren, great grandchildren, etc
gch/o, ggch/o, etc - grandchildren of, great grandchildren of, etc
gdau, ggdau, etc - granddaughter, great granddaughter, etc
gd/o, ggd/o, etc - granddaughter of, great granddaughter of, etc
gf, ggf, etc - grandfather, great grandfather, etc
gf/o, ggf/o, etc - grandfather of, great grandfather of, etc
gm, ggm, etc - grandmother, great grandmother, etc
gm/o, ggm/o, etc - grandmother of, great grandmother of, etc
gs, ggs, etc - grandson, great grandson, etc
gs/o, ggs/o, etc - grandson of, great grandson of, etc

ae - aged
b - born
bro - brother(s)
bro/o - brother(s) of
ch - children
ch/o - children of
d - died/death
dau - daughter(s)
d/o - daughter of
dob - date of birth
dod - date of death
f - father
f/o - father of
h - husband
h/o - husband of

m - married
mo - mother
m/o - mother of
mn - maiden name
pb - place born
pd - place died
s - son
s/o - son of
sib - sibling(s)
sis - sister(s)
sis/o - sister(s) of
w - wife
w/o - wife of
wid - widow(er)
wid/o - widow(er) of

General

(A) - Article
abt - about
AC - Americus Couincil
aft - after
aftn - afternoon
ag - agriculture/agriculturist
AL - American Legion
AMR - American Red Cross
assist - assistant
assoc - association
Assoc P - Associated Press
ave - avenue
biz - business
bfr - before
bldg - building
B of - Board of
BNY - Brooklyn Naval Yard
B&L - Building and Loan
bldg - building
btwn - between
C - Confederate, the South
CBL- Catholic Benevolent Legion
CC - City Council
CE - Court Elizabeth
celeb - celebrate(d)
cem - cemetery
chap - chapter
Chapl - Chaplain
co - company/county
CoC - Chamber of Commerce
com- commission(er)/(ed)
comm - committee
ComC - Common Council
conf - conference
CP - Chief of Police
CSMA - Confederated Southern Memorial Assoc
cuz - cousin
DAR - Daughters of the American Revolution
DC - District of Columbia
Dem - Democrat
Dep - Deputy
dept - department
Desc - decendant/decended
dis - discontinue(d)
disb - disbanded
DL - Daughters of Liberty
E(rn) - East(ern)
EDJ - Elizabeth Daily Journal
EF(A) - Exempt Fireman (Association)
EL - Essex Lodge
Eliz - Elizabeth, New Jersey
employ -employ /employed / employee
Encmp - encampment / encamp(ed)
Engage - engagements
ERL - Esther Rebecca Lodge
est - established/establishment
eve - evening
Exp - experience(s)
F/F - funeral
(F) - Funeral article
F&AM - Free and Accepted Masons
fam - family
FD - Fire Department
Fed - Federal
FHC - Father Henry Council
fm - from
FOA - Foresters of America
for yrs - for many yrs/many years/for several years
fqt - frequent(ly)
gen - general
gens - generation(s)

xviii

H - hospital
hist - historic(al)/history
HL - Herman Lodge
HNS - Holy Name Society
HRS - Holy Rosary Society
imp - important
imm - immigrated/immigration
incld - including
Inst - Institute
int - interred
intl - international
IOF - Independent Order of Foresters
IOOF - Independent Order of Odd Fellows
IORM - Improved Order of Red Men
JL - Jerusalem Lodge
JP - Justice of the Peace
Jr - Junior
KP - Knights of Pithias
KT - Knights Templar
LCA - Letter Carriers Association
LH&L - Lafayette Hook and Ladder
LI - Long Island
LL - Lafayette Lodge
LoyL - Loyal Legion
LRC - Ladies' Relief Corps
manu - manufacture / manufacturing
MDAY - Memorial Day
mem - member
mos - months
mrng - morning
mu/i - muster(ed)(ing) in
mu/o - muster(ed)(ing) out
natl - national
NE - New England
ngt - night
NJJ - New Jersey Journal

n/o - number of
N(rn) - North(ern)
NYC - New York City
OB - Olive Branch
obit - obituary
occ - occupation
ocnl - occasional
OL - Orient Lodge
org - organization/organizer
otbrk - outbreak
ovr - over
P - Pastor
(P) - Picture
PC - Police Commissioner
PD - Police Department
PF - Police Force
PHL - Philadelphia, Pennsylvania
PJ - Police Justice
Pl - Place
PL - Progressive Lodge
PM - Postmaster
PO - Post Office
pos - position
PrS - private school(s)
Pres - President
PS - Public school(s)
Pub - publish(ed)(ing)
RA - Royal Arcanum
RC - Resolute Council
rcvd - received
Rd - Road
R - reunion
Repub - Republican
res - resident/resided/lived
ret - retired
riv - river
RJE - Red Jacket Engine
RR - railroad
S(m) - South(ern)
SAR - Sons of the American Revolution

SB - Shepherds of Bethlehem
SBS - Sick Benefit Society
Sec - Secretary
Sem - Seminary
S'H - (Disabled/Old) Soldiers' Home
SI - Staten Island
Singer - versions of: Singer Manufacturing Works, Singer Plant, Singer Sewing machine works, Singer Manufacturing Company, Singer Machine Company, Singer sewing machine, Singer Works
SL - Sons of Liberty
Soc - Society
SOCV - Sons of Confederate Vets
S&S' - Soldiers and Sailors'
S&D of L - Sons' and Daughters' of Liberty
sol - soldier(s)
SoV - Sons of Vets
Sq - Square
SS - Sunday school
st - street
ST - Sons of Temperance
surv - survivors
super - superintendent
SVA - Singer Vets Association
svc - service
svrl - several
sys - system
tdy - today
Theo - Theological/theology
TL - Tyrian Lodge
Tp - township
trans - transferred
transp - transportation
Treas - Treasurer/Treasury
U - Union, the North
UCV - United Confederate Vets

Univ - University
VA - Vets Association
vcnty - vicinity
VP - Vice President
VVFA - Vet Vol Firemen's Association
W(rn) - West(ern)
WCTU - Women's Christian Temperance Union
wk - week
WL - Washington Lodge
WRC - Women's Relief Corps
yng(st) - young(est)
yr - year(s)
ystdy - yesterday

Days of the Week: / Mon / Tue / Wed / Thu / Fri / Sat / Sun/
Months: / Jan / Feb / Mar / Apr / May /Jun / Jul / Aug / Sep/ Oct / Nov / Dec /

States: Abbreviated in two letter PO format. Ex: New Jersey =NJ.

NJ Grand Army of the Republic Posts

GVH3	Geo. Van Houten	Jersey City	Hudson Co
JAG4	James A Garfield	Newark	Essex Co
B8	Bayard	Trenton	Mercer Co
L11	Lincoln	Newark	Essex Co
UD12	Uzal Dodd	Orange	Essex Co
HW13	Henry Wilson	Jersey City	Hudson Co
AW23	Aaron Wilkes	Trenton	Mercer Co
UD25	Ulric Dahlgren	Elizabeth	Union Co
WFB27	William F Barry	Rahway	Union Co
JH32	Joe Hooker	Atlantic City	Atlantic Co
Z38	Zabriskie	Jersey City	Hudson Co
W45	Washington	Bordentown	Burlington Co
JBM46	James B Morris	Long Branch	Monmouth Co
LB48	Lambert Bowman	Flemington	Hunterdon Co
JBM52	James B McPherson	Hackensack	Bergen Co
A61	Arrowsmith	Red Bank	Monmouth Co
JK64	Judson Kilpatrick	Elizabeth	Union Co
BJ67	Boggs-Janeway	New Brunswick	Middlesex Co
WS73	Winfield Scott	Plainfield	Union Co
FL79	Frank Lloyd	South River	Middlesex Co
WCB85	William C Berry	Woodbridge	Middlesex Co
MLW88	Marcuc L Ward	Newark	Essex Co
EHW96	Edward H Wade	Millburn	Essex Co
GS100	Gen Sherman	Bayonne	Hudson Co
MA109	Maj Anderson	Plainfield	Union Co
USG117	U. S. Grant	Chatham	Morris Co

The NJ GAR reached its peak in 1892, when there were 117 Posts with abt 9,000 mem. At the beginning of 1933, there were only 119 CW Vets left. Thu Mar 30, 1933.

Military

Adj - Adjutant
AC - Army of the Cumberland
AJ - Army of the James
ANVA - Army of Northern VA
AP - Army of the Potomac
Art - Artillery
AW - Army of Washington
B&G - Blue and Gray
Bat - Battery
Brev - Brevet(ed)
Brig - Brigade
Brig Gen - Brigadier General
Btln - Battalion
Cav - Cavalry
cmd - command
Cmdr - Commander
CO - Commanding Officer
Co - Company
Col - Colonel
Comdt - Commandant
C - Confederate forces
Cpl - Corporal
CW - Civil War
Cwo - Chief Warrant Officer
disc - discharge(d)
Div - Division
Eng - Engineer
enl - enlisted
Ens - Ensign
GAR - Grand Army of the Republic
Gen - General
HQ - Headquarters
Inf - Infantry
IW - Indian War(s) (1790-1811)
KIA - Killed in Action

Lt - Lieutenant
Lt Col - Lieutenant Colonel
Lt Cmdr - Lieutenant Commander
Maj - Major
Major General
mil - militia/military
MW - Mexican War (1846-48)
NCO - Non Commissioned Officer
NG - National Guard
OD - Officer of the Day
pens - pension(ed)
PO - Petty Officer
POW - Prisoner of War
promo - promoted
Qtmstr - Quartermaster
Reg - Regiment
reup - reenlisted
RW - Revolutionary War (1775-1783)
S/AW - Spanish American War (1898)
serv - service
Sgt - Sargeant
Sgt Maj - Sargeant Major
U - Union forces
V - Vice
Vol - Volunteer
1812 - War of 1812 (1812-15)
WIA - Wounded in action
WP - West Point
WW - World War (I)
Z - Zouaves

Religious

AME - African Methodist Episcopalian

Bapt - Baptist

Chh - Church(es)

Cong - Congregational

Episc - Episcopal

Luth - Lutheran

Meth - Methodist

ME - Methodist Episcopalian

Presby - Presbyterian

Prot - Protestant

RC - Roman Catholic

CHAPTER 1

OBITUARIES OF CW VETS

A

ABBOTT, WILLIAM T, REV, 89, d Wed ngt May 27, 1925, at home, Asbury Park. Chapl of the NJ Dept GAR. **MEM:** New Brunswick ME Conf. Thu May 28. Opened the 44th annual GAR encmp of the Dept of NJ Thu mrng in the Masonic Temple, Trenton, with a prayer. Fri May19, 1911.

ACKERMAN, PHILIP, 67, d Thu Dec 8, 1910, at home, 537 Grier Ave, Eliz. **SURV:** ch George, Wharton, Philip, Jr, Newark, Mrs R Cook and J J, E, and Mrs G Lindemar, Dover. **SERV:** Co E, 7th Reg Inf, NJ Vol. Fri Dec 9.

ACKLEY, GEORGE F, 75, d Sun ngt Jun 27, 1915, at home, 91 Albert St, Rahway. **SURV:** w/ch Mrs Mary? Brandt, Mrs Carl D. Drake, Mabel, Olive, Wilbur, George, Robert and Edwin. 8 gch. Eng for the PA RR Co Ferry btwn Jersey City and NYC. **MEM:** R Lodge 25, AOUW, WFB27, and the RR Relief Assoc. **F:** Wed aftn, Albert St, Rev C S Kemble, P, Trinity ME. Mon Jun 28.

ADAMS, CHARLES C, b 1844, West Camp, Ulster Co, NY, d Mon ngt May 19, 1913, at old homestead of Adams fam, W Camp. **SURV:** w/sib Jeremiah E and James B, Eliz, and Mrs Henry L Norton, Jamaica, LI. Res Eliz 30+ yrs. In the coal biz. **MEM:** Charter mem UD25. **CHH:** Meth. **SERV:** 14th NJ Vol Inf 3 yrs. **F:** Int West Camp. May 20.

ADAMS, HUGH WHITE, MAJ, b 1843, Barbourville, KY, d Sun ngt Aug 6, 1916, at home, 252 Palisade Ave, Yonkers, NY. Res once in Eliz. **SERV:** Believed to be the yngst officer to cmd a Reg. Tue Aug 8.

ADAMS, JEREMIAH ELIGH, 77, b West Camp, NY, d early

1

Tue mrng Jun 22, 1915, at home, 134 Jefferson Ave, Eliz. **SURV:** 2/w. ch Mrs Amos Febrey, Samuel H, J E, Jr, and Mrs Herbert Loveland, E. 4 gch. bro-in-law of Henry L. Norton. Res E 50+ yrs. E 50+ yrs. Upon arrival, opened one of 1st grocery stores downtown. **MEM:** EL F&AM, and the Osceola Hose Co of Vol FD. One of 1st Repub of now 2nd Ward, with many primaries and election meetings held at his 1st St and Broadway store. Usually spent summers at Ocean Grove. **SERV:** Enl Brooklyn, NY, Reg, next day aft hearing war sermon preached by late Bishop Hurst of Fulton St ME. Tue Jun 22. (See: Norton, Henry L, Mr & Mrs, **"Living Vets"**)

AERZT, JOSEPH, d Sat Mar 26, 1904, Park Ridge. **MEM:** UD25. **F:** Int Mon. Tue Mar 29.

ALLEN, DAVID S, CAPT, b near Dover, d Wed mrng Dec 31, 1913, at home, Dover. **SURV:** ch Mrs E L Perry, 263 Orchard St, Eliz. Res D entire life. In plumbing and tinning biz. Dir D Trust Co, Park Union Lumber Co, and D B&L Co. **MEM:** B of Trade. **CHH:** D Presby. **SERV:** Co K, 39th NJ Vol, 9 mos. Recruited another Co, and Capt to end. WIA Petersburg, VA. Fri Jan 2, 1914.

ALLEN, JAMES WARNER, d NC, drowned on the Burnside Expedition to NC. Body brought back to NJ State Capital and taken to the State House. Apr 5, 1911.

ALLEN, JOHN C, 95, d Wed Nov 17, 1937, at home of dau Mrs John H. Gregg, Atlantic City. One of the last 2 CW Vets here. The only surv now is John Spanger, who moved here fm Phl a few yrs ago. **MEM:** JH32. Thu Nov 18.

There's no one left for John Allen, 94, to chat with about the war of '61 - no one, that is, who knows what it was all about. The d last Sun of his comrade-in-arms, Enos F Hann, 92, left Allen the sole surv mem of JH32. Allen walked feebly with Vets of more recent wars to his comrade's F ystdy and gave him a farewell salute. Thu Dec 10, 1936.

ALLEN, WILLIAM O, COL, 87, d Tue Sep 22, 1931, S'H, Kearny. **MEM:** Junior V-Cmdr GAR, Cmdr Emeritus Vets

Alliance Essex Co, Pres 39th NJ Vol Inf Assoc, frmr VP of B of Managers of the S'H. **SERV:** Enl Navy 1863, shipped on the bark "Midnight" for 1 yr, then enl Army. Tue Sep 22.

Allen, William O, of Newark, GAR Cmdr Dept of NJ, in charge of installing UD25 officers Tue ngt. Tue Jan 8, 1924.

ANDERSON, HANS, d Tue Apr 20, 1909, Brooklyn (See **Monitor**).

ANTHONY, JOSEPH, 81, b Alsace-Lorraine, d Sun Mar 31, 1929, at home, 849 Pond St, Eliz. **SURV:** ch Mrs Frances Scholl and Mrs Sylvia McCoy, E, Mrs Lorenzo Jenkins and Joseph, Jr, Paterson. Imm USA at an early age. Came to E fm Paterson 15 yrs ago. Employ by the Motor Transp Co. **CHH:** Sacred Heart. Mon Apr 1.

APGAR, ABRAHAM, 64, native of Cokesbury, Warren Co, d Thu ngt Apr 25, 1907, at home, 13 Baltic St, Eliz. **SURV:** w/ch John B, Charles F, Mrs William Whiting, Lillian and Minnie. Res E abt 25 yrs. **MEM:** UD25, and Carpenters Local Union 167. **SERV:** Enl Co F, 2nd NJ Cav, disc 1865 Vicksburg, MS. In many imp battles. **F:** Sun aftn at home. Int, by request, in S&S' plot, Evergreen. Fri Apr 26.

APPLEGET, THOMAS B, REV, 64, d Tue Feb 23, 1904, Cooper H, Camden. **SURV:** w/dau/s, PM at Hightstown, Mercer Co, Auditor of the West Jersey RR, Fqt visitor to Eliz. **CHH:** Meth clergyman. **SERV:** 9th NJ Vet Vol as Sgt, promo to Maj, disc 1865. **F:** Fri mrng at home, Hightstown. Thu Feb 25.

ARRIGHI, ANTONIO A, REV, 88, b Barga, Italy, d Sun eve Feb 25, 1923, at home of dau, in the boulevard, Westfield. **SURV:** ch Mrs Edwin H Oswald, W, Garry, Charles, Roswell, George and Howard, NY. Educ for ministry in Florence, Italy, and Boston Theo Sem. Meth preacher, then a Presby minister. P Emeritus of Broome St Tabernacle, NY, where a P for 40 yrs. Ret 10 yrs ago. Personal friend of Lincoln. Author of many books, incldg *Reminescences of Lincoln* and *Antonio, The Galley Slave*. Composed svrl revival hyms. Rem to W 4 yrs ago aft wife d. **SERV:** Drummer boy in Garibaldi's army in Italy. In CW, at

Wilson Creek. Mon Feb 26.

ASH, GEORGE W, 60, d last wk City H, Newark. Frmr res Eliz. Employ as clerk in meat markets in Cranford and Eliz. **SERV**: Enl ae 16 Co A, 1st NJ Vol. Mon Jun 8, 1914.

ASHE, SAMUEL, CAPT, 97, d Wed ngt Aug 31, 1938, at home, Raleigh, NC. Elected V-Cmdr C Vets in abstentia on Tue at 48th R in Columbia, SC. A newspaperman, hist, and Fed clerk. At Reunion, sol heard Pres J Rion McKissick, Univ of SC, say the signing of the Secession Ordinance was "the most solemn and impressive public ceremony in the hist of this state." Thu Sep 1.

ASHTON, JAMES YARD, REV, 91, d Feb 1902, Phl, PA. A Tamaqua, PA, ME minister, known as "The War Horse" during the CW because of his intense patriotism and strong U allegiance. Preached fiery sermons, with people coming to hear them from surrounding towns. Used his pulpit to denounce the C rebels while espousing the policies of Lincoln. It was said he bore a striking resemblance to Lincoln. "Upon svrl occasions, he was mistaken for the war president while in Phl and other cities," the Tamaqua Courier reported. "He was very proud of this resemblance, declaring that it was an honor to even resemble in appearance the greatest patriot that ever lived." **SERV**: Chapl for 4 mos in the field for PA troops in the early part of the CW. U Chapl did much more than preach to the troops. (See **Experiences**, Chaplains.) Times News (PA): Sat Apr 6, 2002, "Early Times Capsule," Jim Zbick, Times News reporter.

AUSTIN, HENRY C, d Wed mrng Nov 2, 1904, Amityville, LI, NY. **SURV**: w/s Harry, Eliz. Res Amityville for yrs. Came to Eliz soon aft CW, worked for late John W Benjamin's express biz btwn Eliz and NYC. Upon election of Benjamin to the CC, chosen as CP. **MEM**: Resolute Baseball Club, managed by Benjamin, and Vet Z, mem to dod as 2nd Lt. **SERV**: 82nd NY Vol, became Sgt. Serv to end, WIA svrl times. Taken prisoner at the Wilderness. POW Andersonville, GA, and Florence, SC. Endured prison life horrors, coming home a skeleton. **F**: Sat eve. Thu Nov 3.

AUSTIN, PERRY, 77, d Thu Nov 3, 1904, at home, Waukegan, Il. Picked by Lincoln to serv as a bodyguard because he was tallest man in Gen Winfield Scott Cav. Serv 17 mos. Spent last few yrs lecturing in schools on "Patriotism." Thu Nov 3.

AVERY, GEORGE B, 77, d Fri 323 pm Dec 10, 1920, at home, 22 Lewis St, Rahway. **SURV:** bro Frank E. Vet never m. Res entire life in R. **MEM:** WFB27. Vet d while Post in session GAR Hall. **SERV:** Co E, 14th NJ Vol, to end. Last surv mem of Co. Mon Dec 13, 1920.

Attended the complimentary dinner for WFB27 mems given by A Edward Woodruff Tue eve May 30, 1911.

AYRES, WILLIAM B, 77, d Fri Feb 21, 1908, Dunellen. **SURV:** 6ch. **MEM:** Howell Div, ST, Plainfield, the Grand Div of NJ, and WS73. **SERV:** Co C, frmr 14th NJ Vol, recruited in Eliz by Capt Chauncey Harris. Sat Feb 22.

B

BACON, SMITH, 75, d Tue Sep 28, 1915, Emergency H, Washington, as a result of being run over by a horse and buggy ystdy. Of Bridgeton, NJ. Tue Sep 28.

BADEY, JOHN, d Fri Feb 9, 1900, New Brunswick. **SERV:** Enl ae 16 9th Reg NJ Vol. Captured at Dreury's Bluff, VA, at the time Gen Drake and others were taken prisoner. Ill for 6 yrs fm exposure in C prisons. His father was killed at his side. Sat Feb 10.

BAKER, RALPH PRIESTLY, 68, b Eliz, s/o late Phineas M, gs/o Ralph Priestly, sol 1812 and res E, d Thu 8 pm Oct 18, 1906, at home, 27 W Grand St, Eliz. **Surv:** ch Ralph P, Jr, Harry C, Mrs Walter H Leveridge, Mrs Florence Hand, Elizabeth, and Lucretia. 8 gch. sib George, David, Mrs Luther Martin, whose h was KIA Gettysburg, and Mrs George Sparks, Brooklyn. w, d/o late Robert Cleveland, d 8 yrs ago. Carpenter by trade, but engaged in wholesale produce biz for yrs. An EF, for yrs mem of frmr Rolls Engine 2. **MEM:** Carpenters Union. **SERV:** Enl otbrk

Co A, 1st NJ Vol, the first recruited in E under the call for 3 yr troops, Capt then Maj David Hatfield, who d E fm battle wounds. **F:** Sun aftn at home, Rev Dr Tomlinson, Central Bapt. Int Evergreen. Fri Oct 19.
BALDWIN, DANIEL W, 64, d Sun ngt May 15, 1910, at home, Caldwell. **SURV:** w/ch Lester, C, and Edward, Newark. Lifelong res C. **SERV:** Drummer. Tue May 17.
BALDWIN, EDWARD, 73, b NYC, s/o late Edward & Elvira, d Sun 1030 pm Apr 19, 1914, at home, 345 Rahway Ave, Eliz. **SURV:** w Elizabeth/ch Edward and Mrs T M Haratt, NYC, and Elvira, E. sib William R, Flemington, and Alfred A, E Orange. 2 gch. Educ NYC PS. Rem to E 30+ yrs ago. **MEM:** UD25, past Cmdr and current Adj. When Alfred Atkins of Roselle Park was Dep Cmdr GAR NJ, he became assist Dep Adj. WL F&AM, E, and Polar Star Lodge IOOF, NYC. **CHH:** St James ME. **SERV:** Enl otbrk Pvt 13th NY BAT of Lgt Art, to end. At Gettysburg, Chancellorsville, Fredericksburg, Lookout Mountain, Chattanooga, Missionary Ridge, and others. Mu/o Lt. Mon Apr 20. (P)
BALDWIN, JOHN M, d Newark. Bro/o Horace, who was murderously assaulted in his Union Tp home a yr or more ago, and who d fm his injuries. **F:** Sat. Int Evergreen, next to bro. Wed Feb 5, 1902.
BALDWIN, WILLIAM R, b Thu Feb 9, 1843, NYC, d Wed 8 am, Oct 10, 1917, at home of dau Mrs H A Zimmerman, 1020 Grove St, Eliz. **SURV:** ch Mrs Zimmerman and Walter. bro Alfred, Newark. gch Mary and Sarah Zimmerman. Came to E 1874 and est a grocery biz with his f, E. Baldwin & Son. Rem 1908 to Flemington. Returned Spring, 1916, and res with dau. **MEM:** Past Cmdr UD25. **CHH:** 1st Presby. **SERV:** Co F, 28th NJ Vol, 3 yrs. Wed Oct 10. (P)
BAUMAN, JULIUS, 67, d noon Mon Apr 4, 1904, at home, 72 Division St, Eliz. **SURV:** w/dau/3s. Res E since 1873. Well-known German-American citizen. One of the bosses at Singer for yrs. **MEM:** Opeeche Tribe 92, IORM, The Plattdeautsch Verein,

UD25, and others. **SERV:** Co D, 8th NY. Mon Apr 4.

BAXTER, ISRAEL P, 72, b England, d Wed noon Jul 27, 1904, St Barnabas H, Newark. **SURV:** ch Mrs Sarah E Eaton, Broad St, Lyons Farms, with whom he res last 12 yrs aft w d, and Mrs Emma Oliver, Quincy, MA. 5 gch. Imm USA when yng. Stock buyer for yrs in partnership with f. **MEM:** UD25, on the detail to raise money for MDAY celeb expense. Spent considerable time each yr having the graves of Evergreen and the adjoining Jewish cem put in order for MDAY. For yrs caretaker of the Jewish cem. **SERV:** Soon aft imm, enl Co I, 36 th NY Vol, to end. **F:** Fri 2 pm at home, the same hour of Mr Pitcairn's F. Thu Jul 28. (See Pitcairn, John M)

BECKER, FREDERICK G, 65, d abt Mon Jan 27, 1902, at home, 842 Spring St, Eliz. **SURV:** sis Mrs Kempel, Meriden, CT. Res E abt 20 yrs. Painter by trade, at one time employ as such with Central RR car shops. **MEM:** JK64. **SERV:** Mu/i Co H, 13th NJ Vol Wed Sep 17, 1862, Trenton. Hon disc Sat Jun 27, 1863, Flemington. Sat Feb 1.

BECKER, JOSEPH, 64, b Berdin, Normandy, d Fri mrng Jun 5, 1908, at home, 67 Fulton St, Eliz. **SURV:** ch Mrs Michael O'Hearn and Ida. Imm USA at an early age, and E 26 yrs ago. Cigar maker by trade. **MEM:** Adj of JK64, Cigar makers Union, of Court Onward, FOA, and the Deutsche Einigkeit Krauken Unterstutzung Verein 1. **SERV:** Enl 1864, Pvt, 8th Reg, MA Vol Hvy Art, Capt Binghams Co, serv 1 yr in the S. Mu/o 1865 Cpl in Co C at Fort Lincoln. Fri Jun 5.

BELT, D. M., 70, d Fri Aug 25, 1911, Lehigh Valley RR crash, Rochester, NY.

BENNET, CAPT, d Thu mrng Feb 19, 1903, at home of dau Mrs Charles Sortor, Elmer St, fm excitement of a fire at Mrs Grants. Agent for Union News Co. Thu Feb 19.

BENNETT, JOHN, b Mon Oct 7, 1839, Brownsburg, PA, d Fri shortly aft 8 pm Jun 9, 1905, at home of dau Mrs Minard, Verona. **SURV:** w, frmr Emma Large, d/o Isaac S, of New Hope, PA. All their ch surv: Annie L (Garrison) Davis and Isaac E,

Brooklyn, Elizabeth A, Englewood, and Sarah T (Duane) Minard, V. Aft short stay in New Hope, worked for Central RR of NJ at Hampton Junction 25 yrs. When Junction car shops closed, was among many mechanics transf to Eliz shops. Res Eliz 9 yrs. Ret 2 mos ago and moved to V. **CHH:** Park ME. **SERV:** Enl 104th Reg, PA Vol, 1862, 3 yrs. **F:** Mon 3 pm, at Montrose Ave home of dau. Int fam plot Friends Burying Ground, Solebury, Bucks Co, PA. Sat Jun 10.

BENNETT, JOHN B W, 75, b Manchester, England, d Mon aftn Feb 11, 1907, at home, 29 Union St, Eliz. **SURV:** 2/w, m Mon Jul 1, 1901, yngst d/o Rev Dr R C Shimcall of NY. 2 s and a dau. Imm USA ae 18. Res E and vcnty 56 yrs, part of that time on a farm near Salem Mills. Carried on an express biz E for yrs. Lifelong Repub, taking pride that his first vote was for Fremont and Dayton in 1856. During past few yrs made svrl trips to Manchester home, and recently visited CA with his w. **MEM:** UD25. **CHH:** 2nd Presby. **SERV:** Pvt Co B, 13th NJ Vol, Capt Lewis. **F:** Thu aftn at home, Rev Dr E. B. Cobb, 2nd Presby. Int Evergreen. Tue Feb 12. (P)

BERGEN, THOMAS, d Thu Oct 11, 1928, in an auto accident, White Plains, NY. Res Eliz for yrs. Frmr Head of the Eliz library. **F:** White Plains Presby. Int Evergreen. Sat Oct 13.

BERGQUIST, JOHN P F, 83, d Tue Jun 14, 1910, at home of s John, Orange. F lived to ae 101. Capt of a vessel that made many trips around the world. **SERV:** MW. CW, on the "Vermont" and "Seneca." Two medals conferred on him by Congress at close of CW. Wed Jun 15.

BERRY, T. HALSEY, 69, d Fri, Jul 2 1915, High Bridge. **SURV:** w Matilda/dau Mrs I E Bennitt, Brooklyn, gs and 5 bro. Frmr res Eliz. Employ Central RR since 1867. **CHH:** Fulton St ME. **F:** Tue mrng at home Hampton. Tue Jul 6.

BLATT, CHARLES, d Wed Aug 8, 1900, 863 Cross St, Eliz. **SURV:** w/s Charles. Employ as an eng at the frmr firm of Crane, Tubbs and Co, E Broad St. For yrs gave exhibitions as the Man Fish. Wed Aug 8.

BLISS, FRANK H, SR, 78, b Nov 1840, Truxton, Cortlandt Co, NY, d Mon May 5, 1919, at home, 120 Jacques Ave, Rahway. SURV: ch William and Frank H, Jr, both R. sib Mrs Mary J Lyon, Chicago, and Mrs Kate M Robinson, Addison, NY. 5 gch. Came to R 62 yrs ago. Councilman-at-Large 2 terms, chairman of the Finance Comm, and Pres of ComC. Resigned latter pos to accept pos of City Treas, serv 2 terms. MEM: GAR. Charter mem LL F&AM.. CHH: St Pauls. SERV: 6th NY Lgt Art. Promo to Cpl and later to Qtmstr Sgt. Tue May 6.
Attended the complimentary dinner for WFB27 mems given by A Edward Woodruff Tue eve May 30, 1911.

BLOODGOOD, BENJAMIN C, 83 next Jun 20, b Woodbridge, d Wed aftn May 19, 1926, at home, 10 Leesville Ave, Rahway. SURV: dau Harriet. Gch Harry Rushton and Mrs N Warren Fellows, Scarsdale, NY. 2 ggs. w d abt 8 yrs ago. Res R nearly all his life. An Ag. SERV: At Gettysburg, Bull Run and other struggles throughout VA. WIA Bull Run. Aft recovery reup, serv to end. Thu May 20.

BLOOMER, DENNIS P, b Tue Mar 11, 1845, Marlboro, Ulster Co, NY, d Wed ngt Jun 3, 1925, at home of dau Mrs Mamie C Smith, 326 Benson Pl, Westfield. SURV: ch Mrs Smith and Mrs Edgar B Wright. 2 gch Winifred and Edgar Wright. Res W 25 yrs. In biz NY until 12 yrs ago. MEM: Honory Watchung Camp, United S/AW Vets, past Cmdr GVH3. Mem for 50+ yrs, Honorary, Martin Wallberg Post 3 AL, and Clark Hyslip Post VFW. As Cmdr Houghton, aided in movement for erection of Sol Monument Bay View Cem. SERV: 1861-65, at 1st Battle of Bull Run, and other battles. WIA. Thu Jun 4.

BODWELL, JAMES L, CAPT, 74, b Ohio, d Fri ngt Feb 6, 1903, at home, Essex St, Rahway. SURV: 2/w, Miss Annie Harvey, d/o vet John. 1/w was Jane Flatt. ch, by 1/w, William J and Mrs Clarence Hatfield. Left OH scarcely ae 23 for 1849-50 Gold Rush. Reaching NYC, deemed it financially unwise to continue and found work in Eliz with William H Flatt, one of the most prominent Eliz carriage makers, and bro/o 1/w. Super of state rifle range, held until otbrk S/AW, when range closed. Aft S/AW carried on the auctioneering biz. Serv as Constable until dod. Bfr CW, a Lt in Capt Cladek Home Guards. **MEM:** WFB27. Vet Z, Eliz. Masonic LL and Lafayette Chap of that order, a Tyler of both. **SERV:** Among 3 mos men, Lincolns first call for 75,000. Enl Capt David Pierson Co, numbering 75 men, mu/i Co B, 3rd NJ State Militia as a Commissary Sgt, and had honor as 1st man sworn into USA serv fm NJ. Heaviest battle recruits fought in was Bull Run, Sun Jul 21, 1861. On Jul 27, men mu/o by reason of expiration of svc. All reup, and those not WIA or disabled fought 3 more yrs. He formed Co E, 14th Reg, for the 3 yrs. WIA in 6 different parts of body, but it took a shell explosion to send him home on Mon Sep 19, 1864. Sat Feb 7. (See HARVEY, JOHN H. Has dau as Laura)

BOGERT, JOHN W, 83, d Wed aftn Dec 17, 1913, at 105 Union St home of William Francis Crane, Montclair, as the Rev Llewellyn S. Fulmer was about to begin funeral svc for Mr Crane. Both men serv in same Reg. Thu Dec 18.

BONNELL, EDWARD C, 83, b Thu Apr 28, 1831, Morris Ave, Eliz, s/o Joel, last Eliz surv of 1812, who d abt 25 yrs ago, d Fri aftn Feb 6,1914, at home, 1159 E Grand St, Eliz. **SURV:** w/ch Mrs Carrie Bonnell and Mrs Belle Hobson, both wid. gs and gd. Last of a fam of svrl ch. Cabinet maker by trade, for yrs in the Singer cabinet dept. **MEM:** UD25. **CHH:** 1st Presby, a worshiper since Rev Dr Nicholas Murray, who d at CW otbrk, was P. **SERV:** Enl Cpl Co A, 1st NJ Vol, Capt David Hatfield. POW 10 mos Andersonville. Reup for 3 yrs. **F:** Rev William Force Whitaker, DD, 1st Presby. Sat Feb 7. (P)

Celebrated his 82nd dob Mon. Last of a fam of 7 ch. Learned the cabinet making trade with William Mulford, on the site of the Hersh bldg, Broad St. Bp by Rev Murray ae 3. When a boy, sang in the chh choir. Tue Apr 29, 1913. (A)(P)

Celebrated his 80th dob Fri. Yngst s/o Joel, who d at his Eliz home in 1880, ae 89, and was int in the 1st Presby Chh cem with military honors. Answered Lincoln's 2nd call for vol, and went to

the front in 1861. Nearly starved to d at Andersonville. Rejoined Reg Richmond, serv to end, mu/o at Trenton. Sat Apr 29, 1911.
BONNELL, ROSWELL V, b Jan, 1842, Eliz, s/o late Albert, gs/o Joel, 1812 Vet, d Sun mrng Dec 3, 1916, S'H, Washington. SURV: ch Mrs Grace Ronnell Deminatus, Rahway and Albert F, Eliz. 1 gs. In plumbing business for 30 yrs. For yrs a Sanitary Inspector Central RR. Ret for last 10 yrs. MEM: UD25 and Plumbers Union Local 245. CHH: 2nd Presby. SERV: 3 yrs AC. Enl 19th Inf NYC, Capt James Mulligan of Eliz. Rank of 1st Sgt. Duty at HQ of 1st Brig, 1st Div. At Corinth, MS; Stone River, TN; Resacca, New Hope Chapel, Kenesaw Mountain, Neal Doro Station, Peach Tree Creek and Jonesboro, GA, as well as Siege of Atlanta, and others. F: In letter to dau, requested the Chapel of A C Haines, 1211 E Broad St, E, during the eve, so GAR and Plumbers Local might attend. Mon Dec 4. (P)
BONNELL, WILLIAM P, d Tue eve Jun 20, 1911 at home, 15 Westfield Ave, Roselle Park. SURV: w of 46 yrs/ch J Nelson, Eliz, Mrs John Dushanek, Westfield, and Mabel, at home. Real estate man. A Repub, svrl yrs as assessor, and also mem B of Educ. MEM: UD25, past Cmrd. SERV: Enl otbrk with bro George, 1st NY Vol Eng, 3 yrs. F: Thu 8 pm at home. Wed Jun 21.(P) (See Bunnell/Bonnell)
BONNETT, D BLAKE, 93, b Sun May 5, 1844, N Moore St, NYC, d Wed aftn Jan 26, 1938, at home of s, 310 W Jersey St, Eliz. SURV: s Louis B. sib Mrs R K Dana, Montclair, and Charles P, New Rochelle, NY. Nephew Carlisle Dana, Upper Montclair, and R Bingham Dana, Scarsdale, NY. G-nieces Laura H and Lucia S Dana, Scarsdale, NY. w d May, 1929. French Hugenot ancestry on his f side and NE Mayflower stock on his mo side. Both f and gf were natives of NYC. N Moore St then was a fine residential district. Pavement on Broadway ended at 23rd St, with dirt road beyond. Madison Sq was open lots and commons. He m early in life his cuz Margaret Augusta Bonnett, and when her fam rem to E in 1874, came with them, res in the old fam home, 414 S Broad St. Educ in NYC PrS then went into

biz in firm of Bonnett, Schenck & Co, wholesale importers of tea, coffee and spices, founded by his f. Concern dissolved about 1875, then devoted his time to the care and management of the large real estate holdings of mo-in-law Mrs M B Bonnett, in the old 8th Ward, until abt 1890. While in NYC, one of the "Gentlemen Trotting Horse Drivers," using present uptown St. Interest in horses switched to newly popular bicycles. 1st man in his section of NJ hitting 20,000 miles on a bike, as mem of old E Wheelmen. Summer res Bay Head 40 yrs, plying waters of Barnegat Bay. Sailed and drove auto to ae 83. For yrs oldest man sailing own boat. The oldest depositor, both in age and seniority of account in the Union Co Trust Co. **CHH:** St Johns Epis. **SERV:** NY 7th Reg. Thu Jan 27.

BOPP, LEONARD, 77, d Tue mrng Jun 22, 1915, at home, 244 E Jersey St, Eliz. **SURV:** w Elizabeth/ch Mrs John H Spargo, Mrs Nathaniel Astfalk, Jr, and Lily. bro Simon, Elgin, IL. Res E 51 yrs. Blacksmith Central RR 44 yrs, ret 7 yrs ago. **SERV:** Co C, 30th NJ Vol Inf, Capt Holland. Stationed for a time in DC. At Aqua Creek, Belle Plains, Chancellorsville and Pollack Mills Creek. Tue Jun 22.

   BOPP, ELIZABETH, MRS, 74, native of Eliz, d Fri ngt Jan 13, 1933, at home, 244 E Jersey St, Eliz. **SURV:** ch Leonard, Mrs Clifford Marshall and Mrs Lily Kiyler. sis Mrs John Conolly, Irvington. gch Mrs John A Lynch, Charlotte and Leonard Astfalk, Leonard Bopp, Jr, and Eugene Kiyler. wid/o LEONARD BOPP. Mem of an old E fam that has res in the downtown section for 100+ yrs. **CHH:** Moravian. Sat Jan 14.

BOUGHTON, STEPHEN E, 80, d Tue mrng Feb 13, 1906, S'H, Kearny. Res Eliz many yrs. Frmr mem of the firm Boughton & Earl, painters, of Eliz. **SERV:** Rescued on the battlefield by Samuel Nichols, per obit Nichols. **F:** Int Eliz, per obit of George K. Lloyd. .

BOYLE, W. COOPER, b 1840 Eliz, d Sun 2 am Sep 2, 1900, at home, 124 Union St, Eliz. **SURV:** sib Mrs John M Clark, Union & Grand Sts, E, and Mrs William H Beach, for yrs res of

Newark, now of E, with whom he res. Engaged as clerk in a dry goods store NYC bfr CW. Aft CW, Govt svc for awhile in Nashville, TN, and other cities. Fqtly invited to preside at the organs of prominent chh. In 1867, joined Howell & Marsh, gen merchants, at 85 Broad St. Remained through firm's existence, and with successor Jonas E. Marsh, until the latter ret. Supporter, and attended most games of, the Resolute Baseball Club, when at height of fame. MEM: UD25. An org of the late Glee & Madrigal Soc. In many of the best musical shows in E during past 30+ yrs. CHH: 1st Presby. At Mr Marsh's suggestion, accepted pos of organist, succeeding Isaac C. Kiggins. Held pos for 26 yrs. Rcvd gold watch fm chh mem a few yrs ago upon ret. SERV: Co B, 13th NJ Vol, Capt Lewis. Co composed of well-known yng men of E and vcnty. F: Wed aftn at home, Rev Dr Cobb. Int Evergreen, by side of par. Mon Sep 3.

BRADY, HUGH, 65, d Wed ngt at home, 16 W 2nd St, Eliz. SURV: w/ch John, Hugh, James, Thomas, Terence, Mrs John Burns, and Agnes. Res E 35 yrs. Watchman at the Cordage Works until destroyed by fire. SERV: 31st Reg NY Vol. July 5, 1901.

BRAGGA, CAMILLO, b Wed Jul 25, 1832, Castile, San Juan, Italy, d Thu ngt Feb 4, 1915, at home, 171 Stiles St, Eliz. SURV: w Fanny/o William. Imm USA aft Crimean War ended, a few yrs bfr CW, settling in E. Landscaper by trade, employ for 45+ yrs as caretaker for the fam of James E. Hedges, 171 Stiles St. An admirer of frmr Pres Roosevelt and Wilson, presenting each a cane he made himself. MEM: UD25, the oldest Vet to march last MDAY. Connected with old Vet Z. SERV: Enl 3rd Reg Italian Legion 1853. At Siege of Sebastopol fm Thu Sep 28, 1854 to Tue Sep 11, 1855. Crimean War Vet. Enl 1862 49th NY Vol Inf, in many battles. WIA Deep Bottom, VA and taken POW, Libby. As he was led into prison, a C sol made an insulting remark to him. He recognized the C as one who had serv with him in the Crimean War. Learning who the prisoner was, the C asked for forgiveness. Mu/o 1865. F: Chapel of A C Haines, 1211 E Broad

St. Fri Feb 5. (P)

BRANDT, HEINRICH, 72, d Mon mrng Sep 30, 1912, at home, 624 Franklin St, Eliz. **SURV**: w/dau/s. Familiarly known as "Squire" Brandt. Res E many yrs. A JP, E. **SERV**: Enl Jul 5, 1860, 1st R. S. Mackenzie, Co K, Btln of US Eng. Hon disc Mon Jan 4, 1864. Mon Sep 30.

BRANSON, WILLIAM W, 62, d Sat mrng May 19, 1906, at home, Commerce St, Rahway. **SURV**: w/ch Harper, Mrs George E Martin, Mrs James T Jaques, and Mrs Albertson. Conductor on the PA RR 35+ yrs. **MEM**: Past Cmdr WFB27, and Post Chapl at dod. **CHH**: Trinity ME, Super of SS, a local preacher, and mem B of Chh Stewards. **SERV**: 1st NJ Cav. **F**: Tue 230 pm, Trinity. Sat May 19.

BRANT, JOSEPH, 79, b Eliz, d Sun 11 am Aug 6, 1922, at home, 248 Westfield Ave, Eliz. **SURV**: dau Mrs Ida M McClaren and 2 gs, Kenneth W and Eugene McClaren. Res E all his life, on Fulton St, and then with dau last 18 yrs. Ret foreman printing shop Central RR, employ for 37 yrs. Previously employ at Singer. **MEM**: Cmdr JK64. Last surv charter mem PL78 KP, and of Franklin Lodge 9 IOOF. **CHH**: Trustee Fulton St Meth, then mem 2nd Presby. **SERV**: 2 yr 9 mos in 1st Reg, NJ Vol, Col Hatfield. **F**: Wed 8 pm at home. Mon Aug 7.

BRAUNE, CHARLES F, 82, b Germany, d Thu mrng Dec 8, 1910, at home, 2458 N 31st St, Phl, PA. **SURV**: w. Res Eliz 25+ yrs, Cherry St, btwn W Jersey & Murray. With the Imm Svc at the old "Castle Garden" station in NY, and when abandoned, transf to Phl. When in Eliz, often took fishing and hunting trips with his intimate friend, ex-Pres Cleveland. **MEM**: Past Cmdr UD25. **SERV**: Capt, Co A, 2nd NJ Cav. **F**: Int Eliz. Thu Dec 8.

BRECKINRIDGE, WILLIAM CAMPBELL PRESTON, COL, 67, Cav in C svc, and Representative in Congress fm KY 1884-95, d Sat Nov 19, 1904. The Youth's Companion - NE Edition Thu Dec 8.

BREEN, MICHAEL, 69, d Sat ngt Jan 13, 1912, at home, 220 Lenox Ave, Westfield. **SURV**: w/sis Mrs Mary Waddles,

Hudson, NY. MEM: R D Lathrop 138. SERV: Enl Co D, 3rd NY Vol. Mon Jan 15.

BRIGGS, LEWIS W, SERV: Co A, 88th PA Vol, and Co C, 86th PA Vol. F: Mon Oct 4, 1915, at home, Eliz, Rev Frank A Smith, P Central Bapt. Large attendance of relatives and friends, incldg 20 mem UD25. Int Evergreen. Tue Oct 5. (P)

BRITTEN, BENNETT, b Jun 16, 1813, Paterson, d Mon 6 am, Oct 25, 1915, Plainfield. SURV: dau Mrs Susan Decastro, Havana, Cuba, her s Chief of the Havana PF. Oldest res of P. Entered hotel biz at 6th Ave & Broadway, NYC, at an early age. Opened hotel in Scotch Plains 25 yrs ago. 5 yrs later rem to P, remaining in hostelry biz. Opened cigar store and poolroom last yr. Staunch anti-suffragist, would have cast vote last Tue against proposed amendment. SERV: Enl otbrk Co B, 1st NY Cav, lying about his age, for 4 yrs. Mon Oct 25.

BRITTIN, DAVID S, s/o late John, d at noon Sat Aug 4, 1900, Alexian H, Eliz. SURV: w/a child. sib Mrs Roswell B Bonnell of Westfield Ave, and Frank. Assoc with his f for yrs in the lamp and oil biz. Painter by trade. Appointed as letter carrier by late PM James T Wiley. Serv under PM Moore, Sheridan and Whelan. Route was on E Broad & Walnut St, Madison & Jefferson Ave. MEM: UD25, mu/i Mon Sep 18, 1882. Branch 67 LCA. SERV: Co I, 13th NY Vol, hon disc. Reup Co B, 35th NJ Vol, late Col Cladek, Rahway. Rank of Cpl. In Shermans march fm Atlanta to the sea. Requested to a relative that Congressman Fowler make sure his wid would get her pens. F: Tue aftn at 314 Linder St home. Sat Aug 4. (See Bonnell, Roswell)

BRONSTETTER, WILLIAM, 75, d Thu mrng Feb 12, 1920, at home of dau Mrs John Demogugne, 441 1st Ave, Eliz. SURV: ch Mrs Demogugne, Mrs Mary Bowme, John and Christopher. sib Mrs Peter Middledorf and Henry. 14 gch. Res E for yrs. CHH: Grace Epis. Thu Feb 12.

BROWN, JOHN, 72, b Short Hills, d Wed aftn Nov 17, 1909, at home of dau Mrs Frederick Morhart, 113 Liberty St, Eliz. SURV: ch Mrs Morhart and Mrs Robert Kessinger, Newark. sib

Mrs John Fitzpatrick, Rahway, and Peter, Newark. Res Rahway up to 2 yrs ago. F: D J Leonard, Elizabeth Ave, Rev Thomas I Coultas, DD, St James Meth. Thu Nov 18.

BROWN, JOHN A, 87, d early Sat mrng Feb 28, 1931, at home of s George, 424 3rd Ave, E, Roselle. **SURV**: w Teresa/ch George and Robert, Brooklyn, NY, Mrs Sarah McElroy, Dumont, and Mrs Isabelle Moore, Chatham, NY. Conducted a carriage trimming biz in Hackensack until 10 yrs ago, ret and rem to R. His biz later gave way to the trimming and upholstering of automobiles and tops. Res Trenton for yrs. **MEM**: Cmdr of JBM52, disb svrl yrs ago as mem dwindled. IOOF Lodge of Trenton 50 yrs, Hackensack Rotary Club, and Bergen Co Hist Soc. Honorary mem AL, VFW, and S/AW Vets, all Hackensack. **SERV**: Co A, 20th MA Vol, of which only surv mem is Justice Oliver Wendell Holmes, US Supreme Court, who was his Lt. WIA Ball's Bluff. POW, held for 124 days. Disc Army, joined Navy. In Battle of Fort Fischer at Plymouth, NC. Said by fam to be last U sol of Libby prison, Richmond, VA. **F**: Mon eve at home. Mon Mar 2.

BRUNT, HARVEY, 68, d Wed May 6, 1908, at home, 238 Maple Ave, Rahway. **SURV**: w/svrl ch. Lifelong res R. **MEM**: WFB27, Post Adj last 8 yrs. Thu May 7.

BRYANT, GEORGE L, b Lyons Farm, d Tue mrng Jul 24, 1906, Lake Hopatcong. **SURV**: w, fmr Miss Rindell, yngst d/o Robert of Cranford. dau Mrs Low, w/o Dr Frederick of High Bridge. f d a few yrs ago, ae 90, and s Robert d within recent yrs. Compositor for NJJ when a boy. Entered svc of Central RR as baggage-master, became conductor, and was once trainmaster at Dunellen then High Bridge, having charge of the German Valley sys. Conducted the Nolan's Point Villa for yrs, and managed the Buckingham Hotel in FL 4 yrs ago. Ret to Lake Hopatcong 3 yrs ago. **SERV**: Lt, 9th NJ Vol, to end. **F**: High Bridge. Tue Jul 24.

BUCKBEE, WILLIAM A, b Fri Oct 14, 1842, Flushing, NY, d Mon ngt Apr 15, 1935, at home, N N Ave, Dunellen. **SURV**: ch William A, Jr, of 252 Winans Ave, Hillside, and Mrs Ida

Sorenson, D. Sgt in Jersey City PD, ret 1901. MEM: Past Dep Cmdr NJ GAR. 65 yr mem IOOF. SERV: 15th NJ Vol, 4 yrs, WIA svrl times. F: Thu ngt at home, assist by vets, all over age 90, fm Jersey City, Eatontown, Trenton and Plainfield. Int Fri at F, LI. Tue Apr 16. (A, Fri Apr 19, said vet d Sun.)

BUCHBEE, WILLIAM A. In the Wed tribute paid to CW Vets, with 27 other NJ Vets and a NY Vet. GAR reunion with colorful parade and amory fete in Eliz. A mem-at-large, represented Plainfield. Thu Mar 30, 1933.

BULL, JAMES HENRY, 77, native of NYC, s/o James, d Mon aftn Apr 25, 1921, at home, 142 Orchard St, Eliz. SURV: 2/w, Mary Looker, m 1900. 1/w, Mary Kane, d 1897. ch Archibald F, Hillside, William D, Plainfield, Mrs James Monohan, Rockville Center, LI, and Mrs John Deroucher, who res in the S. sib Mrs Charles Smith, New Haven, CT, Mrs James Woodruff, Brooklyn, and Benjamin, E. 12 gch. 9 ggch. Step ch Augustus G Pool and Mrs Ida Bogart, both of E. Came to E abt 45 yrs ago. Followed the carpentry and painting trades, ret svrl yrs ago. CHH: 1st Bapt. SERV: Enl ae 17 Co I, 66th Reg, NY Vol, Cmdr James H. Bull, his f. Enl without knowledge or consent of par. His f not being aware of s presence in the Reg until the latter came to him in uniform. Saw much svc on Srn battlefields. Bcmg ill, assigned to recruiting duty on eve of Battle of Gettysburg, the 66th playing a prominent part. f was shot and killed by a sharpshooter while heading a party of sol in the construction of a pontoon bridge across a small stream near Gettysburg. Disc Fri Nov 4, 1864. Tue Apr 26. (See obit of Archibald H Bull, **Relatives**)

BUNKERHOEF, JOHN, 83, d Tue ngt Oct 24, 1911, Westfield. SURV: sis, Roselle. Mem Sandy Hook Life Saving Crew. Wed Oct 25.

BUNN, DAVID J, 68, b Woodbridge Tp, Middlesex Co, d Sat aftn Jun 28, 1902, at home of dau Mrs Arthur S Wilkins, Rahway. SURV: 2s/2dau, all m. sib Constable Isaac, Ellis, Matthias, and 2 sis. w d a little more than a yr ago. An almost lifelong res R. Bodymaker by trade. Bfr CW and some yrs aft, an ardent Dem, elected 1865 assessor of the 1st Ward, beating Repub William H. Moore by one majority. Some yrs past became ardent Repub, holding svrl minor offices, one being PJ. MEM: WFB27, tending resignation as Cmdr a few days ago due to illness. SERV: Enl Sgt Mon Apr 22, 1861, 3rd NJ Vol 3 mos. Enl Sgt Sat Feb 1,1862, Co I, 2nd Reg, DC Vol. Disc Sat Nov 1, 1862. F: Tue 2 pm 27 E Grand St res of Mrs Wilkins, Rev F C Mooney, P First ME. Mon Jun 30.

BUNN, MATTHIAS, 70, d Sat 8 am Mar 4, 1916, at home, 17 Commerce St, Rahway. SURV: sib Elizabeth and Margaret of R. bro/o frmr PJ David and Capt Isaac, both d. Vet never m. Res R abt 60 yrs. A carpenter. SERV: 14th NJ Vol. F: WFB27 in charge of svc. Sat Mar 4.

Attended the complimentary dinner for WFB27 mems given by A Edward Woodruff Tue eve May 30, 1911.

BUNNELL/BONNEL, GEORGE C, d Fri mrng Feb 19, 1904, at home, Union Tp. SURV: w, an heir of the Fair Estate. bro William P, CW Vet, in same unit. Res U all his life. MEM: UD25. SERV: 1st NY Vol Eng. F: Mon 230 pm. Fri Feb 19.

BUTLER, JOHN T, 78, b Brooklyn, d Tue Mar 2, 1920, 45 Orchard St, where he boarded, Eliz. Res E 37 yrs. MEM: JK64. CHH: 1st Bapt, while res in Brooklyn. SERV: 1 yr with 11th NY Eng. POW Libby. F: August F. Schmidt & Son. Wed Mar 3.

C

CARKHUFF, PHILIP E, b Centreville, Hunterdon Co, Mon Mar 7, 1831, d Fri May 30, 1902, at home of s Lorenzo, 417 Fay Ave, Eliz. SURV: w/ch John W, Bayonne, Mrs Digan, Lebanon, Lorenzo W, Philip A, Garwood, Jacob S, NY, Mrs Joseph Oakley, E, Ida, Harriet, and Mrs Hallaway, Newark. Res for a time in Newark, where he was mem Passaic Riv Yachting Club. Res E since 1869, with Lorenzo since 1892. In E, entered the svc of late Phineas M. Baker on W Grand St. In later yrs traveled in the interest of Richardson Saw Works. SERV: Army. F: Mon

aftn, Rev Dr Wilding. Int in vault of s in Evergreen. Sat May 31.
CARLTON, WILLIAM J, b Fri Sep 14, 1838, Winchester, NH, d early Fri mrng Jul 18, 1902, at home, 236 W Grand St, Eliz. **SURV**: 3 dau/2s. w, frmr Helen M Newcomb, d/o Thomas of Albany, m Wed Oct 25, 1865, d Jun, 1893. Res E 40 yrs. Serv svrl terms on both the B of Educ and CC. **MEM**: UD25, WL F&AM, and took interest in the NY Commandery of the Military Order of LoyL. **CHH**: Closely identified with Meth in E for 40 yrs. Treas St James past 25 yrs. **SERV**: Enl Pvt otbrk 58th NY Vol. AJ, promo to Capt Jul, 1863, and brev Maj at end. Fri Jul 18.
CARMAN, JAMES L, CAPT, 81, native of Newark, d Sat Jun 23, 1923, Rahway (Dateline). **SURV**: ch Emma D, Florence I and Lt James L, Jr, stationed at Fort Hamilton. 5 gch. sib Mrs William H Wright, w/o the City Treas, 111 Central Ave, and Henry C, 103 Bryant St. Res 70 Pierson Rd, Maplewood. **MEM**: GAR and LoyL. **SERV**: Cmdr of a Co in the 13th NJ Vol, under his bro Col E A Carman. WIA. **F**: Sun aftn. Int Metuchen. Mon Jun 25.
CARROLL, PAUL, d Mon Apr 23, 1900, S'H, Kearny. **SURV**: w/ch Paul, Jr, Joseph, May E and Mrs George Hoffman. Res Eliz for yrs, frmr employ of the oil cloth factories. **SERV**: Co K, 3rd NJ Vol, late Capt Whelan. Mon Apr 23.
CARROLL, ROBERT, 71, b Ireland, s/o late Robert, d Sun mrng Jan 22, 1917, at home, 128 Washington Ave, Eliz. **SURV**: ch Mrs Ralph Brundage and Mrs William Sheeran. 7 gch. 1 ggch. Last of his fam. Imm USA with par ae 8, trip taking a month, settled in E. A spoke turner for yrs, and more recently a city employee. At one time a Vol fireman, mem Engine Co 2. **MEM**: EFA, rcvd the 6th Exempt Certificate issued by E. UD25. **CHH**: St Marys. **SERV**: Enl otbrk Co K, 3rd Reg Vol Inf, late Capt John Whelan, Col George W. Taylor and Col Henry O Brown. Reg org at Camp Olden, Trenton, and to Washington Fri Jun 28, 1861. Attached to 2nd Brig of Runyon Reserve Div. At Bull Run and the Defense of Washington. In Mar 1862 attached to Kearny

Brig, AP. At Munson Hill, Springfield Station and Burke's Station. In Apr 1862 moved to VA peninsular, attached to 1st Div, 6th Army Corps. In Siege of Yorktown, and at West Point, Oak Grove, Gaine's Mills, Charles City Crossroads, Malvern Hill, Bull Run Bridge, and the 2nd Bull Run. Also in Seven Day's Battle and the battle bfr Richmond. WIA at 2nd Bull Run, hon disc Tue Feb 17,1863. In Oct 1872, enl in Sedgwick Guards, mem Co B, 3rd Reg, NJNG. Mon Jan 22.

On the Honor Roll for bravery. 50th anniv of 1st Brig Tue Jul 18, 1911.

CARY, JOHNSON W, 65, b Arkport, NY, d announced Tue eve Jan 20, 1903, Eliz. **SURV**: s Charles. Res E abt 25 yrs, for some time at 42 Sayre St. Expert machinist with Singer since CW. Long time foreman of the tool dept. **MEM**: UD25, a regular attendant at Post encmp, the current one where his d was announced. **SERV**: Sgt Co C, 173rd NY Vol. **F**: Thu aftn, Rev Otis A. Glazebrook, DD. Wed Jan 21

CHATTIN, CHARLES F, 77, b Sep, 1848, OH, d Wed Aug 4, 1926, Alexian Bros H, Eliz. w d abt 5 yrs ago. Moved to E only recently, at 501 N Broad St past 3 wks. When ae 7 emigrated with par across the Wrn plains ovr the "Covered Wagon" trail, settling in what is now Summerville, OR. Butcher by trade. In E to look up some GAR mem and compare notes. Had 6 older bro also in CW, and 10 yrs ago held fam reunion with all present. All are gone now. **SERV**: Went to IA and enl, in all active campaigns last 2 yrs. **F**: F C & H C Ogden. Thu Aug 5.

CHEESEMAN, DAVID AUGUST, 79, native of South River, d Tue aftn Oct 17, 1911, at home of dau Mrs William Forman, 1061 Lafayette St, Eliz. **SURV**: ch Mrs Forman, Mrs George McClure, Highland Park and Mrs Whittenack, New Brunswick. 5 gch. Res S R until a month ago. **MEM**: FL79, and Enterprise Lodge 29 KP, S R. **SERV**: Co K, 6th Reg, NJ Vol. Wed Oct 18.

CHUBB, HENRY C, 81, b Cleveland, OH, d Sat ngt Feb 26, 1927, at home, 354 Lincoln Ave, Cranford. **SURV**: w Ida G. bro Walter M, Cleveland, OH. Niece Irene Robus, NYC. Res C 5 yrs.

Employ for yrs as cashier for the Railway Steel Spring Co, NYC. MEM: Azure Lodge F&AM, and KP. SERV: Navy. Mon Feb 28.

CLARK, CHARLES HOMER/C, 63, d Sun Jun 6, 1909, at home of dau, Huntington, MA. SURV: w/dau Mrs Jenkins. A s, who d svrl yrs ago, m a d/o Cranford Tp Collector T A Crane. Res Cranford for yrs, on Walnut Ave. MEM: Cranford Council, RA, once lodge collector. UD25 when res NJ, then took card E. CHH: Deacon 1st Presby, one time a choir mem. SERV: Enl as musician fm NE. F: Tue, assist by Lee Grand Post. Mon Jun 7.

CLARK, CORNELIUS HYER, 75, b Thu Apr 13, 1843, NYC, d Fri Feb 22, 1918, at home, 502 Jefferson Ave, Eliz. SURV: w, frmr Miss Sarah Mather Smith of NYC. sis Mary. Educ in NYC schools. Came to E 1868. Joined the clerical force of a Wall St financial house aft CW. Serv a term as mem B of Educ. MEM: Lafayette Post GAR NYC, fm its formation. CHH: Westminster, Clerk of the Session for yrs. SERV: 22nd Reg, NY Vol, to end. Enl twice, a Lt at close. Sat Feb 23.

CLARK, THERON B, 89, b Walkill, NY, s/o late Mortimer A & Mary J, d abt midnight Aug 1-2, 1924, at home, 26 Vista Ave, Eliz. SURV: ch Mrs Robert J Aljoe(?) Mrs Bryant Marsh, E, and Arthur B, NY. 8 gch. 11 ggch. bro James, Middletown, NY. Educ in Middletown. In 1858 m Miss Mary Elizabeth Stevenson. Res Middletown for a short time, then Brooklyn, Jersey City, and later in the W. Came to E abt 50 yrs ago. Res downtown for yrs, Livingston St abt 13 yrs, W Grand St abt 24 yrs, then Vista Ave 3 yrs ago. Worked at Singer for yrs. In partnership with George Gibbs, est the firm Clark & Gibbs, coal and feed merchants in Front St, near E Jersey St. Ret 12 yrs ago. MEM: RJE Co 4, Vol FD. EFA. PL78 KP. Charter mem CE1 IOF. Hoffman Lodge F&AM, Middletown, joining 65 yrs ago. Dir Excelsior B&L Assoc. CHH: 1st Presby as a boy. On Wed May 28, 1879, became mem Marshall St chh, which became the Greystone 29 yrs ago. On Wed Mar 30, 1887, installed as Elder, and for abt 10 yrs was assist Super of the SS. SERV: U forces. Sat Aug 2. (P)

CLARK, WILLIAM JACKSON, REV, b Fri Dec 28, 1832, Perry County, IL, s/o William of SC & Sarah Joy, of MA, d Thu Sep 10, 1920, at home of dau, Eliz. SURV: ch Mrs Thomas F Russum, 916 E Jersey St, E, and Paul Haskell, Beloit, WI. sis Mrs George Tracey Williams, Page Ave, E Cleveland. Attended Grinnel College, Davenport, IA til CW, returned to college aft CW at Amherst. Entered Chicago Theo Sem. Had Pastorates in OR and CA. Bfr coming to E, res Hinsdale, IL, where he m in 1891 Miss Eliza Norton Haskell. SERV: 5th IL Cav, to end. Fri Sep 10.

CLAYTON, ASHER M, 78 next Mon, b Freehold, d Thu ngt Feb 27, 1913, Alexian H, Eliz. SURV: w Laura/ch Mrs Emily O'Keefe, Mrs Joseph Conrad, Mrs Edward Mergens and Maurice. For yrs employ with James O. Brokaw, 115 Broad St. Came to Essex Co in 1872 with Nicholson Paving Co. A Dem, proud that his Mar 3rd dob was the day before a Pres election (sic), esp this yr with a Dem being inaugurated as Chief Exec. CHH: Sacred Heart. SERV: One of two surv in E of the 28th NJ Vol, he being in Co F. Fri Feb 28.

CLEM, JOHN LINCOLN, 86, d Thu ngt May 13, 1937, San Antonio, TX. SURV: w Elizabeth/ch John and Elizabeth. SERV: Famed "Drummer Boy of Chickamauga." Joined 23rd MI Inf when barely past ae 10. At Shiloh 1862 he beat the lead drum. A yr later he was allowed to carry a gun. Remained in Army aft CW, 14 yrs in San Antonio, coming as a 2nd Lt in 1871. Qtmstr for 8th Corps for yrs. Rank of Maj Gen, Ret, at dod. Fri May 14.

CLEVELAND, EDMUND J, b Fri Nov 25, 1842, Eliz, s/o Joseph, d announced Jul 9, 1902, Hartford, CT. f was a pioneer Meth of Eliz, and operated a bakery on Washington Ave for yrs. SURV: Leaves a fam. Aft CW was Sec and Treas of Elizabeth & Newark Horse RR Co for yrs. Engaged in real estate, and in 1886 rem to Hartford, having previously m a Miss Brogaw, and engaged in the brokerage biz. A numismatician, having one of the largest collections of coins in the USA. Authored a n/o poems under the nom de plume VIDI. SERV: Enl Aug, 1862, Co A, 2nd

NJ Vol, disc due to illness, then attached to Co K, 9th Reg, same month. Had to wait for 3 yr term to expire, when 9th signed for CW, to reup. Disc Jun,1865. Performed every duty in a faithful, intelligent and fearless manner, as his published biography says. While in army, found time to write letters to the NJJ, giving his experiences as a sol and telling numerous experiences of camp life. Wed Jul 9.

CLIFFORD, CHARLES J, b 1831, Newark, d Wed ngt Mar 2, 1910, at home, 372 1st Ave, Eliz. **SURV**: w Marietta Huntsman Clifford/ch Mrs Oscar C Cramer, Cleveland, OH, Mrs Benjamin Baxter, Elkhart, IN and Henrietta F, Columbus, OH. 4gch. Res E for yrs. For a time res Chicago, but back to E abt 8 yrs ago. Master mechanic for Rogers Locomotive Works, Paterson. Traveled extensively, visiting many countries where, under his supervision, locomotives shipped fm Paterson were put together and placed in com. One of his last trips was to Peru. Ret for svrl yrs. **MEM**: EL49 F&AM, 51 yrs, 2nd oldest on the roll. **SERV**: On the US man-of-war "Home." **F**: East Bapt, Rev John V Ellson. Thu Mar 3.

COATES, JOHN, 70, CW Vet of Wellsville, d abt Nov 7, 1918, Cuba, NY. Drowned in Cuba Lake, along with Lloyd Gardner of Hornells, ae 29, while fishing. A shotgun accidently discharged and blew a hole in the steel boat. Neither could swim. Fri Nov 7.

COEYMAN, WILLIAM, 71, native of NYC, d Sat mrng Jun 23, 1917, at home, 435 Meadow St, Eliz. **SURV**: w Martha J Hughes Coeyman/ch Mrs Alfred H Pickens, Newburgh, NY and William John. Res E for yrs. Engaged in cabinet making. **SERV**: Enl otbrk Co A, 16 th Reg, US Vol Reserve Corps, Capt Henry C Kerr. Gave his name as William Freeman, as he did not want his par to know he joined the Army. Hon disc Mon Aug 1, 1894, and reup Co A, 3rd Reg, on Mon Jan 9, 1865. Disc Mon Dec 4, 1865. In a n/o engage. Sat Jun 23.

COLE, EDMUND LEWIS/R, COL, 64, d Thu shortly aft 7 am Dec 26, 1907, at home, Elm St, Westfield. **SURV**: w. Couple had no ch. Lawyer with offices in City Hall, NY. Thu Dec 26.

COLLINS, FERGUS, returning fm a CW meeting, where he had rcvd svrl hundred dollars bounty, was waylaid near the frmr home of Isaac M Littell, who long res at 417 Elizabeth Ave, Eliz, by two men, murdered and his body carried across vacant lots and thrown into the Elizabeth Riv. The men were arrested, one was executed in the old Courthouse, while the other was sent to State prison. He escaped, but recaptured, and serv the balance of his time. Fri Apr 21, 1911. (No date of event given)

COLYER, JOSEPH, JR, d Sun mrng Aug 19, 1906, Grand Central Station, Chicago, on his way home fm the natl encmp at Minneapolis, MN, where he had been elected a mem of the Council of Administation. w rcvd letter Mon written in MN less than 12 hr bfr he d, mailing the letter as he was about to board the train. A manu of carriages in Newark for yrs. **MEM**: Past Jr V-Dep Cmdr of NJ GAR. **SERV**: Enl ae 17 13th NJ Vol, 2 wks aft at Antietam, MD. At Gettysburg and Chancellorsville. On duty Fords Theater, Washington, when Lincoln was shot, saw Mrs Surratt and other conspirators executed, and was one of the squad of soldiers which had charge of Booth's body aft the murderer was killed. Tue Aug 21.

COMPTON, NATHAN V, b Tue Nov 2, 1841, Liberty Corners, Somerset Co, s/o Alvah & Ann Marie Ayres Compton, d Mon 115 pm Jan 29, 1917, Rahway. **SURV**: w Emma L Briant Compton, d/o Mr & Mrs John A Briant of Newark. ch Mrs William R Gibbons, R, and Mrs John A Herrmann, Jersey City. 1 gdau. 1 niece. Res 64 W Milton Ave. Fam came fm SI and is of English origin. Ayres fam is of Scottish origin. ggf Jacob fought in RW, and gf Oliver in 1812. Rcvd a common school educ, then worked as a grocery clerk in New Brunswick, then Plainfield. Learned silver platter trade in Newark until CW. Aft CW took a pos with a Newark mercantile house for 5 yrs when he engaged in real estate and insurance in R. Assessor R for yrs. Appointed as one of the Com of Taxes and Assessment by late Chancellor William J Magie, then Supreme Court Justice, when R became involved in post CW biz depression. When normal taxation not psbl, appointed as one of the special Com of Taxation by Gov Leon Abbett, renewed by Gov George T Werts. Fm this, appointed on B of Finance by R major, and helped to restore R financial standing. A Dir of the Workmens B&L Assoc, R. Ret 2 yrs ago, being first city employee to rcv a pens. **MEM**: WFB27, Adj and frmr Co officer of NJNG, being Capt and Paymaster of 3rd Reg under Col B A Lee. A Mason, initiated into St Albans Lodge 68 F&AM, Newark, the year bfr m. In 1871, affiliated with LL27 R, and Worshipful Master 1878. Made a Royal Arch Mason in 1872 Lafayette Chapter 26, RAM, becoming High Priest in the Grand Chap of NJ by James H Durand, Grand Master of Masonry. Mem A&A Scottish Rite Bodies of the Valley of Jersey City up to and incldg the 32nd degree. **CHH**: 2nd Presby. **SERV**: Enl Aug 1862 Co H, 13th NJ Vol, Col John J Cladek, in that Co with the AP at Fredericksburg and Chancellorsville. POW latter battle, held Libby for short time. Tue Jan 30. (P)

Compton, N V, Adj, WFB27, attended the complimentary dinner for Post mems given by A Edward Woodruff Tue eve May 30, 1911.

CONAWAY, WINGATE/WRIGHT B, 64, b MD, d Wed eve Feb 24, 1904, at home, 17 Bloomfield Ave, Newark. **SURV**: w/4 s/dau. Frmr res Eliz, connected with Central RR NJ, and a few yrs bfr with the DE, Lackawanna & Wm RR as div super. Res N for yrs. **MEM**: CE IOF. **SERV**: Navy, at the evacuation of Charleston, SC, at end of CW. Hon disc. **F**: Sat 2 pm. Int Evergreen. Fri Feb 26

CONGER, WILLIAM, native of Rahway, almost 89, d Tue 7 pm, Jan 3, 1928, Rahway. **SURV**: w Caroline/dau Mrs Ester Jean Bennett, 9 Mary St, Carteret. gdau Mrs E A Webb at frmr address. sib George, 194 Bryant St, for yrs head of R PD, and Jeremiah, Tenafly. A skillful carriage trimmer for 35+ yrs, when R was a leader in carriage making. Worked for D B Dunham & Son. Also a printer by trade, working at the old Mershon plant, R. Mem Vol FD. **CHH**: Free Meth early then Trinity Meth. **SERV**:

Enl otbrk 3 mos Co B, 3rd Reg, NJ Vol Inf, Mon Apr 22, 1861. With McDowell army around Alexandria & London railway, and at Bull Run. Reup for 3 yrs. Co K, 9th Reg, NY State Militia Inf, which was subsequently detached and designated 6th Ind Bat, NY Lgt Art, Capts Bunting and the late Joseph W Martin. Attached to 2nd Div of 3rd Army Corps, AP. At Pritchard's Mills, Point of Rocks, Ball's Bluff, Siege of Yorktown, two battles of Fair Oaks, Seven Pines, seven days before Richmond, Malvern Hill, Harrison's Landing, Defense of Washington, where he was attached to 1st Brig, Horse Art, Pleasanton 1st Div of Cav.

At Chancellorsville, Kelly's Ford, Beverly Ford, Upperville, Gettysburg, Culpepper Courthouse, White Sulphur Springs, St Stephens Church, Auburn, Bristol, Mine Run, Locust Grove, Parker's Store, the Wilderness, Todd's Tavern, Sheridan's Raid, Nordun River, Yellow Tavern, Island Station, around Richmond fortifications, Pamunky River, Hanovertown, Hawes Shop, Totopotamy Creek, Cold Harbor, Defense of Washington, completing his 2nd enl. Mu/o Columbus, OH, Fri Feb 23, 1866. On Jul 4, 1866, rcvd an honorable testimonial fm Gov Marcus Ward. F: H B Leech, Trinity Meth, and Rev S W Townsend of Bayonne, frmr P of Trinity. Wed Jan 4.

Attended the complimentary dinner for WFB27 mems given by A Edward Woodruff Tue eve May 30, 1911.

CONNOLLY, THOMAS, 61, d Mon Jun 26, 1905, S'H, Kearny. **SURV**: s James, Eliz. Inmate of the S&S' Home, Hampton, VA, was on furlough to visit relatives in Bayonne when he became ill. Admitted to Kearny Home Fri. **SERV**: Navy. Wed Jun 28.

CONNORS, PATRICK, 81, d Fri Jul 1, 1910, at his 12 Willow St home, Newark, less than ½ hr aft talking with his w.

CONRAD, LOUIS, b Sun Oct 17, 1847, Bavaria, Germany, d Wed mrng Oct 15, 1930, at home, 108 Sayre St, Eliz. **SURV**: w Louise, ae 81, and a dau in Asbury Park. ch Edward, Mrs Henry Schmidt and Mrs James Hill, E, Mrs James Jones and Mrs Charles Hockenbury, Asbury Park, and Fannie, Spring Lake. 13

gch. sib Dora and Frederick, E. Imm USA to E ae 3. Couple celebrated 51st m anniv last Mar. Often gave addresses to school pupils about CW. **MEM**: UD25, V-Cmdr. **SERV**: Tried to enl ae 17 Jersey City near close of war, but rejected, lack of par consent, then went to Newark. Accepted for 9th NY Inf, serv 5 mos. **F**: J S Stiners Home for Svc, 97 W Grand St. Wed Oct 15.

Installed as officer of the day at the UD25 meeting Tue ngt. In 9th NJ Inf. Imm USA with parents. Tue Jan 8, 1924. (P)

Attended Christmas party for CW Vets given by WRC27 Tue ngt. Wed Dec 23, 1925. (P)

Attended annual UD25 Christmas party. Thu Dec 30, 1926. (P) Honored at MDAY services. Sat May 31, 1930. (P)

CONRAD, LOUISE C, MRS, 86, d Wed eve Jun 24, 1931, at home of dau Mrs Henry Schmidt, 108 Sayre St, Eliz. **SURV**: ch Mrs Schmidt, Edward, Mrs James Hill and Mrs James Jones, E, Mrs Charles Hockenbury, Asbury Park, and Fannie, Spring Lake. sib Charles and John Menge, CA. wid/o LOUIS CONRAD. **MEM**: Star of E Lodge 68, SB. **CHH**: Epworth ME. Thu Jun 25.

MENGE, WILLIAM MCKINLEY, b Eliz, d "somewhere in France" the latter part of Dec, ae 20. **SURV**: mo Mrs Mary Menge, Warren, MI, who was notified by the War Dept on d of s. sis, Mrs Lydia E Menge, 741 Livingston St, E, who learned of his d in a letter fm her mo, who rem fm Livingston St to the Detroit suburb soon aft her s enl. gf, Adolphe Menge, is a CW Vet, as is an uncle, Louis Conrad, 138 Sayre St. Svrl cuz are in serv to Uncle Sam in various branches. Among the first to enl, at the Broad St recruiting station early in May. Assigned to Medical Corps and sent to France. Grad of PS9. Worked at the American Can Co Kenilworth plant bfr enl. Wed Jan 2, 1918.

COOK, ALFORD B, 78, b Rahway, d Sat Jan 29, 1921, at home of s, 33 Montgomery St, Rahway. **SURV**: w/s Clarence J. sib Edward, 222 Main St, Clarence W, 66 Main St, and Mrs Jennie Larrison, 66 Milton Ave. 5 gch. Lifelong res R, Milton Ave until 8 wks ago. Police Court Judge for years, a JP for 5 yrs. 21 yrs on B of Educ. Painter by trade, ret svrl yrs ago. **MEM**: WFB27, past

Cmdr. V-Cmdr State Dept GAR. **SERV:** Enl otbrk in DC unit, Co I, 2nd DC Vol, to end. WIA. **F:** Tue 730 pm, Rev F G Merrill, 1st Bapt. Mon Jan 31. Attended the complimentary dinner for WFB27 mems given by A Edward Woodruff Tue eve May 30, 1911.

COOK, JOHN, d late Tue May 17, 1910, at home of dau Mrs Keifer Carr, Church St, Boonton. Wed May 18.

COOPER, GEORGE W, 79, d Mon Feb 17, 1908, Eliz. **SURV:** w/ch Mrs Cornelia C Smith and Mrs Amy L Abel. Res E but a short time at 364 S Broad St. Worked for Harper Brothers and the NY Life Ins Co for yrs. **MEM:** Chancellor Walworth Lodge of Free Masons, NY. 71st NY Vet Assoc. **SERV:** 127th NY Vol. **F:** Thu aftn, Rev Dr William Force Whitaker, 1st Presby. Int Woodlawn, NY. Wed Feb 19.

COOPER, JOHN W, 91, of Largo, FL, d Thu ngt Jul 7, 1938, Carlisle H, Carlisle, PA, while attending the 75th, and final, B&G Reunion at Gettysburg. **SERV:** C sol.

CORY, ENOS W, 72, b Fri Nov 23, 1832, NY, d Wed 943 am Sep 23, 1914, Linden. **SURV:** w Emma C, m Sat Nov 23, 1867. ch Mrs Amy E Esdaile and Frederic N, Linden, Mrs William B Devoe, Orchard St, Eliz, Mrs R E Diston, Ironia, H L, OH, and William. A sis, Mrs Sarah Spences, Chicago, ae 81, d 3 wks ago, and another sis, Mrs Phebe Ennis, Eliz, d Sep 11. Res Elm St, L, since Apr, moving fm NY with fam. Regarded as one of the greatest experts in the country on cement. **MEM:** Noah Farnham Post GAR and Pacific Lodge F&AM, both NY. NY Gen Soc of Mechanics and Trades, and the EF of the W Hoboken Vol FD. **F:** Sun 230 pm at home, Rev A G Schatzman, Meth P. Cremation at Rosedale. Wed Sep 23.

COWIE, GEORGE W, CAPT, b Scotland 1846, d Fri 2 am May 23, 1902, Rahway. **SURV:** w/s George H, an assist to the NY Corp Counsel. bro Thomas A, Navy paymaster. Imm USA as a yng man. Struck Thu abt 10 pm by the Washington, PHL & Boston Express. Res at corner of Briant & Commerce St. **SERV:** Enl Navy 1863, under Adm Farragut. Rose to Chief Eng as Capt.

During S/AW on battleship "Indiana," sent to Philippines at end of war. Later assigned to shore duty BNY. Fri May 23.

COX, ANDREW, 68, native of Plainboro, d Sun mrng, Mar 24, 1907, Plainfield. SURV: w/ch Mrs John Reed, Newark, and Albert, Easton. sib Mrs John Middleton, Newark, and Mrs Mary Mershon, Louisville, KY. A mason and builder. Took part in building all imp city structures past 20 yrs, among them the Pond Tool Works, Potter Printing Press Works, Scott Press Works, Babcock Bldg, and 3 of the PS. Assoc for yrs with William Panghorn, Contractor. MEM: WS73. SERV: Enl Trenton Co B, 1st Reg, 1861. In all the largest battles fm Bull Run to Gettysburg. F: Tue. Mon Mar 25.

COYLE, CHARLES JOSEPH, 104, b Manchester, England, d Thu Aug 12, 1937, Fort Lauderdale, FL. Imm USA a yng man. Newspaper reporter in NY and Chicago, then went to FL as a farmer. Ret 10 yrs ago. Credited with being the oldest mem of the Masonic Order in the USA. SERV: Army. Thu Aug 12.

CRANE, BENJAMIN P, b Fri Feb 22, 1822, Galloping Hill Rd, Union Tp, s/o late John B & Mary Wade Crane, ggs/o Col William, RW, d Tue ngt May 21, 1912, at home of George H Wenkie, 330 Grieg Ave, Eliz. SURV: w Jennie. Last of a fam of 5s/5dau. Visiting Wenkie when stricken. Aft finishing grammar school, apprenticed to Belcher Woodruff, a builder, and learned the mason trade. Employ a long time with Joseph Davis and helped to erect City Hall abt 50 yrs ago. Ret 6 yrs ago. Last yr climbed to the roof of his 1069 William St home and repaired the chimney. Belonged to Whig party during the 1840 Pres campaign, voting for Henry Clay and Theodore Frelinghuysen. Voted in his life for 16 Pres candidates, and res in the administrations of all but the first 5. MEM: Color bearer for UD25 until a short time ago. CHH: Mt. Zion Chapel. SERV: Enl Newark 8th Reg, NJ Vol, seeing much svc in VA. Mu/o in DC. One of few surv of the Co, for yrs under Capt James Jenkins. In the centennial Battle of Trenton celebrations, taking part with the force representing the Hessians. Wed May 22. (P)

CRANE, EDWARD S, 79, b NYC, d Tue mrng Aug 21, 1917, at home, 307 Walnut Ave, Cranford. SURV: w/ch Mrs Abbler Davis, Phoenixville, PA, Mrs George A Watson and Edward D, C. For yrs res on a farm in South Cranford. Assessor in C, one time on the Tp Comm. MEM: UD25. SERV: 7th Reg, NY. Tue Aug 21.

CRANE, ISAAC, 74, d Sun ngt Feb 3, 1918, Rahway City H, Rahway. Res R for years, res at 137 Main St, at the plumbing establishment of J J Marsh, where employ. SERV: 6th Ind Bat of NY. Mon Feb 4.

Attended the complimentary dinner for WFB27 mems given by A Edward Woodruff Tue eve May 30, 1911.

CRANE, WILLIAM FRANCIS, d Newark. F: Dec 18, 1913. Vet D W Bogert d at his bier. Both men in same Reg. Obit Bogert Dec 18.

CROSS, BENJAMIN F, 61, b in New York State, d Mon 630 am Oct 22, 1900, at home, 26 Prospect St, Eliz. SURV: w Mary L Avery, d/o James. ch 3 s and 2 dau. One s Richard serv in the S/AW, 3rd Reg, and is a Lt, Co C, 2nd Reg. Res E abt 20 yrs. Painter with PA RR. SERV: Co I, 8th NY Vol. Mon Oct 22.

CROWELL, THEODORE, disappeared Feb 22, 1901 ae abt 60. Found Apr 18 in a slip at Pier 6 coal docks, Eliz. SURV: w/3 s/dau. One s, Augustus, identified his f. Res E for yrs. Carpenter at the Crescent Shipyard. Res 163 Livingston St. MEM: UD25. SERV: 4th NY Heavy Art. F: August F. Schmidt Undertaking. Thu Apr 18.

CULVER, AUGUSTUS P, 64, b Pottsville, PA, s/o Jonathan, d Thu aftn Mar 3,1910, at home, Parker Rd, Eliz. SURV: w/2(?) s/dau. 2 s were killed in 1901. On Wed May 15, Bertram M, a line man, in a fall while at work in the city yard, and on Thu Nov 14, Arthur, fm wounds rcvd while fighting in the Philippines. He was int Evergreen Jan 2, 1902. Res E 35+ yrs, for 25 yrs Super of Reservoirs of the Elizabethtown Water Co. For 10 yrs worked at his carpentry trade. MEM: JK64. SERV: Pvt Co A, 28th NJ Vol Inf, as was his f. F: Mon, Rev 1st Bapt Chh. Fri Mar 4. (P)

CULVER, GEORGE, 78, d Mon 740 pm May 22, 1905, Eliz. SURV: bro Stephen, Point Pleasant. Struck and instantly killed by a Baltimore & Ohio train bound east on the Central RR 100 yds east of the signal tower at the Elizabethport station. On a 60 day furlough fm S'H, Kearny, confirmed by Martin Morgue of which Mr Martin's f, who d a few yrs ago, serv in the same CW Reg. Entered S'H last Dec 26. SERV: Co K, 28th Reg, NJ Vol. F: S'H, if body not claimed. Tue May 23.

CULVER, JONATHAN, 94, d abt Mon May 20, 1907, South Amboy. SURV: s Augustus P, Eliz Town Water Co pumping station super, on Parker Rd, and is V-Cmdr JK 64. SERV: F and s both enl Co A, 28th Reg of Vol. S was abt 18 at enl, returning fm Freehold wearing his uniform. f, then abt 50, remarked that he would give his s a surprise the next day, went to Freehold, enl, and returned home wearing his uniform. Wed May 22.

CUMMINGS, ALEXANDER M, 82, d bfr noon Wed Aug 25, 1924, at home, 27 Grant Ave, W, Roselle Park. SURV: w Susie/ch Mrs A Soper, Somerville, Mrs N Taynor, R P, A E, William and Fred A, R P. 13 gch. 4 ggch. Res R P 49 yrs, for 33 yrs on B of Elections, and at one time mem B of Health. MEM: Past Master Azure Lodge 129 F&AM, the Masonic VA, Newark. CHH: 1st ME. SERV: 1st Lt 27th Inf, in 26 battles, including Gettysburg. Thu Aug 26.

CUMMINGS, JOSEPH, 60, d Wed aftn Aug 24, 1910, Gen H, Eliz. Walking fm home in Huntington to the S'H in Kearny, took ill in E. Thu Aug 25.

CURRIDEN, BENJAMIN, 84, d Tue mrng Jun 9, 1914, at home. Tue Jun 9.

CURTIS, ARTHUR R, BRIG GEN, 82, one of the few remaining CW Gen, d early Wed Apr 8, 1925, natl S'H, Milwaukee, WI. Wed Apr 8.

D

DALLAS, WILLIAM, 73, b Scotland, d Thu aftn Mar 27, 1919, at home, 135 N Euclid Ave, Westfield. SURV: w/ch Jessie, Mary and Lindsay, all W. Imm USA when a boy. Since 1900, manager of the wholesale tea house of Carter & Mason, NY. MEM: WS73. Plainfield Kennel Club. W Club and the W branch SPCA. CHH: St Pauls Epis, mem Mens Club. Mon Jan 13.

DANNEBERGER, JOHN J, 65, native of PHL, d Wed mrng Feb 27, 1907, S'H, Kearny. SURV: w/ch Charles F, Newark, Mrs Robert Waters and Mrs John J Hogan. sib Joseph, Broadway, Eliz, Anthony, ret mem Newark PF, and Mrs Charles Brown, P. Came to Eliz when a boy. Conducted a barber shop. At Kearny last 7 yrs. MEM: UD25. EFA. SERV: Enl Eliz Co H, 4th NJ Vol. He and bro Joseph attended many reunions of Vets and sang, both having good voices. Wed Feb 27.

DAUBNER, JOHN, 87, b Germany, d Tue mrng Sep 30, 1913, at home, 625 S St, Eliz. SURV: ch John, George, Leonard, Joseph, all E, and Frank, Washington. 15 gch. 5 ggch. Res E for yrs. Carpenter by trade, ret yrs ago. MEM: UD25. CHH: A founder of St Michaels, mem St Michaels Soc. SERV: Sgt Co A, 1st NJ Vol, in a n/o battles. WIA. Tue Sep 30.

As a yng man, serv in the German Army, in the days when Germany had not yet found itself a combined empire and when the many provinces were girding themselves for the great conflict with France, the Franco-Prussian War. Imm USA in time to join CW. Had imm primarily to better himself in a biz way, but found war even more evident in the new country than the old. Could not resist the war spirit when the call for arms came, and enl, his svc invaluable because of his sound military training rcvd abroad. A Repub aft imm. However, during the CW became a Dem, not on any principles, but because of insulting remarks cast toward Dems by Repub at the front. Heard it said time and time again that there were no Dem in the N and that people of the N did not know what Dem were. For this and other reasons, returned fm war a full fledged Dem. Fri Feb 3, 1911.

DAVIS, ANDREW, of PHL, d toward end of 1928. Second to last surv mem PHL Corn Exchange Reg. Obit of Henry H

Fri, Feb 22, 1929.

DAVIS, JOHN R, 67, d Tue Jan 2, 1906, at home, Toms River. **SURV**: s Walter E, Eliz. **CHH**: Bapt. **SERV**: C Army, standing by his state, VA, when it seceded. **F**: Buried Sat aftn. Mon Jan 8.

DAVIS, THOMAS, d Sat mrng Jan 9, 1909, at home of dau Mrs John J McLean, 81 Court St, Eliz. **SURV**: ch Mrs McLean, with whom he res, Mrs Frank Trowbridge and Mrs Thomas Gorringe, E, and Mrs Augustus A Bahr, Indianapolis, IN. Res E for yrs. Employ by Singer as doorman at the main entrance of the big factory. **CHH**: 1st Cong. **SERV**: Navy. Sat Jan 9.

DAY, ALLEN H, CAPT, 68, d Sat Nov 25, 1905, Dunellen. Worked Central RR, well known to many commuters fm early runs Dunellen to Jersey City and return. Long resided D. **MEM**: Mercer Lodge 50 F&AM, Trenton. **SERV**: Co I, 15th NJ Vol. **F**: Tue aftn. Tue Nov 28.

DAY, DANIEL C, b Newark, s/o Vincent, d early Sun mrng Jun 24, 1906, Gen H, Eliz. **SURV**: 2dau/2s, one s ae 6. w d Springfield 2 yrs ago, and he rem to E, 29 Crane St. When yng, rem to IL. **SERV**: Enl ae 18 Bat A, 1st IL Art. **F**: Tue 2 pm, Parlor of W J R Knowles, 262 Morris Ave, Rev Dr Cobb, with GAR ceremony. Int S&S' plot Evergreen. Mon Jun 25.

DAY, WILLIAM H, 71, d Wed Feb 5, 1913, at home of dau, Rahway. **SURV**: w/dau Mrs S C Terrill, 134 Hamilton St. 3 gch. Res R 18 yrs, past 12 yrs as clerk in the Special Delivery Dept, R PO. Res Irvington bfr, in the grocery biz. **MEM**: LL27 F&AM. JG4. **SERV**: Enl otbrk, 8th Reg, NJ Vol Inf. At Gettysburg and nearly all the struggles of the AP, to end. 4 bros went through CW successfully, but have since d, he being last of his fam. **F**: Sat 8 pm at home of dau. Rev H R Rose, P, Chh of the Redeemer, Newark. Int Irvington. Thu Feb 6.

DECKER, AMOS A, b Sat Mar 26 1836, NYC, d Tue Feb 22, 1910, at home, 16 Ball St, Irvington. **SURV**: w/ch Mrs William Allen, I, Mrs Joseph Struck, Newark, and Harry A. Half-bros George and Henry Struck, Newark. Rem with par as a boy to Rahway. Learned the coachsmith and blacksmith trade with his uncle, Samuel Ross. Earned 9c/day plus board during 5 yr apprenticeship. With the old Rahway Vol FD. **MEM:** Past Cmdr I VA. Honorary mem I Vol FD. **SERV:** Pvt 6th Ind Bat of NY. Thu Feb 24.

DECKER, CHARLES S, 83, native of Jamaica, LI, d Sun Jan 12, 1919, Ridgewood. **SURV:** s Henry C, Jersey City. **F:** F Chapel, Jefferson Ave & E Jersey St. Mon Jan 13.

DECKER, GEORGE WILLIAM, b Thu Feb 26, 1846, native of Eliz, s/o late Ann Crane & John Decker, d Mon mrng Feb 13, 1922, at home, 48 Charles St, Roselle Park. **SURV:** w Georgiana Caniff Decker. sib J Albert, Frank C and Mrs Menta C Glaser, all E, and Edwin T, Brooklyn. Res E except past 3 yrs. **MEM:** UD25, past 2 term Cmdr. Honorary mem E Post VFW when frmd. **SERV:** Enl Mon Feb 17, 1862, Brooklyn, Co I, 67th Reg, NY Vol Inf, attached to 2nd Brig of the 1st Div of the 4th Army Corps. At Siege of Yorktown, and at Williamsburg, Fair Oaks, Rappahannock and the Wilderness. Hon Disc Fri Feb 17, 1865, St Petersburg, VA. Mon Feb 13.

DECKER, HENRY, "CAPTAIN", 83, d Mon mrng May 2, 1927, Rahway H, Rahway. Rcvd title of "Captain" when he operated a boat on the Rahway Riv and SI Sound. **SERV:** Hvy Art with the AP. Mon May 2.

b Chelsea, SI, would have been 85 next Mon. **SURV:** w Elizabeth/step-ch incldg Mrs Adrian Martin, Brooklyn, Mrs Julia LaPoint, Newark, Mrs Mary DeWolff and Mrs Stephen Tucker, Jersey City, Mrs J H Levy, NY, and Charles and Arthur, Phl. "gch", incldg Franklin LaPoint, Phl, Evelyn and Gertrude Tucker, Jersey City, Mrs Harry Zbinden, Brooklyn, Mrs Carl Mier, Mrs Harold Hansel, Mrs George Springer and Mrs H H Roxford, Newark. Res Richmond, SI, bfr rem to R. In the oyster biz, operated boats on the riv and sound. **MEM:** Richmond Post 524 SI. Honorary mem Mulvey Ditmars Post VFW, R. **CHH:** 1st Bapt, and the Mens Brotherhood. **SERV:** Throughout. Bat E, 4th Reg, NY Vol Hvy Art, Capt J Alston and Col Thomas Doubleday. In the defense of Washington, then serv with 22nd

Army Corps. At the Wilderness, Piny Branch Church, Laurel Hill, Spottsylvania Courthouse, North Anna River, Pamunky River, Totopotomay, Cold Harbor, Petersburg Siege and capture, Jerusalem Plank Road, Deep Bottom, Strawberry Plain, Ream Station, Poplar Grove Church, Hatcher's Run, Dabney's Mill, Boynton White Oak Road, Amelia Springs, Sailor's Creek, Farmville, Appomattox Courthouse, present at Lee's surrender and marched in the Grand Review at Washington, Tue May 23, 1865. Expanded obit Tue May 3.

DECKER, JAMES H, 65, b SI, d Tue ngt Dec 17, 1907, Alexian H, Eliz. **SURV**: w/sib Richard and William. Res at 211 Geneva St. Res E 50+ yrs. Worked for NY & SI Ferry Co. **MEM**: Past 2 term Cmdr JK64. **SERV**: Co C, 4th NY Heavy Art, 3 yrs, in svrl imp battles. **F**: Thu 2 pm, Howard T Scheckler, Super of E Rescue Mission. At his request, buried with GAR ceremony. Int S&S' lot, Evergreen. Wed Dec 18.

DECKER, RICHARD, 66 yrs, 4 mos, b Eliz, d Tue Jun 13, 1911, at home, 42 Geneva St, Eliz. **SURV**: w Loriena/ch Isaac, Richard, John, Alfred, George, Mrs Charles O'Brien and Mrs Alfred Duheau. 15 gch. bro William. Life long res E. **SERV**: Cpl in Co B, 11th Reg, NJ Vol. Disc while in camp near DC, Tue Jun 6, 1865. 40 yrs ago during a Jul 4th celebration, crippled for life and rendered blind. With a number of other men he was about to fire a cannon in front of the old Courthouse, when the cannon exploded. He had his right arm and 2 fingers on his left hand blown off. Wed Jun 14. (See Van Pelt, John W.)

DENTON, ANTHONY W, 65, d Thu Jan 26, 1905, S'H, Kearny. **SURV**: Relatives in Rahway and Eliz. A wid. Inmate S'H 12 yrs. **SERV**: Co G, 39th NJ Vol. **F**: Int Sat Evergreen. Mon Jan 30, 1905.

DENTON, CHARLES C, SR, 71, b Eliz in the old hist bldg on Washington St, near the Siloam Presby Chh, s/o Nathan F & Lydia, d Mon 1210 pm, Jan 11, 1909, at home, 19 Catherine St, Eliz. **SURV**: w Julia/s Charles C, Jr, with the Elizabethtown Gas Co. 7 gch. Par d yrs ago. When yng, rem with par to Newark,

where he conducted a newspaper and stationery store. Returned to E 20 yrs ago. Past janitor Morrel St PS. Marched on MDAYs with UD25. SERV: Enl Newark Pvt Co B, 9th Reg, Vol Inf. Mon Jan 11.
DEPREZ, JOHN, abt 65, b Somerville, d Tue Jan 30, 1912, at home, 848 Martin St, Eliz. SURV: 3 dau. For yrs a mem PD, detailed on duty at the uptown RR sta when the PA and Central Stas were combined. In 1885 appointed mail clerk, a senior clerk at the local PO at dod. Yrs ago serv on CC, the Dem from the old 3rd Ward. MEM: Hansa Lodge 165 IOOF, HL81 F&AM. UD25. Treas Postal Clerks & LCA. SERV: Navy. Wed Jan 31. (P)
DERREVERE, MATTHIAS, 83, d Mon mrng Feb 8, 1904, at home, St George Ave, Rahway. SURV: w/svrl ch. Conducted a cartage and express biz for yrs. Mon Feb 8.
DEVINE, EDWARD M, d Sat eve, Aug 7, 1909, at home, Plainfield. SURV: w/dau. Conducted a coal biz in P for yrs. MEM: WS73. Mon Aug 9.
DEVLAN, CHARLES F, d Sat Feb 7, 1920, Idaho Springs, ID. A bro-in-law of Mrs Hattie Darling, 326 1/2 Murray St, Eliz. Frmr res Eliz. CHH: Frmr mem Fulton St ME. SERV: Enl PHL 1861, assigned to Cav in the AP. In 52 battles, often inside enemy lines, with most svc Co K, 6th PA Cav. F: Eliz. Thu Feb 12.
DI CESNOLA, LOUIS PALMA, GEN, 72, Vet of the Italian war for independence, Brig-Gen in the U Army, and Dir of the Metropolitan Museum of Art in NY since 1878, d Mon Nov 21, 1904. The Youth's Companion - NE Edition, Thu Dec 8.
DICKIE, ROBERT B, CAPT, 81, WIA many times, and serv as a Guard at the bier of Abraham Lincoln, d Mon May 3, 1920. May 3, Dateline Pittsfield, MA.
DIETRICH, JOHN, COL, b Thu Mar 15, 1821, Belvidere, d announced Tue Mar 1, 1910, at home, Arlington Ave, Plainfield. SURV: A dau, Concord, NH, and 3 nieces. Came to P 1876. Educ at Stone Academy, Belvidere. A "49'r," went to CA, where he prospered, then rem aft 2 yrs to Bloomington, IL, where he became acquainted with Lincoln, Douglas and Grant. Had a place

in the Treas Dept in DC, resigning in 1863. Aft CW appointed as Surveyor of Customs, Galveston, TX, and PM, Calvert, TX. **SERV:** Enl 1863. Went to Vicksburg and assigned to Qtmstr Dept until Vicksburg fell and the first meridian organized. Appointed Col of the 1st MS Reg, on guard at Vicksburg. Tue Mar 1.

DIXON, JOHN J, 80, b SI, d early Mon mrng Apr 7, 1919, at home, 121 Elizabeth Ave, Eliz. **SURV:** ch Mrs Isaac King, Mrs Lillian McFee, Mrs Ida Bruggy, William A, and Alfred. Res downtown E 70 yrs, at Elizabeth Ave. When a boy, followed the sea for a short period. Aft CW appointed to the PD, a patrolman for 12 yrs, then a plainclothesman for 3 yrs. Ret, then engaged in the furniture biz. Past 15 yrs, had a shop at 121 Elizabeth Ave, and dealt in articles that were brought fm all sections of the world by seafaring men. **MEM:** Franklin Lodge 9 IOOF, and OB78 KP. **SERV:** At otbrk., went to NYC and vol his svc to the Cmdr of a new Reg of Inf, and accepted. Fought under Grant 3 yrs. Mon Apr 7.

DIXON, WALTER, 77, b Eliz, s/o late Alexander, d Tue ngt Nov 21, 1922, at home of dau Mrs Paul Saxer, 15 Butler St, Eliz. **SURV:** ch Mrs Isaac Van Pelt, Mrs Harry Gordon, Mrs William J E Cocker, Mrs Saxer, Mrs John Halberstadt, and Walter, all E, Robert, Roselle, and G Arthur, Roselle Park 36 gch, 19 ggch. sib William H and Alexander, E. w d 12 yrs ago. Life long res E. A dock builder by trade, ret 12+ yrs ago. **MEM:** RJE Co 4, E Vol FD. EFA. PL78 KP. Hon mem VFW. Senior V-Cmdr JK64. **CHH:** Grace Epis. **SERV:** In Aug 1862, then ae 17, walked fm E to Trenton to enl in Co B, 11th NJ Vol. At Fredericksburg, Chancellorsville, Gettysburg, Watting Heights, Spottsylvania Court House, Cold Harbor and Petersburg encounters at Kelly's Ford, Locust Grove, Mine Run, skirmishes abt North Anna River and Barker's Mills, and the Wilderness. Hon Disc Tue Jun 6, 1865. F: Sat aftn at home. Wed Nov 22.

DIXON, ROBERT E, PVT, 17, s/o Mr & Mrs Robert, 43 S 2nd St, Eliz, and gs/o CW Vet Walter, is stationed at Camp

McClellan with Co G, 113th Inf. Enl Sep 19, 1917. Wed Feb 13, 1918. (P)

DOBBS, JOHN, 92, d Fri Mar 1, 1918, S'H, Kearny. SURV: ch Mrs P J McCartney, Rahway, and John, Montclair. 5 gch. Oldest inmate of S'H. Frmr res Rahway. Sat Mar 2.

DOHMEYER, CHARLES B, 63, native of LI, d Sat Nov 25, 1911, Eliz. SURV: w/ch Mrs Henry Gebhardt and Mrs Alfred Grieves. Res 900 E Jersey St, and E abt 40 yrs. Engaged in the cigar biz at E Jersey & Division St. MEM: UD25. Vet Z. CHH: German Luth. SERV: Enl Co B, 3rd NY Vol. F: At home, Rev Christian G Fisher. Int Evergreen. Mon Nov 27.

DOOLEY, MICHAEL F, 69, b 1843 Cohoes, NY, d Fri ngt Jan 26, 1912, at home of dau Mrs C O'Donnell, 24 W 26th St, Bayonne. SURV: ch Mrs O'Donnell, John J, ex-School Com, Eliz, Charles E, agent for the Plumbers Union, Cranford, William E, Thomas H, Mrs James H Daugherty and Mrs John F Dooley, Bayonne, and Mrs John Anderson, Newark. 15 gch. sib John F, Jersey City, James J and Mrs John Welsh, C, and Mrs M A McCusker, B. Res 846 E Jersey St, Eliz. Fm 1868 to 1884 in charge of the Singer cabinet making dept at North Bend, IN. Transf to Eliz 1884, in charge same dept. Left Co 1896, rem to B, started own biz, and ret 1904. MEM: GS100, past Cmdr, and the Adj and Treas at dod. CHH: A founder Holy Rosary. Sat Jan 27.

DONOVAN, JOSEPH, LT, 66, b London, England, d Fri ngt Oct 4, 1901, at home, 1157 Mary St, Eliz. SURV: w. An orphan. Imm USA to E as a boy and spent early yrs on a farm in the suburbs. Learned the carpentry trade, becoming a successful builder. When Gen Harrison was elected and Samuel S Moore was appointed PM, appointed as assist PM, serv until succeeded by William J Whelan, who aft became PM. A founder of the Repub party, active in the frmr 5th Ward, and fqtly chosen Judge of Election. MEM: UD25, Cmdr. Frmr mem WL33 F&AM for yrs. Initiated into Lodge when he came home fm Army on furlough. SERV: 1st Lt Co A, 2nd NJ Vol, principally recruited in E, late Capt James Wilson, to end. Severely WIA. In one battle the Co flag was in danger, and he, being the last of the guard of 7 who had defended it, at the risk of his life secured the highly-prized emblem, and wrapping it about his body saved it from falling into the hands of the C. The act was considered one of the most heroic which was performed during the rebellion and won the praise and admiration of the Vets. The flag was in his possession and will be placed on his casket. F: Tue aftn, Post in attendance. Bearers Vets of old Reg. Sat Oct 5.

HEROES LIVED AMONGST US, EVEN BEFORE CAMERAS RECORDED THEM

One cannot be unmoved watching our flag being raised at ground zero. A most proper connection was made to the raising of the flag at Iwo Jima. The names of those at Iwo are known to historians, and hopefully the names of those at the tragedy Sept. 11 are known and will join the former in the history books. These events are milestones in the history of our nation, rallying points that focused needed efforts to defeat those who would destroy our country. What of the age before pictures? Did such heroes exist and we do not remember them because there are no pictures to look at?

Yes they did, and I wish to remember one now by the name of Lt. Joseph Donovan. Donovan was born in London, England, about 1835, and came to the United States as a boy, settling in the vicinity of Elizabeth. He was an orphan. At the outbreak of the Civil War, he volunteered and served as first lieutenant of Company A, Second New Jersey Volunteers, which recruited men principally from Elizabeth, under the command of Capt. James Wilson.

Donovan served throughout the war, and was severely wounded. In one battle, the company's flag was in danger, and, being the last of the guard of seven who had defended it, at the risk of his life he secured the highly-prized emblem, and wrapping it about his body, saving it from falling into the hands of the Confederates. The act was considered one of the most heroic which was performed during the rebellion and won the praise and admiration of the veterans. The flag was in possession of Donovan at the time of his death. This information came from his obituary of Oct. 5, 1901, headlined "He was the last of a brave color guard" and "Flag he saved from enemy to be on his casket."We have no pictures of what Donovan did that day, but his heroic act was remembered for the next 35 years. What Donovan protected in the heat of battle protected him on his final day. This man who began life as a London orphan could say then, "I am an American!" We can call him hero.

Harry G. Woodworth
Willingboro

Letter to the Editor, Burlington County (NJ) Times, Sun, Dec 2, 2001.

DORAN, JOSEPH, b Sun Dec 10, 1843, Eliz, d Thu mrng Jan 1, 1925, Alexian Bros H, Eliz. **SURV**: bro, a RC Priest in Phl. Res with par Race St for yrs. Aft par d, kept house with sis, Sarah, until she d 1912. Sold homestead, then boarded at various downtown addresses. For svrl yrs res at S'H, Kearny, but returned to E, at Laurie Hotel, 78 E Jersey St. Cabinet maker and carpenter. During WW, in spite of being ae 75, accepted for guard duty at Standard Aircraft Corp, serv until Armistice. **CHH**: St Marys. **SERV**: Enl 1861 as a Vol, 9th NJ Reg, seeing much active svc. **F**: Sat mrng St Marys. Fri Jan 2.

DOTY, ALONZO, 92, d Tue Apr 4, 1933. One of Morris Co 6 surv CW Vets. Custodian of one of the PS, ret 1912. Tue Apr 4, Dateline Morristown.

DOTY, JOHN H, 93, b Newark, s/o Samuel, d Mon aftn Jan 4, 1937, Disabled Vets Home, Menlo Park. **SURV**: ch Mrs Wright, Eliz, and s S C, Hillside and E H. gch and ggch. w Charlotte d 1923, just bfr his ret fm Central RR. Partial Obit Tue Jan 5. (P)

Only surv Roselle CW Vet, rode in place of honor at the head of the MDAY parade Wed mrng. Serv in 1st Corps, 1st Div, enl with a NJ Vol Reg as Drummer Boy, ae 18. At Gettysburg and others of imp. Rode in the car owned by his gs, Fire Chief George S Wright, who is Jr V-Cmdr Unity Post 229, Inc, AL. Thu May 24, 1934.(P)

A MDAY svc was held for the late John H Doty Wed eve. Resolution adopted, as follows:

"Whereas, John H Doty, the last surv mem of the U Army to res in either Roselle or Roselle Park, has passed away and whereas: John H Doty had an outstanding record earned in the svc of his country due to his active engage in the historic Battle of Fredericksburg. Therefore, be it resolved, that the mems of Unity Post 229 AL Inc, of Roselle and Roselle Park, express sincere regret and extend sympathies to the mems of the fam of the late John H Doty."

DOUGHERTY, HENRY, 64, d Sun mrng,_____, at home, 87 Central Ave, Westfield. **SURV:** w/ch William E, George H, and Mrs Carrie Gaskill, W, and Mrs Charles T Marsh, Eliz. Came to W 30 yrs ago. In blacksmithing biz with s William at shop on N Ave. **MEM:** WS73. **SERV:** Enl 30th Inf, NJ Vol. F: Tomorrow 230 pm at home, Rev George A Francis, P 1st Bapt, W. Int Fairview. Obit _____.

DOUGLAS, H. FRANK, CAPT, native of Hanover Neck, Morris Co, d Mon Nov 19, 1906, Daytona, FL. w, d/o late Enos Woodruff, d svrl yrs ago. Res Eliz for yrs. Conducted mens furnishing goods store at 1st & Court St. For yrs a purser on line of steamers plying btwn NY and Sandy Hook. For yrs a clerk in a spice store in NY. Visited Eliz a few mos ago fm FL, where he held a Govt pos. **SERV:** Qtmstr 1st NJ Brig. Wed Nov 21.

DOUGLASS, FRANK W, 69, d Mon Jun 24, 1912, S'H, Kearny. **SURV:** dau Mrs Alvin R. Eaton, Jr. Frmr res downtown Eliz. **MEM:** JK64. **SERV:** Enl Tue Aug 19, 1862, Co C, 141st PA Vol. WIA Wilderness Fri May 6, 1864. Hon disc as Sgt Thu Jul 6, 1865. Tue Jun 25.

DRAKE, CHARLES, 73, d Fri May 5, 1911, Rahway. **SURV**: w/ch Theodore A, Eliz, and Robert A, Newark. sib James, Newark, and Mrs J E Moore, Main St, Eliz. Res 46 Fulton Ave, and R for yrs. **CHH**: Trinity Meth. **SERV**: 13th Reg NJ Vol. F: Mon aftn, P Rev C C Woodruff. Fri May 5.

DRAKE, CHARLES N, 70, b Eliz, yngst s/o late James S, d Fri aftn May 5, 1916, at home, 7 Orange Ave, Cranford. **SURV**: 2/w frmr Miss Hannah Johnson of Union/ch Mrs Watson Milder, Rutherford, and Charles N, Jr, and Emily, C. sib Edward K, Eliz, Mrs Charles Vermule, Asbury Park and Mrs Benjamin H Norris, 6 others having d, one being Gen J Madison Drake, Cmdr of the Z, and another Silas D, of Lincoln, mem of his CW Co. Res C 35 yrs. f at one time was an owner and editor of the NJJ. When ae 10 indentured to a Trenton man to learn marble cutting trade. At 17, ran away to enl CW. Aft CW worked in the office of the NY World. 26 yrs ago last Sep became a compositor in the office of the EDJ, ret last Fall. The first reporter for the EDJ in C. A Repub, mem of the C Tp Comm. **MEM**: In Grants campaign a mem of the Boys in Blue, and campaign club of Eliz. Vet Z, which disb in Eliz a few yrs ago. UD25, color bearer. Made many trips with GAR, and helped aid the surv of the Vets train wreck in Buffalo a few yrs ago. C Council, Royal Arcanum. Typographical Union 150 Eliz. **CHH**: C Presby. **SERV**: 20th PA Cav. Sat May 6. (P)

DRAKE, JONATHAN BAKER, b Mon Jan 18, 1841, Westfield, oldest s/o Ezra & Mary Baker Drake, d Sun Jun 26, 1904, at home, 137 Jefferson Ave, Eliz. **SERV**: Co B, 30th NJ Vol, H Steward. (Partial obit) Mon Jun 27.

DRAKE, SILAS DOWNER, b Feb, 1843, Eliz, 3rd s/o James S & Eunice, d Wed eve Jul 15, 1908, at home Beechwood Heights, suburb of Bound Brook. **SURV**: w frmr Miss Alice Van Houten, m E 1865, Rev Dr Robert Aikman, P 3rd Presby/ch Louis L, Boston, Edward R, Louisville, KY, and Arthur G, Bound Brook. 4 gch. sib Gen J Madison, E, frmr Capt 9th NJ Vol, Edward K, newspaper writer, long assoc with the EDJ, Charles N, Cranford,

printer with the EDJ, and CW Vet 20th PA Cav, Mrs Isaac Faulks, Mrs George A Mooney, and Mrs Hampton Norris, E, and Mrs Charles Vermeule, Asbury Park. f was a prominent publisher, a mem of the firm Foote & Drake, who published the NJJ, issued as a weekly in 1843. Attended local schools then joined f to learn printer trade at the NJJ, then rem to Trenton. Worked with f at intervals at the State Gazette and True American, and the Mercer Standard, a weekly. At close of CW opened a stationery store, then became traveling salesman for Prince Metallic Paint Co, visiting almost every state. Entered real estate, with Westfield ave, opening up that section of E, a tribute to him. Founded Lorraine, and Dewey Park, suburb of Lincoln, and named aft Adm Dewey whom he admired. Elected Mayor, and appointed PM, Lincoln. While Mayor, appointed an all-woman Town Council. Attended a natl convention of Mayors in Lincoln, NE, taking this "Petticoat Govt." At Lorraine built a strictly non-denominational chh with his own money. When one soc tried a grab, he closed it. It later passed to Mrs Hannah Randolph and is now the Wesley ME. Its pews had been part of the furnishings of the old Cranford Presby. Erected the theater on E Jersey St, E, now known as Proctor's Theater. Pres of many realty cos. Rem to Beechwood 10 yrs ago. Gave a lot of land to the FD for a hose house. **MEM:** One of first E Vets to join GAR in its infancy at Newark, then UD25, ending with AW23. **CHH:** Epis. **SERV:** Enl 1864 Co C, 14th NJ Vol Inf, Capt Chauncey Harris. Bro Charles enl 4 days later. At Winchester, Shenadoah Valley, WIA by a minie ball right arm. Active svc 19 days, but mos in H on invalid list. Hon disc and pens for life. Always wore minie ball attached to his GAR badge. Vet Z, E, eldest bro Gen J Madison, Cmdr. **F:** At home. Laid to rest in GAR uniform. Thu Jul 16. (P)
DRAKE, WILLIS SANFORD, d Sun mrng Feb 7, 1926, Eliz. (See **Monitor**)
DREYER, FRANK, b Oct 8, 1837, Markolden, Germany, d Thu 10 am Oct 10, 1912, at home, 20 Palmer St, Eliz. **SURV:** w Meta, couple celebrating their 50th m anniv Aug 14/ch Mrs Peter

Miska, Mrs Charles Wenke, Mrs George Zingler, Frank, Jr, and August. Imm USA 1859 to E. A building contractor, had charge of part of the construction work on the bridge built across Newark Bay for the Central RR. He, among other builders, erected 1st German Presby chh. **MEM**: A founder of the Plattdeutsch Verein, and one of the first Pres. Charter mem HL81 F&AM. Harmonia B&L Assoc, VP at dod. **CHH**: German Luth. **SERV**: Enl otbrk U Army, to end. Engaged in building pontoon bridges and other construction work. Thu Oct 10.

DUBON, WILLIAM, d Sun Mar 24, 1907, at home, Frenchtown. **SURV**: w/ch Mrs Benjamin Dalrymple and Walter J, Eliz, and Mrs Grant Haver, Flemington. To F only a short time ago. In Eliz, assist s-in-law Dalrymple in his grocery at 3rd & Franklin St. **MEM**: GAR. Masonic Fraternity. Order of the Patrons of Husbandry. **CHH**: Bapt. **SERV**: 38th NJ Vol. **F**: Took place in F Bapt, Rev Mr Austin. Sat Apr 6.

DUNHAM, SAMUEL, b near Rahway, d Sun Jan 26, 1902, at home, 317 Pearl St, Eliz. **SURV**: w/3s/dau. Res E for yrs. A painter. **MEM**: E Painters Union. **SERV**: Enl Spring 1861 Co A, 1st NJ Vol, late Maj David Hetfield, first Co in NJ to enl for 3 yrs. Later, serv in Co C, 14th Reg. **F**: Wed aftn at home, Rev Dr Tomlinson. Int sol plot Evergreen. Mon Jan 27.

DUNN, LEWIS A, 61 next Thu, s/o late Theodore, d Sun mrng, May 25, 1902, Pasadena, CA. **SURV**: w/2 s. Frmly of Plainfield. Head of Dunn & Case, who had a news and stationery store in Eliz, and later Dunn Bros, news agents on the NJ Central, until underbid by the present Union News Co. **CHH**: 7th Day Bapt, P. **SERV**: A Lt at CW end. Tue May 27.

DUNN, MICHAEL W, d Tue ngt Mar 30, 1909, at home, 238 2nd St, Eliz. **SURV**: w Johanna/ch Joseph and Michael. Res E 55 yrs, always on 2nd St. Ret for 15 yrs. **CHH**: A founder of 50 yr old St Patricks. **SERV**: 37th NY Vol, and 14th NJ, enl latter Reg in E. **F**: Fri mrng St Patricks. Wed Mar 31.

DURBAN, THEODORE, CAPT, 77, b Mainz, Germany, d Wed Aug 6, 1902, Eliz. Imm USA to NYC as a yng man. Long res at 152 Livingston St, E. Conducted a saloon on 1st St, btwn Livingston St & Broadway. MEM: JK64. SERV: Rallied a number of yng men around him at otbrk, who followed him in Co G, 45th NY Vol. WIA, granted a pens. F: Fri 2 pm JK64 HQ. Thu Aug 7.

DURIE, WILLIAM BRITTEN, 75, d Sun Jan 17, 1916, at home, 56 Jaques Ave, Rahway. SURV: w/ch Samuel C and William Britten, Jr, of R, and Mrs Frank, Marlboro. Res R 43 yrs, coming when Lincoln School was built, and took charge of the high school then conducted in that bldg, the Principal for 5 yrs. Principal of School 24, Jersey City, 35 yrs. Serv svrl terms as a CC and B of Educ mem. Treas of the Workmens B&L Assoc 25 yrs, resigning 3 yrs ago. MEM: WFB27. R Council 884 RA. CHH: Trinity ME, 30+ yrs. SERV: NCO Co B, 30th NJ Vol, and later 39th NJ Reg. F: Int Chatham. Mon Jan 17.

b Mar 16,1839, lifelong friend of William H Miller. (See Miller)

DUSENBERRY, AUGUST, b Newark, d Fri mrng Mar 13, 1914, at home, Park Pl, Newark. SURV: 3 ch. sib Mrs J E Buzby, and J P, Treas of Public Serv Corp, both N. Life long res N. Hardware biz, ret 5+ yrs. Mem CC 1882-93, then serv as a PC svrl yrs. SERV: POW Libby. Fri Mar 13.

DUTROW, ADAM L. 86, native of Baltimore, MD, d Sun mrng Dec 9, 1928, at home, 19 New Brunswick Ave, Rahway. SURV: w Henrietta/ch Leonard, 29 Church St, R, and Milison M, at home. bro George. (Psbly others, incomplete obit.) Res R aft CW. Est a large lumber biz, having a branch at Spring Lake. Became Super of Egyptian Lacquer Co, which erected its plant on the site of his frmr lumberyard at Lewis & Dock St, remaining in that pos for yrs. A Repub. MEM: GAR. LL27 F&AM. The old Vulcan Co Vol FD, when the old hand-pumping engine was in use. CHH: 2nd Presby. SERV: Ran away fm home to enter U side. Impressed with the NY Ind Bat when he saw it in B, enl, serv 3 yrs/7 mos. At Gettsburg, Bull Run, Antietam and others. One of the 3 surv mem of the 6th Ind NY Bat, made up largely of

R men. F: Tue 730 pm at home. Int Wed 10 am fam plot R. Mon Dec 10.

DWIGHT, H O, REV, 74, b Constantinople, Turkey, d Tue 3 am Jun 19, 1917, at home, 151 6th Ave, W, Roselle. **SURV:** w frmr Miss Frances Warner of Roselle, m 1901/ch Mrs L T Reed, Mrs J R Lewis, Mrs H H Fisher, Mary L, Adelaide F and s H E Dwight. Step-ch Warren and Howard Mulford, R. Imm USA at an early age. Res R 16 yrs. Educ in PS then entered college in OH. Aft CW, completed college then became a civil eng. In 1866 rem to Northampton, MA, where he was engaged in the building of a street RR. Began studying theo, and in 1868 returned to Constantinople as fiscal agent for American Bible Soc. In 1880 completed religious studies in Turkey and became a missionary in Constantinople. Engaged in translation of literary work until 1899. Rem to USA 1906, becoming corresponding Sec ABS, held until dod. A well-known author. LLD degree conferred on him at Amherst College 1896. **CHH:** 1st Presby, although being a Cong. **SERV:** Enl otbrk Pvt 20th OH Vol, to end. Disc as Capt, the pos awarded him for bravery. Tue Jun 19.

DWYER, PATRICK, d Tue Dec 14, 1912, Eliz. **SURV:** ch William J F, Aloyisus F and Joseph F. bro Rev William, P of St Andrews, Erie, Pa. sis-in-law Mrs Edward Cullen, Jersey City. Res E 40+ yrs, 38 yrs employ at Singer. An expert detective on counterfeit money, making a n/o arrests shortly aft CW. **MEM:** The old RJE Co 4, when the old hand-engines were used. JK64. **CHH:** A founder of St Patricks, but with Holy Rosary for yrs. **SERV:** Co H, 13th NJ Inf; Co C, 13th NY Art; and 6th NJ Art, to end, hon disc. Sat Dec 18, 1912.

E

ECKERT, JOHN, paternal gf/o WW sol William F Eckert, serv 4 yrs with 26th NY Eng. Wed Sep 4, 1918.

EDSON, JOHN HENRY, COL, 84, b 1830 BNY, s/o late Capt Alvin, US Marine Corps, d Wed Feb 11, 1914, at home, 218 W Jersey St, Eliz. **SURV**: ch Frederick C, Mary L and Mrs James Provost Thomas. m frmr Miss Frances Clarke, d/o late Gen Newman Clarke, E, abt 54 yrs ago. She d 1905. The late Col James Bomford was his bro-in-law. Rcvd early educ in Boston, MA. entered WP 1847, grad 1852. Went W, serv in Regular Army, engaged in the IW, and stationed for a time on the TX border. While W, ret fm svc and went into biz until CW. Aft CW, employ for some time NYC Custom House, ret yrs ago. **CHH**: St Johns. **SERV**: Enl Col otbrk in a VT Reg of Vol. Thu Feb 12.

EDWARDS, JOSEPH, 67, b Tue Oct 10, 1843, Meadow St, Eliz, d Fri aftn May 5, 1911, at home, 950 William St, Eliz. **SURV**: ch Mrs Mabel Scrimshaw, Mrs Grace Herlich, Robert C and Joseph E. 10 gch. m twice. Employ at Singer for yrs, Pres of the shipping dept SBS. **MEM**: AC25 OUAM, 16 yrs, presiding officer 2 terms, known among mem as "Uncle Joe," "War Horse," "Father of AC" and "Old Reliable." **CHH**: Park ME. **SERV**: Cast his first vote for Lincoln, and at whose Mon Jun 10, 1861, call for troops he enl Co K, 73rd NY Vol, Sickles Brig, Hookers Div of the 3rd Army Corps. Sat May 6. (P)

ELLIS, WILLIAM A, 83, b Mattopoisette (near New Bedford), MA, d Wed 330 am Sep 15, 1926, at home, 22 Donald Pl, Eliz. **SURV**: w Clarice/ch William A and George A, E, and Mrs E B Atken, West Roxbury, MA. sib Arthur W, Newark, Herbert E, Mrs John Traftin, Roselle, and Mrs Albert Carter, Perth Amboy. 10 gch. 4 ggch. Res E 60 yrs. In the oil biz as W A Ellis & Son at the foot of Elizabeth Ave. Sold co in 1913 to Standard Oil, worked for them a few yrs, then ret 1914. **CHH**: Epworth ME. **SERV**: Revenue Cutter Service, enl otbrk New Bedford. Wed Sep 15.

    Mr & Mrs William A Ellis of 238 Donald Pl, Eliz, celeb their 50th m anniv Thu ngt, and rcvd a purse of gold. Works for Standard Oil. Among those attending were Mr & Mrs Arthur Ellis, Newark, Mr & Mrs William H Ellis, Mr & Mrs George

Ellis, M Estella Ellis, Clarissa K Ellis, Jennie M Ellis, George A Ellis, Jr, William K Ellis, Arthur W Ellis, Jr, Newark, Edward B Ellis, J Harold Ellis, and Herbert L Ellis. Also, Mrs E B Aiken, Boston, John T Trafton and Albert Carter, Perth Amboy. Fri Jun 5, 1914.(P) (More names of attendees are listed.)

ENNIS, WILLIAM, 71, native of NY, d Sat ngt May 9, 1908, Eliz Gen H, Eliz. SURV: w frmr Mrs William Syers of E, m 44 yrs ago, and whose h had been a CW Vet, 5th NJ Vol/ch 2s/2steps. sib Rev Dr George, Bapt, and 2 sis, all Nyack, NY. Res 84 Broad St, and E since CW. MEM: UD25, on the firing squad MDAYs and F for Post mems. Long a caretaker of HQ. F: Rev Dr Eben B Cobb. Int Evergreen. Mon May 11.

ERNST, FRANCIS, native of Weile, Jutland, Denmark, d Tue, Apr 9, 1907, at the 852 Rebecca Pl home of the Mogensen fam, Eliz. Res USA 40 yrs, Bayonne first, then E since 1870. For yrs an inmate of the S'H, Kearny, and the last 3 yrs with the Mogensens. A flag man at the Schiller St crossing of the Central RR. CHH: Holy Trinity Luth. SERV: Enl 1861 Co K, 15th Reg, NY Vol, 2 yrs. Reup Co K, 33rd Reg, NJ Vol, 3 yrs. F: Thu aftn, Rev Frederick C Knapf. Int Evergreen, next to w, who d abt 12 yrs ago. Wed Apr 10.

ESSEX, EDWARD, native of England, d Fri eve, Mar 21, 1902, Eliz Gen H, Eliz. SURV: w/s/dau. Res NJ 32 yrs, most of the time in E. Machinist for the Central RR carshops. MEM: UD25. CHH: Memorial Bapt fm start, then Central Bapt. SERV: Enl otbrk Co A, 2nd NJ Vol, in many of the most imp battles. F: At home Tue 2 pm, Rev Dr Tomlinson. Int Fairmount, Newark. Sat Mar 22.

ESTABROOKE, EDWARD MANNING, b St John, New Brunswick, d Tue 10 am Dec 22, 1903, at home, 41 Broad St, Eliz. SURV: w mn Moore, and who was Mrs M B Crane at his m/ch s by a former m, in MI, and an adopted dau, New Haven. sib bro in ME, bro in the West Indies, and a sis in MI. Apprenticed to a photographer when yng. Went to ME, then later opened a gallery on Broadway, NY. Rem to E and purchased a galley at 110 Broad St fm W Harry Hill, now of Pasadena, CA. In later yrs relocated to 41 Broad St. Published many books on photography. **MEM**: Treas RC, RA. Crescent Lodge of Free Masons, Brooklyn, attending its 50th anniv a few mos ago, of which he rcvd a handsome souvenir. UD25, Trustee. **CHH**: Bapt, being bp ae 21 in a riv near his home in St John. Mem Memorial Bapt while in NY. In E, Central Bapt 8 yrs, and 4 yrs ago united with 1st Bapt. **SERV**: When a yng res of ME, became mem of the Band of the 1st Cav. Rode with it through E on his way to DC. **F**: Rev Travis B Thames, DD, P 1st Bapt. Int New Haven. Tue Dec 22.

F

FAULKS, WILLIAM, 89, b Newark, d Thu mrng Jan 3, 1929, at home, 701 Maple Ave, South Plainfield. **SURV**: ch N W, S Orange, Mrs Harry Tappen, Frank, Mrs Howard Snowden and Mrs Harry J Manning, S P. 5gch. 5ggch. Aft his Tue Jun 4, 1867, m to Miss Emma Webster, rem to Eliz for abt 5 yrs, where he conducted a meat market with an uncle. **MEM**: WS73. **CHH**: 1st Presby, when in Eliz. **SERV**: Abt a yr with 2nd NJ Vol. In the 1st Battle of Bull Run, City Point and the 7 day Battle of Gaius Mill. WIA on the 2nd day. Disc fm H. Fri Jan 4

FAY, JOHN C, 67, native of Eliz, s/o late Prof Julius Augustus, d abt Wed Sep 10, 1913, in his Corcoran Office Bldg, DC. His body was sitting in a chair in front of a window in his office which looks out upon the Treas Bldg in full view of thousands of people who pass there every day. **SURV**: w Eva/ch Mrs Lillian Brakely and Julius Augustus. w and ch were at Asbury Park summer home at dod. sis Mrs Arthur Nelson Trimble, 338 Rahway Ave, Eliz. Late bro Gen J Augustus Fay was Co Prosecutor for 10 yrs, and at one time Adj-Gen of the state. Educ in his f's school, 408 Rahway Ave. After CW moved to DC with f and studied law at Columbia Law School. Began practicing and became a claim lawyer of note. At one time assist Attorney-Gen

in charge of Govt interests before the Court of Claims. **MEM:** UD25, HQ at 109 Broad St. **SERV:** Ran away fm home and, underage, enl Co F, 1st NJ Cav. f worked to get him out, incldg a personal appeal to Lincoln, successful aft a yr. Bfr his disc, was in svrl battles incldg the Wilderness, where he had 2 horses shot out fm under him, and was WIA. Wed Sep 17.
FEALDS, FRANK D, 60, d early last wk St Margarets H, Kansas City, KS. Res Rahway for yrs. Conducted the Opera Bowling Alleys. Rem to Roselle Tp and opened a road house on St George's Ave until less than a yr ago, when he and fam started W. Fri Nov 8, 1901.
FEE, THOMAS J, 62, b Huntington, PA, d Thu abt 10 am Sep 24, 1908, Eliz. **SURV:** w/ch Edward, William R, and Frederick B. sib John, Frank, George and Harry, all res PA. bro-in-law William H Rankin. Res E for 26 yrs. Super Barrett Manu Co, where he d instantly while talking to bro-in-law. Bfr E worked as an eng for PA RR. **MEM:** Monshaunn Lodge F&AM. **CHH:** Greystone Presby. **SERV:** Lt 22nd PA Cav, brev. Thu Sep 24.
FIELD, GEORGE H, d Thu Feb 10, 1910, Hollywood, CA. **SURV:** w, in Hollywood/s and dau in the E. CC Hollywood. Res for yrs with fam Westfield Ave, Roselle Park, a property owner. In Hollywood since res in the W. Sat Feb 26.
FINK, JAMES W, 71, b Jersey Shore, PA, d Fri mrng Mar 7, 1919, at home, 433 E Dudley Ave, Westfield. **SURV:** w/ch Mildred and Mary W, and Cpl Arthur, with US forces in France. Rem to W 35 yrs ago. County Road Super, 25 yrs next month. **MEM:** WS Post. **CHH:** W Presby. **SERV:** Enl Sat Feb 27, 1864, disc Fri Aug 11, 1865. Fri Mar 7.
FLOOD, EDWARD, d Sat, Aug 17, 1901, Eliz. Vet never m. Res 446 Schiller St. Watchman at Singer. **MEM:** JK64. **F:** Tue mrng St Patricks. Int Holy Cross, Brooklyn. Mon Aug 19.
FLOWERS, JOHN, DR, 74, d Thu Jun 15, 1911, at home of sis Mrs Samuel H Cooper, 400 Fay Ave. Ocean Grove. Res with sis past 15 yrs. A practicing physician in Bristol, PA, at CW otbrk, enl as assist surgeon 52nd PA Vol, to end, mu/o a surgeon. Took

up practice in PHL, but ret in a yr due to illness. Mon Jun 19.
FLYNN, PETER, d Thu mrng Aug 5, 1909, at home of dau, 564 2nd Ave, Eliz. **SURV**: ch Mrs William Sheridan and Thomas, E, and Cornelius, Cambridge, MA. Res E 45 yrs, on the PF 14 yrs. **MEM**: JK64. **CHH**: Holy Rosary. St Patricks Alliance. Thu Aug 5.
FORGUS, WILLIAM F, 72, d Sun Jan 16, 1916, S'H, Kearny. Past res Eliz, entered S'H 1907. **SERV**: Co G, 3rd NJ Vol Inf. Mon Jan 17.
FOSSELMAN, CHARLES H, d announced. Frmr res Eliz. When yng, a student taught by the late F W Foote. Many relatives in Eliz and vcnty, cuz to Mrs J W Carkhuff, Bayonne, and related to Capt Aaron Bennett. **SERV**: Maj, 7th NJ Vol. Fri May 23, 1902.
FOX, THOMAS J, 92, d Mon ngt May 25, 1936, at home of dau Mrs Joseph F Levine, Rahway Ave, Eliz. **SURV**: 2 s/4dau, one being Mrs George F Schuble, a nurse in the Parochial Schools of Newark. sis. 16 gch. w was late Caroline Lind Fox. **MEM**: EFA. **CHH**: St Marys. HNS. **SERV**: Enl fm Union Co, mu/i Pvt, Trenton, Mon Sep 2, 1861, assigned to Co G, 8th Reg, NJ Vol Inf. Left for DC Sep 14 and did duty there until Apr, 1862, being later assigned to the AP. WIA Aug 13, 1862, and sent to H in Phl. Hon disc Wed Nov 5, 1862. Reup Navy Sat Aug 13, 1864. Assigned to steamer "Pawtucket" as a coal heaver. Cruised along the coast of NC, participating in NC blockade. At the attack on Fort Fisher, the Sugar Loaf Bat and the attack on Fort Anderson. Hon disc Tue Jun 13, 1865. **F**: Mon ngt at home of Mrs Levine, Solemn High Mass St Marys, Rev Walter G Jarvis of the faculty of Seton College, a g-nephew, celebrant, assist by Rev Thomas J Conroy, St Marys, and Rev Thomas Padians, St Patricks. Int Fri mrng Mt Olivet. Fri May 29, 1936.

Another dau Mrs Ellen Bransfield. Mon Jan 6, 1936.
On E MDAY celebrations. Thu May 31, 1934.(P)
Memories of '61 recalled. Mon Jun 1, 1931.(P)
In the Wed tribute paid to CW Vets with 27 other NJ Vets and

1 NY Vet, GAR reunion with colorful parade and armory fete in E. 3 GAR mem-at-large represented E. Thu Mar 30, 1933.
Honored at MDAY svc. Sat May 31, 1930.(P)
Attended annual UD25 Christmas party. Was Cmdr. Thu Dec 30, 1926.(P)
Installed Senior V-Cmdr at the UD25 meeting Tue ngt. Res 15 Cherry St. Tue Jan 8, 1924.

FRANKLIN, FREDERICK H, b Pittston, ME, d Sun ngt Feb 20, 1910, at home, 54 W Jersey St, Eliz. SURV: 2/w. s Walter. sib Joseph J and Mrs Arthur B Clark, Brooklyn, James J, E, and Mrs Charles Morgan, Boston. Res E since abt 1860, employ with J B Cooley, dealer in lumber yards, located at the foot of E Jersey St. Later worked for E G Brown, ice dealer, principle office in lower section of E. Next worked for Reeve & Williams. Became Super 10 yrs ago when Reeve d. Connected with E Ice Co since org, being its Super and one of its Dir. A Repub, for many terms represented old 1st Ward in CC. MEM: UD25. EL49. Masonic Fraternity. SERV: Co C, 14th NJ Vol. Mon Feb 21.

FRAZEE, JOHN H, REV DR, d a few days ago, Knoxville, TN. His w d a few wks ago. In yng yrs was Sec of the NJ Ag Soc, and editor of a Somerville newspaper. CHH: Twice P of Presby chh in Toms River, then part of New Brunswick Presby. P 1st Presby Knoxville 20+ yrs. Chapl 3rd TN Reg NG at dod. SERV: Chapl 3rd NJ Cav. Fri Oct 11, 1907.

FREEMAN, UEL, 90, d Tue Oct 19, 1926, at home of dau, 194 Elm Ave, Rahway. SURV: ch Edward S, 100 Milton Ave, W, William C, 200 Elm Ave, Walter, 210 Elm St, and Mrs W H C Coles, all R. A carriage manu bfr CW. In real estate biz past 40 yrs. MEM: B of Educ for yrs. SERV: 6th NY Ind Bat. Tue Oct 19.

FREEMAN, WILLIAM - see COEYMAN, WILLIAM.

FROMM, JOHN, b Wed Jan 16, 1839, d Sun 5 pm Dec 8, 1912, Gen H, Eliz. SURV: w Mary/ch Mrs Bertha Byer, Brooklyn, Mrs Lucy Herter, PHL, Edward and Louis, at their Lafayette St home. Came to E ae 1. At 19, opened the first barber shop on Broad St, opposite the Union Station, in biz for 42 yrs, ret 12 yrs ago. For yrs his barber shop was in the old Sheridan Hotel, where the new Courthouse stands. **MEM:** An org of UD25. A founder of the EFA. LH&L 30+ yrs. **CHH:** German Luth. **SERV:** Enl Sat Aug 30, 1862, Co H, 30th NJ Vol Inf. Dec 9.

G

GABRIEL, HENRY H, 88, b Milford, CT, d Mon ngt Feb 6,1922, at home, 13 Clinton St, Rahway. **SURV:** w Cornelia W, m 65 yrs ago/ch John H, Jacksonville, FL, Mrs Margaret Kune, Dallas, TX, Mrs Mildred Lynn and Mrs Martha G Moore, of 13 Clinton St, and Mrs Grace A Collins, Avon. 16 gch. 8 ggch. sib Mrs Annie Fisher, NY, Mrs Martha Taylor, Flushing, LI, Theodore, IL, and Charles, Cleveland, OH. Res R abt 70 yrs. Expert coach builder by trade. **MEM:** Past Cmdr WFB27, OD at dod. **CHH:** 1st Bapt. **SERV:** Co C, 30th NJ Vol, in a n/o imp battles. Tue Feb 7.

Attended the complimentary dinner for WFB27 mems given by A Edward Woodruff Tue eve May 30, 1911.

GAFFNEY, MICHAEL F, 96, b Dublin, Ireland, d Sun Apr 3, 1938, at home of a dau, West Orange. Imm USA 1845, res Newark and W O. **SERV:** 3 yrs. At the Wilderness, Gettysburg, Antietam and the 2nd Bull Run. Heard Lincoln deliver his Gettysburg address. Mon Apr 4.

GALLAGHER, THOMAS, b overseas, d Mon ngt, Nov 19, 1906, at home, 1055 E Grand St, Eliz. **SURV:** 2 s/6dau. Imm USA a yng man. A gardener employ by US Senator John Kean. **SERV:** Enl Co H, 150 NY Vol as Cpl, with Sherman in march to sea, and in many battles. At Gettysburg. An orderly to Gen Grant. F: Wed 2 pm, Rev Dr E B Cobb, 2nd Presby. Int Evergreen. Tue Nov 20.

GARBONATI, FRED, 80, d Wed May 2, 1917, Gen H, Eliz. w and dau d some yrs ago. Res Rahway and vcnty abt 40 yrs. Res Westfield Ave, Clark Tp, near the Rahway line. Since fam d, lived alone among his flowers and pets in Clark Tp, and a regular exibitor at the Rahway library annual Rose Show. **MEM**: WFB27. **SERV**: First man in RI to enl when the first call for Vol was issued, serv in a RI Bat and made Lt. Reup in a NY Reg, to end. Svrly WIA, which caused lifelong inconvenience. Mem famous Walker Expedition. Joined the J Madison Drake Vet Z, crossing the continent with that body. **F**: Sat. Int sol plot Hazelwood. Thu May 3.

Attended the complimentary dinner for WFB27 mems given by A Edward Woodruff Tue eve May 30, 1911.

GARDINER, WILLIAM H, 81, b Wed Mar 22, 1843, Newark, d Sat Jul 12, 1924, at home, 688 Pennsylvania Ave, Eliz. **SURV**: ch William H, Jr, Elizabeth I and Mrs Estelle Gardner. Fireman and eng with the PA RR 31 yrs, ret 12 yrs ago. **MEM**: Last surv charter mem St Chrysostom Lodge 3, KP, Newark. Winfield Scott Council 53, Jr, OUAM, E, Treas 20 yrs. **SERV**: Ran away ae 17 to Washington, enl U Army, to end. Mon Jul 14.

GARTHWAITE, SAMUEL, b Roselle, found d in bed. (No date mentioned.)

GARTZ, WILLIAM H, b 1845 NYC, s/o late Frederick and Louise, d Sat Jan 8, 1910, Bernardsville. **SURV**: w/2ch. Came to Eliz 1847. Attended school in both the old Presby chh bldg, Marshall St, and the old PS1. Aft CW in building biz lower section Eliz until 1894. Rem to B, doing same work. **SERV**: Enl Navy otbrk. One of the "Otsego" surv, torpedoed in the Roanoke River. Mon Jan 10.

GERKE, REINHARD, 80, b Soast, Westphalen, Germany, d Sun 5 am Jan 31, 1904, at home, 520 1st Ave, Eliz. **SURV**: ch Robert, Julius and Mrs Hattie Trauman. sis Mrs Matilda Terstegen. 7 gch. Imm USA 1854. Res E 4 yrs, rem to PHL aft m. In the silverware and jewelry biz. Aft CW, back to E and est jewelry biz on 1st St. In 1870 chosen assessor of the old 1st Ward, holding pos until a yr ago. In the real estate and insurance biz. Dir Central B&L Assoc, Harmonia B&L Assoc, and Union Co Mutual Fire Ins Co. **MEM**: Past Cmdr JK64. Hansa Lodge of

Odd Fellows, Platt Deutscher Verein, Leiderkranz Singing Soc. **SERV:** Enl otbrk Co A, 75th PA Vol, 1st Lt. Upon d of Capt, promo to Capt, holding the rank to end. In one battle a bullet penetrated his clothing and struck a watch in his vest pocket. He carried the watch until dod. F: Tue 8 pm at home. Cremation at Fresh Pond Wed. Mon Feb 1.

GIBSON, HENRY RICHARD, 100+, d Wed May 25, 1938, Washington (Dateline). Believed by fam to have been the oldest living frmr Congressman. Not certain whether he was b Christmas Eve 1836 or 1837, a difference which he always dismissed as "nothing to worry about." Practiced law at Knoxville, TN, where he founded the Repub Party in 1881. A few yrs later became editor of the Knoxville Daily Chronicle. Represented the 2nd TN district in the House 1895-1905. **SERV:** U Army Commissary Dept. Thu May 26.

GIEGER, JOHN, d last week. A founder of St Michaels. (A on John Daubner, Fri Feb 3, 1911.)

GILBERT, CALVIN, 100, b Gettysburg, PA, d Wed ngt Sep 13, 1939, Gettysburg, PA. Last surv of the U Army b Gettysburg. **SERV:** Commissary Dept, rcvd a Capt Com fm Lincoln, and later made Brev Maj by Pres Johnson. Thu Sep 14.

One hundred candles flickered on the cake of a Vet once rejected for war svc in 1861 as unable to stand the rigors of CW. Pres Roosevelt joined a host of friends in extending greetings to the Maj, who recalled "my health improved in the svc." Vet opened a foundry at end of CW and cast hundreds of cannon and gun carriages for the battlefield cem, a Natl shrine. Roosevelt wrote "I hope the day will bring you many pleasant reminiscenses and that you will accept my best wishes for your health and happiness." Sat Apr 8, 1939.

GILLEN, JAMES P, 84, d Sun ngt Dec 29, 1913, at home of sis, Altoona, PA. Vet of the MW and CW, a ret US Naval gunner, and the last surv of the Perry Expedition, which opened the ports of Japan to the USA in 1853. Mon Dec 29.

GOOD, JOHN H, 84, b Eliz, s/o late Adam & Euphemia, d Sun

Oct 23, 1927, Alexian Bros H, Eliz. **SURV**: w Mary Miller Good/ch John A, Mrs Elijah Stout and Mrs W Earl Bradley, E, and Mrs William Houston, Waterbury, CT. 4 gch. 8 ggch. Lived 606 Floral Ave, a lifelong res E. Worked 50+ yrs as a carpenter at Singer, ret abt 4 yrs ago. **MEM**: SVA. **CHH**: 1st Bapt. **SERV**: Enl otbrk 9th Reg, NJ Vol, promo to Cpl in the Inf, serv 4 yrs. With the 1862 expedition which sailed under sealed orders for the coast of NC and took part in the Battles of Roanoke and New Bern. At Antietem, South Mountain, Fredericksburg, the Wilderness and Petersburg. Oct 24.

Mr & Mrs John Hoffman Good, 118 Orchard St, Eliz, celebrated their 50th m anniv Tue ngt, he ae 75, she ae 68, both natives of E. He serv in Co K, 9th NJ Vol. She is mem WRC, GAR, and the Womens Auxiliary YMCA. He is foreman of the Singer table dept. Among those attending were Mr & Mrs W C Houston, Virginia Houston, Mr & Mrs E Stout, Katherine Stout, Mr & Mrs John A Good, Emma Good, and Mr & Mrs W E Bradley. Wed Dec 20, 1916.(P) (More names of attendees listed.)

GORHAM, CHARLES H, 72, b NY, d Sat Sep 11, 1909, at home, 4 Underhill Pl, Rahway. **SURV**: w. Res R for yrs. **MEM**: WFB27. **CHH**: First ME. **SERV**: Co P, 38th NY Reg Vol Inf, doing considerable Scout duty. **F**: Tue, Rev J B Heard, WFB27 in charge. Mon Sep 13.

GRACE, JOSEPH, 55, d Tue ngt Sep 27, 1900, at home, 224 3rd St, Eliz. **SURV**: w. Employ at Singer. Res E abt 20 yrs. **SERV**: Co A, 1st Reg CT Vol, Hvy Art. **F**: Fri mrng. Wed Sep 28.

GRAFF, EMIL, d announcement Sat Apr 3, 1926, St Cloud, FL. Mem of the Last Mans Club, begun with a roster of 34 1st MN Vol Inf vets. Only 3 left, John S Goff, St Paul, MN, Charles Lockwood, Chamberlaid, SD and Peter Hall, Atwater, MN. The merry group first met Tue Jul 26, 1885, and gathered annually at Stillwater, MN, for a banquet. A bottle of wine, which has reposed in a bank vault since the first meeting will be opened by the last surv mem, to toast his departed comrades. The 3 remaining Vets plan to gather next Jul 21st, the bottle of wine will be brought forth and placed on the festive board, but not opened. Sat Apr 3, 1926.

GRANT, GABRIEL, DR, b 1830, Newark, d Mon Nov 8, 1909, at home, NYC. **SERV**: In Jun, 1861, appointed as Surgeon of the 2nd NJ Vol, later promo to Surgeon US Vol, to end. His gallantry and fearlessness won for him the admiration of officers and men alike, and gained for him **THE CONGRESSIONAL MEDAL OF HONOR**, presented to him by order of Pres Lincoln. Surgeon of the Medal of Honor Legion, USA, reappointed at the reunion of the Legion at the Hotel Astor last mos. Tue Nov 9.

GREEN, JOHN S, 83, native of Flemington, d Sat Aug 6, 1927, Avenel. **SURV**: w frmr Mrs Josephine Hann of Eliz, m in Eliz/ch Mrs Ruth Klosky, Newark, Spencer and Harvey, A. Cuz Spencer Fisher, Orchard St, Eliz. Spent early life in F, 12 yrs in Eliz, and in A since Mar, on Remsen Ave. **MEM**: GAR F, Jr Mechanics and IORM. **CHH**: Park ME, when in Eliz. **SERV**: Co A, 15th NJ Vol, 6th Corps, in many battles. **F**: Int sol plot, Kearny-Arlington, Rev George A Law, P, 1st Meth, this city. Mon Aug 8. (Rahway Dateline.)

GREEN, WILLIAM H, b Mon Dec 18, 1843, Spring Valley, NY, d Sat ngt Feb 3, 1917, at home, 470 Monroe Ave, Eliz. **SURV**: w frmr Miss Elizabeth A Jones, m 1869, res Eliz since then/ch Nellie R, Mrs D A Gillespie, Roosevelt, Carrie E and Lilian M, Principal PS5. 2 gch, Blanche A and James H Gillespie, Roosevelt. Employ Singer 40 yrs. **MEM**: On Fri Feb 23, 1872, org TL134 F&AM, made first Master. Oldest past Master in NJ. PL78 KP. Charter mem Elizabethport B&L Assoc. **CHH**: 3rd Presby. **SERV**: Enl otbrk Pvt, Anderson Z, 62nd NY State Vol. At Seven Pines, Fair Oaks, Gettysburg, Rappahannock Station, the Wilderness, Fredericksburg and Cold Spring Harbor. WIA Cold Spring. Promo to Cpl Thu Mar 10, 1864. Reup Mon Jul 10, 1865, 1st NY Eng. Mon Feb 5.

GROAT, JAMES ELLIOTT, b Tue May 19, 1846, NY, d Sat ngt May 9, 1936, Jersey City. **SURV**: 2/w Mrs Mate Bernard Groat/ch Mrs George Weber, Westwood, Mrs Lloyd Jeffries,

Teaneck and Mrs Ernest Kull, Rahway. 8 gch. 1/w was late Mrs Augusta Albright Groat of Eliz. Past res Eliz, res J C last 20 yrs. Locomotive eng Central RR for yrs, and later with Lehigh Valley RR, pens abt 10 yrs ago. **MEM:** With the frmr UD25. **SERV:** Drummer Boy. Mem Vet Z under Gen Drake. Commended by Grant for his horsemanship. **F:** Tue in J C. Mon May 11.

H

HAGERMAN, JAMES E, 85, b Englishtown, d Fri Dec 10, 1926, at home of gs George B Ford, with whom he res, 705 Monroe Ave, Eliz. **SURV:** ch Forrest, Brooklyn, Frank, E, Mrs Roy Stout, Irvington and Mrs Mary B Ford, Monroe Ave. Res E 50 yrs. **MEM:** Old E Produce Exchange. **CHH:** Tennent Presby, Monmouth Co. **SERV:** Enl twice, 29th, and then 38th, NJ Inf. Fri Dec 10.

HALL, ASA, d announced Fri Apr 12, 1912. Middletown, NY (Dateline). Found near the Ellensville Station of the Ontario & Western Railway Fri. Prbly murdered. Police are in the dark, because his watch and money were intact. Fri Apr 12.

HAMMOND, THOMAS B, 58, d Wed ngt Oct 25, 1905, at home, 22 S 5th St, Eliz. **SURV:** 2/w, frmr Miss Caroline C Lang/3ch. Shipping clerk 30 yrs for John T Norton at the coal wharves, and recently clerk of the Central RR of NJ. **MEM:** Orient Council 46 Jr Order. United American Mechanics. **CHH:** Greystone Presby. **SERV:** Enl ae 14 Drummer in one of the NJ Reg of Vol. **F:** Sat 230 pm at home. Thu Oct 26.

HAND, WILLIAM, CAPT, 78, b 1838 just outside Plainfield, d Mon aftn Feb 14, 1916, at home of Edward G Townley, whom he was visiting, 638 W Broad St, Westfield. **SURV:** ch Recorder Fred, P, and Milton, Jersey City. Sib David P and Mrs A L Jameison, P, and Hezekiah, Scotch Plains. Res of P. Pob was his f's farm, one of the largest estates in this part of NJ. The land is now covered with residences and is known as the Netherwood section of P. On one part of the property stood the old Jackson district school house, where he went with Arthur Brisbane, editor of the NY Journal. Engaged for yrs with s in heavy trucking and storage biz. **MEM:** Charter mem WS73. **SERV:** Co B, 11th Reg, NJ Vol Inf. In 38 imp battles, incldg Gettysburg and Chancellorsville. In 1907 celebrated 50th m anniv by entertaining all the living mem of Co B at a large banquet given in Truell Hall.

HANEY, WILLIAM, 70, d, along with 2 other Vets since last Sun, S'H, Kearny, fm the effects of the heat wave. Had res Livingston. **SERV:** Co H, 1st Reg, NJ Militia. Thu Jul 26, 1900.

HANN, ENOS F, 92, d Sun Dec 6, 1936, Atlantic City (Dateline). (A on John Allen as lone GAR survivor. See obit John C Allen)

HARRIS, CHAUNCEY, COL, b Wed Aug 26, 1829, Bethlehem, NY, s/o Francis & Elizabeth, d Mon 715 am Mar 20, 1911, at home, 90 Westfield Ave, Eliz. **SURV:** 2/w, mn Baker/ch Mrs Theodore F Stanford, Cherry St, E, Mrs Herbert U Beebe, MN, Luella G and Grace E. 6 gch. 3 ggch. Of 8 sib, leaves George W, E, for yrs Sec of the Gas Co, Mrs David T Crane and Amanda, Ocean Grove, and Mrs Martin Crane, Amsterdam, NY, the h for yrs assoc with frmr 1st Natl Bank, E. 1/w m Tue Feb 14, 1856, Beverly, MA, d E shortly bfr CW. Rem to E when yng. Long engaged with f and bros in the milling biz on Westfield Ave, near where fam res for yrs. Chief Eng of the FD 5 yrs and attended formal opening of the Brooklyn Water Works. Aft CW appointed as PM by Lincoln, who signed his first com, and serv under next 5 Pres. He introduced the free delivery system in E on Tue Jul 1, 1873. A founder of the NJ Repub party in 1856, and in 1848 had cast 1st Pres ballot for Taylor and Donaldson. On CC frmr 6th Ward yrs ago. Mem Grand Jury which met in the new Courthouse. **MEM:** UD25, chosen presiding officer at the dedication of the 1906 S&S' monument. Frmr Pres 14th Reg Assoc. **CHH:** Senior Elder 2nd Presby. Chosen Marshall of a procession in which hundreds of boys and girls marched fm City Hall to Jefferson Park for the centennial of the Robert Raikes SS

Movement. **SERV**: At otbrk org Co C, attached to 14ᵗʰ NY Vol, Col Truex, who serv in MW. This E Co was composed largely of firemen. 14ᵗʰ participated in many imp battles. At Monocacy Junction, MD, Sat Jul 9, 1864, assist in saving DC fm C capture, and severely WIA. Disc Dec 1864. At dod possessed the battle-scarred flag of the 14ᵗʰ Reg, which he displayed on special occasions. Brev Lt Col for bravery at Monocacy. A few yrs ago attended Reg reunion at site of Monocacy, when the Govt erected a costly shaft. w attended unveiling ceremonies, as battle was fought near her frmr home. **F**: Wed 230 pm, Rev Dr E B Cobb. No GAR svc. Mon Mar 20. (P)

HARVEY, JOHN H, 84, d Sat mrng Jun 24, 1905, at home, Monroe St, near Lawrence, Rahway. **SURV**: ch George W, Mrs Laura Bodwell, wid/o James L, and Mrs Edward Terrill, all R. **MEM**: WFB27. **SERV**: Co E, Fourtenth (sic) NJ V, disc as a Cpl. **F**: Tue 230 pm 2ⁿᵈ Presby, Rev W T Stuchell. Sat Jun 24.

HAUGHWOUT, WILLIAM B, **F**: Fri Apr 21, 1916, at home, 411 Fulton St, Eliz, Rev Levi B McMickle, P, Fulton St ME, assist by Rev Enoch Meachem, New Providence, frmr P of the Chh, and Rev George Q Baccus, P, 1ˢᵗ Meth Prot. Large attendance of relatives and friends, incldg U/D25 and Port Richmond 66 F&AM, SI. Int Sat Evergreen. Vet was a frmr eng of SI Ferry. Sat Apr 22.(P)

HAZARD, THOMAS TILLEY, b Tue Apr 23, 1839, Newport, RI, d Sat ngt Jul 8, 1911, at home, 702 Newark Ave, Eliz. **SURV**: w frmr Margaret A Kellogg of NY, m btwn 1857 and the CW yrs/ch L K, Thomas T, Sallie, Margaret and Abigail, all E, and Mrs F W Field, Bound Brook. f ancestors were among the founders of N in 1639; and William Tilley, mo ancestor, started the first "Rope Walk" in this country in Boston. Tilley went to N and est a "Walk" there in 1736. Vet rem to NY in 1857 and entered the wholesale linen trade with Watson Bros. In early 1860s became gen salesman for H B Claflin & Co, with the firm until abt 1880, when he launched into biz for himself. In his trade at dod. Had rem with fam to E in 1870 and for yrs res in home where he d. An enthusiastic horseman when yng, some of the finest kept in his stables. MEM: Soc of the Cincinnati, and SAR, through ancestry. RA. One of the first mem of the E Athletic Club. CHH: Westminster. SERV: 22nd Reg, NYNG, promo to 1st Sgt. Transf to 7th Reg, going out with them in 1865, seeing active svc. F: Rev Louis B Crane, P. Mon Jul 10. (P)

HEADY, CHARLES L, 80, d announced Fri Apr 29, 1927, on a visit to Bath, NY. SURV: ch Mrs Gertrude Heady Irving, 1 Brown Pl, Pres of the Rahway Biz & Professional Womans Club, with whom he frmly res, and Mrs Charles Carroll, Binghampton, with whom he res past 25 yrs. SERV: One of the POW Fed sol, Libby. F: Int fam plot Oxford, NY. Fri Apr 29.

HECTOR, GEORGE, 81, b Feb, 1834, Verdun, France, d early Fri, Feb 14, 1915, Eliz. SURV: ch Mrs Madeline Schumann, and Emil, Buffalo. w d abt 5 yrs ago. Res 641 E Jersey St at dod, and in E for yrs. Imm USA 1860. At one time engaged in manu of eyeglasses with a factory on Broadway, E. MEM: In 1883, Vet Z, a Bugler, going with them on their 1891 Srn trip. SERV: At ae 17 enl French Army, 1st Reg of the Lion, 5 yrs. Enl 1854 Crimean War, to end. Few yrs later enl 1st Reg British Foreign Legion and serv at Sepoy, India, during the 1857 Indian mutiny. In CW enl 55th NY Reg (Guard Lafayette) otbrk, mu/o 1862 Battle of Antietam. Also serv as a musician. Sat Feb 15. (P)

HEEGE, JACOB, 74, d Fri mrng Feb 9, 1917, at home, Jamesburg. SURV: w/ch Mrs David Brinley and Mrs William Streep, Eliz, Mrs R McLaughlin, SI, Alfred, Eliz, and Lester, Jamesburg. 8 gch. 3 ggch. Frmr res Eliz. MEM: JK64. Sat Feb 10.

HENDERSON, ARCHIBALD, 61, native of Scotland, d Mon 2 am Feb 1, 1904, at home, 1065 Mary St, Eliz. SURV: w. Res E long time. Worked 25 yrs at Singer. MEM: UD25. Vol Lodge 110 KP. CHH: His last days administered by Rev William B Hamilton, Westminster Hope Chapel. SERV: Sgt Co A, 70th Reg NY Vol, and Sgt Co E, 86th NJ Vol, where he lost a leg at Gettysburg. F: Wed 2 pm. Int Evergreen. Mon Feb 1.

HENDERSON, THOMAS B, 75, b Lincoln, Scotland, d Fri Apr 30, 1909, at home, Springfield. Imm USA ae 25, starting in biz as a steam eng. **SERV:** Enl otbrk 47th NY Inf, 3 1/2 yrs. **F:** Sun aftn at home, Rev William Hoppaugh, Presby. Sat May 1.
HENNESSY, JAMES, almost 70, b Ireland, d Tue mrng Jul 26, 1904, at home of dau Mrs Maguire, 242 Franklin St, Eliz. **SURV:** ch Mrs Maguire, Patrick and Mrs John Cosgrove, w/o E's Walking Delegate. w d last Oct. Imm USA a yng man, just bfr CW. Watchman at the Central RR freight yards. **MEM:** JK64. **CHH:** St Patrick. **SERV:** Navy, under Adm Farragut. In Battle of Mobile and others. **F:** James J Higgins in charge. Tue Jul 26.
HENRY, ALEXANDER, 73, native of Ireland, d Mon Jan 9, 1905, at home, 607 2nd Ave, Eliz. w d last summer. Imm USA to E 50+ yrs ago. Carried on carpet weaving with his w. **SERV:** Throughout. A pens. Serv in English Army when yng, seeing svc in India. **F:** Thu aftn. Int Evergreen. Tue Jan 10.
HENRY, WILLIAM, 66, b Ireland, d Thu aftn Apr 26, 1906, in the Emergency H while waiting to see a doctor, Eliz. **SURV:** w frmr Miss Ellen Hopkins/ch Lewis, John, James, William, Mrs Susan Bedell and Mrs Anna Lott. 7 gch. Imm USA a yng man. Res 29 Rahway Ave, almost opposite the H. Landscape gardener for numerous well known fams. **MEM:** UD25. On MDAYs, one of the Vets assigned to address students in the PS, speaking last at the Julia St school. **SERV:** Enl Co C, 14th NJ Vol, in many battles. WIA twice. Long time pens. The day bfr d, expressed the hope that he could attend the coming Fall anniv of the Battle of Monacacy Junction, MD, with other E and vcnty 14th Vets for the dedication of the monument marking the place where the Reg took a bold stand in defense of DC. **F:** Sun 2 pm at home, Rev Dr Glazebrook. Int Evergreen. Fri Apr 27.
HERMES, MICHAEL, 67, native of Olive, Germany, d Thu eve May 29, 1913, at the stable of s-in-law School Com George B Cladek, Irving St, Rahway. **SURV:** w/ch Mrs George B Cladek, Mrs J T Dunn, Mrs J E Dunham, Elizabeth R and Mrs J J Lynch, Eliz. 4 gch Mrs George Levi, Eliz, and Emma Cladek,

Jack Dunn and Alfred Dunham, R. sib Mrs M Kessler, Charles and Albert, Newark. Imm USA ae abt. 7 to R, res 60 yrs. Stockholder and Dir of the R Mutual Fire Ins Co and a large property owner. **MEM**: WFB27. **CHH**: St Marks German Catholic. **SERV**: 30th NY Reg and later in the Navy 3 yrs, aboard the "Nyack," for which svc he recently rcvd a **Medal of Honor**, being one of two R men to be thus honored. **F**: Mon mrng, Rev F R Rhabanus. Int R. Sat May 31.

Hermes, Senior V-Cmdr WFB27, attended the complimentary dinner for Post mems given by **A Edward Woodruff** Tue eve May 30, 1911.

HERRICK, GEORGE WASHINGTON, 99, b Thu Jan 22, 1835, d Tue Oct 30, 1934, Willimantic, CT. **SURV**: 3gch. Oldest CW Vet in CT, and one of the oldest in NE. **SERV**: Enl Jul, 1862, 18th CT Vol as a waggoner. At many major engage in Mar, 1864, and POW Andersonville 18 mos. Tue Oct 30.

HEYER, WILLIAM D, DR, b Norwalk, CT, s/o late Rev William G, DD, Prot Epis Chh, d Sat aftn Feb 5, 1916, at home, 523 S Broad St, Eliz. **SURV**: ch Irma, E, and Mrs E E Howe, Hazelton, PA. 3 gch. sis Mrs J H Parker, New Rochelle, NY. Rcvd early educ NY state, grad fm Univ of the City of NY. Started school work Essex Co, NJ, 1854. Went S and became principal of boys high school in New Orleans, LA, at one time Prof of physics and astronomy Homes College, LA. Aft CW, rem N and taught in NYC. Rem to E 1873, appointed as principal PS3, remaining there until 1900, transf to PS9, and ret 1913. **MEM**: American Assoc for the Advancement of Science, Microscopical Union, Soc of Pedagogic Research, NJ Club of Scientific Review, and others. OL126 F&AM, past Master. Grand Lodge, Washington Chap and St Johns Commandery. **SERV**: Drafted otbrk 9th LA Inf, C Army, Sgt, then com a Lt. Mu/o. **F**: Conducted by OL. Mon Feb 7.

HIGGINS, FRANCIS H, CAPT, 78, native of Bordentown, d Thu ngt Nov 2, 1911, at home of dau Mrs H L Lamphear, 171 Main St, Rahway. **SURV**: ch Frank H, Trenton, A E, Emaus, PA, and Mrs Lamphear. 7 gch. 4 ggch. Spent much of his life in B. Res past 9 yrs with dau. Super for the large iron works at Tyconia, PA. In charge of placing the iron stairways in the Washington Monument, structural work in the Congressional Hall, and the Public Bldg and Penn Statue in PHL. Serv term as Councilman at B. MEM: KP, and W45. CHH Bapt. SERV: Enl otbrk Co B, 23rd Reg, NJ Vol, rising to Capt. In many imp battles. F: Sat eve at home, Rev T C Mayham, Newark, frmly P of Trinity Meth. Int B. Sat Nov 4.

HIGGINS, G. BARTON, 65, d Thu mrng Mar 14, 1907, dropping d on Church St, Flemington. Had a store in F. **SERV**: Co F, 9th NJ Vol, 3 yrs. Fri Mar 15.

HIGGINS, TIMOTHY, 90, b Ireland, d Mon ngt Nov 25, 1929, at home of nephew Edward J Flynn, 464 Monroe Ave, Eliz. **SURV**: Svrl nephews/nieces. Imm USA 78 yrs ago. Res NYC 72 yrs, following the carpenter trade, then rem to E to res with nephew. **MEM**: Joseph B Calfin Post GAR, NYC. **CHH**: Sacred Heart. **SERV**: 55th NY Inf. When the ranks of that Reg were greatly depleted, he was attached to the 40th NY Inf. Tue Nov 26.

HIGGINS, TIMOTHY E, b overseas, d Fri mrng Jun 3, 1910, at home, 401 Magnolia Ave, Eliz. **SURV**: w/ch Timothy E, John F, Mary L and Anna N. Sib Mrs Bernard Sharkey and Margaret. Mrs Sharkey is confined to bed, and Margaret in the H, aft being struck by a car E Jersey St, aft they visited their sick bro. Imm USA when a boy, spent early yrs in the S, then rem to NY bfr CW. Aft CW rem to E and opened a saloon in the downtown section. Oldest saloon keeper in E. **MEM**: Ancient Order of Hibernians Div 1. **CHH**: St Patricks. HNS. **SERV**: U Army throughout. Fri Jun 3.

HIGGINSON, MICHAEL W, 83, b Dublin, Ireland, d Sun ngt Feb 6, 1916, at home, 1114 Hampton Pl, Eliz. **SURV**: w frmr Miss Caroline Briant, d/o late Samuel & Sarah, m 18th St Presby chh, NYC/ch Mary E and William H, Newark. 1 gch. Named aft his mo bro, Sir Michael Smith, mem of the British Parliament. Imm USA 50+ yrs ago, the greater part res E. When yng learned trade of wood carving, ret some yrs ago. CHH: 2nd Presby. SERV: Enl otbrk, Pvt, Co A, 8th NY Inf, in 1st Battle of Bull Run. Mon Feb 7. (P)

Mr & Mrs M W Higginson, 1141 Hampton Pl, Eliz, celebrated their 55th m anniv Mon. He is a wood carver, employed in NY bfr ret. The couple jokingly referred to their "golden-wooden" wedding. They do not believe in the fallacy of the superstition attached to the number "13," their day of choice for their m. Their gdau is Ida W Higginson, Newark. Tue Nov 14, 1911. (P) (Article states both were natives of NY.)

HILL, CHARLES EDWARD, REV, 84, b Sep, 1824, DC, d Wed Oct 14, 1908, Red Bank. SURV: s/5dau, the eldest Mrs Charles E Hill, 118 Mt Pleasant Ave, Newark. Ordained Meth Chh ae 20. CHH: P of many famous NJ chh, among them being Pitman of New Brunswick, Meth of Seabright, 1st Meth of Camden, Old Front of Trenton and the leading chh of Bridgeton and Red Bank. Ret 10 yrs ago. Lifelong mem NJ Conf of his chh. MEM: For past few yrs State Chapl NJ Div GAR, being mem Arrowsmith 61. SERV: At otbrk made Chapl 118th PA Vol, known as the "Corn Exchange" Reg, having been raised by the PA Corn Exchange. At Shepherdstown and Fredericksburg, with especial distinction. Did yeoman work in his field throughout. F: Sun at home of another dau. Thu Oct 15.

HILLER, FREDERICK, 62, f/o Charles M, 652 Elizabeth Ave, d Fri Jun 12, 1903, Alexian H, Eliz. SERV: a NY Reg. F: Mon. Sat Jun 13.

HODGE, WILLIAM, 85, b Rahway, d early Thu mrng Sep 23, 1926, Gen H, Eliz. SURV: s Lawson, with whom he res for a yr, 905 Cross Ave. gd Helen Hodge, mem EDJ advertising dept. Res Jersey City for yrs. MEM: GAR. SERV: Enl otbrk, serv to the Wilderness, where WIA. F: Sat aftn J S Stiner Home For Svc, 97 W Grand St. Int Grove chh, New Durham. Thu Sep 23.

HOFFMANN, JOHN T, 85, b 1831, PHL, d Wed mrng Feb 16, 1916, at home, 939 Grove St, Eliz. SURV: w/ch Catherine, Virginia, Jacob, PHL, and a s in E. Res E past 34 yrs. A "49'r," sailing around "The Horn" to CA. **SERV**: Enl otbrk 1st PHL Vol Inf as a "3 mos man," seeing active svc in many of the early engage, incldg the Baltimore riots. Wed Feb 16. (s in E was named, but blurred.)

HOLMES, BENJAMIN P, COL, d Fri aftn Jan 20, 1922, at home, Pine Grove Ave, Summit. Res yrs ago Eliz, employ as agent for the Central RR. **SERV**: In CW in his youth. Mem NJNG in the old 3rd Reg. Promo to Capt and inspector of rifle practice on Mon Mar 3, 1880, Maj on Wed Dec 7, 1887 and Lt Col on Tue Mar 18, 1890. Lt Col 3rd Reg, NJ Vol Inf Wed Apr 27, 1898, to end. S/A W. **F**: Sun 330 pm Calvary Epis, Woodland Ave, S. Sat Jan 21.

HOOTON, SAMUEL B, 83, b Brooklyn, d Sun Feb 16, 1930, Brooklyn. **SURV**: w. Res Westfield up to 3 mos ago for 9 ½ yrs. **SERV**: Sailor, enl Brooklyn. Sole surv CW Vet in Westfield. Feb 1.

HOUSTON, JAMES, b Sat Dec 28, 1839, Brooklyn, s/o James, d Fri 210 am Mar 10, 1911, at home, 234 Fulton St, Eliz. **SURV**: w/ch Warren G, Fulton St, Wilbur D, Newark, Reba E, a teacher in PS10, and Mrs Frank Carberry, West Orange. Sib ex-Sheriff Robert G, E, Mrs Mary Ten Eyck, Cherry St, E, and Samuel, Sr, East Summit. Par were among the 1st res of the downtown section, on Fulton St, when Elizabethport was only sparely settled. Started work in the old rope walk factory working, as was the custom, sunrise to sunset. In the eve went to Cooper Inst. Became an apprentice ironmolder at the foundry of late Samuel L Moore, Sr, at the foot of Pine St. Rem ae 18 to Sparta, IL, where he and a cousin farmed on the Prairie. Aft CW returned East and went for Spuyten Duyvil, where he resumed his trade. Res Summit 7 yrs, working in the wagon biz with bro Samuel. Rem to E with fam and purchased property at 500 and 508 E Jersey St, where he built a wagon, blacksmith and paint shop. Aft 10 yrs installed sewing machines and rented to an overall manu, then manu overalls himself. Mem of the comm in charge of unveiling the Sol Monument. **MEM**: JK64, Senior Order of

Stationary Eng, and the Ironmolders Union, past Pres. Frmr mem IORM. **SERV**: IL Home Guard Co, made 1st Lt. With little chance of going to the front, rem to MO, and serv with Co F, to end. At Shiloh and Antietam. Fri Mar 10. (P)

HOWARD, LT, d early Jan, 1900, Washington. (See **Monitor**)

HOWELL, B C, b 75 yrs ago, Ithaca, NY, d early Wed mrng Jan 6, 1915, Haverstraw, NY, where he had gone to spend Christmas. SURV: w m at Groton, NY, celeb 50th m anniv Wed Feb 22, 1911/ch Mrs P W Moore, Plainfield, Mrs E E Stryker, Somerville, Mrs David P Finney and W R V Howell, Westfield, and B C, Jr, Lebanon, OH. 15 gch. Res Westfield 15 yrs, 243 Chestnut St. Res Cranford at one time. Of colonial stock, gf in the RW. Civil eng and mining expert, ret for some yrs. For the past yr or so, the Forester for Westfield. **SERV**: 76th NY Vol. 3 bro also in CW. Wed Jan 6.

HUBBARD, J. FRANKLIN, CAPT, b Sat Jun 23, 1827, Berlin, Rensaaeler Co, NY, d Mon 130 pm Jun 26, 1905, at home, Plainfield. Shortly aft b, par rem to Scott, Cortlandt Co, NY. Rcvd educ here in common and academic schools, and learned carpentry trade. At ae 22 rem to Alleghany Co, NY, as a carpenter and builder. In same yr, m Miss Elizabeth Grace Green. Rem to P in 1854. Aft CW entered printing press biz, in the trade to 1879. Various ventures aft 37 yrs on Union Co B of Freeholders, 17 yrs as Dean. At recent May meeting chosen for 18th consecutive time. **SERV**: Enl otbrk 30th NJ Inf, Capt, to end. In many battles, incldg Fredericksburg and Chancellorsburg. Mon Jun 26. (P)

HUGG, WILLIAM H, 88, b 1845, NC, d early Wed mrng Jun 6, 1934, MD Gen H, Baltimore, MD. **SURV**: ch Harvey and Mrs J T Sinclair, Cranford, and Mrs Emory S Towson, Berkley Springs, VA. 6 gch and a ggch. mo's gf Robert Ashley fought in RW under Gen Nathaniel Green, and f's gf fell in 1812 while with the forces trying to repulse the British in their march fm Washington to Baltimore. Traveled extensively in his youth. Res Eliz nearly 40 yrs at 225 Murray St. Rem to Cranford 11 yrs ago, res at 306 N Ave, E. Inventor and experimenter with Singer for yrs, ret for 9 yrs. **MEM**: SAR, The Union Co Hist Soc, the Singer Club, the Liederkrants Singing Soc Washington Chap 16, Royal Arch Masons, and Tall Cedars of Lebanon Eliz Forest 6. **SERV**: C soldier, carried along as a prisoner by Sherman men in their march to the sea. Wed Jun 6, 1934.

HUGHES, GEORGE ISAAC, 97, d Thu May 20, 1937. **SURV**: 2/w, ae 28/ch Franklin Roosevelt, ae 28 mos, and Mary Gertrude, ae abt a yr, as well as ch by 1/w. Had 16 ch by 1/w. The spread of time btwn the oldest and yngst was 63 yrs. His record of bcmg a f aft passing ae 94 astonished the medical world. **SERV**: C soldier. May 20, New Bern, NC, Dateline.

Impending b of 2nd ch announced to assoc editor of the Kingston Morning Herald. Aft b of 1st ch, his case was authenticated by medical records and an account published in the American Medical Journal. Vet lives on a small Govt pens. Mon Feb 17, 1936, New Berne, NC, Dateline.

HUGHES, HUGH, 80, d Sun Jun 3, 1917, at home, 234 Main St, Rahway. **SURV**: sis Mrs Eunice Crane, wid/o Augustus B, Eliz. Came to R aft CW. Stone mason by trade. **MEM**: Frmr WFB27. Brown Garrison 92 Army & Navy Union. Mon Jun 4.

HUGHES, WILLIAM H, lifelong res Eliz, d Tue mrng Sep 21, 1909, at his lower Main St home, Rahway. Would have been 70 early Nov. **SURV**: sib Benjamin W, St Com, Hugh, and Mrs Eunice Crane. Vet, as bro Hugh, never m, and res together keeping Bachelors Hall. Followed, with Hugh, the biz of relaying sidewalks and setting curb and gutter stones. **SERV**: Enl ae 21 on Tue Aug 6, 1861, Pvt, 6th NY Ind Btln, a gunner. Made Cpl early, but at his request went back to Pvt. Hon disc Tue Aug 16, 1864. At Boliva, Williamsburg, Fair Oaks, Malvern Hill, (both battles), Kelly's Ford, Chancellorsville, Brandy Station, Gettysburg, Shepherdstown, Sulphur Springs, Auburn, Bristoe Station, New Hope Church, Parker's Store, Culpepper Ford, Corbin's Run, Broad Road, Todd's Tavern (2 engage), Glenvale, Island Ford, Ashland, St Stephen's Church, Richmond Hill,

Ennols Chapel and Sheridan's Raid. **F**: Home of R W Hughes, 90 Essex St. Wed Sep 22.

HULL, CHARLES F, REV DD, b Mon Mar 28, 1842, NYC, d Mon ngt Aug 6, 1906, at home, the parsonage of the ME chh, Woodbridge. **SURV**: w/s/dau, Mrs William H Hayward, Roseville. Res NYC to CW. Entered Madison now Colgate Univ. Aft taking collegiate and post grad courses, entered active work of the Ministry. **CHH**: First appointment Mt Hope, 1877; Woodrow, SI, 1878-80; Otisville, NY, 1881; Rockland Lake, NY, 1882-84; Bayonne, 1885-87; Rahway, 1889-90, at 2nd now Trinity ME; Tottenville, SI, 1891-93; Jersey City, 1894-97, Linden Ave; Paterson, 1898-1900; Newark, 1901-05; W, 1906. **SERV**: Enl Pvt 5th NY Vol, Duryee Z. Transf Navy, to end. **F**: Thu 2 pm W ME. Int Rahway. Tue Aug 7.

HURT, BENJAMIN F, 60, b Eliz, d Thu Aug 19, 1909, at home, Malta, IL. **SURV**: w Jeanette/s Herbert. sib Frederick, Edward, mem of the firm Hurt & Woodall, 30 W Scott Pl, and Mrs George R Townley, also E. When res E, at Chilton St. Left E as a yng man. Conducted a grocery store at M. **SERV**: Drummer Boy in one of the Wm Reg. Fri Aug 20.

HUTCHINSON, JOHN S, MAJ, b Jul 20, 1819, Princeton, d Wed mrng Apr 5, 1911 at home of s Fitz, 450 Elizabeth Ave, Eliz. **SURV**: ch Fitz and Mrs Henry J Elms, 74 Broad St, E. 4 gch. 3 ggch, ch/o his gd Mrs G Harley (Elms), 17 DeHart Pl. His w, mn Covert, d a few yrs ago. When yng, Cmdr Princeton Blues, the surv of the cmd, which often took part in celebrations of the Battles of Trenton and Princeton. Conducted the Princeton Hotel, where stagecoaches making NY to Phl trip exchanged horses, and the passengers dined, for yrs. Worked for the Camden & Amboy RR, in charge of a construction train for yrs. Rem to Trenton. In 1878 rem to Bergen Pt, serv yrs as the first Station Agent at 8th St. Resigned and rem to Jersey City, appointed as Sgt of police. Rem to Bergen Pt and became a contractor. In 1882 rem to E, for yrs res in the frmr 4th Ward, then on Chestnut St, where his w d. A clerk in the Jersey City offices of the Central RR, pens in 1909. A Dem, elected PJ 4th Ward. **SERV**: Com at otbrk by Gov Charles S Olden to muster the home guards of Trenton, Mercer Co, for duty, many of whom aft went to the front. Wed Apr 5.

I

INSLEE, ISAAC, CAPT, d Wed mrng Aug 19, 1903, Woodbridge. **SURV**: w/dau. **MEM**: WFB27. **CHH**: Cong. **SERV**: 28th NJ Reg. Wed Aug 19.
IRONS, GEORGE GIBERSON, LT, d Sun May 1, 1904, Toms River. **SURV**: w frmr Miss Lydia Jeffrey, whom he m in Camp at Trenton a few days bfr his Reg embarked on the Burnside Expedition to NC/2s/dau. Older s, Longstreet, res Eliz for yrs, a telegraph operator at Jersey City for Central RR. Lifelong res T R. Engaged in farming. **SERV**: 1st Lt, an org of Co D, 9th NJ Vol, Co composed of Ocean Co men. Tue May 3.
IVANS, THEODORE ALONZO, 71, native of NYC, d Sat Jul 27, 1912, Brooklyn, NY. **SURV**: w Mary McClain Ivans/sis Mrs Margarett Ann Farewell, Eliz. Worked in the BNY. Employ at one time in shipping dept of Standard Oil Co. **SERV**: A Man-of-Wars-Man, enl twice. On the "Merrimac" and "Powhatan," in a n/o engage. **F**: Mon ngt at his 24 Devoe St home. Int Greenwood. Tue Jul 30.

J

JACKSON, GEORGE W, 62, d Fri mrng Sep 15, 1909, at home, 10 Whittier St, Rahway. **SURV**: w/dau/2s. On R PF 13 yrs. **SERV**: Co H, 5th NJ Vol. Fri Sep 15.
JACKSON, THOMAS H, 70, d Tue Sep 20, 1910, at home, Monroe Ave, Kenilworth. **SURV**: w. Came to K fm Norristown, PA, abt 5 yrs ago, and a few yrs aft started a candy store, conducting it to dod. A musician of ability. **SERV**: Musician in Co L, 45th Inf. **F**: Fri noon at home, Rev W M C Hawes, P 1st

Bapt. Int in Linden. Thu Sep 22.

JARVIS, JOHN RICHARDSON, 75, b Kingston, Canada, d Tue ngt Jan 11, 1921, at home, 120 W Grand St, Eliz. **SURV**: ch Altha C, Bayonne, William E, Indianapolis, and Grace E, of the Battin High School faculty. 2 gch, Mrs Clifford Townley, Bayonne, and Walter M Jarvis, Yonkers, NY. w, frmr Katherine Harrison, m 1868, NYC, d a n/o yrs ago. f and gf had been officers in the Canadian Home Forces. Aft his elementary educ, par sent him to a college in Buffalo, NY. Rem to Albany in 1863. Aft CW, rem to Jersey City, in 1873 to Roselle Park, and in 1889 to E, where he and fam est res. Followed the hardware biz, working for any firm. Ret Oct, 1919. **MEM**: UD25. **CHH**: Trinity Epis. **SERV**: Enl 1863, Albany, 10th Reg of Inf, NY Vol. In a large n/o engage bfr Cold Harbor, where he was com fm Pvt to 1st Lt for conspicuous gallantry. Later captured, POW Libby, Andersonville and Salisbury for 6 mos. Soon aft disc, became mem 22nd Reg, NYNG, then the 9th Reg, Coast Art, NYC, 1st Sgt to 1873. **F**: Thu eve at home, Rev W S, P, Trinity. Wed Jan 12.

JONES, ERNST, 83, b Germany, d Fri 3 am Nov 6, 1908, at home, 320 Centre St, Eliz. **SURV**: w/step-ch fm her prev m, Frank R Fricke, Charles W Fricke, Louis J Fricke, Mrs Albert Prescher, Annie Fricke, Mrs Henry Siess, Ernest Fricke and William H Fricke. Imm USA a yng man. Res E 50+ yrs. Employ Central RR, ret abt 8 yrs. **CHH**: German Lutheran, being a founder. Serv on official B of the Chh, and mem parish SBS. **F**: Chh, Sun aftn. Fri Nov 6.

JONES, PATRICK HENRY, GEN, b Sat Nov 20, 1830, Westmeath, Ireland, d at home, Ann St, Port Richmond, SI. **SURV**: w/4s. Imm USA 1840 with par to upper part of NY state. Aft CW, rem to Ellicottville, NY. In 1865 elected Clerk of the NY Court of Appeals, 3 yrs. On Thu Apr 1, 1869, appointed as NYC PM and serv during Grant 1st term, afterwards practicing law. In 1875 elected Register of the City and County of NY, 3 yrs. **SERV**: Enl otbrk 37th NY Vol, as 2nd Lt, then Adj and Maj. Became Col 154th NY Vol. On Sun Dec 4, 1864, com Brig Gen

of Vol, to end, when he resigned. Wed Jul 25, 1900.
JONES, WOODRUFF, 86, d Mon Sep 17, 1928, at home, Germantown, PHL. SURV: Mrs Conover English, Eliz, and 2 other m daus. 10 gch. One of PHL oldest fam. VP and Treas of John T Lewis Bros, manu of white lead and paint for yrs. Wed Sep 19.
JOYCE, MICHAEL, 69, d Tue mrng Dec 6, 1910, at home, 358 Magnolia Ave, Eliz. SURV: w Bridget/ch Delia, Nora, and Michael A, Jr. sib Martin and Patrick. Res E 50 yrs. Worked for Central RR, E, 40 yrs. MEM: UD25. CHH: St Patricks. Tue Dec 6.

K

KEILER, VALENTINE, 60, d Sun ngt Jan 28, 1906, State H, Morris Plains. SURV: No relatives in USA, own immediate fam long d. Res Rahway for yrs. Inmate of S'H, Kearny, then rem to State. MEM: WFB27. SERV: Pvt 9th NJ Vol, hon disc with a recommendation which he had reason to feel proud. F: Thu 2 pm St Marks, Rahway. Tue Jan 30.
KEIMIG, CHARLES B, 72, native of Germany, d Sat 545 pm Apr 8, 1911, at home of s Charles, 880 Livingston St, Eliz. SURV: 2/w. ch Charles M B, Peter, Fred W, Mrs Henry Essex and Mrs Adam Morhart. Imm USA 1853. Worked yrs for Samuel Gale, who manu womens shoes at W Jersey & Union Sts. Aft CW est a restaurant Elizabeth Ave, having it 35 yrs. A fireman, at one time assist Chief. Serv 5 yrs as foreman of LH&L, assoc with co for 35 yrs, with his restaurant as HQ, and then reunions. MEM: UD25. CHH: St Michaels. SERV: 3rd NJ Vol, Capt John Whelan, in many of the most imp battles. F: Home of s. Mon Apr 10. (P)
KEIPER, DANIEL, 84, b Pa, d Wed aftn Apr 7, 1920, S'H, Kearny. SURV: ch Mrs F Haiges, Mauch Chunch, PA, Mrs F E Walter, Kansas City, MO, Mrs George J Reiss, Grove St, Allan M and Howard L, Eliz, Rene D, PHL, and Lillie J, Rochester,

PA. bro H Alfred, White Haven, PA. F: Home of Mrs Reis. Thu Apr 8. (Note: Mauch Chunch is the present day Jim Thorpe)
KELBER, JOHN, d but recently. A founder of St Michaels. (A on John Daubner Fri Feb 3, 1911.)
KELLY, PATRICK, 77, b Thu Aug 15, 1846, Ireland, d Thu aftn Mar 13, 1924, at home, 155 Bond St, where he res 60 yrs, Eliz. SURV: w Bridget C/ch Mrs Katherine Haggerty and Mary, E, Mrs Elizabeth Dooley, Cranford, John and James, E, William, Joseph and Francis, Brooklyn. 13 (+) gch. Imm USA ae 8 with par, settling in E. Stationary eng with Gen Chemical Co, Bayonne, ret svrl yrs ago. Mem Hibernia Engine Co 5 Vol FD. MEM: J/K64. EFA. Honorary mem E post, VFW. CHH: St Patricks. HNS. A founder of the Father Matthew TAB Soc. SERV: Enl Thu Aug 18, 1864, 14th NJ Vol Inf. In many battles, incldg Winchester, Fisher's Hill, Cedar Creek, Sailor's Creek and Petersburg Farm. Present at Lee's surrender Appomattox. Fri Mar 14.
KELLY, PATRICK, b Ireland, d Sun mrng Dec 2, 1928, at home of dau, 523 Spring St, Eliz, ae thought to be abt 85, but never told to anyone. SURV: ch Martin, William, Mrs George Kornmeyer, Mrs Frank Mulhearn, and Anna. bro John. 5 gch. All res E. Imm USA abt ae 8. Par res on a farm in NY for a time, and later in CT. Began work in a sewing machine factory, and later worked with Singer in NY. When the E plant was built, came to E and remained until ret. Res downtown for yrs. MEM: UD25. CHH: St Patricks, then Sacred Heart when he rem to Spring St. SERV: Enl too yng, so mo obtained his release. Enl again under another name and serv 2 yrs. Mon Dec 3.
KENNEDY, PETER, 79, b Ireland, d early Fri mrng Jan 4, 1924, at home, 516 S Park St, Eliz. SURV: ch Mrs William Snyder and Mrs William Rogers, both E. 10 gch. Imm USA 68 yrs ago, to Hoboken. Res E 50 yrs. MEM: Mount Zion Chapel, and PL78 KP. SERV: Enl otbrk 28th Reg, NY Inf. Became Cpl Co H, to end. Fri Jan 4.
KENNELLY, MAURICE V, 80, d Thu Aug 28, 1924 at home

of s Ralph, 632 Arlington Ave, Westfield. **SURV:** ch Albert L, White Plains, frmly of Cranford, Ralph V and Mrs James M Scott, Roselle, with whom he res for 10 yrs. For yrs in the contracting biz, Jersey City. **MEM:** GVH3. **SERV:** 176th Co, NY Vol. Fri Aug 29.

KERR, JOHN B, 79, b Kingwood Tp, Hunterdon Co, d Sun aftn May 22, 1927, at home of dau Mrs Harvey Worman, with whom he res, 305 Trinity Pl, E. **SURV:** ch Mrs Worman, Joseph, John and Wilson, Flemington, and Fredrick, Morrisville, PA. 22 gch. 12 ggch. Came to E 1888, res with dau 20 yrs, a home of 4 gens, the Vet, his dau, her dau Mrs Harriet McCandless, and Harriet's ch. A bricklayer. **MEM:** Bricklayers Protective Union. LB48. **SERV:** Ran away fm home ae 16 and enl in that body of troops later known as the "Game Chicken Reg," Col E Bird Grubb. Reg was a "100-day unit," so called as it was the belief then that a period of 100 days would see the end of the war. Reuped 50th Reg, PA Vol, to end. Mon May 23.

KIBBE, ISAAC PEASE, b Sun Apr 12, 1846, Coos Co, NH, d Thu ngt Nov 2, 1916, at home, 300 Poplar St, Roselle. **SURV:** w frmr Sallie Frances Carpenter, m 1872, Victoria, TX/ch William J, 254 E 3rd Ave, R, Preston, NY, Louis G, Torrington, CT, Irvin, Victoria, TX, Frank W and Isaac St. J, Brownsville, TX. A dau d bfr him. Ancestors came fm England in 1632, settling in NE. Shortly aft b, par rem to TX. A Dem. When TX passed laws to protect the fish and oyster industries, selected as State Com to enforce them. His work rcvd special recognition from the US Bureau of Fish and Fisheries. Rem to R 1908 to be with some of his s, and took up real estate. **MEM:** Victoria Lodge F&AM, and a 32nd Degree Scottish Rite Mason of the Galveston Shrine. **CHH:** Elder of Presby at Victoria. **SERV:** Throughout, Greens TX Brig. **F:** Sat aft at home. Int Victoria, TX. Sat Nov 4.

KING, CHARLES, GEN, 88, b Sat Oct 12, 1844, Albany, NY, s/o Rufus & Susan Eliot King, d Fri Mar 17, 1933, Milwaukee, WI. On Wcd Nov 20, 1872, m Miss Adelaide Lavender Yorke of

Carrol Parish, LA, and had 3 dau and a s. ggf was RW Capt and had 2 s, Rufus, a Maj in the LI campaign, and Charles, Col, 1812, his gf, who became Pres Columbia Univ. f grad WP 1833, serv in the Eng Corps, and later Adj-Gen NY. s Rufus III went to Annapolis by appointment of Pres Roosevelt. **MEM**: Military orgs. A Mason. **SERV**: Left studies at Columbia to become mounted messenger to his f, who had been recalled to svc as Brig Gen. Rcvd appointment to WP fm Lincoln 1862. Aft grad, stationed in New Orleans, and later an instructor of military tactics at WP. Transf to 5th Cav, in the 1871 campaign in which Custer was massacred. In IW with Buffalo Bill. Ret 1879 due to IW wounds. **F**: Tentative Tue, pending word fm s, Cmdr Rufus, US Navy, on duty Gulf of Mexico. Sat Mar 18. (P)

KING, CHARLES H, d at home of s, Keyport, d announced Fri Jan 8, 1915. Frmr res Eliz. **F**: was held Tue Jan 5. Int K. Fri Jan 8.

KING, RUFUS, MAJ, b Bleecker St, NY, d at home, 477 Central Park W, NYC. ggs of Gen Rufus, 1st Minister to the Court of St James, 1796-1803. s/o late William Gracie, and eldest gs/o late Charles, Pres of Columbia. Res on N Ave, E, for yrs. **MEM**: Military Order of LoyL, and of Lafayette Post, GAR, NY. 7th Reg VA. **SERV**: Ret officer Regular Army. Capt of the Art in CW, cmd a Bat at Gettysburg, then promo to Maj. Recently Congress awarded him a **Medal Of Honor.** In early days mem old 7th Reg NY. Mem staff of Vet Z, E. During Gov Green administration, serv on Gov staff. (Partial obit not dated. He d same day as Eliz Bauman.)

KYTE, GEORGE, 54, b NY, s/o Charles, d Sat ngt May 5, 1900, at home, Fanwood. **SURV**: w/3s/2dau. Res F for yrs. A Repub, svrl terms as assembly mem, and a term as Co Sheriff 1894-97. Mayor F last 2 yrs. Svrl terms on F Tp Comm, and also mem Union Co B of Freeholders. Developed property along the Central RR of NJ. Sec of the Central NJ Land Improvement Co, office in NY. **SERV**: 21st Reg NY. **F**: Tue 3 pm, Bapt chh, Scotch Plains. Mon May 7. (C)

L

LACOMBE, LOUIS, 82, b Oswega, NY, d mon ngt Jan 1, 1930, Alexian Bros H, Eliz. **SURV**: dau Elizabeth. Res E last 29 yrs, his home at 55 Geneva St. **MEM**: UD25. **CHH**: St Patricks. HNS. **SERV**: Co K, 104th NY Vol. Tue Jan 2.
Attended annual UD25 Christmas party ystdy. Thu Dec 30, 1926. (P)

LA FULEY, EDWARD, 71, native of Albany, NY, d Thu aftn Dec 19, 1911, Gen H, Eliz. Vet never m. Boarded for yrs on Harrison St, but recently on Bond St. A few yrs aft CW, rem to E and obtained work at Singer as a machinist, ret a few yrs ago. Watchman at the Union Co Trust Co. **MEM**: UD25. Loyalty to America (?) Council, DL, the Jr OUAM, and Orient Council F&AM. **SERV**: 11th NY Bat of Art. WIA Gettysburg, long time in H. Returned to Bat at Mine Run, VA. WIA. Fri Dec 20.

LAING, NOAH B, 83, d Sun Jun 24, 1917, at home of dau, W Grand St, Rahway. **SURV**: ch Mrs Harry C Coulter and Barry, R. Lifelong res R. In the trucking biz. **MEM**: WFB27. **SERV**: 6th Ind Bat of NY 1861-63. WIA. Mon Jun 25.

LAMBERT, ALBERT, 68, d Sat Feb 12, 1910, at home, 335 St George Ave, Rahway. **SURV**: w/steps George Schwindinger. Res R 30+ yrs. Proprietor of St George Hotel at St George & Westfield Ave. **MEM**: WFB27. **CHH**: St Marys. **SERV**: Co B, 30th NJ Vol. F: Tue St Marys. Mon Feb 14.

LAMBOT, JULES C, b Paris, France, d Sat Nov 1, 1924, at home of dau Mrs Albert F Messig, Neshanic. **SURV**: ch Mrs William G Aiken and William, Los Angeles, CA, Mrs William Sands, Dunellen, Mrs Messig, and Mrs Benedict Maskevich and Victor, Eliz. sis Mrs Fred Emmerick, NYC. 5 gch. Came to Eliz when Singer moved its plant there. In the adjustment dept 50 yrs, pens 2 yrs ago. **MEM**: Founder and 1st Cmdr JK64. SVA. **SERV**: Enl Co A, 1st NJ Inf 1861, 3 yrs/9 mos. At Gettysburg, the Wilderness, and many others. Mon Nov 3. (P)

LANCE, JOHN W, b Fri Dec 10, 1847, Berwick, PA, d Fri ngt Nov 17, 1916, Gen H, Eliz. SURV: w Laura Fonda Lance/dau Mrs John Errickson, NYC. First followed the sea. Circled the globe twice, and in 1868 lived with the Esquimaux in Iceland for 6 mos when his merchant vessel became imprisoned in ice. Worked next for Perth Amboy coal dealers, then some yrs later in the traffic dept Central RR, Bayonne. In 1892 assoc with the Lehigh & Wilkes Barre Coal Co, E, as a salesman. In Sep 1910 became line sales agent, in pos up to last Jun. SERV: Enl Co K, 194th PA Vol, 1864. Disc next yr and reup Co A, 74th PA Vol, to end. F: The F Chapel, Jefferson & E Jersey St. Sat Nov 18.

LANE, E CLARKSON, 89, d Fri ngt Jan 20, 1933, at home of s Clifford, Newton. SURV: ch John W, Glen Ridge, Clifford, and Mrs Joseph Crawn, Swartswood. One of the 5 surv Vets in Sussex Co. Clerk, co Election Board. Charter Mem Hercules Fire Co. SERV: 27th NJ Vol. F: Mon Christ Epis. Int N.

LANE, HENRY B, 70, d Sun ngt Mar 2, 1902, at home, 140 Elizabeth Ave, Eliz. SURV: w/ch William, E, and Thomas, Pittsburgh, PA. Came to E fm the W 25 yrs ago. Worked for Elizabethport Cordage Co. MEM: JK64. SERV: Pvt Co K, 102nd PA Vol. F: Wed aftn. Int sol plot, Evergreen. Mon Mar 3.

LAROSA, ANDREW OTTISON, 64, b Brooklyn, d Sat 3 pm Jul 16, 1910, at home, Downer St, Westfield. SURV: sib Mrs Tompkins, Mrs Joseph, Frank W, and a bro in Meriden, CT. Vet never m. Came to W 25 yrs ago and commenced an express biz until a few wks ago, selling it to his nephew Charles Tompkins. EF with Hose Co 1. MEM: Trustee of the W Firemans Relief Assoc at dod. SERV: Enl Drummer Boy, Brooklyn Reg. Mon Jul 18.

LAWRENCE, BENJAMIN L, COL, 86, b Toms River, s/o Joseph & Rachael Stout Borden Lawrence, d Mon Mar 4, 1929, at home of dau, Glen Ridge. SURV: ch Mrs Mathias Steelman and Alice, Eliz, and Mrs Frederick L Hutchinson, Glen Ridge, whom he was visiting dod. bro William Borden Lawrence, Red Bank. Came to Eliz in his early 20s, res for 60 yrs. Dr William

A Newell, his cuz, acted as Lincoln fam physician during the CW and later was elected Gov of NJ. Through his friendship with Horace Greely, a printer for the old NY Tribune, and later in the same capacity by the EDJ when Drake and Davis owned and pub the paper. Later entered the retail and wholesale grocery biz, HQ at 227 Broad St. Res 18 Orchard St dod. **MEM:** WL F&AM. UD25, 2 terms as Cmdr. Only 16 mem remain. First mem Eliz B of Trade, his fam saving the certificate of mem. **CHH:** St James ME. **SERV:** Org Co H, 29th NJ Reg. At Fredericksville and Chancellorsville. Mu/o day bfr Gettysburg. Often told the story concerning the days when the Govt was so poor that it was behind in its payment of salaries to the AP. **F:** Int Eliz. Tue Mar 5. (See **Experiences**)

LEATHERBURY, WILLIAM, LT, 68, d Mon ngt Feb 8, 1909, at home, Fieldsboro, Burlington Co. **MEM:** Personal friend for 50+ yrs of Edward K Drake and with him initiated as a mem Excelsior Div 4, ST of Trenton Mon Jan 17, 1859. **SERV:** A "First Defender," being one of the first yng men in Trenton to respond to the call of Lincoln for troops to serv 3 mos. An officer in a Trenton Co in 14th Reg. Severely WIA Battle of Cold Harbor, VA. Thu Feb 11.

LEDLEY, JOHN M, and w, 632 S Ave, Westfield, found d in bed at 3 pm Wed Jan 2, 1918. Gas fume victims. **SURV:** ch Mrs George Cox, w/o the Overseer of the Poor, Downer St, Frank M, Garwood, and Ellesworth, Plainfield. John M, b Sun Dec 27, 1846, Rahway, rem to W ae 11 and remained. Ret mason contractor. Built many houses in this section and at one time constructed many bridges for the co. Lifelong Repub, Councilman fm the 4th Ward 2 terms. **MEM:** WS73. **SERV:** Enl otbrk Co B, 30th Reg NJ Inf. Hon disc Sat Jun 27, 1863, Flemington. Reup Thu Mar 10, 1864, Co L, 1st Reg NJ Vol Cav. WIA Jul 12 Petersburg, VA. On Sun Jan 1, 1865, promo to Cpl, and on Mon Jul 24, 1865, hon disc at the Grand Review in Washington.

Mrs Ledley, b Frankfort, PA, d in her 60th yr, and res W 15 yrs.

She was 2/w. Thu Jan 3.

LEE, WILLIAM, 62, d Sun Feb 1, 1903, at home, Eliz. **SERV:** 3rd MS Vol. Mon Feb 2.

LEONHARD, JACOB, 90, native of Baden Baden, Germany, d Thu Jan 19, 1933, at home, 416 Marshall St, Eliz. **SURV:** ch Lillian, E, Mrs Emma Hasson, Ozone Park, NY, and Jacob, Jr. 8 gch. 8 ggch. Imm USA 76 yrs ago, res E 34 yrs. Employ of Singer, ret 15 yrs ago. **CHH:** Greystone Presby. **SERV:** Enl 1861 Co F, Hawkins Z, 9th Reg, Regular NY Vol. Reuped 1863 Co L, Hvy Art, 15th NY Reg. Hon disc 1865. In first period at Newport News Fri Jul 5, 1861, Hattress Wed-Thu Aug 28-29, 1861, Roanoke Island Sat Feb 8, 1862, Camden, NC, Fri Apr 18, 1862, Rainbow Banks Wed Jul 9, 1862, and Plymouth Sun Aug 3, 1862. Fri Jan 20. (P)

LESTER, DANIEL K, d early Thu mrng Dec 25, 1924, Eliz. (See **Monitor**)

LEVI, RICHARD, 68 yrs, 10 mos, b Woodbridge, d Sat aftn Apr 21, 1917, at home, 13 Clinton St, Rahway. **SURV:** w/ch Mrs Newton Hatfield, Eliz, Mrs Edward Tunison, Linden, Mrs John Roarke, Morristown, Roscoe C and George H, Eliz, Joseph B, Baltimore, and Charles A, W. 7 gch. Res W until 5 mos ago. Worked 21 yrs for the PA RR. **MEM:** WCB85. **SERV:** Sailor on the "Niagra." Mon Apr 23.

LEWIS, W S, 86, bodyguard to Lincoln during the CW, and for 35 yrs mail clerk at the White House, where he was well known to 12 Pres, d Thu Sep 28, 1911. Became ill 3 wks ago while standing before his desk. Thu Sep 28.

LITTLE, JAMES A, 85, native of Eliz, d Sat eve Dec 27, 1924, at home, 424 Linden St, Eliz. **SURV:** ch Rutherford, NY, Chester, Newark, and Mrs Edith Mains, Bradley Park. Blacksmith by trade, conducted a wagon repair shop at Westfield & Morris Aves. **MEM:** UD25 last 27 yrs. **SERV:** Enl Co B, 19th Inf, latter part of 1861, to end. Twice WIA. Reg sent to the Dept of the Tennessee in 1862, and took part in the attack on Atlanta, GA. At Chickamauga, Stone River, Missionary Ridge, Kenesaw

Mountain, and Harper's Shoals, where he was taken prisoner. With Sherman on his march to the sea. Promo to a Sergeantcy bfr hon disc. Mon Dec 29, 1924.

LITTLE, THOMAS A, 63, b Morris Ave, Eliz, d Sat eve Mar 9, 1907, at home, 19 Sayre St, Eliz. **SURV**: w. An agent at the Broad St station Central RR for abt 25 yrs, then the station at the foot of Liberty St, NY, for abt 15 yrs. A Repub. Represented the frmr 6th Ward, B of Educ, 1 term. **MEM**: UD25 fm formation. Past Cmdr. **SERV**: Orderly Sgt Co B, 30th NJ Vol, Capt Lewis. F: Tue eve at home, Rev John T Kerr. Int Wed mrng Rosedale and Linden Park. Mon Mar 11.

LLOYD, GEORGE KILPATRICK, 71, b Eliz, d Thu aftn Mar 22, 1906, at home of dau Kate, Catherine St, Eliz. **SURV**: ch James, William, Oliver, Samuel, Thomas, Mrs Kate Greenough, Mrs James Houston, and Georgia. w, frmr Nellie Smith, a d/o David, whose ancestors were among the early settlers of Elizabeth Town, d last mo, and he then res with dau. Carriage painter and stripper employ by late Councilman Thomas H Price, when this trade was extensively carried on in E long bfr CW. EF of frmr Rolla Steam Fire Engine 2. A Repub and mem of the Fremont and Dayton club. A gifted singer, often in entertainments as a minstrel. **MEM**: Z in 1867, attending anniv at home of Gen Drake on his 69th birthday last Jan. **SERV**: Enl Apr 1861, at the call of Lincoln for 3 yr troops, Co A, 1st NJ Vol, Capt David Hetfield. POW, Libby. Disc for disability Wed Feb 4, 1863. F: Sat 230 pm at home of s William, 437 Meadow St. Int per request in Z uniform. Fri Mar 23.

LONG, DAVID, 82, d Mon Feb 15, 1915, PHL.

LONG, JOHN W, b 1844, Salem, NJ, d early Sat mrng Mar 4, 1911, at home, 226 Westfield Ave, Eliz. **SURV**: w Emma, sis/o Robert A Mulford, Morris Ave/ch Walter M, Robert C, and Mrs Alvah O Boyer. bro Quinton J, Atlantic City. Taught school for awhile. Rem to E 35 yrs ago. Long employ downtown telegraph office Central RR, in the super dept. Recent yrs inspector in the NY Customs House, ngt duty. Ret 2 yrs ago. **MEM**: UD25, librarian at one time. Past councilor Winfield Scott Council, Jr, OUAM. Farragut Assoc. CE IOF. Odd Fellows in S 40 yrs. **CHH:** Became mem Central Bapt Dec 1889. **SERV:** Enl navy ae 18 Qtmstr, on the "Alert." Engaged a C vessel on the Nansumand Riv, near Hampton Roads, in 1863. All "Alert" sailors were WIA or KIA, with Vet losing an arm and eye. **F:** Rev Dr Tomlinson, his P. Sat Mar 4.

LONG, STEPHEN M, b Mon Mar 25, 1844, NYC, d Sun ngt Apr 9, 1905, at home, E Orange. City Clerk of E O. **MEM:** Past Cmdr UD12. Natl Assoc of U Ex-POW, Dept Cmdr 1903-04. **SERV:** Enl otbrk Pres's Life Guard. Later transf to PHL Fire Z. At Cheat Mountain and Ball's Bluff 1861, and the Seven Day's fight 1862, which incld Fair Oaks, Peach Orchard, Antietam and Savage's Station, where WIA and captured, POW Libby, then Belle Isle. Exchanged, returned to Reg, and at Fredericksburg and Gettysburg. Tue Apr 11.

LONGHORST, GUSTAVUS, 60, b NY, d Fri Jul 8, 1904, DC. **SURV:** ch Mrs George Keller and Fannie, NY, Lulu, Atlantic City, and Gustavus, George and Jacob, Eliz. Res Eliz many yrs. Worked for Singer, foreman needle dept. **SERV:** Enl 1861 Co E, 73rd NY Vol, hon disc. **F:** Int Evergreen. Tue Jul 12.

LORING, CHARLES B, 63, b Portland, ME, d Tue 830 am Feb 10, 1914, at home, 1126 Washington St, Eliz. **SURV:** w Julia/ch Mrs Michael Kennedy, Plainfield, and Charles, Jr. 4 gch. Res E 35 yrs. Carpenter by trade and in the jobbing biz. **CHH:** St Johns. Tue Feb 10.

LOVELL, JOHN L, 77, b Chemung Co, NY, d Mon aftn Nov 11, 1907, at home of s Charles, 32 Locust St, Roselle Park. **SURV:** w frmr Miss Sarah M Berry of Elmira, NY, m 1851/ch Mrs W B Jones, Bloomington, IL, William J, Roselle, and Charles F, R P. Res R P 8 yrs. **CHH:** Became a Christian ae 16, mem 1st Bapt. **SERV:** Pvt 107th NY Vol Inf, Co D. Joined Com at Chattanooga under Gen Sherman, with him during the march fm Atlanta to the sea. Pens since 1890, the 1st papers made out in Binghamton, NY. Later the amount was increased, and during the 1905-06 winter the late Joseph D Lowden gave untiring efforts for another. On Mon Mar 12, 1906, the request was granted and the pens doubled. Vet had the pleasure of seeing them signed last wk. F: Wed aftn at last home. Int Elmira, NY. Tue Nov 12.

LUM, WILLIAM B, 58, b CT, d Thu ngt Oct 28, 1909, at home, 40 Union St, Rahway. SURV: w. Res R for yrs. SERV: Navy. Sat Oct 30.

LUNGER, JACOB S, 88, d Wed Jan 1, 1936, at home of dau Mrs James B Lunger, 149 Lincoln Ave, W, Roselle Park. SURV: ch Stanley J, Miami, FL, Mrs Lunger, and Mrs Charles H Coe, Maplewood. sib (bro) Guile R, Union and Mrs Mary Puterbauch, Mansfield, PA. 7 gch. 5 ggch. Mem Newark PD for years, ret 21 yrs ago as Lt. MEM: L11, until disb. SERV: Enl abt ae 15. At Bull Run, Gettysburg, and the Wilderness. F: Schmidt Memorial F Home, 139 Westfield Ave, Eliz. Thu Jan 2.

LUSHEAR, ALFRED, 73, b Boonton, d Mon eve Apr 28, 1913, at home, N Main St, Springfield. SURV: ch Clarence and Anna, both Springfield. Rem to Springfield when a boy. MEM: EHW96. SERV: Enl otbrk Co F, 27th NJ Vol, for abt a yr. F: Wed 230 pm, Rev T Stuart Molyneaux, P ME Chh. Int Main St Presby. Tue Apr 29.

LUSTER, ROBERT CRANE, 73, b Eliz, d Wed mrng May 8, 1907, at home, 14 S Reid St, Eliz. SURV: w/ch Edward, Frank, George, Mrs Ida Grant and Mrs Cameron. sib Albert, E, Theodore, Passaic, and Mrs Chetwood Bird, Trenton. SERV: Enl 5th Reg NJ Vol, to end. Badly WIA Chancellorsville. Wed May 8.

LUTZ, JOHN A, b Thu Oct 21, 1847, NY, s/o late Capt John B, Co K, 3rd NJ Vol, d Fri ngt Oct 13, 1905, Newark. SURV: w/2 s/2 bro/sis Mrs Feininger, Paris. One bro res Eliz. Res E 30 yrs then rem to Newark. In 1899 entered the War Dept Serv at the Gen Depot of the Qtmstr Dept, NYC, as an inspector, then secured a pos in the Newark Water Dept. MEM: L11. 35th Reg, NJ Vet Vol, Sec 10 yrs, Pres 1 term. SERV: Enl as recruit Co H,

35th Reg, NJ Vol Wed Sep 7, 1864. At Meriden, MS, Resaca, New Hope Church, Dallas, Big Shanty, Kenesaw mountain, Rosewells Mills, Bluff Mills, Decatur and Siege of Atlanta, GA. Detailed as Orderly at HQ of Gen Mauer and Manning Force, 1st Div, 17th Army Corps, to end CW. Mon Oct 16.

LYNCH, RICHARD H, 70, d Mon Nov 8, 1909, at home, 27 E Grand, Rahway. SURV: W. ch Edgar and Joseph. Res R for some time. CHH: St Marys. F: Thu St Marys. Tue Nov 9.

LYONS, JOHN B, b Sun Mar 27, 1842, Ireland, s/o late Murtagh, d Mon ngt Nov 3, 1930, at home of dau Mrs A M Horton, 812 Kilsyth Rd, Eliz. Divided his time living with dau, and 321 Rahway Ave home of s. Imm USA ae 5 with par. Cabin boy on a Mississippi Riv steamboat, in S when CW broke out. Aft CW learned trade of bricklayer, ret svrl yrs ago. Vol fireman in old Engine Co 1, where he manned a pumper. When co bought a steamer, he worked at that boiler. SERV: At otbrk, for N. While watching the "Louisiana Tigers" drilling, determined to go N. Waiting for an opportunity, finally left vessel when it reached Carroll on its trip fm New Orleans. Enl Army at Newark, 2 yrs, WIA Gettysburg. Transf to Navy, assigned to "Valley City" as a fireman down in the hold of the craft. (Partial Obit) Tue Nov 4.

Attended a Christmas party for CW Vets given by the WRC 27 Tue ngt. Wed Dec 23, 1925. (P)

Attended annual UD25 Christmas party Wed. Thu Dec 30, 1926. (P)

M

MACGREGOR, ALEXANDER, b Sun Aug 21, 1842, Scotland, d Tue aftn Dec 2, 1919, at home, 1141 E Jersey St, Eliz. SURV: ch Dr James, Bayonne, Mrs Abraham Schleimer, Rutherford, Mrs William B Martin, Mrs E N Parcis and Jane, all E. w, frmr Miss Lucy Henry of E, m 1866, d abt 12 yrs ago. Imm USA ae 12 with par, res E almost all his life. Connected with Standard Oil, Bayonne plant, 30 yrs. MEM: Mason, Master of

TL 3 consec terms. UD25, Cmdr a n/o yrs. **CHH:** 2nd Presby. **SERV:** Enl ae 18 otbrk Co A, 1st NJ Vol, 4 yrs. At Bull Run, Antietam, Fredericksburg, Gettysburg, Rappahannock, the Wilderness and Spottsylvania Courthouse. Wed Dec 3. On the Honor Roll for bravery. 50th anniv of 1st Brig article Tue Jul 18, 1911.

MACKEY, WILLIAM HENRY, 62, d Fri 5 am May 24, 1907, at home, 316 Fulton St, Eliz. **SURV:** w/ch Joseph H, William H, and Mary. A gch. sib Mrs A Wooden, Jersey City. Res more than half his life in E, arriving in 1875. Practiced dentistry, with an office on Fulton St. Accepted a pos in the Jappaning dept at Singer, holding the pos until dod. **MEM:** IOOF, and various other councils and lodges. **CHH:** East Bapt, Deacon for yrs. **SERV:** Enl otbrk Co I, 14th NY Vol. In 1st Bull Run 1861. Reup, 3 yrs, Co K, 48th NY(?) Vol, WIA 3 times. **F:** Mon aftn, Rev John V Ellson. Fri May 24.

MACQUAIDE, THOMAS G, b Northfield, Essex Co, d Wed May 9, 1900, at home in NY. **SURV:** w/only s Samuel H. Long an inspector in the Custom House of that city, in that pos at dod. **SERV:** WIA Battle of Newbern, NC, Mar 14, 1862, refused to leave the firing line. Continued to load and fire until too weak to keep on his feet, then taken to field H. A surv of Co K, now living in Eliz, stood by his side in many battles fm Roanoke Island to the Siege of Petersburg. **F:** Fri eve. Int Northfield, where he spent his boyhood days. Fri May 11.

MAHER, PATRICK, b near Clonmel, Co Tipperary, Ireland, d Tue 10 pm, Feb 21, 1904, Eliz Gen H, Eliz. Would have been ae 65 next St Patrick's Day. A wid, res on Morris Ave for yrs. Imm USA during CW. A farmer, locating in Cranford, Union Co, aft CW, bringing a large quantity of vegetables daily into E. **CHH:** St Marys. **SERV:** A farmer on LI. When his employer was drafted, vol as a sub, driving a supply wagon in the AP. Wed Feb 22.

MANDEVILLE, CHARLES A, 81, d Sun 830 pm Feb 17, 1918, Rahway City H, Rahway. **SURV:** s Charles W, Oliver St, with whom he res. bro Frank, R. Worked for the Elizabeth Herald as compositor for yrs, and later as head of the make-up dept, holding this pos when the paper was discontinued some yrs ago. MEM: Typographical Union. WFB27. SERV: 2nd Lt, 3rd NJ Inf, to end. Mon Feb 18.

MANNON, EDWARD P, 85, b 1839, Lebanon, s/o Nicholas & Elizabeth, d Mon Oct 20, 1924, Alexian Bros H, Eliz. SURV: s Asa L, St Petersburg, FL. 2 gch. 3 ggch. sib Mary A and Mrs Elizabeth Pierce, Neshanic, both ae 90+. Res E for yrs with gdau Mrs Richard A Norman, 148 Orchard St. MEM: UD25. SERV: Co A, 31st Reg NJ Inf Vol, to end. F: Chapel of A C Haines, 1211 E Broad St. Tue Oct 21.

MANVEL, JOHN, 56, b Eliz, s/o late Cyrus, d Fri eve, Apr 25, 1902, at home, 545 Westminster Ave, Eliz. SURV: w frmr Miss Mary Moore, d/o late Samuel L/s Herbert E. Educ school at Greenwich and New Haven, CT. Began a biz career in f's E iron foundry. In later yrs the firm was John & Frederick Manvel, the latter his bro. Deputy Comptroller E 16 yrs. Cashier of Citizens Bank 2 yrs, then aft private Sec and Treas of the Moore Bros Co. Fm there entered employ of NY Metal Co. At dod cashier of American Smelting & Refining Co, HQ NYC. 6 mos ago rem fm 1071 Elizabeth Ave home to 545, where he had erected a handsome home. MEM: A Mason, EL49, Washington Chapter 16, and St Johns Commandery 9, KT. SERV: 2 yrs in a NJ Reg. Sat Apr 26.

MARSH, WILLIAM J, 85, b NYC, d Sat Aug 18, 1928, Alexian Bros H, E. SURV: ch Harry R, Dayton, NJ, Mrs William A Sauer, with whom he res since w d, until a yr ago, Pennington St, Mrs Walter Crist and Mrs Percy Mulford, all of E. 4 gs, Harry C and Allan F Sauer, and Harry W and Joseph Marsh. Res Rahway for yrs then rem to E 22 yrs ago, res at 52 Orchard St. Steam eng, worked for yrs at Mershon Printing Plant, Rahway, ret for 12 yrs. SERV: Enl ae 19 Pvt Co B, 30th NJ Inf, Wed Sep 3, 1862, until Jun 1863. In the AP, Maj Gen Ambrose E Burnside, Fredericksburg. Often told of shaking hands with

Lincoln when visiting the troops. Mon Aug 20.

MARSHALL, SAMUEL, 77, native of PA, d Mon Jul 21, 1919, S'H, Kearny. **SURV**: ch Charles, Boston Ave, and Clara Lamoreaux, Long Ave, Hillside, where his f res abt 5 yrs, Anna, Helsinstein, PA, Robert, Locustdale, PA, and William, W Nanticoke, PA. Res S'H since Oct. **SERV**: Enl Pottsville, PA, Tue Feb 28, 1865, assigned to Co C, 93rd PA Inf Vol, disc following Jun. **F**: At home of Charles. Tue Jul 22.

MARTIN, AMOS, 110, b Scotland in 1798, d Tue Aug 4, 1908, Newcastle, PA. Had never been ill prior. Lived in 3 centuries. **SERV**: Vet of 3 wars, 1812, MW and CW. WIA 2nd Battle of Bull Run. Tue Aug 4.

MARTIN, BALTHANSER, CW Vet and h/o **Marie, CW Vet**.

MARTIN, FREDERICK, COL, 68, b 1834 PHL, d Tue 1030 pm Sep 2, 1902, at home, 207 Holly St, Cranford. **SURV**: w/2s. Gen manager of the Brooklyn "L" Road for yrs, having started as Construction Officer. Succeeded in building this RR aft svrl receivers were applied for. Submitted the plan, which was adopted, for the two-platform terminal for the Brooklyn Bridge cable cars. Ret for yrs. **SERV**: With a NY Reg, '61-'67, Lt Col under Gens Ord, Terry and Benjamin F Butler. Military Mayor of Richmond aft its surrender. Mu/o officer AJ. **F**: Fri 11 am at home. Wed Sep 3.

MARTIN, JOSEPH WILLIAM, CAPT, 70, b Rahway, s/o the 2/w of late Dr Lewis Drake, her 1/h a Martin, d Fri 1140 am Nov 13, 1908, at home, 99 Main St, Rahway. **SURV**: w/ch William, Louis, Harry Stone, until svrl mos ago organist at the State Reformatory, and is organist at St Pauls, a pos held for yrs, and Manton, for some time Sec to his f at the State Reformatory. Engaged in a big tobacco warehouse NYC. In 1902, appointed as assist Super of NJ State Reformatory, and in 1907 Super, a successor to the 1st Super, James D Heg. A Repub, elected in the early 70s mem ComC. **MEM**: WFB27. A Free Mason, past Master LL27, and in 1881 Grand Master of NJ. **CHH**: St Pauls Epis, R, for yrs mem official board. **SERV**: Capt 6th NY Ind Bat, first known as the Bramhall Bat. Fri Nov 13. (P)

MARTIN, MARIE, 91 last Nov, b Germany, d Tue Jun 26, 1928, at home, 914 E Grand St, Eliz. **SURV**: ch Mrs Minnie Henry, with whom she res last 5 yrs, Jacob, Belmar, Charles, Newark, and Conrad, Maplewood. 16 gch. 14 ggch. Her h Balthanser, CW Vet, d 15 yrs ago. Imm USA 69 yrs ago in a sailboat, trip requiring 75 days. **SERV**: 2 wks aft m, h enl. Desiring to serv adopted country, registered as a nurse, and serv for the duration, taking part in a n/o battles, administering to the sick and WIA. Stationed for a time at a field H. One of the few remaining CW nurses. Wed Jun 27.

Martin, Mary, celebrated her 80th dob at dau Mrs Minnie Henry's 914 E Grand St home Sun ngt, and it was in the nature of a fam reunion. One who aided in the entertainment was Miss Ethel Mader, a ggdau, who sang and danced. In 1861 m Balthasar Martin. In CW, stationed at Bunker Hill, MD. Has 6 ch, Jacob, Mrs Minnie Henry, Conrad, Charles, Mrs Elizabeth Turner and George; and 15 gch, John William Henry, Florence and Edna Henry, Mrs Marie Robinson, Mrs Katherine Mader, Joseph Turner, Miss May Turner, Miss May Martin, Joseph Martin, John Martin, George Martin, Andrew Martin, Lucy Martin, Miss Veronica Martin, and Raymond Martin. Mon, 27, 1916.

MARTIN, WILLIAM J, 70, d Thu Jun 17, 1915, at home of dau, Roselle. **SURV**: ch Mrs J A Bedford, 319 1st Ave, W, and Edward L, Brooklyn, NY. Res R 10 yrs. **MEM**: Reno Post, NY. **F**: Sat 2 pm at home, Rev Charles F Goodall, P, 1st Bapt Chh. Int Evergreen. Fri Jun 18.

MATSON, MORRIS M, CAPT, 73, b Montgomery Co, PA, d Mon 4 am May 13, 1907, at home, 1094 Elizabeth Ave, Eliz. **SURV**: ch Luke, a detective, Mrs Otto Zimmerman and Mrs Edward S Keefer. 2 gch. A ggch. sis Mrs Frederick Loney of PA. Came to E soon aft CW. Health Inspector, holding that pos during epidemic of smallpox of abt 30 yrs ago. St Comm abt 15 ~rs. **MEM**: UD25, Cmdr. Vet Z. **SERV**: Enl 1st PA Reserves.

WIA. F: Wed aftn at Williamson & S St home of dau Zimmerman, with GAR svc, per request. City Hall flag put at half mast, at req of Mayor Ryan. (Partial Obit) Mon May 13. (P) **MATTOX, WILLIAM R**, b Mon Nov 21, 1836, Newark, d Sun Mar 23, 1902, Plainfield. **SURV**: w/6 ch, eldest s William one of the Roundsmen of the city police. Rem to P 30 yrs ago, one of the first policemen of the city. As a yng man attached to the Newark Theatre, now known as Waldmanns, filling the pos of property man for yrs. Later joined Hendersons Stock Co and played in nearly every city in the E. Well acquainted with Joe Jefferson, William J Florence, Edwin Varey and Tom Keene, having filled minor rolls in their cos. **MEM**: Howell Div, ST, P. GAR. **SERV**: Enl otbrk Co F, 1st NJ Reg. Mon Mar 24.

MAXFIELD, CHARLES WILLIAM, b Mon Jan 14, 1839, eldest s/o late John Gillen & Mary Elizabeth Maxfield, East Chester, NY, d Sun Aug 21, 1910, at home, 548 Westminster Ave, Eliz. **SURV**: ch Charles Evans, Newark, John Guion, Springfield, MA, Edwin Rogers, E, Howard Hoyt, Trenton, and Mrs Mary Guion Rollinson, E. sib John F and Joseph B, Mrs Thomas Oakes, Mrs Joseph Hague and Mrs John A Lawrence, all of Bloomfield. Late w was frmr Ellen Scriven Evans, m Apr 1862. On mo side, direct desc of the Guion fam, among the first Huguenots to arrive. b in the old Guion homestead, a house dating back to Rev times. First biz was with Central Bank, Brooklyn, rising to teller. Resigned to go into the wholesale fruit and produce biz in NY. Res Bloomfield when yng. Res Metuchen for 10 yrs bfr rem to E 25 yrs ago. **MEM**: UD25. VA of the 23rd Reg. A Mason, WL, E. **CHH**: Washington Ave Bapt, Brooklyn, ae 18. 1st Bapt in Metuchen, then E, a Deacon, Trustee and Super of the SS. At dod was teacher of the Baraca class, begun 1899, only teacher class ever had. **SERV**: Joined 23rd Reg of Brooklyn. Put on H staff to treat Gettysburg WIA. Reg recalled to do riot duty in NY. Disc shortly aft, as Sgt. Mon Aug 22. F: Tue aftn at home, Rev Dr Thomas Vassar. Wed Aug 24. **MAY, FREDERICK THOMPSON**, b Mon Jan 4, 1830, Hull,

Yorkshire, England, s/o late Thomas M & Mary Gray May, of Lincolnshire, d Wed Dec 14, 1916, at home, 849 Kilsyth Rd, Eliz. **SURV**: w frmr Eliza Jane Thompson of Merion, PA, m 48 yrs ago/ch Mary, Ann, Mrs F D Van Arsdale, and Frederick T, a SI undertaker. bro Richard C, Los Angeles, CA. 2 gch, Frank D, Jr and Frederick T Van Arsdale. Imm USA with par ae 5 in a sailing vessel and settled in NYC. Later, on a trip to the island of St Thomas, he and his f got yellow fever, fatal for the f. Attended the Friends school and the Columbia school, and for a time a boys school in CT. Fam summered in SI. Engaged in fishing for yrs, taking many trips on schooners to the Grand Banks. When gold was discovered in CA, he and 2 bro went to the gold fields via the Isthmus of Panama. He returned, the bro stayed. Res E 33 yrs, ret for the greater part. **MEM**: Vol FD. **SERV**: He and other FD comrades began a special Co when the first call for troops was issued. Thu Dec 14.

MAY, JOHN A, 65, b NYC, d Sun 930 pm Jul 15, 1900, at home, Westfield Ave, Lorraine. **SURV**: ch George F, Mrs Gertrude E Rau, and Mrs Carrie L Johnson, L, and Charles A, Washington Territory. 6 gch. w d 10 yrs ago. When m, went W, res CA for a time. Rem fam to Eliz 1889, on Wall St, Elizabethport. Rem to L in 1892, one of the first res of that place. For 2 yrs conducted the PO free of charge as an accommodation to his fellow townsmen. Govt made the L PO a remunerative one 3 yrs ago, and a substation of the Eliz PO. **MEM**: UD25. Became a free Mason while in CA. **SERV**: Went to Governor's Island ae 11, learned to drum, and enl MW, Gen Scott, to end. Drum Maj 8th NY and 47th NY Vol. Enl CW, Capt Hinchman. WIA 1st Bull Run. In 27 battles. **F**: Tue 230 pm at home. Int Evergreen.

MAYS, EDMOND, 94, d Tue Jun 9, 1936, at home, 201 E Hazelwood Ave, Rahway. Last of the R CW Vets. **F**: Thu, with military honors, at the fam plot, Hazelwood, Rev James W Laurie, Pastor 2nd Presby. Fri Jun 12. (F)

b England. **SURV**: ch Mrs Andrew H Glendinning and Estella,

201 E Hazelwood Ave. sis Mrs Bertha Perrine, Central and Esterbrooke Aves, R. 3 gch, Mrs George Wilson and Warren Glendinning, 201 E Hazelwood Ave, and John Edmond Glendinning, Denville. 3 ggch, Virginia Wilson, and Ralph and Bruce Glendinning, Denville. w, Alice Stell Mays, d 11 yrs ago. Imm USA ae 3 with par, in Brooklyn a short time. Rem to a large farm on the outskirts of R and Linden, where the present day River View Inn bldg is. Fam homestead for yrs and where his f lived to ae 92. Wholesale milk dealer by trade, had large dairy farm in Clark Tp, near Goodmans Crossing. In 1920 purchased present home. Owned many large sailboats at different periods and made fqt trips up the Hudson Riv. Brought the first 75 lamp posts used in R for the original street gas lights on his boat fm Poughkeepsie. His last craft, "Middlesex," sank in the Rahway Riv at the bend just below Haydock St, and accumulating silt has formed an island around the hulk. **MEM:** GAR. **CHH:** 2nd Presby. **SERV:** Enl Newark, at the Newark Enl Post in the old market place, now Military Park, 8th NY Cav. At Gettysburg, Antietam, Petersburg and other battles and skirmishes. Wed Jun 10.

Attended the complimentary dinner for Barry 27 mems given by A Edward Woodruff Tue eve May 30, 1911.

MCCANDLESS, DAVID, 95 last Jan, b overseas, d Sun eve Feb 17, 1907, at home of s-in-law James C Manahan, 149 Orchard St, Eliz. **SURV:** w frmr Miss Mary Place, m bfr imm, she now 88/ch John, a decorative painter, Robert (See **Living CW Vets**), Mrs Henry Fulton, Mrs Wallace Lang, and Mrs Manahan. 21 gch. 19 ggch. Older s is ae 64. Imm USA 66 yrs ago, soon aft m, induced by a bro who preceded him and res E. Worked in the Singer cabinet making dept 10 yrs, ret 15 yrs ago. A Repub, voting in 1856 for Fremont and Dayton, the first Repub party candidates. **MEM:** UD25. The "Brethren," a religious group he and Mr Manahan belonged to. **SERV:** Enl 1861 ae 50 9th NJ Vol, Capt J Peter Ritter, to end. S John wanted to enl, but f though best he learn a trade instead, so enl in his stead. Followed the fortunes of Burnside's NC campaigns, incldg Newberne. Could not accompany surv of Reg last summer to Newberne, where a monument was dedicated to the memory of the d of the 9th buried there. F: No GAR svc, per fam request. Mon Feb 18.

MCCANN, JAMES, 65, d Tue eve Mar 29, 1910, at home of sis Mrs James Holt, 75 Fulton St, Eliz. SURV: sib Mrs Holt and Daniel. Nephews and nieces, James and Mary McCann, Plainfield, John McCann, E, James and Thomas Holt and Mrs James Quilty. A ret biz man. Rem to E 2 yrs ago fm NY, Wed Mar 30.

MCCLINTOCK, FERDINAND, 68 (?), d announced in Newark. SERV: Co A, 1st NJ Vet Vol, the first Co of 3 yr troops raised in Eliz. F: Sun aftn at home in Caldwell. Oct 20, 1900.

MCCORMICK, THOMAS, 77, b Ireland, d Mon ngt Jan 31, 1916, St Eliz H, Eliz. SURV: w Margare/ ch Mrs M J Kennedy, John, William and Thomas F. 6 gch.4 ggch. Imm USA and settled in E 50 yrs ago. An old vol fireman, at one time mem Protection Engine Co 1. MEM: EFA. CHH: St Marys, but of late Holy Rosary. SERV: Enl otbrk Co K, 9th NJ Inf, to end. F: At home of Mrs Kennedy, 402 1st Ave. Tue Feb 1.

MCCOTTER, DOUGLASS GRANT, 88, b Plattsburg, NY, d Tue Sep 3, 1907, at his summer home, Smithtown, LI. SURV: w/2dau/3s. Res Eliz abt 15 yrs, 410 W Jersey St. Ret real estate dealer. In 1849, a CA gold seeker, and had visited almost every part of the world. SERV: Capt of a Co of Vol. F: Sat mrng at home. Thu Sep 5.

MCCUDDEN, JAMES, d mon mrng Oct 9, 1905, at home, 68 Livingston St, Eliz. SURV: w/6ch. s Andrew was killed in a trolley accident 6 mos ago. Old E res, worked for Singer. MEM: JK64. SERV: Co D, 1st Reg, NY Vol Inf. Mon Oct 9.

MCCREA, JOHN E, d reported Tue May 9, 1911, at home, Newark. A Repub, was Super of the St, Water, and Lighting Dept. SERV: Carried imp dispatches fm Lincoln to Sheridan, on his march to the sea. Tue May 9.

MCCREEDY, GEORGE D, 91, native of Glens Falls, NY, d Sun Dec 22, 1935, at home of s George B, Pikesville, near Baltimore, MD. SURV: w Louise/s George D. 2 gch, Patricia and Jane McCreedy, P. Res Rahway since 1913, at 96 W Grand Ave. Mon Dec 23.

MCDEDE, ANTHONY, 67, d Sat Jan 15, 1910, at home, Cumberland St, Westfield. SURV: w/ch Anson, Anthony, Mrs A W Stiles, and Mary W, Mrs Raymond Robinson, Roseville, and Mrs William Lynch, New Milford. Res W 14 yrs. Tue Jan 18.

MCDERMOTT, PATRICK, d Fri Jul 20, 1900, S'H, Kearny. An old Eliz res. MEM: UD 25. SERV: Co H, 2nd NJ Vol, with Sherman in march to the sea, Co A, 35th NJ Vol. Sat Jul 21.

MCDONALD, DENNIS, b Ireland, d Thu mrng Dec 21, 1916, at home, 813 S St, Eliz. SURV: w Julia/ch Julia C, John F and James E. Rev John McDonald, Ridgefield Park, is a nephew. Last of a fam of 14. Imm USA when a boy, settled in E. A mason by trade, ret for yrs. CHH: St Marys. FHC CBL. SERV: Enl otbrk with 2 other bros Co K, 3rd NJ Vol, late Capt Whelan, and in Gen Phil Kearny Brig. Serv to end, in most of the principal engage, incldg Gettysburg. Thu Dec 21, 1916.

MCGLYNN, JOHN, d announced Tue Jul 30, 1901. SURV: w/ch John J, Frank, Nellie and Mrs B L Farrell, the latter of Milburn. sib Mrs Whelan, wid/o Capt John H. Res Milburn, Essex Co, for a while. Res Eliz 48 yrs. MEM: Carpenters Union 167. CHH: St Marys Chh of the Assumption. HNS, FHC 267, CBL. SERV: Res in S at otbrk. Enl LA Reg, C Army. A bro was killed in the service. F: Thu mrng, St Marys. Int Milburn. Wed Jul 31.

MCGRATH, EDWARD, s/o CW VET William. SERV: 1st NY Mounted Rifles, hon disc.

MCGRATH, WILLIAM, d Thu abt 2 am Dec 29, 1904, at home of s Edward J, Eliz. SURV: ch Edward J, at one time Chief Eng E FD and now Super E Alms House, John and William. w d 25 yrs ago. Came to E a yng man. A contractor.

CHH: When he came to E, there was no RC Chh, so he walked to Newark to attend Mass. A founder of St Marys of the Assumption. Recently attended St Michaels. SERV: 1st NY Mounted Rifles, as did son Edward. Both rcvd hon disc. Oldest E Vet, and a pens. Thu Dec 29, 1904.

MCKENZIE, JAMES S, 68, b CT, d Thu mrng Jan 26, 1911, at home, 1170 Chestnut St, Eliz. SURV: w/s/relatives in CT. Came to E abt 35 yrs ago. Janitor of the GAR HQ in the Cory St bldg, Broad St, for yrs, and of the Madison Ave Presby Chh last 5 yrs. Also worked as a sign painter. MEM: UD25. SERV: With a CT Reg. Jan 26.

MCKEON, CHRISTOPHER, 85, b NYC, d Thu Feb 12, 1932, at home of niece Miss Julia McKeon, 144 Smith St, Eliz. SURV: s Raymond. Svrl nieces and nephews. Res NYC most of his life, rem to E a yr ago shortly aft w d. MEM: A E Kimball Post 100 GAR, NY. CHH: Immaculate Conception. SERV: 95th NY Inf. Fri Feb 13.

MCKIERNAN, JOHN, CAPT, d Sat Mar 4, 1905, Paterson. Treas of the State Firemens Assoc for the past 26 yrs, frmr Chief of the P FD, and a prominent biz man. SERV: Org and named Capt Co A, 25th NJ Vol, made up largely of firemen. Co mu/i Sep, 1862, and became part of Col Derrom Reg. In many battles, incldg Fredericksburg. Disc Jun, 1863, but serv in Qtmstr Dept Newbern, NC, 2 yrs. Tue Mar 7.

MCVICKER, LOUIS J, CAPT, b Sun Jan 7, 1844, SI, d Thu 1 am Mar 26, 1908, at home, 622 Pearl St, Eliz. SURV: w frmr Miss Mary A Longstreet, d/o late Isaac M, Rahway/ch Louis E, John L, Charles P, Bessie and Mary. 4 gch. His mo d Jan at an advanced age, int SI. Res E 25 yrs. A bookkeeper. MEM: UD25, Cmdr in 1905. SERV: Enl ae 18 4th NY Hvy Art, promo to Sgt-Maj. Joined Co E, frmr 3rd Reg, NG, 1886, then transf to Maj Shailer Gun Det, and in 1897 appointed Commissary Sgt of the Reg. Lt Co E 1888-90, when appointed Adj of the Reg, up to S/AW. F: Int S&S' lot, Evergreen, per request. Thu Mar 26. (P)

MEAD, JOSEPH T, 82 yrs, 6 mos, b Rahway, d Tue aftn Mar

16, 1926, Rahway. SURV: w frmr Miss Tamaseen L Keller/ch Arthur E and Clara L, both 16 Thorn St. gdau Mrs Wilson E Sofield, Woodbridge. Another s, Benjamin C, who d a few yrs ago, was in real estate and insurance biz with f. In those biz for abt 50 yrs, his office on Cherry St. Prior to that had conducted one of the largest grocery stores in R, in what was then known as the Union Hall Bldg at Irving and Cherry St, now Griggs hardware store. CHH: 2nd Presby, B of Trustees. SERV: Fm Mon Jul 21, 1862, to Thu Jun 8, 1865, Co A, 13th NJ Vol. Attached to 3rd Brig, 1st Div, 12th Corps, AP. Later transf to 2nd Brig, 1st Div, 20th Corps, AC. Promo to Cpl, and in line for Lt. At Antietam, Chancellorsville, Gettysburg, Dallas, Pine Knob, Kulp's Farm, Kenesaw Mountain, Shermans march to the sea, Sandersonville, Montieth Swamp, the capture of Savannah, Averyshore, Portsmouth, Rocky Road Ridge, Resaca, Cornwall and others. At Gettysburg, narrowly missed d, a bullet striking the tintype picture of Tamaseen. Wed Mar 17.

MEEKER, JOHN J, b Sat Jun 29, 1833, in the historic Meeker Inn, Union, d Sat Dec 7, 1912, at home of dau Mrs E O Runyon, Irvington. Res in I for yrs. A carpenter and builder. In later yrs rem to Newark. SERV: Co D, 5th NJ Vol Inf. F: Wed aftn. Thu Dec 12.

MEEKER, WILLIAM H, 66, b Newark, s/o late Jonathan M, d announced Fri Jan 8, 1909, Pasadena, CA, where visiting with w and dau for his health. SURV: w frmr Miss Julia Hicks, d/o late Jason, for yrs ticket agent for the PA RR/ch S Merchant and Mrs Nellie Dorr. sib Theodore F, Eliz, Rev Jonathan M, DD, Pres of the Centenary Collegiate Inst, Hackettstown, and Mrs William M Morse. bro/o frmr Assemblyman Ellis R, who d Mon Sep 28, 1908, at his Elm St home, and whose w, Fannie Gilbert Meeker, d 2 hrs bfr. For some yrs res at 376 Morris Ave. As a yng man, ran a grocery store on Broad St up to CW. In partnership with f in real estate biz. For 30 yrs agent in Eliz for Merchants Ins Co, Newark, and other cos, his office on E Jersey St, near the corner of Broad St. For yrs his s has been in biz with him. A Repub. Sec of the B of Educ many terms. **MEM:** UD25. A Free Mason, WL33 F&AM, its Worshipful Master in 1877, 1878 and 1881. Washington Chap, Royal Arch Masons, and a past Cmdr St Johns Commandery, Masonic KT. **CHH:** 1st Bapt. **SERV:** Enl Cpl Co A, 1st NJ Vol, Capt David Hatfield, who is now int Evergreen, and in whose honor old David Hatfield Camp 2 SoV was org in Eliz. Promo Capt, Co B, 11th NJ Vol. Sat Jan 9, 1909. (P)

MERRICK, LOUIS, 72, d Tue Apr 30, 1912, at home of dau Mrs George Umber, Park St & E Milton Ave, Rahway. **SURV:** ch Mrs Umber and Mrs Alfred C Feakes, E Grand St, R. sib George, Manasquan, Albert, Newark, Mrs Mary Thompson and Mrs William Howard, Central Ave, R. 3 gch. **MEM:** WFB27. First NY Assoc. **CHH:** 2nd Presby. **SERV:** 5th NY Hvy Art, in many battles. **F:** Fri aftn at Mrs Umber's home, Rev W T Stuchell, P. Tue Apr 30.

Attended the complimentary dinner for WFB27 mems given by A Edward Woodruff Tue eve, May 30, 1911.

MEYER, JACOB, CPL, 78, native of Wales, d Fri noon Dec 6, 1907, at home, Belvidere. **SURV:** w/s. Imm USA when a lad. **SERV:** One of the first Warren Co men to enl 1861, Co H, 9th NJ Vol. Hon disc Wed Jul 12, 1865. Mon Dec 9.

MILLER, GOTTLIEB, 76, b Baden, Germany, d Tue ngt Jun 5, 1917, at home of dau Mrs John Farawell, 576 Adams Ave, Eliz. **SURV:** ch Mrs Edward Welch, Mrs James McGuire, Mrs Fred Welcome, Mrs Farawell, with whom he res, Louis, Frederick, Charles, George and John. 21 gch. Res E 55 yrs. Tailor by trade. **MEM:** UD25. **CHH:** German Lutheran. **SERV:** Co H, 22nd Reg, NY Cav. Wed Jun 6.

MILLER, JACOB, b Germany, d Fri ngt Feb 13, 1920, Gen H, Eliz. **SURV:** ch Mrs Nicholas Brady, Mrs John Goretski, of West New York, NJ, Mrs Miles Bishop, CT, Fred and Joseph. 4 gch. 3 ggch. sis Mrs Rosanna Grody, NY. dau Mrs William F Pender d abt 6 yrs ago. Imm USA 50 yrs ago, most of the time in E. Worked in the Singer oil milling dept 25 yrs. Res 408

Broadway. Sat Feb 14.

MILLER, JAMES, 64, native of New Brunswick, d Thu Jan 23, 1908, S'H, Kearny. **SURV**: sib Edward, 230 Vine St, Eliz, and William, NY. Vet never m. **SERV**: Enl Navy, on the monitor "Patapsco," which bombed Fort Sumter. She was struck by a torpedo in Charleston Harbor and sank in a few min, with a loss of nearly 100 men. Among the few who escaped by going into the turret and remaining there until the vessel went down with her colors flying, then jumped into the water and rescued. Remained in govt svc til end of CW, then returned to N B. **F**: Last Sat aftn, N B, Rev Dr Pockman, Reformed Chh. Int Elmwood. Mon Jan 27.

MILLER, JOHN LEWIS, 76, d Tue Jan 30, 1917, at home of dau Mrs Edward S Welch, 218 S Elmer St, Westfield. **SURV**: w, Newark/ch John, Arnold, and Mrs Welch, W, Henry and Lewis, Newark, and Mrs J A Mooney, Syracuse, NY. Res W since last Nov. Wed Jan 31.

MILLER, WILLIAM H, b Mar 16, 1840, s/o Smith & Catherine Coddington Miller, native of Chatham, Morris Co, d Mon eve Mar 12, 1912, at home, 213 Stiles St, Eliz. **SURV**: ch William H, Jr, ME, Mrs George W Dowers, with whom he res, and Mrs Charles E Carlton, Asbury Park. 3 gch. w d Sep. Ancestors were in the AW. Spent early yrs in Brooklyn. Res E 35 yrs, at Lafayette St a long time. Res of Tarrytown for a while. Aft CW appointed to the NY Customs House as messenger. Worked 40 yrs, ret 3 yrs ago as examiner of lace goods. **MEM**: UD25, past Cmdr. **CHH**: Park ME, up to his rem to the NW section of E, then Epworth, where w was a mem. **SERV**: Enl Cpl Co C, 83rd NY Vol. In 2nd day's fight at Gettysburg, lost an arm. Tue Mar 12. (P)

Returning home aft visiting his dau, William H Miller was surprised at being the recipient of 71 carnations fm William B Durie of Rahway, for his 71st dob. The two, as boys, res at New Providence, where they attended the same school. Met ocnly in later yrs, and both enl 1861. Both were b on the same day in

1839. The f/o his s-in-law George Dowers was in the same reg as he, and through their friendship, their ch became acquainted, and m followed. A founder of Park ME Chh. Aft he lost an arm at Gettysburg was taken to a H in PHL, and aft many wks went home to Brooklyn. Mon Mar 27, 1911.(P)

MILLS, EMORY JAMES, b Mon Oct 11, 1847, Sparta, Ontario, Canada, d Sat Jun 12, 1920, at home, 618 Highland Ave, Westfield. SURV: w/ch Cecil R and Ella Louise. 2 gch, Marion and Robert Mills, W. Res Oak Park, a suburb of Chicago, rem to W 3 ½ yrs ago. MEM: Free Masons and RA in Chicago. CHH: Presby. SERV: 19th NY Field Art. Mon Jun 14.

MINGUS, HENRY H, 83, native of Blackwood, d Thu aft Feb 21, 1929, at home, Rahway. SURV: w Martha/ch William H, Pitman, George W, 141 Central Ave, R, and Harriet L, 92 Seminary Ave, R. A gdau, Barbara Mingus, 141 Central Ave, R. Desc of an old Colonial fam fm Scotland. Svrl relatives in RW, an uncle losing a leg in the Battle of Trenton. Res in PHL most of his life, rem to R 21 yrs ago. Connected with PA RR 46+ yrs, ret abt 15 yrs ago fm pos of Through Baggage Master on NY Div fm NY to Pittsburgh. Crossed the continent 7 times on special trips. Seriously inj in a western PA train disaster. MEM: For yrs Cmdr GAR Post, PHL. RR Relief Assoc, and others. Order of Independent Americans of PHI. CHH: Raised Meth, attended Presby often. SERV: Enl Co G, 118th PA Vol Inf, the PHL "Corn Exchange" Reg, Sat Aug 9, 1862, to end. WIA. Transf 2nd Btln, 32nd Corps. At Antietam, Fredericksburg, Chancellorsville, Gettysburg, the Wilderness, Spottsylvania, Totopotomy Creek, Cold Harbor, and in many engage and skirmishes. WIA twice bfr ae 16. Last man mu/i Corn Exchange Reg and the last surv mem of the Reg, his buddy Andrew Davis having d some mos ago. Name is on the PA monument at the Gettysburg Monument and because of his accurate knowledge and comprehensive view of the battle, sought out by educators, and designated an official guide, making at least 62 trips there. On Mon Jul 4, 1927, shown special honor at Gettysburg, occupying a place of prominence, and being showered with roses by the ch. **F:** Rev George A Law, Pastor 1st Meth. Cremation at Rosehill, Linden. Fri Feb 22.

Mingus, Martha M, 84, b Sat Aug 21, 1847, native of PHL, d Tue 1140 pm Sep 8, 1931, Rahway. **SURV:** ch George W, 145 Central Ave, R, William H, Pitman, and Harriet, 92 Seminary Ave, with whom she res. Her h, a CW Vet and lifelong PA RR employee, d Feb 21, 1929. Celebrated her 84th birthday at home of s George. **MEM:** Greble Council 1, SL & DL, Phl. **CHH:** Meth, earlier in life. **F:** Rev George A Law, of N Plainfield, officiating. Cremation, with int Pitman.

MISKA, HERMAN O P, 69, b Eliz, d Sun Feb 11, 1917, at home, 633 Elizabeth Ave, Eliz. **SURV:** w Catherine Miller Miska. A moulder by trade, but employ by St Dept. **MEM:** Court Washington IOF. **CHH:** Christ. **SERV:** Co I, 37th Reg, NY Vol. Mon Feb 12.

MITCHELL, JAMES, b Tue Mar 8, 1836, Ireland, d Fri Oct 4, 1912, Alexian H, Eliz. **SURV:** ch Mrs David McConnell, St Louis, MO, and William, US Army Cav unit, WP. sis Mrs Joseph Moore, E. W, Mary, d last yr. Imm USA, settled in Jersey City. Once was a miner near Reynoldsville, PA. Aft CW rem to E, employ as watchman for Singer 14 yrs. Rem to St Louis 7 yrs ago, returning to E when w d. **MEM:** Charter mem Harmony Lodge 99 KP. JK64. **SERV:** Enl Pvt Jersey City 1862, Co A, 21st Reg, NJ Vol, 3 yrs. **F:** August F Schmidt Parlor, 63 3rd St. Sat Oct 5, 1912.

Made his home with Detective Luke Matson, 140 E Jersey St, since d of w. Fri Oct 4.

MITCHELL, ROBERT M, 75, d Wed aftn Feb 19, 1913, at home, Cumberland St, Eliz. **SURV:** w/ch Walter, Toronto, Canada, and 2 daus out W. **MEM:** WS73, one of 8 Vets there. **SERV:** Enl US Army May, 1861, Co F, 13th IL Vol Inf. Under Gen Curtis during the Pea Ridge campaign. WIA Lookout Mountain, hon disc. In Navy, under Adm Farragut in the blockading squad May 1864 to Sep 1865. On the USS "Arizona" until she was destroyed by fire at the mouth of the Mississippi

Riv on Mon Feb 27, 1865. He escaped the fate of many companions by jumping overboard and swimming to shore. Also on the USS "Oneida." On Wed Dec 6, 1911, rcvd a medal fm the Sec of the US Naval Dept as a reward for svc during the CW. Thu Feb 20.

MOFFETT, ELMORE DRAKE, 84, d Sun May 7, 1905, at home, Plainfield. Appointed assist Union Co Clerk under James Vosseller in 1882, ret during Co Clerk Howard's 1st yr. A Dem. Elected to the Common Council of P 1890, 2 terms, one as Pres. **MEM**: MA109, past Cmdr when it merged with WS73. JL26 F&M. **CHH**: 1st Bapt. **SERV**: Co G, 32nd NY Vol. **F**: Wed aftn, buried fm 1st Bapt, P, per own request. Tue May 9.

MONEYHAM, WILLIAM, 101, d announced Mon Aug 1, 1921, Benton, IL (Dateline). **SURV**: 82 living desc. **MEM**: GAR, since its inception. **SERV**: 81st IL Inf.

MOORE, GEORGE W, 80, native of Rahway, d Mon Jul 28, 1919, at home, Adams St, Rahway. **SURV**: sib John E, R, and Robert W, Glen Ridge. A mason and builder by trade, had charge of many imp building enterprises in NY. **SERV**: Enl otbrk 6th NY Ind Bat. Reup and serv to end. At many big battles. **F**: At home Wed 330 pm, Rev C L Cooder, DD, Glen Ridge. Tue Jul 29.

MORRISON, JAMES H, nearly 87, native of Parsonfield, ME, d Thu Apr 15, 1926, Rahway. **SURV**: w Ella D. Nephews William and Charles Waterman, Montclair, and Dr George Waterman, Boston. Niece Mrs Alice Thayer, Boston. Res Lawrence, MA, 60 yrs and conducted a boarding house. Rem to R 2 yrs ago, res 166 Central Ave. **MEM**: Lawton Post GAR and Tuscon Lodge F&AM, Lawrence. **CHH**: Advent, Lawrence. **SERV**: 2nd Co Reg, in engage in the Wrn part of the country. **F**: Rem to Lawrence. Fri Apr 16.

MORSE, WILLIAM MULFORD, 75, b Eliz, d 405 am Wed Feb 15, 1911, at home, 350 Union Ave, Eliz. **SURV**: ch Mrs Thomas H Faulks and Mabel I M. 2 gch. Desc of RW Capt Amos Morse. w, frmr Miss Mary B Meeker, d/o late Jonathan

Magie Meeker, m Wed Feb 6, 1856, d Wed Jun 29, 1910. Worked 40 yrs with the firm of Henry E Frankenberger, Broome St, NY, up to 4 yrs ago. **CHH:** 2nd Presby. **SERV:** Co B, 30th Reg, NJ Vol. Wed Feb 15.

MUECK, OTTO, 68, b Neustadt, Germany, d Fri mrng Mar 19, 1915, at home, 593 Madison Ave, Eliz. **SURV:** w Margaret/ch Otto F, E, and Emil, Newark. bro Emil, Chicago. 2 gch. Frmr res Plainfield, rem to E abt 8 yrs ago. Chief clerk of the Military Service Inst on Governor's Island for yrs. **MEM:** JL F&AM Plainfield, frmr High Priest. Also mem Jerusalem Chap Trinity Commandery 17 and Plainfield Council 711 RA. Fri Mar 19.

MUIR, WILLIAM FREDERICK, (1) d Sat Jan 19, 1929, S'H, Kearny. **SURV:** s Frederick, Eliz. Res S'H since 1912. **SERV:** Co E, 14th NJ Inf, and Co D, 2nd NJ Inf. Mu/o as Cpl. **F:** Int sol Circle, Arlington. Mon Jan 21.

(2) b Tue Oct 12, 1847, native of Rahway, s/o William W, d Sun Jan 20, 1929, at the Kearny H, Rahway (Dateline). **SURV:** w, Louise Lehleiter. s Frederick, 316 Grier Ave, Eliz. Lifelong res R. **MEM:** WFB27. **SERV:** Enl Pvt Co E, 14th Reg, NJ Vol Inf. Transf to Co D, 2nd Reg, and promo to Cpl. At the Wilderness, Gettysburg, Cold Harbor, Chancellorsville, Fredericksburg and Spottsylvania Courthouse. Mu/o end of CW at Hall's Hill, VA. Aft CW in Co F, NG, rose to 1st Lt. Last surv mem Drake Vet Z, Eliz. A Sgt, traveled across the continent with late Gen J Madison Drake aft CW. **F:** Albert E Lehrer F Home, 12 Main St, R, Rev Robert W Elliott, Rector Holy Comforter. Mon Jan 21.

MULDOON, PHILIP, 71, d Wed ngt Jul 22, 1914. Res 280 9th St, Jersey City. Frmr Super of Sewers and a ret cigar dealer. Thu Jul 23.

MUNN, FRANCIS W, b Irvington, Essex Co, d Thu 7 pm May 16, 1907, at home, 38 Chestnut St, Newark. **SURV:** w frmr Miss Mary Emily Kent, m 1868. When yng rem to CT. Res Eliz for yrs. Super of the frmr Newark & Eliz Horse Car RR. Dir of the Fire & Marine Ins Co, and Dir of svrl B&L Assoc. **MEM:** L11. **CHH:** While in Eliz, 3rd Presby. **SERV:** Enl otbrk 25th Reg, CT.

WIA Irish Bend, taken prisoner, and afterwards recaptured. F: Mon 230 pm, Rev Dr Ingliss, his P, assisted by Rev John T Kerr, 3rd Presby. Fri May 17.

MURPHY, JAMES B, 56, d Wed mrng Dec 16, 1903, at home, 72 Court St, Eliz. **SURV**: w/ch James, Thomas, Bernard, Mrs Benjamin O'Neill, Mrs Oscar Wiengart and Lillian. Res E 40 yrs. Worked at Singer as a machine polisher. **CHH**: St Patricks. HNS. **SERV**: At CW otbrk was in 6th US Inf, saw much serv in campaigns among the Indians in the far W. Disc regular Army, and enl 4th MA Vol, in svrl battles incldg Bull Run. Wed Dec 16.

MURPHY, JOHN, 66, b Ireland, d Thu Feb 21, 1901, at home, 224 Geneva St, Eliz. **SURV**: w. Res E 35 yrs, a large part of that time working at the frmr Elizabethport Cordage Works. **SERV**: Enl May 14, xxxx, Co G, 74th NY Vol, then Co F, 2nd NJ Vol. **F**: Int S&S' lot Evergreen Sun, a detail of JK64 as bearers.

MURRAY, SAMUEL, 70, b in the N of Ireland, d Sun Mar 24, 1901, at home, 129 Liberty St, Eliz. **SURV**: ch William, OK, Samuel, employ at Singer, and Annie. w, a sis/o late frmr Sheriff Thomas Forsyth, d svrl yrs ago. Res E abt 45 yrs. Long employ in the frmr Albro Oilcloth Factory as a painter. At one time janitor of City Hall, and in later yrs serv a term as Councilman fm the frmr 8th Ward. A Repub, fqt delegate fm his Ward to city conventions. When Elizabeth Ave was repaved a few yrs ago, appointed inspector. **SERV**: Enl Co G, 9th NJ Vet Vol, and serv with the Reg. **F**: Wed aftn, Rev Dr Wilding. Mon Mar 25.

MYER, CHARLES L, b Saugerties, NY, s/o Peter B, d early Mon mrng Jan 25, 1904, at home, 16 Sayre St, Eliz. **SURV**: w a d/o Mr & Mrs Gilbert Mount of Freehold. A dau d a few yrs ago. f was com in 1836 by NY Gov William L Marcy as Capt of Troop A, 1st NY Cav. Came to E soon aft end of CW. Appointed assist freight agent by Col James W Woodruff, and promo when freight agent Ogden Woodruff transf to Newark. Took 4 trips to FL trying to improve his health. **MEM**: E Lodge, Ancient Order United Workmen. **CHH**: 1st Bapt. **SERV**: Enl Co G, 20th NY Vol, hon disc. **F**: Wed aftn, Rev Travis B Thames, DD. Int

Evergreen. Mon Jan 25.

N

NAEBOR, JOHN, 70, b Germany, d Tue mrng Dec 12, 1916, at home, 146 4th St, Eliz. **SURV**: ch Frank, James, Andrew, Joseph, Daniel and Arthur. 24 gch. Imm USA to NYC yrs ago. Aft CW worked for Singer, and rem to E when the co relocated to E. Foreman in the assembling and old gear room, employ for 40 yrs. **MEM**: Singer SBS. JK64. **SERV**: Enl otbrk in a NY Reg of Z, to end. Tue Dec 12.

NAYLOR, JOHN H, SCOUT, 69, d Sat ngt Jul 17, 1909, State Asylum, Morris Plains. **SURV**: w/2bro. Res 277 Morris Ave, Eliz. Known as "Buck" Naylor in his yng days. Scout in IW for yrs with Buffalo Bill. Left the circus and rem to E, starting a riding academy. Entered the express biz, doing trucking for the local 5 & 10-cent store. Also a RR eng. **SERV**: Co B, 5th NJ Vol, 3 yrs. **F**: Tue. Int Sol plot Evergreen. Mon Jul 19.

NEAL, WILLIAM T, 59, s/o late John, frmr contractor, d Sun ngt Nov 9, 1902, at home of bro Edward, 227 Centre St, Eliz. **SURV**: A fam. In the Hack biz for yrs, and later a produce dealer. **SERV**: Enl ae 17 1st Reg NJ Vol. Lost an arm at the Wilderness. Mon Nov 10.

NEEFUS, DAVID, 91, b Brooklyn, d Thu Dec 25, 1913, at home, Passaic Ave, Chatham. **SURV**: ch James and H W. f/o late David of 20 Lyon Pl, for yrs assessor in the 10th Ward. Sat Dec 27.

NEILL, EDWARD K, 68, b Eliz, E Jersey & Spring St, s/o late John, a well known contractor, d Thu Apr 13, 1911, at home, 459 Walnut St, Eliz. **SURV**: w/ch Thomas J, Edwin W, Mrs C C Harris, Mrs A Hendry and Anna. 7 gch. **MEM**: AC OUAM. **SERV**: Enl Co A, 1st NJ Vol, attached to Kearny Brig 3 yrs, bcmg Qtmstr. **F**: Rev Dr Eben B Cobb. Fri Apr 14.

NEVIUS, HENRY N, b Sat Jan 30, 1841, near Freehold, d reported Mon Jan 30, 1911, Red Bank (Dateline). Educ in the Freehold Inst, then went to Grand Rapids, MI. Studied law in the offices of Russell A Alger, aftward Sec of War. Lawyer by trade. Judge of the Circuit Court 1896-1903, and Prosecutor of the Common Pleas in Monmouth Co 1904 until Oct, 1908. **MEM**: GAR, natl cmdr in 1909. **SERV**: Enl 1st NY, Capt Reynolds. Promo for gallantry to 2nd Lt in 2nd MI Cav. Lost an arm in an engage near Washington. Mon Jan 30.

NICHOLS, SAMUEL, 73, b Northampton Co, PA, d Sat ngt, May 31, 1902, at home, 1072 Lafayette St, Eliz. **SURV**: ch Arthur L and 3 daus. W d 6 yrs ago. When yng rem to Brooklyn, where he was m. Res E for yrs. Apprenticed to the late John Ogden, f/o F dir Ogden, as cabinet maker, in his employ for yrs. At otbrk MW, went to Governor's Island with a companion named Davis. Mr Ogden thought his apprentice too yng and secured his release. Aft CW worked for Ogden, then for James C Ogden. Ret past few yrs. **SERV**: Enl otbrk Co A, 1st NJ Vol, 3 yrs, in all engage. Stephen E Boughton owes his life to him having been rescued on the battlefield. **F**: Private, Wed aftn. Int next to w. Mon Jun 2.

NOE, NOAH S, 71, d Tue Sep 17, 1901, S'H, Kearny. **SURV**: Sis Mrs Susan Geery, Eliz. Vet never m. Lifelong res Eliz. Coachmaker by trade. At close of CW went into farming. **SERV**: Pvt Co B, 30th Reg, NY Vol, Capt Lewis. Co B was recruited in Eliz and Rahway. Wed Sep 18.

O

OESE, VICTOR, 57, d Wed ngt Aug 22, 1900, at home, 611 Franklin St, Eliz. Worked in the Singer shipping dept for yrs. **MEM**: Kolte Post 32 GAR, Dept of NY. AC, Order of United American Mechanics. **SERV**: Co A, 15th NY Vol. **F**: Evergreen. Thu Aug 23.

O'KEEFE, DANIEL, 60, native of Ireland, d Fri aftn Mar 23,

1906, Alexian H, Eliz. **SURV**: Cuz John Brosnan, E. Imm USA 50 yrs ago. Boarded 128 Trumbull St. Carpenter, worked for awhile at the BNY. Recent yrs worked for Singer. **SERV**: Navy. Obtained considerable prize money. **F**: J S Stiner, Wed mrng St Patricks. Mon Mar 26.

OLIVER, JOSEPH BROWN, 71, b Cherry St, Rahway, d Sun 745 pm May 3, 1914, at home of sis Mrs S B Morss, 57 Seminary Ave, Rahway. **SURV**: sib Mrs Morss, with whom he res, Mrs C R Danforth, Richmond Hill, NY, and Ella W, Seminary Ave. Vet never m. PM R 1866-70. **SERV**: Enl Sat Jun 15, 1861, Co K, 9th NY Reg, then 6th Ind NY Btln, AP. In 1861, at Bolivar, VA, Wed Oct 6, and Ball's Bluff Sun Oct 27. In 1862, at the extensive Peninsula Campaign, Siege of Yorktown Thu Apr 3 to Sun May 4, Williamsburg Mon May 5, Fair Oaks or Seven Pines Sat May 31 and Sun Jun 1, Savage Station Sun Jun 29, White Oak Swamp Mon Jun 30, Malvern Hill Tue Jul 1 and Tue Aug 5. In 1863, at Kelley's Ford Tue Mar 17, Chancellorsville Fri May 1 to Tue May 5, Brandy Station Tue Jun 9, WIA, Gettysburg Wed Jul 1 to Fri Jul 3, Shepherdstown Thu Jul 16, Sulphur Springs Mon Oct 12, St Stephens Church Wed Oct 14, Auburn Wed Oct 14, Bristol Station Wed Oct 14, New Hope Church Fri Nov 27, Parker's Store Sun Nov 29, and Culpepper Ford Tue Dec 1. In 1864, at the Wilderness, Thu May 5 to Sat May 7, Spottsylvania Sun May 8 to Wed May 18, including Rock Rd, Fri May 6, Todd's Tavern Sat May 7 and Sun May 8, Glendale Mon May 9, Island Ford Tue May 10, Beaver Dam Tue May 10, Ashland Station Wed May 11, Glen Allen Wed May 11, Richmond Hill Thu May 12, and Emmon's Chapel, Tolopotomy Creek Sat May 28, where he lost his left leg. Mu/o Thu Aug 18, 1864. In a strange coincidence, Gen Daniel Sickles, who cmd his Corps at Gettysburg, d Sun ngt. The Gen also lost a leg in the CW. **F**: Thu aftn at home, Rev L Y Graham, Pastor 1st Presby. Int R. Mon May 4.

OPIE, DAVID B, 82, b Bedminster, s/o late Isaac Voorhees & Eliza Gould Opie, d Mon Dec 7, 1931, at home of dau Mrs John

H Newsome, 42 Chilton St, Eliz. **SURV**: ch Mrs Newsome, with whom he res, Mrs Emma Perty, Edmester, NY, Mrs Maud Carkhuffs, Linden, and Mrs George C Sullivan, Indianapolis. 8 gch. Res E 55 yrs. Employ 49 yrs Bowker Chemical, Carteret, ret 15 yrs ago. **MEM**: UD25 at one time. **SERV**: Pvt 38th Reg NJ. Tue Dec 8.

O'SULLIVAN, DANIEL, 73, b Ireland, d Mon ngt Oct 26, 1914, at home, 227 Magnolia Ave, Eliz. **SURV**: ch Dennis L, William D, Mrs Michael French, Mrs Thomas H Fox and Sister Petronilla, who is connected with Father Drumgool's Mission on SI. sib Patrick, Syracuse, NY, and James, E. 19 gch. Imm USA when a boy. Worked for yrs as a stationary eng for Central RR. Res downtown E 55 yrs. A Dem, 2 terms on the B of Freeholders. **MEM**: JK64. **CHH**: St Patricks. HNS. FHC CBL. **SERV**: Enl otbrk Co F, 38th NY Vol Inf. POW Libby. When released enl Navy. Tue Oct 27.

OTIS, ELWELL STEPHEN, MAJ GEN, b Sun Mar 25, 1838, Frederick, MD, d early Thu Oct 21, 1909, at home, Gates, near Rochester, NY. **SURV**: w/3 dau/a m bro. Rem to Rochester ae 2. Educ R PS. Grad Univ of R 1858, then took law course Harvard. **SERV**: Enl Capt 1862 Co D, 140th NY Vol. Promo Col aft the Wilderness when leader Col O'Rourke was KIA. WIA 1864, Chapin's Farm, but in time to be Brev Brig Gen of Vol for conspicuous gallantry at Spottsylvania. Mu/o 1865, returning to R to practice law. In Jan 1866, enl Regular Army as Lt Col 2nd Inf, Col 1867 and Brig Gen 1893. At S/AW otbrk appointed as Maj Gen of Vol, then in 2 yrs Maj Gen Regular Army, holding rank until 1902 ret. Saw many IW battles during Wm Posts svc. Judge Advocate of the Court which condemned Capt O M Carter for the Savannah frauds. Succeeded Gen Merritt in the Philippines in 1898, rcvg a commendation fm Pres Mckinley. Left the islands in 1900, then in cmd of the Dept of the Lakes until ret. Thu Oct 21.

OW, ALEXANDER, 77, b New Brighton, PA, d Fri aftn Feb 23, 1923, at home, 443 Grier Ave, Eliz. **SURV**: w Mattie E. Res

E past 15 yrs. Pattern maker for Durant Motor Car Co. **MEM:** Edwin M Stanton Post GAR, Qtmstr one term. Robertson Lodge 450 IOOF. Social Lodge 54 KP. **SERV:** Pvt Co F, 55th Reg, PA Inf. Sat Feb 24.

P

PACKARD, JOSEPH C, HEAD OF GAR, DIES WITHIN 12 HRS OF W, FANNIE G.

Mr Packard, 83, s/o <u>CW Vet Joseph White Packard</u>, b Jun 1, 1844, NYC, d 4 am Wed May 9, 1928 at home, 314 Drake Ave, Roselle. Desc of the Packards who settled in MA in the 17th century. **MEM:** UD25. SAR. SoV of CW. Lincoln Camp 2. **CHH:** Wesley ME. **SERV:** Enl Mon Aug 18, 1862, Co F, 139th Reg, NY Vol Inf. Co sent fm Brooklyn to Fortress Monroe, VA, and thence to Williamsburgh. In the Fall of 1863, went to Coinjock, NC, where the unit remained until the campaign of 1864, when it returned to VA and joined the 18th Corps at Yorktown. At Williamsburgh, April 1863, Crumps Farms, Jun 1863, Fort Darling, Drury's Bluff, VA, May 12-16, 1864, and Cold Harbor, VA, Jun 1-2, 1864, WIA and sent to H. Upon returning to Reg, sent to Fortress Monroe until end. Mu/o Fri Jun 30, 1865.

Mrs Packard, 73, d/o Robert Denison, b Tue Jul 11, 1854, Brooklyn, m Thu Jun 25, 1874, Eliz, d Tue aftn at home. The Denisons are rich in the hist of the colonial govt, arriving America in 1631.The couple res Eliz many yrs, rem to R abt 10 yrs ago. **SURV:** ch Mrs William Post, 314 Drake Ave, Mrs William Thomas, Jersey City, Robert, Plainfield, and David, Rahway. 7 gch. Vet has sis Mrs Mayra (Maria) Donnell, Lakeland, FL, and his w 2 sis, Mrs Lulia Nelson, St Louis, MO, and Caroline, Lynbrook, LI. **MEM:** WRC 27, Sons of CW Vets Aux 15. Wed May 9. (P of Cmdr)

F: At their home. Svc ME Chh, Rev J Clark Calender, P, and Chapl Warren Pattencoon, frmr P. Sat May 12.(P of couple)

Mr & Mrs Joseph C Packard celeb their 50th m anniv at their home last ngt. He is actively engaged in GAR work, and left tdy for the GAR convention at Asbury Park. Those present were: Mr & Mrs Joseph C Packard; Mr & Mrs R W Packard and Robert W Packard, Jr, Plainfield; Mr & Mrs W F Thomas and Cornelia F Thomas, Jersey City; Mr & Mrs D N Packard, Leslie F and Edwin J Packard, and Miss Margaret C Packard, Jersey City; Miss Caroline Denison, Lynbrook, NY; Mrs Emma Packard, Eliz; the Misses Ellen and Lillian Hefti, and Mrs Vioia Louis, Plainfield; Miss Beatrice Brink, Mauch Chunk, PA: Edward Marr, Jr, Newark; and, Mr & Mrs W Post, Miss Linda Clark, Mr & Mrs George S Vought, and Rev EA Quimby, Roselle. Thu Jun 26, 1924. (A-Dateline Roselle)(P of couple) (Note: Mauch Chunk is the present day Jim Thorpe)

Attended a Christmas party for CW Vets given by WRC27 Tue ngt in Eliz. Wed Dec 23, 1925. (P)

Installed as Cmdr at the U/D25 meeting Tue ngt. Was Cmdr many yrs ago. Tue Jan 8, 1924. (P)

PACKARD, JOSEPH WHITE, b Nov 2, 1820, Clinton, NY, s/o Nathaniel Rawson, 1812 Vet, and Elizabeth (Clary) Packard, d Tue Jan 27, 1891, m, Catherine Ann Angus, b Mar 14, 1820, d/o James of Eliz, & Mary (Brower) Angus, d Sat Oct 7, 1899, Eliz. They had 7 ch: Joseph Clary, CW Vet; Algernon Sidney, b Sat Oct 11, 1845, d 1846; Mary Elizabeth, b Tue Jan 25, 1848, d Fri Nov 22, 1918; Ida, b Mon May 5, 1851, d 1853; William C, b Tue Dec 14, 1852, d Mon Apr 5, 1920; Marie C, b Mon May 18, 1857, d 1935; and Frank B, b Sun Nov 25, 1860, d Aug, 1865. Ch 1-3 & 6 b NYC, and ch 5 Brooklyn.

Nathaniel Rawson Packard serv 1812, Pvt, Capt John Smith's Co, 4th Reg, Sweets MA Militia, Sep 12-25, 1814. Place of res is shown as Readfield.

Joseph White Packard, 1st Sgt, Co F, 139th Reg, NY Vol Inf. Enrolled Brooklyn Aug 19, 1862, 3 yrs, mu/i Sep 9, 1862, Brooklyn. Promo 2nd Lt, assigned to Co C, 139th Reg. Promo Capt Mar 25, 1865, assigned to Co B, 139th Reg. Hon disc as

Capt, at Richmond, VA, Jun 19, 1865. The 139th belonged to the 18th Corps, AJ. Captain Packard cmd clipper ships in the China trade btwn NYC and the Orient. He skippered for the firms of A A Low and the Black Ball Line bfr CW. The clippers were fast sailing ships. Aft CW he again went to sea, his s William C 1st Mate. Last ship was in the banana trade btwn NYC and the W Indies (in steam ships). He belonged to the old John St Meth Chh NYC. He played the flute and is believed to have sung in the choir. He reportedly gained the distinction of being one of the Christian Sea Captains. His favorite hymns were "Father is at the Wheel" and "A Shelter in the Time of Storm."

Catherine Ann Angus was the w/o Joseph White Packard and mo/o Joseph Clary Packard. Her f was James Angus of Eliz and her mo Mary Brower. Catherine was thought to have been b Rahway Sep 19, 1794, and was desc fm James Angus, b 1751, fm Aberdeen, Scotland. He imm America bfr the RW and was Commissary Gen and Messenger in the Nern Rev Army. He res in Albany, NY , and had 6 s and 3 dau. Catherine Ann Angus was 1st cuz of James Winans Angus, who res in the old stone house on Elizabeth Ave, corner of Reid St, Eliz. He desc fm early settlers of Elizabeth Town, Mayflower, and French Huguenots. Ref: Annie Stockton Chapter DAR, Packard & Allied Fam Assoc, War records furnished by War Dept, Washington, DC.

PANGBORN EDWARD, DR, 70, d Fri aftn Aug 25, 1911, Manchester, near Clifton Springs, NY. Of Brooklyn. Killed in a Lehigh Valley RR train wreck. One of 27 dead, with others badly inj. Sat Aug 26.

PARKER, JAMES A, native of Pottstown, near Baton Rouge, LA, d Mon aftn Jun 17, 1929, at home, 28 Newton St, Rahway. **SURV**: w Amy T. Came to R 50 yrs ago. A mason by trade. **MEM**: Connected with a Brooklyn GAR Post. **CHH**: Silver Leaf Club of Ebenezer AME, Pres B of Trustees for yrs, a class leader. Hon mem Ruth Missionary Circle, 2nd Bapt. **SERV**: Enl U as a messenger boy 1862, to end. While aboard a naval vessel,

lost an eye by the premature explosion of a shell. F: Ebenezer. Tue Jun 18. (No mention of color. Obit specifies chh as AME.)
PARKIN, PAUL G, 73, d Sun ngt Oct 18, 1914, at home, 82 Franklin Pl, Summit. **SURV**: 5 ch, all live in S. Res S 32 yrs. **MEM**: USG117. IORM. F: Rev John F Butterworth, frmr Rector Cavalry Epis. Tue Oct 20.
PAYTON, THOMAS, d Sun Apr 14, 1901, the 40th Anniv of CW otbrk, Alexian H, Eliz. A wid. Res E many yrs. Carpenter by trade. A founder of Jefferson Engine Co 6, one time its foreman. Recently admitted to S'H, Kearny. **SERV**: Co B, 35th NJ Vol, enl Mon Sep 21, 1863, hon disc Sat Jun 24, 1865. F: Mr Martin in charge. Mon Apr 15.
PEEPLES, THOMAS WINSTON, native of Harrisburg, PA, d Sat Apr 27, 1907, East Orange. **SURV**: s/dau. Had remarked to fam mems that he was going to see his gs, Clarence Bruen, who d abt a yr ago, fell asleep, and d. Once res Chestnut St, Eliz. Rem to E O 30 yrs ago. When yng entered svc PA RR, being made a master mechanic of the Harrisburg Div by ae 21. Appointed to a pos with the Jersey Central RR, staying until 1874, when made Chief Eng NY Elevated Roads, staying for 23 yrs. **SERV**: Org at otbrk a Co of RR men and went to front with Co E, 201st PA Vol. Tue Apr 30.
PENDLETON, SAMUEL HEISLER, 77, b Wed Jan 27, 1841, s/o James L & Anna L, Richmond, VA, d Sat mrng Sep 28, 1918, at home of s Arthur T, 1201 Fairmont Ave, Eliz. **SURV**: w frmr Miss Sallie Ann Pendleton, m Thu Dec 15, 1864, Warsaw, a small town near Richmond/s Arthur T. 3 gch. Attended a Richmond PrS as a lad. At close of CW rem to NY and engaged in the grain biz as a corn merchant. 2 yrs later rem to E. Ret last 25 yrs, and res with s. A Dem, supporting the party except when he supported the gold faction of the Dem party during the Bryan Free Silver campaign. **CHH**: With Trinity as it was being frmd, serv as both a Vestryman and Warden. Rem to St Johns when Dr Otis A Glazebrook came to E as Rector. The 2 men were boyhood playmates. **SERV**: Enl otbrk Richmond

Howitzers Art Co, to end. In Dec, 1864, passed through the U lines on his way back to VA, and m w. To get back to Reg, had to pass through the lines a 2nd time. Sat Sep 28.

PENNINGTON, JAMES O, 71, d Fri Mar 3, 1911, at home of dau Mrs George Lukens, 367 St George Ave, Rahway. **SURV**: w/6dau/4 s. Res Beverly, was visiting dau last 2 mos. A farmer. **SERV**: C sol, fighting under Lee in 31 engage. At Gettysburg, in one of the Reg which took part in the last fatal charge on the U Bat. F: Tue aftn, Beverly. Sat Mar 4.

PIERSON, CHARLES W, 59, s/o late Joseph & Ann, d Wed mrng Apr 25, 1907, St Francis H, Trenton. Desc of John Hartling, one of the signers of the Declaration of Independence. Fam mems have serv in every war. **SERV**: Wanted to enl otbrk, but too yng, even tho unusually large and strong. At ae 14, 3 mos, could easily pass for ae 17, in 1864. Enl Co B, 4th Reg, Capt Robert E Johnson, until Reg mu/o at end. Youngest Drummer Boy. Thu Apr 25.

PIERSON, HENRY W, 76, killed by a train Sat aftn Mar 19, 1904, near Chatham. **SURV**: w/dau Mrs George E Hale, C. bro-in-Law Thomas B Budd, Eliz. Res C. **SERV**: Pvt Co C, 14th NJ Vol, Capt Chauncey Harris, Eliz, to end. Mon Mar 21.

PITCAIRN, JOHN M, d Tue mrng Jul 26, 1904, Long Branch. **SURV**: 2/w a frmr res of CT/ch Mrs Martha (William M) Smith, 27 W Grand St, Eliz, and a dau by the frmr m. 2 s d bfr him. Couple lived with Mrs Smith, and they were all visiting Ocean Grove for his health. Came to Eliz when frmr Councilman Thomas H Smith located his hat factory on Orchard St, having worked for him long bfr in NY. Aft many yrs at the factory, became a mem PF for a long time. For awhile night watchman at the trolley co barns at the foot of E Jersey St. Ret, but fqtly chosen as a juryman. A Repub, chosen mem B of Chosen Freeholders frmr 5th Ward. A CC candidate, but defeated by Dem Jacob W Sheppard. Owner of considerable real estate. **MEM**: UD25, on financial committee 1904, and a delegate with G Dwight Stone to the recent Asbury Park encmp. OL126 F&AM.

SERV: Enl 71st NY Vol, and aft Co H, 10th NY Vol. Tue Jul 26, 1904.

PITMAN, JOHN, BRIG GEN, 90, b RI, d Tue Aug 29, 1933, Orange. SURV: w Anne de Miller Pitman/ch John R, Orange and Joseph L, Springfield, MA. An authority on small arms ammunition. SERV: Appointed to WP, gradually rose through the ranks until ret 1906 as Brig Gen. F: Int fam plot Providence, RI. Tue Aug 29.

Pitman, John R, Brig Gen, 90, b Providence, RI, d Tue Aug 29, 1933, at home, 611 Berkeley Ave, Orange. SURV: 2/w Miss Anna De Miller, m 1903/ch John R, VP Orange B of Educ, and Dr J Livingston, Springfield, MA. 4 gch, including Lt J R, US Army. 1/w d 1901. Of colonial NE ancestry. When quite yng, his f, John T, became the head of a patent office in London, England, and he was sent to college in Brunswick, Germany. Just bfr CW otbrk, f and s returned to USA. MEM: Military Academy Alumni Assoc, for yrs an attendant at Jun meetings at WP, the oldest mem last Jun. Military Order of the LoyL of the US. SERV: Both f and s enl U Army, he as a Lt with 1st RI Vol Reg. In 1863 appointed by Lincoln to WP, grad 1867, and detailed to the Ordnance Dept, US Army. A Col in S/AW, in charge of the ordnance camp Augusta, GA. Became a small arms expert, continuing his study aft 1906 ret as Brig Gen. Possessed a collection of detailed drawings of small arms used in this country since pre-RW days, and had a notable collection of cartridges. F: Orange. Int Providence, RI. NYT obit Aug 30. (P)

PITMAN, JOHN T, f/o Brig Gen John R Pitman, enl Col 9th RI Vol Reg.

PLUM, GEORGE M, 92, native of NYC, d Sun ngt Dec 24, 1933, Rahway. SURV: ch frmr Water Com Frank H, 72 Esterbrook Ave, and Mrs Abram R Shotwell, 59 Maple Ave, R. 4 gch Roger Nelson Plum and Mrs Janet Kingsbury, 72 Esterbrook, Robert Shotwell, 59 Maple Ave, R, and George Plum 3rd, Maplewood. A sis in Newburgh, NY. George, Jr, was killed in an auto accident abt 5 yrs ago, while Miss Flora, frmr

Principal of Lincoln School, d abt 3 yrs ago. Res R nearly 90 yrs. **SERV**: Enl 6th NY Bat, known as Bramhall and Martin Bat. At Gettysburg, Bull Run and many others. WIA twice, leaving him crippled for life. **F**: Tue aftn at home, Rev Finley Keech, P 1st Bapt. Int R. Tue Dec 26.

PONTIN, HENRY B, 61, b 1852 NYC, d Mon 7 pm Mar 31, 1913, at home, 440 Magie St, Eliz. **SURV**: w Mary J/ch Elmer, Herbert L and Frederick H, all E. f Frederick Henry, ae 85, NYC. bro Frederick G, Brooklyn. Res E 35 yrs, 32 yrs in the downtown section at 3rd & Marshall. Res uptown last 3 yrs, first 2 on Orchard St. Completed the Magie and Stiles St home last yr. 15+ yrs ago started a lighterage biz in E, H B Pontin & Son, boats plying btwn E, Perth Amboy and NYC, his dock at the foot of Baltic St. **MEM**: OL126 F&AM, past Master. Orient Council 40 Jr OUAM, and CE IOF. **CHH**: Grace Epis and the Brotherhood of St Andrew. **SERV**: Enl Navy when a boy, on USS "General Foster," in many engage. Reup 1867, and hon disc 1873. Visited many foreign ports. As a keepsake, had a long blue ribbon on which was written in gold letters the names of the ports which he visited. In the center was a picture of the USS "Portsmouth," on which he serv. Tue Apr 1.

PORAPP, WILIAM, 60, native of Germany, d Wed aftn Aug 22, 1906, at home, 13 Spring St, Eliz. **SURV**: ch Mrs Aaron Williams, William and Albert. 2 gch. Res E 55 yrs. Long in the employ of Edwards & King, and an expert painter and decorator. **MEM**: Vet Z. Painters Local 59. **SERV**: Ind Bat, Lgt Art, NJ Vol. **F**: Sat aftn at home, Rev Brockholst Morgan. Int fam plot Evergreen. Thu Aug 23.

POTTER, ERASTUS E, 66, b Mon Aug 10, 1840, East Killingly, Windham Co, CT, yngst of 11 ch/o Stephen Hazard & Esther (Burgess) Potter, d Thu Dec 6, 1906, Wharton. **SURV**: w frmr Henrietta N Himes, d/o a CT cotton manu, m Thu Sep 21, 1865/ch Mrs William H Roe, Newark, Mrs Anna Williams, Julia and Catherine, W. Aft leaving a cotton mill, entered CT schools, then Westfield Academy, and Lapham Inst at North Scituate, RI.

Taught up to CW. Aft CW, taught at E Killingly to 1870, then rem to NJ, in charge for a yr of a Green Village, Morris Co, school. In 1871, rem to Port Oram (now W) for a month trial and stayed, celeb 35th anniv last Fri. Known statewide as the "Yankee Schoolmaster." A political radical. In 1898 ran for US Senator, as a Dem against the reelection of James Smith, Jr. **SERV**: Enl Sat Aug 9, 1862, Co K, 18th CT Vol, to end. Captured Jun, 1863, Winchester, VA. POW Libby, then Belle Isle, then exchanged. Fri Dec 7.

POTTER, HENRY LANDON, COL, 79, d Fri ngt Mar 29, 1907, at home, St George Ave, Rahway, Linden Tp. **SURV**: w/svrl ch. Held a pos at the NY Customs House. **MEM**: Legion of Honor. GAR, at one time an officer. A Mason. **SERV**: Military career dates fm 1856-58 when joined Gen Walker's cmd during the Nicaraguan Episode. Gen at that time was Sec of War. Aft that campaign became Lt Col 71st Reg, NY Vol, to end CW. In 16 battles, rcvd 6 bullet wounds. Nearly KIA by a horse which was shot out fm under him, crushing him to the earth. Wore as a watch charm the bullet which rendered his left arm useless. Another memento was a sabre upon the blade of which he inscribed the names and dates of his battles. **F**: Private, Tue 2 pm at home.

POWELL, STEPHEN H, b NYC, d Mon Apr 8, 1918, at home of dau Mrs Bertha Lufburrow, Atlantic Highlands. **SURV**: w Elizabeth, A H/ch Mrs Lufburrow, with whom he res, Mrs Joseph Vanderwater and Stephen A, Montclair, Mrs Morris M Cleveland, Bridgeport, CT, and William H, Westfield. Went to Eliz ae 20. Contractor and builder by trade, ret nearly 30 yrs ago. Rem to A H 25 yrs ago. **MEM**: UD25. **CHH**: The old St Pauls ME while res Eliz. **SERV**: Enl NJ Vol, Capt Harris, 3 yrs. In many battles. Lost a leg at Manassas Junction, disc. Tue Apr 9.

PRICE, DANIEL, 91, of Marion, IN, d at the Jul 7, 1938, 75th B&G R at Gettysburg. A C sol.

PRICE, GEORGE W, 70, d Thu Jun 5, 1913, in his room at the Dudley Boarding House, Asbury Park. Frmr home was in New

Brunswick. Was going to attend Gettysburg celeb in Jul. At the Dudley House, told of having recovered a bible which he lost on the Gettysburg field. Asbury Park Evening Press, Fri Jun 6.
PRICE, SYDNEY, 78, d announced Sat May 2, 1903, Germantown, Hunterdon Co. SURV: 2 ch. Res Eliz for yrs. A wealthy harnessmaker. SERV: In many imp battles. Sat May 2.
PRINK, JACOB, 53, d along with 2 other Vets since last Sun, at the S'H, Kearny, fm effects of the heat. Res Home for yrs. SERV: Co K, 2nd NJ Vol. Thu Jul 26, 1900.
PROUT, HENRY GOSLEE, COL, 81, b Fairfax Co, VA, s/o late William & Amanda Goslee Prout, d Wed Jan 26, 1927, at home, 615 Springfield Ave, Summit. SURV: w/ch Miss Elizabeth Page, who will be m Feb to Archibald W MacDonald of the "Brittain," 1025 E Jersey St, Mrs Pierpont V Davis, frmly of 851 N Broad St, now of Ossining-on-the-Hudson, Henry B, Boston, whose w was frmr Miss Eloise Willett of Eliz, Curtis, Waterbury, CT, and Mrs Paul G Tomlinson, Princeton. 8 gch. Desc of Timothy Prout, who landed in Boston 1664. Came to S abt 3 yrs ago, had res Eliz abt 3 yrs. Boyhood was spent in MA. Aft CW went to Univ of MI, obtaining a degree of Civil Eng. Worked on the Geodetic Survey of the Great Lakes, running RR surveys through the Rocky Mts, and later went to Egypt. In Egypt 1872-78, during part of which he was Gov Gen of the Equator Provinces. Col Prout rcvd his title fm the Khedive of Egypt in whose svc he spent svrl yrs as Maj of Engs. Among the interesting problems he solved was the transp of an 80 ft screw propelled steamer ovr a strip of 60 miles of broken country on the backs of Negro bearers. The steamer was re-assembled at Dufli, and in it went to meet the explorer Stanley at the time of the famous rescue. Returning to USA, became signal eng for a co which became the Union Switch & Signal Co. In Mar 1887 became editor of the RR Gazette for 16 yrs, then became Gen Manager and later Pres of the U S & S Co, ret 1916. MEM: American Soc of Civil Eng, American Geographic Soc, Century, RR, and Univ clubs. SERV: Enl otbrk 57th MA Reg, to end. At

the Wilderness and Lee's surrender. F: Int fam plot Evergreen. Jan 27.

PROUT, JOHN W, 70, d Sat May 22, 1915, at home, Newark. Mem of the PD for 43+ yrs, ret last Oct. **SERV:** Navy. Sat May 22.

PROVOST, W W, SGT, b New Brunswick, d announced Mon May 14, 1900. **SURV:** bro and other relatives, Eliz. **SERV:** 12th VA Reg. **F:** Tue aftn Fords Parlors. Mon May 14.

PUGH, WASHINGTON S, 80, b 1844, New Hanover, PA, d Sun aftn Aug 17, 1924, Pomona, NY. **SURV:** ch Alexander L and Harry W. 7 gch. w, frmr Mrs Sarah Wooley Johnson. d while on a trip with Alexander. f d when he was a boy. In 1867 studied at Eastman Biz College, Poughkeepsie, where he met his future w. Engaged in biz in NY and CT, then rem fm Jersey City to Eliz in 1873. Worked for Singer 45 yrs, chief timekeeper 30 yrs, ret 1918. **MEM:** UD25, serv as senior V-Cmdr and trustee. **CHH:** 3rd Presby 50+ yrs. **SERV:** Enl Pottstown ae 18 Co H, 68th Reg, Vol Inf of PA. Assist in defense of Washington, campaigned in Nrn VA and MD, and at Fredericksburg, Chancellorsville, Gettysburg and others. In Dec, 1863, Reg made into a provost guard org, in charge of C prisoners to end. Hon disc 1865, Hart's Island, NY. **F:** Int Evergreen. Mon Aug 18.

PUTNAM, BENJAMIN PARKER, d Fri Oct 27, 1911, at home, 17 Bond St, Rahway. **SURV:** w/2s/dau. Worked for PA RR for yrs. Res R only a short time, rem fm Camden. **MEM:** Farnsworth Lodge 143 Odd Fellow, Camden. **SERV:** Enl New Brunswick 14th Reg, NJ Vol. **F:** Mon aftn at home, Rev C C Woodruff, P Trinity Meth. Int Rahway. Sat Oct 28.

PUTNAM, JAMES H, CAPT, 81, d Wed ngt Feb 3, 1920, at home, 42 Monroe St, Rahway. **SURV:** dau Mrs Charles Stoll, R. **MEM:** Adj WFB27. **SERV:** Capt 30th NJ Inf, to end. Thu Feb 4.

Attended the complimentary dinner for WFB27 mems given by A Edward Woodruff Tue eve May 30, 1911.

R

RANDOLPH, GEORGE W F, 72, b Plainfield, d Sat Mar 24, 1900, Plainfield. SURV: w/dau Mrs John Groendyke. Always res P. A Repub, serv svrl terms B of Freeholders, and a mem of the CC and St Com svrl yrs. Under his admin the 1st telford paving in P was made. For yrs held pos in the Qtmstr office of the Dept of the E in the NY Army bldg. SERV: Throughout. Mon Mar 26.

RANDOLPH, WILLIAM H, SR, 78, d Mon ngt Mar 8, 1909, S'H, Kearny. SURV: ch William H, frmr School Com and present mem B of Health, and 2 dau, one of Nutley, the other of Westfield. Res Rahway for yrs, living with s bfr the Home, which he entered 2 mos ago. A blacksmith. SERV: 6th NY Ind Bat. F: Wed eve at Irving St & Elizabeth Ave home of s. Wed Mar 10.

REA, JAMES, 79, d Thu aftn Aug 31, 1911, at home, 321 Fulton St, Eliz. SURV: w/ch Frank, Robert and Richard. Gch. 1ggch. Res downtown E 59 yrs. Org Fire Engine 2, when the old hand-engine was in use, and became mem RJE Co 4, after vol went out of existence. MEM: EFA. JK64. CHH: Grace Epis. SERV: Enl otbrk Co H, 30th Reg, NJ Inf, to end. F: Rev Henry Gifford, Ph D, Rector, Grace. Fri Sep 1.

READING, JOHN, 70, d Wed 2 am Sep 14, 1904, at home, Bonnell St, Flemington. SURV: w/svrl ch. Thu Sep 15.

REDDY, DANIEL F, d Sat mrng Jan 4, 1902, at home, 119 Bond St, Eliz. Res E 22 yrs. Shipcaulker by trade. SERV: Cav, Co A, 118th NY Reg. F: JK64 will provide a detail Sun mrng. Mon Jan 6.

REESE, SAMUEL WIDDOWS, b Thu Sep 14, 1843, Clifton, PA, d Mon aftn May 28, 1913, at home, Elmer St, Westfield. SURV: w/ch Charles D, Franklin E and Sherman E, who was assoc with him in biz. Aft CW res Eliz for a time, then rem to Chicago. Returned E 1876 and started in biz in NY. Res W 30 yrs. Senior mem S W Reese & Co, manu of metal goods at 44 Vesey St, NYC. Held many offices in local govt and for yrs on the B of Educ. **MEM:** Central Council, Jr, OUAM of W. WS73. **SERV:** Enl 1st PA Reserve Cav, to end. WIA and captured at Brandy Station. POW Libby for a month, then exchanged. Tue May 29.

REGAN, JOHN, b Oct 26, 1847, Ireland, d Fri ngt Oct 11, 1935, at home of dau Mrs Ernest Holdorf, 510 1st Ave, Eliz. **SURV:** ch Mrs Holdorf and George, NY. 9 gch. 9 ggch. bro Thomas, NY. Imm USA ae 6 mos. Rem to E fm NYC when Singer plant opened 56 yrs ago, worked 37 yrs. Rem to NYC and worked for Dept of Public Works. Ret yrs ago, res in E. **MEM:** SVA. Saw 2 GAR posts disb as the ranks dwindled. First with JK64, Cmdr when it was disb in Jul 1925, when only 4 names were on the roster. Joined UD25, which disb Jan 1932, with only 2 active mem. There were 7 CW Vets in E at that time, and now only 3, with d of a Red Bank Vet Thu. There are 60 left in NJ. **CHH:** St Patricks, then Holy Rosary. **SERV:** Enl NYC Thu May 9, 1861, Co D, 37th Inf, known as the "Irish Rifles." Co was disb. Joined 15th CT Inf, later consolidated with 99th NY Inf. At Bull Run, Fredericksburg, Antietam and Gettysburg. Captured in a skirmish bfr Kingston, NC, on the return with Sherman fm the sea on Wed Mar 8, 1865. POW Libby. Paroled Mar 26 then fought at Yorktown, Williamsburg and White Oaks Swamp. Sat Oct 12. (P)

In the Wed tribute paid to CW Vets, with 27 other NJ Vets and one NY Vet, in E, GAR reunion with colorful parade and armory fete. Thu Mar 30, 1933.

Article Thu May 31, 1934, on E MDAY celebration. (P)

REID, ANN, NURSE, d on MDAY, 1910, at home of s H M Reid, 53 Beachwood Ave, Eliz. Only surv CW nurse and last pens on that list. wid/o Hugh, and wid at time of CW. Had the distinction of having a bro, Col Angus McIntosh Williamson, C, and a s, Judge John Reid, U sol. She nursed both C and U sol in the W bldgs at Baltimore. Fri Jun 3.

REITCHMYER, JAMES H, 99, d Sun Feb 5, 1939, at home of dau Mrs Gertrude Simmons, Union City (Dateline). Believed to be last CW Vet Hudson Co. Ret wood worker. MEM: Haverstraw NY GAR Post. SERV: Sgt 120th NY Vol Inf, Co K, WIA Fredericksburg. Mon Feb 6.

REYNOLDS, FORMAN J, 78, b Harmony, Monmouth Co, d Tue Jan 5, 1915, at home, 20 Rector St, Newark. Employ 25 yrs N B of Health as an Inspector. MEM: Dept Cmdr of the GAR NJ branch, elected last May 14 at Atlantic City by an almost unanimous vote, and under suspension of the rules, the highest tribute. SERV: Enl otbrk Freehold 28th Vol Inf Reg, in all the principal battles. First man to enter Fredericksburg aft its capture, and promo fm Pvt to Sgt that ngt. WIA 2 days later and sent N. Svrl mos later reup Co B, 3rd NJ Cav, WIA the Wilderness. A few mos later WIA when his horse was shot fm under him. Sent to Ward Army H, N. Hon disc Thu Jul 6, 1865. F: At home. Int Sat, Freehold. Thu Jan 7.

One of 11 candidates for 9 delegates, to be elected during the 44th annual encmp of the Dept of NJ GAR, to the natl encmp Fri May 19, 1911.

RHODES, GEORGE H, b Wed Sep 7, 1845, Rockaway, LI, d Sat 7 am Jan 10, 1925, at home, 414 Cherry St, Eliz. SURV: 2/w Mrs Anna Schardien of E, m 19 yrs ago/dau Georgia. Step-ch Fred Goodale, John A Schardien, Mrs William H Haviland, and Mrs John Mackenzie. 9 gch. 5 ggch. All of E. 1/w d 26 yrs ago, she also m twice. Res E 49 yrs. Aft CW began dock building, working on the construction of the Long Branch RR bridge ovr the Raritan Riv at Perth Amboy. For yrs worked for E G Brown, then super for Eli Young, who was then principal dock builder along SI Sound. In 1894 with Louis Quien and the late Charles H Moore. Org the NJ Dock & Bridge Building Co. In 1902 went into partnership with Herbert E Manvel, frmg the Rhodes & Manvel Co, then R & M, Inc, of 90 W St, NY, Pres at dod. Many waterfront structures along SI Sound, fm Newark Bay to Raritan Bay were designed and built under his direction. Had a wide reputation as a designer of docks and bulkheads. MEM: UD25. Masons. Tall Cedars, KP, and Elks. In 1921 presented with a 50 yr jewel by PL78 KP, having joined Wed Jun 21, 1871, the 43rd mem of the order to get one in this section of NJ, and the 2nd Elizabethan. SERV: Enl ae 16 11th NJ Vol fm Perth Amboy, in all Reg engage in the 4 yrs, WIA svrl times. Present at Lee's surrender. Hon disc Aug 1865 as Capt. Sat Jan 10. (P)

F: Tue at home, Rev Harold J Sweeny, Rector Grace Epis. Floral tributes Tyrian Lodge 134 F&AM, PL78 KP, Lodge 289 BPO Elks, UD25, and the E Turn Verein. Bearers were relatives, Harold and John Schardien, William H and William F Haviland, and John H and John M Mackenzie. Int fam plot Evergreen. Wed Jan 14.(P)

RHODES, NATHAN C, 72, b Providence, RI, d Mon ngt Feb 26, 1917, at home, 1149 Magnolia Ave, Eliz. SURV: ch Mrs Matthew Baird and Mrs George Kunz, E, and Mrs Lillian M Chapin, Cambridge, MA. 9 gch. Res E since boyhood. Eng for Central RR 45 yrs, pens many yrs ago. MEM: TL F&AM. UD25. Brotherhood of Locomotive Eng 688, and the Mutual Aid Soc of 688. SERV: Enl otbrk Co A, 1st NJ Inf, to end. At Bull Run. WIA Gettysburg. Tue Feb 27.

RICHARDS, ALFRED H, 72, b NYC, d Thu mrng Jun 1, 1916, Eliz. SURV: w/s Wallace. Stcp-sis Mrs L Jacobs, Somerville. Res E 30+ yrs. Worked as eng for Joseph W North & Sons 24 yrs, ret and pens last month. MEM: UD25, past Cmdr. CHH: 1st Meth Prot. SERV: Enl otbrk Co I, 5th NY Cav, to end, at various times with Gens Banks, Hatch and Siegel. In the Shenandoah Valley Campaign, at Little Round Top during the 3-day engage. An aide to Gen Dan Sickles, with him when the Gen was WIA so severely that he lost a leg. Took part in the Raid on Richmond, VA, with Col Dahlgren in 1864, and on Fri Mar 4, 1864, taken prisoner with 8 others of his Co. POW Andersonville 9 mos, when he and another were paroled, the other 6 having d. His companion d svrl yrs ago. At Antietam, Cedar Mountain, Chancellorsville and Fredericksburg. Hon disc

Sun Jan 15, 1865. Thu Jun 1. (P)

Res SI bfr E. Res 126 2nd St. Enl Tue Oct 15, 1861. Paroled in Savannah, GA, Wed Nov 23, 1864. Installed as Cmdr UD25 last wk. Mon Jan 12, 1914. (P)

RICHTERS, FREDERICK J, 80, b Germany, while his par were on a visit abroad, d early Sun mrng Nov 4, 1923, St Elizabeth H, Eliz. SURV: ch G Frederick, Percy W, J Charles, and Mrs Harry Conrad, Perth Amboy. 6 gch. w d abt 10 yrs ago. For yrs res in Charleston, SC. Came to E abt 25 yrs ago, and started a real estate biz in NYC. Employ 6 yrs in mailing dept of Singer, ret last yr. Serv a term as a City Council mem, 10th Ward, abt 15 yrs ago. CHH: Presby. SERV: 71st NY Reg, in many imp engage. Mon Nov 5.

RICKETTS, GEORGE ROBERT ASHE, b Tue Aug 4, 1840, St Louis, MO, d Tue mrng Jan 29, 1929, at home of dau Mrs Robert C Bogart, 712 Westminster Ave, Eliz. SURV: ch Mrs Bogart, Maude de Peyster Ricketts, West Willination, CT, with whom he res until recently, John K, Ocean Grove and Philip B, 1252 Clinton Pl, E. w, frmr Laura Virginia Ring, m E, d abt a yr ago, 4 yrs aft 50th m anniv. Frnr res with Philip, and res E 60 yrs. Rcvd early educ St Louis, rem to Rye, NY, for svrl yrs, then to E abt 1869. SERV: 2nd Co, 7th Reg NYNG. Believed to be last surv mem of Honor Guard of 16 men placed around the body of Lincoln as it lay in state at City Hall, NYC. Enl 1864, serv til 1871, participating in the Orange riots. F: Thu 230 pm at home of Mrs Bogart, Rev Lyttleton E Hubard, DD, Rector, St Johns Epis. Tue Jan 29.

RIEFENSTAHL, WILLIAM F, 72, d early Wed mrng May 20, 1908, at home, Lehigh Ave, S Cranford. SURV: w/s/dau. Res S C 15+ yrs. Employ at Aeolian Works at Garwood. Wed May 20.

RIKER, ABRAM, SR, d Thu May 1, 1930, Linden. Res 111 Main St. F: Sat May 3, David, Jr, a bearer. Mon May 5.

RINDELL, ANTHONY C, 80, b 1827 Linden Tp, d Wed Aug 7, 1907, Newark. SURV: w frmr Mary E Conklin, m 1851/ch John G and Charles R. Res N 60 yrs. MEM: Newark Lodge 7,

F&AM. VA. **CHH:** Clinton Bapt, the oldest Deacon. **SERV:** Co D, 13th NJ Vol, 3 yrs/10 mos. Thu Aug 8.

ROBERTS, WILLIAM H, 92, d Sun mrng Aug 14, 1932, at home, 126 Orchard St, Eliz. **SURV:** w Emma Van Wart Roberts/ch Edward, Brooklyn, Percy, SI, Mrs F A Davis, Mrs Emma Ford and Mrs H L Shoemaker, E, and Mrs Hoover Browning, Atlantic City. 7 gch, Mrs Fred Schmidt, W Orange, Mrs Clifford Osgood, SI, Mrs Ethel Davis, E, Mrs Blake Francis, Glen Falls, NY, James and William Roberts, Roselle, and Thomas Roberts, NY. 6 ggch. sis Ida L Harrison, NY. Res E 30 yrs since ret as a provision dealer in NYC. **MEM:** UD25. Republic Lodge 690 F&AM, NYC. Frmr vol fireman NYC and mem VVFA. **SERV:** 9th NY Inf, at Gettysburg, Bull Run and Antietam. Mon Aug 15.

Mr & Mrs William H Roberts, 135 Orchard St, celeb their 50th m anniv Sat ngt. He was b in the old NYC 9th Ward, which at that time was called "The American Ward." gs of Capt James L Roberts and Capt James (?)rt, both 1812. She was also b NYC in the old Greenwich Village section and desc fm Isaac Van Wart, who, with Paulding and Williams, captured Maj Andre of the British Army during the RW. **MEM:** Mason, and a vet fireman of NYC. **SERV:** 9th NY Vol. Among those attending were Mr & Mrs F A Davis, Mr & Mrs Hoover Browning, Mr & Mrs Frederick Schmidt, Jr, William H Roberts, Jr, Perry Roberts, Edward L Roberts, and Blake White Francis. May 12, xxxx.

ROBINSON, HENRY F, b MA, d Wed 10 am Mar 6, 1907, at home, 133 W Jersey St, Eliz. **SURV:** w a d/o late Baylis Hathaway. Came to E abt 42 yrs ago. For yrs a clerk Central RR, then transf to the transp dept as a purser on the steamboats of the Elizabethport & NY Ferry, mostly on the "Chancellor." When ferry was dis, entered the employ of Singer, in the office. A Repub. Represented the old 1st Ward in B of Educ for many terms. Judge of Elections, and when city redistricted, cont in one of the 4th Ward districts. **MEM:** A founder of CE IOF, and its financial Sec. EL F&AM, UD25. **SERV:** Co G, 42nd MA Vol

Inf. Wed Mar 6.

ROBINSON, JULIUS A, d Sat Jun 22, 1901, St Nicholas Hotel, NYC. In early life, res Elizabeth Ave, Eliz. Entered the hotel biz at Saratoga Springs, later owning other large hotels. **SERV**: At otbk, orderly to Col Graham in Sickle Brig, and aft a Pvt Co B, 30th NJ Vol, Capt Lewis, composed of a large n/o men of this vcnty. Placed in charge of the road, engine and car shops of the E TN & GA RR when given to that co by the US govt. Tue Jun 25.

ROBSON, JAMES JOSEPH, 73, d Fri ngt May 8, 1914, Alexian Bros H, Eliz. Res 143 Jaques Ave. **F**: J R Lambert Home, L Y Graham, Jr, Pastor 1st Presby. Int Rahway. Sat May 9.

ROCKETT, THOMAS P, b Albany, d Tue Sep 25, 1928, at home of dau and only surv Mrs Fred W Aschenbach, 400 5th Ave, W, Roselle. Res R for a yr, rem fm Jersey City. Worked for Harper & Bros, NY publishing firm, ret 13 yrs ago. **MEM**: Sec Emeritus Bergen Lodge F&AM, Sec 40 yrs. Past Cmdr Z38. **SERV**: Enl 17th Reg of Vol, being in IL at otbk. Tue Sep 25.

ROGERS, PETER F, MAJ, 79, d announced Mon May 10, 1915, Arlington. **SURV**: w. For yrs Newark PC, and also St Com. In 1878 became super of the S'H for 32 yrs, ret, then sat on B of Managers. **MEM**: Prominent in NJ GAR. **SERV**: Under Gen Burnside and Hooker. **F**: Wed, Rev John Ferguson. Mon May 10.

ROGERS, WILLIAM Y, 86, b Beacon, NY, d Wed ngt Dec 19, 1938, at home of dau Mrs Clara Chase, 144 Jefferson Ave, Eliz. **SURV**: ch Mrs Chase, with whom he res, Mrs William Schreiber, Roselle, Mrs Arthur Lecour, Orange, Charles, E, and Arthur, E Orange. 10 gch. 5 ggch. Res E 20 yrs. **MEM**: GAR Beacon. **SERV**: Enl Mon Apr 22, 1861, Co F, 1st Reg Inf, NY. During a 7 day engage, near Richmond, WIA. Remained on the field unaided for days bfr found by the C, and taken to their field H. Upon recovery turned out in his underclothes and succeeded in making his way back to U lines. Disc Fri May 8, 1863, for effects of wound. Thu Dec 20.

ROLL, JONATHAN S, 73, b Westfield, d Thu 10 am Mar 10, 1904, Eliz. **SURV**: ch Mrs Maurice H Stratemeyer, E, and Joseph H, Somerville. 8 gch. w, a d/o late Capt John Kidd, d 15 mos ago at the Spring St home. He d while reading the book *Sunshine and Shadow in New York* sitting in an armchair in the Broad & Washington St cigar store of his s-in-law Maurice, with dau and a gs present. Res E near 40 yrs, with dau aft d of w. Celeb 50th m anniv 4 yrs ago. **MEM**: Boss Mason. **CHH**: Christ. **SERV**: Mu/i at Ovid, NY. Thu Mar 10.

ROOLVINK, GERARD, 79, b Holland, d Sun Feb 12, 1922, at home, 1005 Magnolia Ave, Eliz. **SURV**: w Elizabeth/ch Godfrey, John, Louise and Mary, E, and Catherine, Washington. Imm USA 58 yrs ago, res Newark. A tutor in French, German and English. Res E 50 yrs. In the painting biz abt 40 yrs. Frmr Excise Com. **MEM**: Master Builders Assoc. **CHH**: Sacred Heart. St Michaels Soc. **SERV**: Co 36, NJ Vol. Mem Vet Z. Mon Feb 13.

ROPES, GEORGE H, frmr Eliz City Attorney, Enl otbrk, d bfr Dec 10, 1912. (A on Henry L Norton.)

ROSE, FRANK B, CHAPLAIN, d Tue Mar 22, 1910, at home, Swarthmore, PA. Chapl of the 14th NJ Vol 3 yrs, under Gens Grant and Sheridan. At Mine Run, the Wilderness, Spotsylvania, Winchester, Petersburg and others. Although ret at S/AW otbrk, applied for and assigned active duty, then ret due to poor health. Spent 30 yrs US Navy, on board the "Lancaster," "Pensacola," "Potomac," "Constitution," and other vessels. Given the rank of Rear Adm by Congress in 1906 in recognition of his CW and S/AW serv. Thu Mar 24.

ROSS, JAMES, 78, b Scotland, d Wed aftn Nov 23, 1921, Gen H, Eliz. **SURV**: dau Mrs William Pabst, NY. 3 gch, Mrs Frederick R Doerrer, Westfield, and Grace and Lillian Pabst, NY. w d svrl yrs ago. Res NY, then Westfield, past 26 yrs. **SERV**: Enl ae 16 Drummer Boy, to end, and made Capt of Co F, 59th Reg, NY Vol. Presented with a handsome sword by the

Co, a relic he prized highly. Fri Nov 25.

ROSS, WILLIAM H, 64, s/o late John, d Tue Jan 3, 1905, S'H, Kearny. **SURV**: bro, Roselle. Res Eliz for yrs, firmly res Plainfield. Inmate S'H many yrs. Long kept a market in frmr Collet Hall bldg, Broad St, Eliz. **SERV**: Co K, 9th NJ Vol, Tue Oct 15, 1861 to Wed Aug 9, 1865. WIA Coldsboro, NC, Fri Dec 19, 1862, and Walthall, VA, Fri May 6, 1864. A pens. Tue Jan 3.

ROUSCH, JOHN, 69, d Tue Feb 13, 1906, at home, McKeesport Gap, this county (Dateline Altoona, PA). One of 6 sol to whom Congress gave **MEDALS OF HONOR** for dislodging and capturing 13 sharpshooters in a log house near Devil's Den, in the Battle of Gettysburg. Wed Feb 14.

ROWLAND, JOHN R, b Wed Aug 7, 1844, Woodbridge Tp, d Wed eve Jun 25, 1902, near his home, Linden Tp (Dateline Rahway). **SURV**: w/2s/2dau. Went fishing in the Sound with Vet Richard Stephens, returning to the city abt 6 pm. While walking on Whittier St toward home, fell ill. s Charles driving by saw f and got him into the wagon, but f d in arms of s. A carpenter and builder. **MEM**: WFB27, elected Cmdr 3 times in succession. **SERV**: Enl 1862 Co C, 30th NJ Vol. **F**: Sun 230 pm First Presby. Fri Jun 27.

RUDRAUFF, JOHN H, b 1840, Germany, d Wed mrng Dec 28, 1910, Alexian H, Eliz. **SURV**: w Mary Matilda/ch Julia, John and Albert, all E. 3 gch. Res E 40 yrs. Car inspector for Central RR. For some time and up to 2 mos ago, res S'H, Kearny. **CHH**: Christ. **SERV**: Enl 1864 Co C, 40th NJ Vol, to end. Mem Vet Z. Wed Dec 28.

RUGG, CALVIN H, 72, b Boston, MA, d Mon mrng May 22, 1916, at home, 75 Myrtle Ave, Plainfield. **SURV**: w/dau Mrs Frederick Van Hausen. Came to NJ as a boy. In coal biz 25 yrs, ret abt 10 yrs ago. **MEM**: Affiliated with all the Masonic Orgs, and serv as Sec of the Masonic Hall Assoc. Treas Queen City Lodge 226 IOOF. **SERV**: Enl otbrk Pvt Co H, 8th NJ Inf, WIA 1862, hon disc. Mon May 22.

RUNYON, NELSON, b Thu Dec 3, 1840, near Greenbrook, Somerset Co, d Mon Jun 28, 1915, at home, E 9th St, Plainfield. SURV: ch Assemblyman William N and Carroll T. sis Mrs John Morrison and Mrs C K Compton. All of P. w, frmr Miss Wilhelmina Trow of P, m Thu Oct 21, 1869, d 1908. 2 s d bfr him. Came with par to P 1854. Studied law at office of Cornelius Boice. Aft CW practiced law with bro Enos, in the firm E W & N Runyon. Enos d in early 80s, and cont alone until 1898, frmg a partnership with s William. 1st City Clerk of P, and City Judge 1880-83. On Wed Apr 10, 1912, a dinner was given in his honor by P lawyers at the Queen City hotel for the 50th anniv if his admission to the Bar. MEM: Charter mem YMCA, on the B of Dir for yrs. CHH: 2nd Bapt, subsequently called Central Bapt, when yng, then helped form 2nd Ave Bapt. SERV: Enl otbrk with bro Francis 13th NJ Vol, 9 mos. Tue Jun 29.

RUNYON, THEODORE I, 74, b Plainfield, d Thu mrng Mar 16, 1911, at home, Plainfield. SURV: w/4dau. Frmr res Eliz. Worked for the Mutual Life Ins Co, Newark. Cuz to the late Chancellor Theodore Runyon, Ambassador to Germany. CHH: 1st Bapt in Eliz, when on W Jersey St. Choir mem. Park Ave Bapt, P, an org and Deacon of that chh. SERV: Co H, 30th NJ Vol, late J Frank Hubbard. F: Fri eve, Rev Dr Maguire. Fri Mar 17.

RUSSELL, WASHINGTON R, MAJ, 77, d Sat Nov 2, 1907, Newark. SURV: A fam. sib William G and Mrs William Brant, both Cherry St, Eliz. Past res Eliz. Cashier of the Newark News Co past 33 yrs. MEM: Masonic fraternity. MLW 88. SERV: Co D, 13th Reg Vol Inf, to end. In many battles, incldg Shermans march to the sea. Seriously WIA Fredericksburg. Aft CW joined NJ State Militia, mem old 5th Reg, rising to Capt. When 5th amalgamated with the 1st Reg, was Reg Qtmstr. Ret Brev Maj. F: Tue aftn. Mon Nov 4.

BRANT, MALANA RUSSELL, MRS, 65, b Fredericksburg, VA, d Fri ngt Sep 2, 1910, Eliz. SURV: ch William, of the Information Bureau of the PA RR in NY, and Gertrude M, 15

Cherry St, with whom she res. Principal of PS7. Dau Louise d abt 2 yrs ago. wid/o Capt William, who distinguished himself in the CW and decorated by Congress. He was an officer of the E PD, and d abt 12 yrs ago. She came N abt 45 yrs ago, under the first flag of truce. Her meeting with Brant was brought about by her bro Maj Russell, who enl CW Newark, and knew him. Aft CW Brant accepted an invite to visit the Russell home. She and Brant m Newark and rem immediately to E, the Brant fam home since colonial times. CHH: 1st Presby. Sat Sep 3.

RYBERG, JOHN WESLEY, d Tue 430 pm Nov 2, 1915, Eliz Gen H, Eliz. SURV: sib Mrs George W Terry, Morris Park, LI, and Mrs Henry C Bogart, Roselle Park. Vet was unmarried. Res with Mrs Bogart since living in NJ. A Repub. SERV: Cpl Co I, 28th Reg of Inf, NYNG. F: At home. Int Evergreen. Wed Nov 3.

RYDER, ALANSON, 82, b Tue Apr 15, 1845, Croton, NY, s/o Henry G, d Thu ngt Aug 25, 1927, at home, 112 Avon St, Roselle Park. SURV: w Margaret/sis Mrs Georgianna Nelson, Jacksonville, Fl. Stage carpenter in a NY theater for yrs, ret abt 25 yrs. Res R P 36 yrs. MEM: UD25. SERV: Enl ae 15 1st NJ Vol, to end. Hon disc Mar, 1865. In many imp battles. Fri Aug 26. Obit lists dod as 1854.

S

SAGE, (1ST name not given), 66, d Wed Aug 12, 1903, at home, Union Village, Warren Tp. f/o assessor Edmund Sage. Res Newark, then Union Village for 25 yrs. Conducted a large dairy. SERV: Spy, attached to Gen McClellan staff. In the slaughter at Antietam with the 5th CT Reg, in which there were only 120 surv of the 1,000 who entered the battle. F: Thu ngt. Int Cromwell, CT. Fri Aug 14.

SANBORN, GEORGE H, b Mon Apr 12, 1847, Laconia, NH, d Sat 1140 am Mar 6, 1909, at home, 518 Madison Ave, Eliz. SURV: w frmr Miss Halstead/3s/dau. Res E, and employ Central RR, 40+ yrs. At ae 17 in charge of the co telegraph office downtown, and finally, by promo, an auditor of the freight traffic dept for yrs. Held lighter pos in Newark and Somerville aft becoming ill. **MEM**: Past Master EL49 F&AM, for yrs its Sec. JK64, acting Adj at dod. Past Grand Master Elizabethport Lodge 116, IOOF. **CHH**: Central Bapt, at one time a Trustee. **SERV**: Co I, 8th NJ Vol, and Co K, 6th NY Vol. In the 8th, under Capt Todd, one of Gen J Madison Drake companions when the latter escaped fm C captors, at Petersburg, VA. Had an exp never forgotten. (See Experiences) Sat Mar 6. (P)

SANBORN, JOSEPH WARREN, 60, native of Salem, MA, d Fri Jul 13, 1906, at 419 S Broad St, Eliz. Vet never m. Long res E. For yrs a conductor Central RR. **MEM**: OL F&AM. **SERV**: In a MA Reg, enl at Salem. **F**: Sun 3 pm, Rev Brockholst Morgan. Int MA. Sat Jul 14.

SANFORD, WILLIAM A, 77, b Englishtown, d Wed ngt Mar 29, 1922, at home, 509 E Broad St, Westfield. **SURV**: w Mary Elizabeth/ch Mrs Mary A Crist, Trenton, Delia and J Horace, W, and Joseph A, Ronan, MT. Ret as a lawyer 20 yrs ago. Mayor of Dunellen 12 yrs ago, where he res at that time. Rem to W abt 10 yrs ago. The originator of the Young America Trading Stamp, credited with being the man who suggested to the govt the use of the green War Thrift Stamp. **SERV**: Cpl, Co G, 11th Reg NJ Vol, which went out fm Englishtown. Lost a finger in one of the battles leading up to Gettysburg. Mar 30.

SAUER, LEONARD, d but recently. A founder of St Michaels Chh. (A on John Daubner, Fri Feb 3, 1911.)

SCHAIBLE, CHRISTIAN, 65, b Germany, d Tue ngt Oct 14, 1913, Gen H, Eliz. **SURV**: w Mary/ch Charles and William. 2 gch. sib Mrs Ernest Reck, Adam and Jacob, Troy, NY, and Michael, Schenectady, NY. Imm USA ae 2. Res Troy greater part of life. Rem to E 6 yrs ago, res 451 Spring St. Worked for some yrs Electric Dynamic Co, Bayonne. **MEM**: UD25. **CHH**: Park ME. **SERV**: Co L, 6th Reg, NY Heavy Art, 1863-65. Wed Oct 15.

SCHLICHTER, FREDERICK, 74, native of Muenster,

Westphalia, Germany, d Thu 700 pm Nov 25, 1915, at home, 542 Chilton St, Eliz. **SURV**: ch Mrs Theodore C Bothmann and Dr Charles H. sis in Germany. Another sis d abt 6 wks ago. Attended Univ of Berlin 2 yrs, then imm USA 1862, settling in NYC. Came to E aft CW. First turned to newspaper work, employ by German Frei Press, published in E. Aft it was dis, corresponded for svrl papers in other cities. Entered the advertising sign biz, 27 yrs, ret 12 yrs ago. A Dem, active in city affairs. Candidate for Freeholder. In the investigation of city financial condition aft E went into bankrupcy. An excise license inspector. **MEM**: Eliz Maennerchor and Turn Verein Vorwaerts. **SERV**: U Army 2 yrs, mu/o 1865. Fri Nov 26.

SCHMIDT, CHARLES H, b 1831 Kaiserlautern, Wissen, Germany, d Wed 7 pm Dec 18, 1907, at home, 10 S Reid St, Eliz. **SURV**: ch Mrs Peter Egenolf and Katherine. w, m 45 yrs, d last Mar. During the Baden rev troubles of 1848-49, became prominent and cast into prison. 2 other sol prisoners also imm USA and achieved distinction in CW, Maj Gen Carl Schurz and Maj Gen Franz Siegel, all men friends for life. Editor and proprietor of the Freie Presse, ret in recent yrs. Rem to E at CW close. **MEM**: Maennerchor, and HL F&AM. **F**: Sat aftn at home. Int fam plot Evergreen. Thu Dec 19. (A on F Mon Dec 23) (P)

SCHNEIDER, AUGUST, b Fri Sep 12, 1845, at Hessen, Germany, d Tue Dec 15, 1925, on his large farm at the Rahway-Woodbridge line. **SURV**: ch Adolphe G, 238 E Milton Ave, H A, 30 Thorn St, and Mrs Richard A Verstig, Woodbridge Rd, all R. 6 gch. w d 1898. Located in R 1869 as foreman at bakery of late Edward Tier. In 1870 went into bakery biz for himself. For 38 yrs had a large bakery on Main St, ret 1908. A Repub. **MEM**: WFB27. Ranks now number only 4. **SERV**: Last surv mem Co 29, 30, 31 and 32, which combined and formed an Ind Bat in Pickens Brig. The 4 Cos were of German and Austrian extraction. At the 2nd Antietam, many others, and in the drive made by Gen Hunter Div. Tue Dec 15.

SCHRAYER, DANIEL, 70, b W Penn, PA, d Sun May 3, 1914,

at home, 555 Livingston St, Eliz. **SURV**: dau Mrs David Aker, with whom he res. Blacksmith by trade, ret yrs ago. Mon May 4.

SCHWARZ, HERMAN E, b Mon Aug 13, 1832, Gehren, Germany, near Erfurt, a well-known fortress, d Fri mrng Apr 25, 1913, at home of dau Mrs S B Whitman, 91 Watson Ave, E Orange. **SURV**: w/ch Mrs Whitman and Mrs Delmar Loveland, Wyoming Ave, Eliz, with whom he res until 2 yrs ago. 7 gch. 6 ggch. A real estate dealer. **MEM**: JAG4. **SERV**: 174th Reg, PA Inf, 1st Lt of Co I. Hon disc Wed Aug 5, 1863. **F**: At home. Sat Apr 26.

SCOTT, HENRY C, 86, b Derby, VT, d Thu ngt Apr 7, 1910, at home of dau Mrs Thomas L Peterson, 551 Adams Ave, Eliz. **SURV**: ch Mrs Peterson, John W, George H and Reuben E, of E. 11 gch. 2 ggch. w d abt 8 yrs ago. Came to NJ when yng. Conducted a leather and findings store in Plainfield. Res E 26 yrs. Res Kearny S'H 3 yrs, then res with dau for many yrs past. **MEM**: JK64. **SERV**: Co A, and H, 2nd Reg NJ. **F**: Mon 230 pm at home. Int Evergreen. Fri Apr 8.

SEBRING, JOHN S, 58, b Mariner's Harbor, SI, d Mon 4 am Jan 29, 1900, at home, 113 Union St, Eliz. **SURV**: w/2s/4dau. Res E most of his life. Last of a fam of 4 s. Painter by trade. In later yrs a gardener. **CHH**: Christ. **SERV**: Enl Drummer 13th NJ Reg, in many campaigns. Mon Jan 29.

SEVERS, CHARLES HENRY, 71, d Wed Jan 24, 1912, pod not mentioned. In early life worked for a Trenton newspaper. Often a visitor to Eliz at the home of Edward K Drake, employ at the same office. For yrs real estate dealer of Parkeville, LI. **MEM**: GAR. **CHH**: Meth, Parkeville. **SERV**: 4th NJ Vol. POW, escaped fm Libby by tunneling. Thu Jan 25.

SEYMOUR, THOMAS H, LT, d "a month ago." Obit of William Ellis, Mon May 11, 1908.

SHAFFER, JOHN, 93, b Northampton Co, PA, d Tue eve Mar 4, 1924, at home of dau Mrs Frank Williams, 15 Mount Prospect Ave, Verona. **SURV**: ch Mrs Williams, contractor George A, 54 W Scott Pl, and Mrs Alberta Williams, 1017 Hampton Pl, V, and

Mrs Henry Dowd, Hazleton, PA. 12 gch. 2 ggch. sis Mrs Rebecca Lake, Hazleton. Came to Eliz in 1904. **MEM:** GAR Post Nazareth, PA. **CHH:** Sexton St Johns, Eliz. **SERV:** With a PA Reg. Wed Mar 5.

John Shaffer of Verona, 79 on Apr 12, the oldest man in NJ who rides a bicycle, makes fqt trips to visit 3 of his ch who live in Eliz. They are Mrs John Williams, John and George. Until 2 yrs ago, used to bike to Hazleton, PA, to visit his dau, staying a wk, then biked back. An enthusiastic 'cyclist for 7 yrs. Rem to V 14 yrs ago aft w d. B Lehigh Co, PA, 1831. Staunch Dem til the 1893 Panic, now votes Repub at natl elections, but nothing else. **CHH:** Dutch Reformed. **SERV:** Sgt Co E, 53rd PA Vol Inf, 1st Div, 2nd Army Corps. Shot thru the hand. Sat Apr 2, 1910.

SHEBBEARD, GEORGE R, 73, b Warren Co, d Thu Jul 19, 1911, Ocean Grove. **CHH:** Meth, 50+ yrs. For past few yrs lived on a cot on a wagon owing to CW injuries, and taken fm place to place by an attendant. Familiar at Ocean Grove past few summers, where he sold the stories of his life, and passed time crocheting. Attended Vet gatherings and was in the procession in Eliz a few yrs ago with the GAR for the 125th anniv of the Battle of Elizabethtown. He d clutching the cap he wore in the Army. **SERV:** Enl otbrk 3 mos. Reup for 3 yrs. Severely WIA in a battle in VA. **F:** Sat, Trenton. Sat Jul 22.

SIMMONDS, S BARTLETT, b Newport, RI, d Wed Apr 13, 1932, Chelsea, MA, a few days aft his 96th dob. f/o Rev Newton M, Washington, frmr P 1st Bapt Chh, Eliz, with whom he res on Madison Ave. Aft CW settled in Taunton, MA, as a contractor and builder. Later res in Fort Payne, AL, then New Bedford, MA. Wed Apr 20.

SIMS, WINFIELD SCOTT, 73, d Mon mrng Jan 7, 1918, St Michaels H, Newark. An inventor and scientist of intl prominence, best known as the inventor of the lynamite breech gun which bears his name. **F:** Wed aft at home, 162 Mt Prospect Ave. Int Mt Pleasant. Tue Jan 8.

SLAVIN, HUGH H, SR, 96, b Scotland, d Wed Sep 8, 1937, at home, 1740 Morris St, PHL. **SURV**: ch Hugh H, Jr, Linden, 4 other s and 3 dau. 22 gch, incldg Vincent DeP and Joseph J, Union, Mrs James T Sullivan, Eliz, and Mrs Joseph Gillick, Linden. 21 ggch. Taken to Ireland by par as a ch, then brought to USA. One of the first employees Standard Oil, ret on pens 1902. **CHH**: A founder of St Thomas Aquinas, PHL. Thu Sep 9.

SMITH, ELIAS DARBY, b Sun Apr 5, 1840, s/o Ogden & Julia Kellogg Smith, d shortly aft noon Apr 1, 1924, at home, 13 S 2nd St, Eliz. **SURV**: dau Mrs Charles S Hamner. Sep, 1866, m Miss Keziah P Martin, d abt 30 yrs ago. Had svrl ch, but only Mrs Hamner surv. f was the first conductor and then first freight agent Central RR. Fam rem to E 1849. Besides Elias, there were sib Elijah K, John J, Walter O, and Mary, now wid/o Judge Joseph Alward. Other surv, Prof Herbert S S Smith, frmly Princeton, now ret Stroudsburg, PA, s/o Elijah K; Howard W, near Pittsburgh, Frank K, NY, and W Percy, AZ, ch/o Walter O; Mrs E B Sexton, NY, Hilda W, Bryn Mawr, PA, Jules K, Kensington, MD, and Helen H, NY, ch/o John J; and Mary Alward, E lawyer, d/o Mary Alward. Entered svc of Central RR in 1855 for 3 yrs, then entered biz on his own. For 20 yrs aft CW conducted a forwarding biz for iron and other heavy freight. In 1884 became assoc of the firm Baker Smith & Co, steam heating eng of NYC, for 10 yrs. Mem B of Educ in the early 70s, Pres 1871-2. Super PS 1875-6. An org of Repub party of E. He and 100 others bolted the party when James G Blaine was Pres candidate in 1884. They published ovr their signatures in the EDJ a circular calling upon Repubs to vote for Cleveland. In 1912 became one of the Progressive Party leaders in Union Co. Made extensive trips throughout USA and abroad. Most notable was the 1908-10 trip with bro Walter O, circumnavigating Africa, with trips into the interior to Victoria Falls. His letters on this trip were published in the EDJ. A founder of the E Rescue Mission. **MEM**: UD25. Quill Club of NY. **CHH**: Elder Greystone Presby 40 yrs, Super of SS 50+ yrs. Mem Presby B of Chh Erection. Serv for many yrs on the Presbytery of E's Comm of Assistance the Siloam Presby Chh for Negroes. The Brotherhood of that chh is named Darby in his honor. **SERV:** Enl Aug 1862 aft Lincoln's 2nd call, Co C, 14th Reg, NJ Vol, fm E, Capt Chauncy Harris, 3 yrs. Disc as Qtmstr-Sgt. Fall 1862-Spring 1863 performed guard duty in MD. Transf in Apr to 6th Div, AP, promo fm Cpl at Mine Run, Nov 1863, the Wilderness, Spottsylvania and North Anna River, all May 1864. Wintered venty Petersburg, VA, then in the Great Advance in Spring 1865, which marked the ending of the CW. His Reg helped drive Lee out of Petersburg and Richmond, VA. Said Vet Smith, "Perhaps the most terrible of all the battles in which our Reg took part was the engage at Cold Harbor, in VA, in Jun 1864. The d were piled up high and the battlefield presented a gruesome sight." Also recalled the battles of Winchester, Cedar Creek and Fisher's Hill. During Gettysburg, his org was in reserve, and later stood ready to help Sherman in the Dept of TN. Disc Jun 1865. Tue Apr 1. (P)

Installed as Chapl at the UD25 meeting Tue ngt. Tue Jan 8, 1924. (P)

SMITH, GEORGE F, b Germany, d Sat mrng Jan 18, 1902, at his and his bro home, 16 Union Pl, Eliz. A wid, his w d last Aug. Imm USA to E at an early age. Barber by trade, his shop at 9 Broad St for some time. **SERV:** Enl 30th NJ Vol, Capt Lewis, composed of men fm E. Sat Jan 18.

SMITH, GILBERT, 78, b New Brunswick, d Fri aftn Jan 8, 1904, at home, 157 Fulton St, Eliz. **SURV:** w/dau Mrs Lawrence Schetzer. 19 gch. Res E 50 yrs. For yrs worked at the frmr Elizabethport Steam Cordage Works. A modern day Robinson Crusoe. When yng shipped before the mast and made 2 to 3 trips around the world. While cruising in the Pacific the ship was lost and he and 3 others were cast on an island. For 2 yrs they lived on fruits and managed to kill a few animals and birds. 2 of the 4 d. A passing vessel saw their constantly displayed signals, and they were rescued. Vessel arrived NY svrl wks later, and he rushed home to N B to fam and friends, who thought he d. **CHH:**

Christ. **SERV**: Co B, 13th NJ Vol, enl Apr 1861, disc 1863, Capt J Frank Hubbard, now Dir B of Chosen Freeholders. **F**: Sun aftn at home, Rev Dr Henry Hale Sleeper. Int Evergreen. Sat Jan 9.
Pvt William Schetzer is the s/o Mr & Mrs Lawrence Schetzer, 315 Elizabeth Ave, and gs/o CW Vet Gilbert Smith. Although b N B, the yng man, ae 23, was reared in E. He is at Camp Dix, having left with his contingent May 27. Tue Jul 23, 1918.(P)
SMITH, JOEL BREWSTER, 85, b SI, d Sat eve Nov 7, 1925, at the Nursing Home, 14 Leslie St, Newark. **SURV**: w Annie R. sib Mrs Martha Stockton and Louise, East Orange. Res at the Home for abt 2 yrs, and was of 700 Madison Ave, Eliz. Res Eliz abt 6 yrs, coming fm Perth Amboy. **SERV**: Pvt Co I, 28th Reg, NJ Inf. **F**: Int Alpine, Perth Amboy. Mon Nov 9.
SMITH, MICHAEL, d Mon Mar 20, 1907, at home, 224 Inslee Pl, Eliz. **SURV**: w/ch Thomas, Mrs Walter Thompson, Jersey City, Mrs Linus Wiltkamp, Richmond, VA, Mary and Anna. Res E near 40 yrs. Proprietor of a boathouse on Newark Bay, near the Central RR bridge, past 25 yrs. **MEM**: JK64. **CHH**: St Patricks. HNS and FHC, CBL. **SERV**: Co D, 133rd NY Vol. Tue Mar 21.
SMITH, WILLIAM H, 60, d Sat ngt Nov 19, 1904, Wells H, New Brunswick. **SERV**: 28th NJ Vol. An officer in the State Encmp GAR. Tue Nov 22.
SMITH, ZACHEUS, d along with 2 other Vets since last Sun, in the S'H, Kearny, fm the effects of the heat. **SERV**: Co G, 8th NJ Vol Inf. Thu Jul 26, 1900.
SNOW, NATHAN C, 66, d announced Wed Apr 18, 1900, Chicopee, MA (Dateline). Res in the house where he d all his life. The house is ovr 300 yrs old (sic). A great source of income to him was the fees he charged for showing hundreds of visitors the place and reciting its interesting hist. Well known as the "Recluse of Johnnycake Hollow." **SERV**: Co A, 37th MA Reg. Wed Apr 18.
SNYDER, WINFIELD SCOTT, 75, b 1848, Easton, PA, d Sun Oct 7, 1923, at home, 15 Sayre St, Eliz. **SURV**: s Harold, E. w Anna d last Jun 15. Educ in Easton PS, then employ in Central

RR yards in Easton and Phillipsburg. In 1858 became a messenger for the American Telegraph Co in Easton. Aft CW worked as a telegraph operator for the Lehigh Valley RR, Easton. Later, transf to E Penn Junction near Allentown, PA, where he sat before his instrument on the Fri night of Apr 14, 1865, and caught the message flashed by the Harrisburg operator: "Pres Lincoln shot at Ford's Theater, Washington, and is dying." Entered employ of Central RR, Mauch Chunk, PA, then to Phillipsburg, White House, NJ, and Somerville, NJ. In 1896 made gen freight agent for the Port Johnson coal docks. In 1907 appointed inspector of Safe Transp of Explosives, being assigned to St Louis, MO. Rem to NJ 1909 becoming custodian Central RR Athletic Assoc in Jersey City. Resigned last May, illness, being employ 50+ yrs Central RR. **MEM**: CE1 IOF. UD25. Dallas Lodge 56 F&AM, Easton. **SERV**: Enl 153rd PA Vol, within 4 wks at the front. At Chancellorsville and Gettysburg. With the AP when reviewed by Lincoln in 1863. Mon Oct 8. (Note: Mauch Chunk is present day Jim Thorpe.).
SOMMER, CHARLES RICHARD, 73, d Thu mrng Mar 1, 1923, at home, 121 Marshal St, Eliz. **SURV**: dau Mrs Louise Drapeau, gch Dorothy and George Drapeau. Came to E when Singer plant built 50 yrs ago, ret fm there 4 yrs ago. **CHH**: Sexton Greystone Presby. **SERV**: Co K, DeKalb Reg, NY Vol, Capt Henry Avens. On Tue Sep 1, 1863, made 1st Sgt. Hon disc Wed May 3, 1865. **F**: Sat 230 pm Parlors of August F Schmidt & Son, 649 Elizabeth Ave. Int Evergreen. Thu Mar 1.
SPAULDING, ISAAC DAVID, b Thu Jun 1, 1826; Ellsworth, OH, his par having been among its pioneers, d Thu Sep 10, 1903, Passaic. **SURV**: w/ch E W, of the Curtis Pub Co, Mrs Albert Kinkel, Mrs Walter Kip and Charlotte King. gf Isaac and ggf Jacob were in RW, and more remote was John, in King Philip's War. Res Eliz for yrs. A school teacher, then engaged in mercantile pursuits. **SERV**: At otbrk raised a large Co in the 125th OH Vol Inf, as Capt, until becoming ill. Hon disc. Breveted Maj, but rejected for physical reasons. One of the original

"squirrel hunters" called out by OH Gov Todd. F: Sun aftn at home of Mrs Kinkel, 344 Grier Ave, Rev John T Kerr. Fri Sep 11.

SPICER, WILLIAM S, 78, b Newark, d Wed 545 am Jul 21, 1915, at home of dau Mrs Frederick Kaufmann, 122 Franklin St, Eliz. SURV: w Harriet/Ch Harry, Isaac, William, Frederick, Charles, and Mrs Joseph Castiaux, Lyons Farms, Mrs Thomas Wheeler, Newark, and Mrs Kaufmann. Spent most of his life in E. Painter by trade, worked abt 33 yrs Central RR Paint Shop. He and w res with Mrs Castiaux 5-6 yrs ago when he became chh Sexton. MEM: AC25 OUAM, and E Council 10 DL. CHH: Elizabeth Ave Presby, Lyons Farms. SERV: Enl otbrk Reg 119, Phl Vol, to end. Charter mem Vet Z. F: Svc by his P, Rev D Newton Dobson, and Rev John V Ellson, East Bapt. Wed Jul 21.

SPICER, HARRIET F, MRS, b Eliz, d Sat Mar 12, 1927, at home of dau Mrs Theodore Wheeler, 12 Chadwick Ave, Newark, within a few days of the 91st anniv of her dob. SURV: ch Mrs Wheeler, Mrs J C Castioux, William and Frederick, all N, Mrs Cornelia Kauffman, Roselle, Harry and Charles, E, and Isaac, Irvington. 27 gch. 45 ggch. wid/o William S. Res E 50+ yrs. MEM: Charter mem E Council 10, S&D of L. ERL20, IOOF. Dames of Malta, E. CHH: East Bapt, E. Mon Mar 14.

SQUIER, THEODORE EUGENE, b Mon Mar 27, 1843, Northfield, s/o John Winans & Sarah Burnett Squire, b Northfield, d announced Mon Jan 14, 1929, Springfield. SURV: ch Mrs James C Stiles, Sr, S, Mrs Sarah B Wardell, E Orange, and Theodore A, Easton. 8 ch. 8 gch. bro A W, S Orange. Desc fm early American stock and claimed kinship with George Washington. Fam mem have serv in all the wars fm RW to WW. Carpenter by trade, apprenticed under Bert Carter, an early S res. Rem to S 51 yrs ago to a farm fronting on Bryant Ave, where his w, frmr Mary Maxwell Johnson, d abt 40 yrs ago. Aft that, his par and sisters res with him. Held svrl terms as Tax Appeal Com then mem B of Educ. Overseer of the Poor past 28 yrs. MEM: Last charter mem EHW96. Delegate many times to natl GAR conventions and attended a short time ago the last state encmp at Cape May. **SERV**: Enl ae 17 Co F, 27th NJ Vol, in many engage with Gen Burnside Brig. Almost buried at sea. (See **Experiences** section). **F**: Mon 2 pm, Rev William Hoppaugh, ret 1st Presby P, Youngs Parlor, Main St, Millburn. Int Presby, Plainfield. Mon Jan 14.

STEIN, ANTHONY, d but recently, a founder of St Michaels. (A on John Daubner, Fri Feb 3, 1911)

STILL, CHARLES R, lifelong res Eliz, d Sat mrng Jul 29, 1905, at 194 Public Lane, Eliz. A wid. **SERV**: Co C, 14th US Colored Vol. **F**: Int sol lot, Evergreen. Sat Jul 29. (No mention of rank/color)

STINE, PETER, b Easton, PA, d on a Sat, early 1915, at home, 136 4th St, Eliz. **SURV**: ch Mrs J P Wreder and James P, Easton, Helen and William E, E, and Bernard L, Passaic. w d svrl yrs ago. Came to E 5 yrs ago. Worked for Central RR, section boss on the Newark-Eliz Div. **CHH**: St Patricks, mem Bishop O'Farrell Council 463 CBL, Philipsburg. **SERV**: Enl otbrk Seymours Bat, 1st US Art, 1st term. Reup, and at Bull Run, Culpepper Courthouse, Spottsylvania, Gettysburg, Fredericksburg, South Mountain, Frederick City, Gaines Mills, Mechanicsville, Petersburg and others. WIA. For a time rode a horse named "Baldy." When Vet was WIA, "Baldy" was turned over to Gen Meade, who rode him in many battles. Aft horse d, the head was stuffed, and inkwells made out of the hoofs, both items lodged at the Lu Lu Temple, PHL. **F**: Int St Bernards, Easton. Obit date not recorded.

STONE, G DWIGHT, b Thu Apr 18, 1839, the anniv date of the ride of Paul Revere, Litchfield, CT, d Fri aftn Mar 13, 1931, S'H, Kearny. **SURV**: Niece Mrs Charles Hutchison, L. w d abt 25 yrs ago. Res S'H 5 wks. Lived yrs at 50 W Scott Pl, Eliz, the res of Cornelius Beatty. Res L to CW. Rem to Eliz 1867, and later for a time in Cranford. Employ for yrs at the old Nixon Shipyards. Selected Law Librarian at the Courthouse Sun Mar 1, 1914, resigning on Thu Jan 1, 1931. Dir of the Eliz Rescue

Mission. **MEM**: UD25, past Cmdr. In later yrs was Adj, and also assist Adj of the NJ Dept. With the ranks thinning, took care of Vet graves at various cem. MDAY in recent yrs meant the placing of 3,000 flags on sol graves. Co Super of S&S' headstones, of all cem in the co. **SERV**: Enl Pvt Co A, 19th CT Inf Reg on Sat Jul 26, 1862. Reg was reorg and converted into a Hvy Art unit (2nd CT Hvy Art) on Mon Nov 23, 1863. Made Cpl then, and on Sat Feb 13, 1864, promo to a Sergeancy. Became a Sgt-Maj Tue Mar 8, 1864, then a 2nd Lt on Thu Feb 23, 1865, and assigned to Co C, same Reg. Often said Cold Harbor, VA, was the bloodiest engage, but he also was with the first Btln that broke through the C lines in the capture of Petersburg, VA. At Spottsylvania, North Anna, Kearns' Station, Openquan, Fisher's Hill, New Market, Cedar Creek and Thatcher's Run. Disc at Fort Ethan Allen, VT, Fri Aug 18, 1865. **F**: J Stiner's Home for Svc, 97 W Grand St, arrangements to be made when Mrs Hutchison arrives. Sat Mar 14. (P)

Vet Stone many mos ago wrote an account of his svc during the CW. (See **Experiences**.)

G Dwight Stone (P) and Walter S Tully, Hillside, will go to the 61st natl encmp of the GAR at Grand Rapids, MI, Sat, to extend fm Sun to the following Fri. Stone is delegate-at-large for the State Dept. NJ delegation will support Frank O Cole, Jersey City, in natl Cmdr-in-Chief election. NJ delegation, which will incld svrl auxiliary orgs, will make the trip on a train departing Hoboken ovr the DE, Lackawanna & Wm RR at 1120 am, stopping at Newark and E Orange, remaining ovrngt in Buffalo, resuming trip next mrng. Return trip begins mrng of Sep 17. Tue Sep 6, 1927.

Attended a Christmas party for CW Vets given by WRC 27 Tue ngt in Eliz. Wed Dec 23, 1925. (P)

Honored at MDAY svc. Sat May 31, 1930. (P)

Attended annual UD25 Christmas party Wed. Thu Dec 30, 1926. (P)

Aft CW, res New Haven, CT, then rem to Eliz. Installed as Adj at the UD25 meeting Tue ngt. Only man to hold Adj-Gen for 2 successive terms. Tue Jan 8, 1924. (P)

STRAUSS, DANIEL, 72, b Alsace-Lorraine, d Wed mrng Mar 28, 1906, at home, 218 W 17th St, NYC. "Old Dan" took part in wars in his native land. Imm USA and enl CW. Aft CW, appointed as a doorman in the PD. At otbrk Franco-Prussian War, returned to Europe and enl French Army, rcvg a medal for bravery. Returned USA and again appointed as doorman PD. Wed Mar 28.

STRAUSS, LEWIS, 65, d Sat mrng Aug 17, 1901, Summit. **SURV**: w/ch David, proprietor of the drug store at 1st & E Jersey St, Max, in the drug business in Bayonne City, Edward and Mrs Jacob Brenner. In S for his health. In early life res Brooklyn, holding a clerkship in the PO. Rem Eliz aft CW. A sewing machine agent with an office on Broad St. For some yrs a collector for the wholesale liquor house of Back & Beck, NY, who frmly did biz at E Jersey & 1st St. **MEM**: An org of JK64, past Cmdr. A founder of HL81 F&AM, past Master. **CHH**: An original mem Congregation B'Nai Israel on E Jersey St, Pres B of Trustees at dod. **SERV**: 14th NY Vol. **F**: At home, 140 E Jersey St. Sat Aug 17. (C)

STRUCK, WILLIAM G, lifelong res Eliz, d Tue Jan 9, 1912, S'H, Kearny. **SURV**: ch Mrs Laura Seymour, Mrs William Leadenham, Joseph, Newark, Charles, Roselle, and Henry, E. A n/o gch and ggch. Wed Jan 10.

STRYKER, WILLIAM S, ADJ-GEN, b 1838 Trenton, d Mon mrng Oct 29, 1900, Trenton. Grad Princeton, studying law. **MEM**: Many Hist Soc. Pres NJ Hist Soc and of the Soc of the Cincinnati. **SERV**: Assist in org 14th NJ Vol 1863, resigning as Lt Col. Com Adj-Gen of NJ 1867, serv til dod. Mon Oct 29.

STUDER, AUGUST H, native of Switzerland, s/o Rev J A, d Tue Mar 1, 1910, at home, 432 Bergen St, Rahway. **SURV**: w/ch frmr assemblyman A C, William, Nyack NY, and Elizabeth. A bro/o Maj A G Studer, frmr US Consul at Singapore, appointed by Grant, and held until raised to a Consulate-Gen by Cleveland.

Imm USA 1852 to R, worked as a carriage trimmer. Returned to Switzerland 1854, then back to USA CW otbrk. Aft CW entered employ of T B Peddie & Co, Newark, 20 yrs. **SERV:** Enl 15th Reg, NJ Vol. In IA, the Maj raised a Co of Vol. Wed Mar 2 **SUYDAM, CHARLES CROOKE, COL**, b Wed Jun 15, 1836, NYC, d Thu mrng Nov 9, 1911, Gen H, Eliz. **SURV:** ch Eliza Gracie, Mrs James N S Brewster, Emily Halsey, Mrs J H Begley, Mrs Everett A Weeks, and Mrs Raymond Stone. 15 gch. Wed Apr 25, 1860, m Miss Eliza Gracie Halsey, d/o Rev Charles & Eliza Gracie King Halsey, d/o Charles King, Pres Columbia College at that time. Grad fm Columbia Jun, 1856, with honors. Came to E 1860. Aft CW admitted to the NY Bar, his office at 206 Broadway, NYC. Had the distinction of never losing a case. Appointed Attorney by the Sec of State for the settlement of claims of US citizens against Spain. **MEM:** A founder of the old Carteret Club. The Holland Society. LoyL. Mattano Club, E. Psi Upsilon frat of Columbia. **SERV:** Enl Pvt Sat Sep 7, 1861, 3rd NJ Vol Inf, then a 1st Lt Co L, NY Vol Cav Thu Oct 31. Org the Ira Harris Cav in NYC, which became Ira Harris Guard, then on Thu Nov 14 org 5th Reg, NY Cav. Left NY for Baltimore and attached to the cmd of Gen Dix until Mar 1862. Became Capt and assist Adj-Gen Thu Mar 6, 1862, assigned to staff of Gen E D Keyes, Cmdr of the 4th Army Corps of the AP. In Jun reassigned as 1st Lt to 5th NY Cav, and in Aug as Lt Col and assist Adj-Gen 4th Army Corps. Corps disb Aug 1863. Reassigned to staff of Gen Pleasanton, Cmdr, Cav Corps, AP. Hon disc Wed Nov 15, 1865, Lt Col. At the Peninsula Campaign, Siege of Yorktown, Williamsburg, Chickahominy, Seven Pines, Malvern Hill, Winchester, Summit Point, Charlestown, Kearneysville, Berryville Pike and Opequan. Captured Sep 21 at Fort Roya, and again at Cupp's Hill, Cedar Creek, while cmdr of Reg. Thu Nov 9.
SWAIN, ROBERT, CAPT, d announced Thu Aug 30, 1900, Salem. **SURV:** w/5ch. **SERV:** Enl Tue Oct 8, 1861, Co I, 9th NJ Vet Vol, a Capt at end, succeeding Capt J Madison Drake of Co

K. Thu Aug 30.

SYRON, MATTHEW V, 66, lifelong res Eliz, s/o late Nathaniel & Abigail, d Fri ngt Mar 16, 1900, at home, 1110 Magnolia Ave, Eliz. **SURV**: ch Mrs George Wilson and 2 s. mo d while he was in the Army, the 3rd s who d and who saw Army svc. m 42 yrs ago. Painter by trade. **SERV**: Enl otbrk, Vol in 3 mos svc, then 35th NJ Vol, with Sherman "from Atlanta to the sea." F: Mon 230 pm. Sat Mar 17.

T

TALIAFERRO, Felix Taylor, b Sun Nov 2, 1845, Orange Court House, VA, 2nd s/o Dr Edmund Pendleton Taliaferro, d Sat aftn Mar 5, 1904, at home, 1165 Chestnut St, Eliz. **SURV**: w frmr Miss Annie Elizabeth Penny, m 1867, of Mobile, AL/ch Mrs F V L Jones, Plainfield, Mrs Arthur T Pendleton, Mrs George Ketchum, Elizabeth Octavia, Edmunt Pendleton, Felix Taylor, Samuel Penny and Clarence Harcourt. Res AL until 1876, in Orange, VA, until 1896, to Bergen Point, then E 2 yrs ago. **SERV**: A student at VA mil inst at otbrk. Enl Army as soon as old enough, serv last 2 yrs. F: Tue mrng at home. Int private, Hillside, Plainfield. Mon Mar 7.

TANTUM, JOSEPH K, b Sat Aug 14, 1841, Crosswicks, d Wed mrng Feb 7, 1917, at his Downer St home, Westfield. **SURV**: w/ch Mrs Lillie Kittell and Mrs Charles Atgar, Weston, and Laura and John R, W. Res C for yrs. Employee PA RR 40+ yrs, ret. **SERV**: Enl otbrk Co E, 21st Reg, NJ Inf, Wed Aug 27, 1862. On Wed Sep 24, assigned to 3rd Brig, AP. At 3 big battles incldg Chancellorsville, VA. Hon disc Fri Jun 19, 1863. Wed Feb 7.

TAYLOR, FRANK, 78, b Calais, France, of English parents, d Thu ngt May 20, 1920, at home of dau, Seattle, WA. The US Army Brig Gen, ret, was a Vet of the CW, IW and S/AW. Fri May 21.

TAYLOR, WILLIAM K/H, 103, b 1827, in that part of Old

Mexico which later became TX, d Fri Dec 26, 1930, Hollywood, CA (Dateline). Came to CA 34 yrs ago. For 25 yrs one of the film colony's most colorful mem. Entered motion pictures in 1910, playing in wrn two-reelers. SERV: "Billy the Scout" joined the Army in 1856 and fought wandering Indian tribes on the Prairies. At CW otbrk enl 78th C VA Reg. At end CW, again joined US Army. Serv under Gen Nelson A Miles, in campaign against Sitting Bull, and a scout for Gen Custer. Spent 20 yrs fighting Indians. Sat Dec 27.

TERRILL, WILLIAM E, 63, b New Brunswick, d Sun ngt Sep 4, 1910, S'H, Kearny. SURV: w Susan Fisher Terrill, m 35 yrs ago last May/dau Mrs Mary Coddington, Plainfield. Rem to Rahway with par, then to Eliz, res last 23 yrs at 1166 ½ Washington St. Inmate S'H near 2 yrs. Took up tool making and employ in E Orange plant of Thomas A Edison 30 yrs, becoming assist super, considered an authority on tool making. Working almost hand-in-hand with Edison, assist him in his new devices, and largely responsible for Edison putting talking dolls on the market. When the Brooklyn Bridge was equipped with electric lights, he turned out most of the special parts required, such as the first special screw. Left Edison 8 yrs ago. Worked 7 yrs for Newark Comb and Brush Works and for a short time in the Wm Elec Instruments Works. SERV: Recruiting officer 3 yrs Co C, 33rd Reg, NJ Vol. Hon disc. Mon Sep 5.

THOMAS, GEORGE W AND CATHERINE A, d Wed ngt Mar 28, 1928, within 2 hrs of each other, at home of Mrs James C Wagstaff, 19 Holly St, Cranford, he ae 84, she ae 83. He was b NY State, rem early to OH, where he was res at CW otbrk. Res Netherwood bfr rem to C abt 25 yrs ago. Ret NY Lawyer. SERV: Qtmstr, attached to staff of Gen Grant, a close friend of him and his fam. Also under Gen, later Pres, Johnson at Gettysburg. In Ford's Theater when Lincoln was shot. w was a Cummings, a relative of a noted Boston dentist. Her only near relatives are Mrs Dorsey W Hyde, frmly Plainfield, now in France, and Deaconess Clark of PHL. Vet is believed to have svrl sis living.

THOMPSON, HUGH SMITH, CAPT, C Army, 68, Gov SC 1882-86, and aft assist Sec of the Treas and Civil Service Commissioner, d Sun Nov 20, 1904. The Youth's Companion - NE Edition, Mon Dec 8, 1904.

THOMPSON, JACOB, b Oct 22, 1819, Newark, d Sun mrng Oct 9, 1910, Lyons Farms. SURV: dau Mrs E A Porter, Newark. Res 1315 N Broad St for 57 yrs. Followed the occ of farming and horticulture. Tended to Evergreen Cem. Many yrs aft d of w, dug his own grave beside her. MEM: UD25, serv as Chapl. CHH: Presby, Senior Deacon for yrs. SERV: Enl otbrk Co B, 30th NJ Vol. Mon Oct 10.

THOMPSON, JOHN D, 77, s/o Sally Ann Ward, d Fri aftn Feb 25, 1910, at home, 325 Belleville Ave, Newark. SURV: w/dau Mrs Vanderbilt Green, Newark. mo was desc of the old Ward fam which settled in Elizabethtown early in the 17th century. MEM: 1st Pres of famous old Joel Parker Assoc of Newark. Jersey City Vol FD and EFA. SERV: In what was known as First Defenders. Sat Feb 26.

THOMPSON, WILLIAM, native of England, d Mon ngt Oct 15, 1906, at home, 703 E Jersey St, Eliz. SURV: w/ch Mary, William, Frank, James and Joseph. Imm USA a yng man. Res E 40 yrs. Worked for Singer, ret for 20 yrs. SERV: Navy, 5 yrs. On board Adm Farragut's Flagship "Hartford" when it entered Mobile Bay. At the taking of New Orleans. F: Thu mrng, Sacred Heart. Tue Oct 16.

THONAN, LEVI E, 75, d Fri Apr 2, 1926, Irvington Gen H, Union (Dateline). Struck by an auto on Springfield Ave Thu ngt while walking fm Newark to Plainfield, near Bertha St, Vaux Hall, just bfr 9 pm. Stepped fm the curb into the path of the auto. Said he lived in IN, and a preacher with no relatives. F: Int sol plot, Evergreen. Sat Apr 3.

THORN, EDWIN, 85, d Sat 1115 am Jul 22, 1916, at home of Mrs W E MacDonald, 221 Elmer St, Westfield. SURV: bro Albert, Plainfield. w d 3 yrs ago. Res W 14+ yrs. For yrs a bookkeeper in James Moffett & Sons office. MEM: Free Mason. Sat Jul 22.

THORN, LINTON ROSCOE, b Mon Mar 29, 1841, at the old Thorn homestead near Westfield, the yngst and latest surv, s/o late Isaac & Catherine B, d Thu aftn Jan 30, 1919, at home, 663 Madison Ave, Eliz. SURV: w frmr Miss Virginia Lounsbury of NYC, m 55 yrs ago/dau Mrs Pauline Lavere. gch Linton Thorn Lavere, Bridgeport, CT, Mrs George Symonds, E, and Mrs Frank Fallon, Springfield, MA. 3 ggch. A ret master mechanic with PA RR. A Repub. MEM: A Mason. CHH: Of Quaker stock. Lifelong Bapt, first with 1st Bapt, Rahway, then Central Bapt, E. SERV: Enl otbrk Co A, 1st Reg, 1st Brig, NJ Vol, to end. Once had to leap at midnight fm a sinking troop ship in Chesapeake Bay, not rescued until daylight by a passing craft. POW 9 mos Libby. Witnessed Lee's surrender at Appomattox. Fri Jan 31.

THORN, THOMPSON, 80, d at midnight Tue/Wed May 25/26, 1920, at home, E Hazelwood Ave, Rahway. SURV: w/ch Mrs Ambrose Hall, Newark, and Mrs Fred Thorn, PHL. sib Louis, R, and Mrs Adele Slater, R. Ret employee PA RR. CHH: 1st Bapt. SERV: 6th NY Ind Bat, one of the 6 surv mem. Remaining are Uel Freeman, George M Plum, Alfred T Crane, Charles Leonard and Adam Dutrow, all R res. F: Fri 3 pm. Thu May 27.

THORNTON, SAMUEL P, b Sat Jan 18, 1840, Bristol, RI, d Thu shrtly aft midnight Aug 26, 1909, Eliz. SURV: w/ch William H and Louis N, E, and Mrs J W Wilson, Cranbury. 3 gch Edith M, Marion H and W Hildreth Thornton. f was a cooper on board of whale ships and d 1850 fm injuries rcvd fm a whale. Res E 47 yrs, 45 yrs in the employ of the NJ Central RR, with the pos of drawbridge and derrick inspector at dod. Until a few yrs ago, res at 327 Marshall St, home for yrs. In 1851 went to sea as a cabin boy at $4/mos, aft increased to $8/mos. Initial voyage was 23 mos. Capt informed him he would be payed for the 3 wks bfr next trip if he signed on. He did, and followed the sea for 13 yrs, incldg CW Navy time. On Sat Jan 9, 1864, entered the employ of the Central RR at the Elizabethport shops as a machinist. Assist in changing the locomotives fm wood to coal burners. Advanced in 1865 to wreckmaster for the road, holding it for yrs. In Mar 1866 super of the taking out of 2 locomotives fm the Bloomsburg Bridge, a difficult feat, as the wrecking derrick was unknown then. Promo in 1875 to road foreman machinist, in charge of the machinery at all drawbridges and water stations on the line, including the NY and LI RRs. When the latter line was opened he installed a number of improvements on the Raritan Riv drawbridge, incldg united rails and expansion points, which attachments were ordered placed on all drawbridges. Constructed the box signal with the diamond top that was in use here for yrs, previous to the elevation of the PA RR at that point. The signals were aft installed on the NY and LB and NJ southern divs. In charge of the scales, crossing gates and coal chutes. Took a trip in 1878 to Wilmington, DE, to super the equip of a test train, consisting of one locomotive and 6 cars with vacuum brakes. Rcvd $50 for appreciation of success of test. **MEM**: UD25, addressing school ch on patriotism. EL49 F&AM. CE1 IOF, and the NJ Central RR VA. Fqt speaker WCTU 1. **CHH**: Fulton St Meth, 37 yrs mem of the official Board, and 14 yrs its Pres. **SERV**: In Matanzas, Cuba, at CW otbrk. When ship arrived Providence, RI, enl Navy, Fri Jul 26, 1861. Sent to PHL and assigned to sloop "Juniata," of the W India Squadron, which proceeded to Norfolk, where the navy yard at that point was destroyed. Abt that time Spain recognized the U and the Squad was sent to arrange matters with that nation. Accomplished, the Squad conveyed the Aspinwall mail steamers and looked for blockade runners, acting as an armors mate, performing all the blacksmith and machine work that was done, for his and other ships in the Squad. Hon disc Fri Dec 4, 1863. Thu Aug 26.

TIER, JAMES EDWARD, 84, lifelong res Rahway, d Tue 535 pm Dec 25, 1923, R. **SURV**: w/ch Walter E, Woodbridge, Frank P T and Mrs Jacques Pfister, both 70 Hamilton St. 2 gdau Carol and Ethel Tier, Woodbridge. Last surv of a fam of 17 bro and sis. **MEM**: Mason 57 yrs, with LL27 F&AM. **CHH**: A Quaker.

SERV: Enl otbrk Co C, 30th NY Vol. At Chancellorsville, Fredericksburg, and in the fighting along the Rappahannock and abt Richmond. Mu/o at expiration of term of svc just bfr Gettysburg. Sec of assoc formed aft CW by Reg mems. (Psbl partial obit) Wed Dec 26.

TILDEN, THOMAS W, 67, d Thu ngt Aug 10, 1905, while seated in the billiard room at the Union League Club, Jersey City. **SURV**: s/2dau. Worked as a freight agent for the Erie RR at the NY office, serv his 2nd term as PC at dod. Super of the NY Bay cem in Greenville. **MEM**: 33rd Degree Mason, past Grand Master of NJ, and past Grand Cmdr KT. Rising Star Lodge 169, Enterprise Chap 2 Royal Arch Masons, Hugh de Payens Commandery 1 KT, various Scottish rite bodies in the valley of J C, and Salaam Temple Mystic Shrine of Newark. J C Fire Board 1871-73. **SERV**: Pvt Co A, 21st NJ Inf, to end. Fri Aug 11.

TIMBROOK, MADISON, b Mon Nov 21, 1831, Montville, s/o Richard & Lydia, d Fri 6 pm May 7, 1909, at home of s Richard, Westfield Ave, Roselle. **SURV**: ch Mrs W J Woodruff, Mrs W H Cox and s Marion, Eliz, and Richard. sib Mrs Jacob Peer, Newark, and Samuel A, Boonton. w frmr Ellen Sanford Walker of Newark. Couple celeb 50th m anniv abt 4 yrs ago. Res Eliz in 1853, a sash and blind maker. Rem to Newark, then back to Eliz 1862. Aft CW made a station agent at the Elberon depot on the Long Branch of the Central RR. Aft 6 mos rem to the El Mora station, staying 30 yrs, ret last Mar 1st and presented with a purse of $50 in gold by El Mora commuters. **MEM**: UD25. RC 808, RA. **SERV**: 7th NJ Vol Inf, 3 yrs. At Gettysburg. Sat May 8. (P)

TINSMAN, GEORGE W, 55, native of NJ, d Sat eve Aug 29, 1903, at home, 406 Jefferson Ave, Eliz. **SURV**: w/ch Mrs William H Neefus, Broad St, E, and Mrs H T Hock, Jefferson Ave. A 4 yr old gd, d/o Mrs Hock, who he was holding when he d. Spent part of his early life in MI and some of his later yrs in Easton, PA. Rem to E 18 yrs ago. Worked 29 yrs for Jersey Central RR as a conductor, then station agent. Recently worked for Prudential Ins Co as an agent. **MEM**: Winfield Scott Council 53 Jr OUAM, E Council 10 DL, and the SB. **SERV**: Co G, 3rd MI Vol, Thu Sep 15, 1864, to Mon May 1, 1865. **F**: Wed 2 pm at home. Int Easton. Mon Aug 31.

TODD, HENRY H, CAPT, native of Scotland, d Mon Jan 6, 1908, at home, Alameda, CA. Imm USA when a lad, settling in Jersey City. Aft CW went W. During the Chicago fire he lost heavily and went to CA, hoping to make another fortune, more or less successful. Spent some yrs in AK, doing fairly well in the mines, until an immense glacier swept away his ore crusher, burying most of his workmen. Owned and operated the Park Hotel at Alameda past few yrs. **SERV**: One of the "First Defenders" fm NJ. Enl otbrk Co K, 2nd NJ Militia. Immediately aft mu/o, joined Co D, 8th NJ, made Sgt-Maj, then 2nd Lt, and in 1864 Capt. Had active part in all the battles of the AP. Captured while leading his Co in a desperate charge in the hand-to-hand struggle at the "Bloody Angle" in the Wilderness May, 1864. POW Richmond, Macon, Savannah and Charleston (See **Experiences**). **F**: Thu.

TOOKER, JOHN K, nearly 78, b Rahway, d Thu mrng Apr 21, 1921, at home, 45 Whittier St, Rahway. **SURV**: w/ch Sam, 37 Harrison St, R, and Mrs Anna S Wraight, 15 Union St, R. 4 gch. Ret employee PA RR. **MEM**: WFB27. EFA. **SERV**: Enl ae 19 Co C, 3rd Reg, NJ Vol Inf, to end. WIA. Fri Apr 22.

TOOKER, NATHAN C, see Tucker.

TOWN, SAMUEL P, COL, 91, d Sat Jul 10, 1937, at home, N PHL. Desc of an old PHL fam. gf Rev John W G Neveling, was a Chapl in AW. **MEM**: GAR, past natl Cmdr. **SERV**: Enl 1864, under Gens Sheridan, Sigel and Hunter. Sat Jul 10.

TOWNLEY, GEORGE R, 72, native of Eliz, d Sun Jul 12, 1914, at home, 561 Chilton Ave, Eliz. **SURV**: w Maria/ch Mrs William Potter and Esther. sib Dewitt and Theodore. Educ in a PrS. Engaged in the grocery biz. Later became a gen collector with Central RR, held for 15+ yrs to dod. **MEM**: UD25. **CHH**: St Johns Episc. **SERV**: Enl otbrk Co K, 9th NJ Inf. Mon Jul 13.

TOWNLEY, JONATHAN, b Sat Dec 14, 1833, Union Tp, s/o John Magie & Elizabeth Cooper Townley, d Fri aft Aug 8, 1919, at home, 139 Murray St, Eliz. Desc of Sir Richard Townley, fm England 1684. As a lad attended PrS of Dr Frederick W Foote, preparing for Princeton Univ, grad 1858. Aft grad, founded a "select classical and English school for boys" in E. French and German were taught by native masters and particular attention given to moral deportment. A well-equipped gym added to school's worth. MEM: Princeton Soc known as "Clio." SERV: Won honors for himself and his city during the CW. Sat Aug 9.
TRAFTON, JOHN E, killed Tue mrng Oct 31, 1905, going to work, at the Spring St station of the Central RR, Eliz. SERV: 2nd ME Reg, of Vol, in some of the hardest fought battles. Declined a tendered com, aft an officer in the US Marine Svc. F: Thu 3 pm at his 558 Jefferson Ave home, Rev Travis B Thames, DD, 1st Bapt. Wed Nov 1.
TRAHON, WILLIAM H, 75, d Sun ngt May 2, 1905, S'H, Kearny. SURV: w. A s, who d in Eliz a few yrs ago, was a sol, and int with military honors, a Co of regulars fm Governor's Island, along with the Island's band. Ancestors were in the AW, and he had a valuable collection of continental money. Res S'H past few yrs. Long a res of NY. Res Eliz for yrs, conducting a market on Broad St, near the Isham bldg, and later on E Grand St. Long engaged in same biz in NY. For some time conducted a hotel on Union St, Eliz, which aft became the HQ of the Gospel Mission, which he identified with aft he gave up hotel biz. A Dem, one time mem B of Chosen Freeholders. MEM: Masonic fraternity, a KT. SERV: 71st NY Vol. F: Alfred C Haines Parlor. Int Evergreen, next to w. (Sic?) Mon May 3.
TRAINOR, THOMAS, 76, b NY, d Sun Jul 29, 1923, S'H, Kearny. SURV: sis Mrs Ellen F Trembley, Eliz, and Mrs Julia Ash, Newark. Res Eliz most of his life. Frmly of 862 Elizabeth Ave. SERV: Enl soon aft otbrk 3rd NJ Vol. In a n/o engage. WIA. F: D J Leonard's Home for F, Elizabeth Ave. Mon Jul 30.
TRAPP, LAWRENCE, 92, b Baden, Germany, d Fri ngt Nov

19, 1909, at home, 611 Cameron Pl, Eliz. **SURV**: ch Mrs Oscar Plum and Mrs Charles Stout. 10 gch and a ggch. Res E 60+ yrs. An oilcloth printer by trade, employ at the old Oilcloth Works, Williamson St. **MEM**: UD25. **SERV**: Co K, 9th NJ Vol, late Capt John B Lutz. Disc as Sgt. Sat Nov 20.

TREMBLEY, JOHN, 73, d Sun Apr 28, 1907, at home, 37 Campbell St, Rahway. **SURV**: w/2s/dau. For yrs worked for Dunham Carriage Factory in R. Witnessed first guns of war at Fort Sumter. **SERV**: Drafted Sun Apr 13, 1862, Co D, 1st Reg, TN Inf. Escaped at first opportunity and joined the Feds, 3 yrs, hon disc. **F**: Tue eve at home, Rev B O Parvin. Int Wed fam plot R. Mon Apr 29. Cor to SERV Tue Apr 30.

TRIMBLE, THOMAS R, 70, b NYC, d Fri mrng Sep 1, 1916, at home, 334 Marshall St, Eliz. **SURV**: ch Thomas R, Jr, May Irene, and Margaret. sib Arthur Nelson, and William H. Aft CW entered the store of Luther T Hand, E PM, on 1st St. When the carrier svc was est Tue Jul 1, 1873, appointed as the first carrier, working for 43 yrs. **MEM**: UD25, past Cmdr. EL49 F&AM, Treas 30 yrs. A founder of Apollo Div, ST. An org of Osceola Hose Co 2. EFA. Natl LCA Branch 67. **SERV**: Enl ae 15 Drummer Boy. Fri Sep 1. (P)

TRIMER, HARVEY G, 61, d Wed ngt Jul 25, 1900, S'H, Kearny. **SURV**: w/svrl ch, at the 216 Centre St fam home. **SERV**: Vet Z. Thu Jul 26.

TRUSSLER, JUSTUS D, 69, lifelong res Rahway, d Sun ngt Jan 23, 1910, S'H, Kearny. **SURV**: sib, 2 sis with whom he res on Campbell St bfr entering S'H a yr ago, and frmr PJ George J, Harrison St. Carriage body maker by trade, worked for yrs in the old F L Graves carriage factory. **MEM**: WFB27. **SERV**: 6th NY Ind Bat, late Capt Joseph W Martin. Tue Jan 25.

TUCKER (TOOKER), NATHAN C, b Sat Jan 7, 1826, Eliz, d Wed ngt Aug 24, 1904, S'H, Kearny. **SURV**: ch Mrs Sarah Leonard, E Jersey St, E, Charles C, 475 2nd St, E Newark, Mrs Elizabeth Synear, Camden, Mrs Mary Chapman, Masonville, and Freeman, PHL. w, sis/o late Capt James Wilson, was b downtown E and d 2 yrs ago on the anniv of their m. Res E until going to S'H 6 mos ago. An oilcloth printer, for yrs employ in the James K Albro Oilcloth Works. Ret, with a $12/mos pens. One of the first E firemen, the first foreman of frmr Washington Engine Co 3, and org of Osceoloa hose Co 2. Had a narrow escape fm the fire that partially destroyed J&SS Thompson lumber yard on Mon Jan 25, 1901, carrying his invalid w fm the house to safety. **SERV:** 2nd NJ, to end. Mem late Capt James Jenkin famous Co, very few surv now. **F:** Sun 2 pm at home of s Charles. Int sol plot, Evergreen. Fri Aug 26.

TUCKER, THEODORE M. 63, b Union Tp, d Tue Jun 16, 1903, in the house where he was b, Union Tp. **SURV:** sis Dr Anna J Crouthers. One of 3 CW Vets to d within a week. **SERV:** Co K, 2nd NJ Vol. Suffered for yrs fm wounds rcvd at the Wilderness, Mar 1864. **F:** Sat 2 pm at the 1120 E Jersey St home of sis. Rev E B Cobb, DD, 2nd Presby. Int fam plot Evergreen. Sat Jun 20.

TUFTS, PHILIP E, b Tue Oct 12, 1841, Blazing Star (Carteret), d Thu aftn Mar 2, 1905, S'H, Kearny. Greater part of life spent in Rahway, rem there in 1872. 4 yr mem of CoC, presiding officer 2 yrs. A finely-framed portrait was awarded him for being the most popular Councilman. Appointed PM R Thu Feb 1, 1894, securing free delivery for Rahway effective Fri Jul 16, 1897. A Dem. **MEM:** WFB27, elected Cmdr in 1882, and appointed Chief Mustering Officer by Cmdr M Nevins in 1883. Elected Senior V-Cmdr of NJ 1885. LL27 F&AM. **CHH:** St Pauls Epis, Rahway, Vestryman and Treas for yrs. **SERV:** Enl Pvt Wed Sep 3, 1862, 30th NJ Vol. Made Cpl Wed Oct 1, 1862. Promo to 2nd Lt and transf to Co C Mon Mar 16, 1863. Made final rank of 1st Lt Wed Apr 1, 1863. Mu/o end CW. **F:** Sat 10 am at the 208 Main St, Rahway, home of sis-in-law Mrs John M Tufts. Rev Charles L Cooder. Int Hazlewood. Sat Mar 4.

TUNISON, WILLIAM, SR, 74, b Somerville, d early Mon eve Aug 13, 1917, at home, 25 N Ace, East, Cranford. **SURV:** w/ch Frederick L and Chief Eng William, Jr, of the C FD, Samuel,

Roselle, and Mrs L Stevens, S. Res C last 25 yrs. Mason by trade. **MEM:** WS73. Local Union 34 Bricklayers and Masons, Garwood. **SERV:** Co E, 2nd Reg, NJ Cav. At Gettysburg and Antietam. Tue Aug 14.

TURNER, WILLIAM FRANKLIN, 65, b NYC, s/o late Louis F & Marguerite G, d Sat Mar 26, 1910, at home, 39 Pierce St, Rahway. **SURV:** w/ch Louis F and Marguerite G. Sib John T, Norwalk, CT, James Randolph, Mt Vernon, NY and Henry, Port Reading. **MEM:** WFB27. **SERV:** Enl Freehold 1862, Co E, 14th NJ Vol Inf, attached to 8th Corps and 1st Brig, 3rd Div, 3rd Brig, AP. Hon disc Fri Aug 26, 1864, reup as ordinary seaman Navy. On the "Manaska," "Ohio," "Allegheny" and others. Disc Wed Jun 14, 1865. At Manassas Gap, Wettma Heights, Culpepper, Bristow Station, Perry Ford, Brandy Station, and WIA Locust Grove. Serv under late Capt James L Bodwell, R, 1st Lt Isaac S Tingley and 2nd Lt K O Bedell. **F:** WFB27 in charge, Rev T C Mayham. Sat Mar 26.

U

URMSTON, DANIEL GARTHWAITE, 68, native of Rahway, d announced Tue Apr 26, 1910, Rahway (Dateline). **SURV:** w/ch Fred W, Joseph W, Alpheus G and Mrs E W Phares(?), 128 Stiles St, Eliz. Sib J J, Frank, Thomas, Mrs James E Stiles, Newark, and Louise. 2 gch. b in the house next to his 111 Union St home. f, John, was for yrs one of the most prominent makers of wooden wagon hubs in the country. Super of the R Water Co. **MEM:** WFB27, Cmdr for yrs and Adj at dod. LL of Masons 44 yrs. The Water Board. **SERV:** Enl Sat Aug 9, 1862, ae 20, Co E, 14th NJ Vol, Cpl later 1st Sgt, AP, in most of their battles. WIA bayonet charge Cold Harbor Wed Jun 1, 1864. On Wed Feb 15, 1865, transf to 51st Co of the 2nd Bat, VRC. Hon disc Aug, 1865. One matter he took great interest in was the collection of data and sketches of all R sol who had serv in CW, and his records were the most complete of any known to exist in regard to local sol. **F**: Fri 230 pm at home. Int R. Wed Apr 27.

V

VAN FLEET, JAMES OSCAR, 86, b in a log cabin in Pontiac, MI, 1840, d Wed 525 am Aug 10, 1927, at home, 34 Elm St, Linden. **SURV**: 2/w, m, 1917, Miss Annie Gulager, a d/o the 1st Mayor of the Boro of Linden. 1/w d 1911. ch Hart S, 139 Westfield Ave, Roselle Park, and Mrs E R Blancke, 403 Henry St. 4 gch J Oscar Van Fleet, Neshanic, Hart Irving Van Fleet, Eliz, Arline and Raymond Blancke, Jr, L. 2 ggch. sib Mrs Mary Wilson, Long Branch, and a bro in Readington. In Pontiac, very friendly with the Indians, and spoke their language. In 1848, his par with their 8 ch made the trip fm Pontiac to Flemington where lived to CW. Rem to L 1872, at 403 Henry St. Builder and contractor by trade, erecting most of the old homes which stand tdy. On the Tp Comm in its earliest yrs. Bldg Inspector 14 yrs. **MEM**: B of Educ. **CHH**: Reformed, life mem of the Consistory. **SERV**: Enl Co F, 9th NJ Inf. At Roanoke and New Berne, NC, under Gen Burnside. Shipwrecked in the transport "Pocahontus." Once shook hands with Lincoln. Believed to be the last Co F surv. Wed Aug 10.

VAN PELT, DAVID II, 76, b SI, d Thu Aug 11, 1921, S'H, Kearny. **SURV**: ch John H, SI, Mrs Theabold G Hedel, Brooklyn, Mrs Egbert Youngkins, SI, and Mrs Sophie Dixon, Mrs John Wilbourne, and Mrs Michael McGarry, Eliz. sib John H, Mrs Isaac King and Mrs Martha Marsh, Eliz, and Mrs William Billings, Linden. 18 gch. 8 ggch. Res Eliz 60+ yrs. Rem to S'H 9 yrs ago. An oysterman, lived on Geneva St. **MEM**: UD25 30+ yrs. **CHH**: East Bapt, Deacon for yrs. **SERV**: Enl end of 1861 Co B, 11th NJ Inf Reg, 3 yrs. WIA Cold Harbor, VA. At Antietam, Thatcher's Run, Deep Bottom, the Wilderness, and Siege at Petersburg, VA. His bro John H also in CW, and WIA. **F**: Mon 230 pm J S Stiners Home for Svc. Int Evergreen. Fri Aug 12.

VAN PELT, JEREMIAH, 75, b SI, s/o late Jeremiah & Catherine Ann, d Sun Dec 1, 1912, at home, 222 Delaware St, Eliz. **SURV**: w Charlotte E. sib Mrs Robert King, Mrs Charles Marsh, Mrs William Billings, John and David. Res E 50 yrs. Conducted a confectionary store 3rd St. **CHH**: East Bapt. **SERV**: Enl Pvt Co B, 1st Reg, NJ Inf, Thu Aug 7, 1862, Capt William H Meeker. Disc Providence, RI, Thu Mar 5, 1863. Mon Dec 2.

VAN PELT, JOHN W, d Sat Jun 6, 1931, at home, 61 Elizabeth Ave, Eliz. Although WIA in CW, a more serious injury in the loss of his left arm and right thumb, firing a salute during an Independence Day celebration in front of the old Courthouse. Even aft accident, considered an expert rifleman. On Mon Oct 2, 1865, joined old RJC4. **MEM**: UD25. EFA. **F**: Tue aft at home, Rev Murray A Cayley, Greystone Presby. Int Evergreen, GAR plot. Mon Jun 8. (See Decker, Richard)

VINCENT, ANTHONY H, 70, b Paris, France, d early Sun mrng Nov 22, 1908, at home, 33 Factory St, Rahway. **SURV**: w/2dau. Imm USA when a boy. Res R for yrs. A watchman for yrs, and until abt 1 yr ago janitor R YMCA. Janitor for R Repub Club when taken ill. **MEM**: WFB27. **CHH**: 1st ME. **F**: Wed at chh, Rev J B Heard. Mon Nov 23.

VOLK, CHARLES P, 77, b Paris, d Tue mrng Mar 16, 1920, Alexian H, Eliz. **SURV**: w Margaret/ch Peter, Jersey City, William, NY, Philip, Lyons Farms, Frank, E, and Mrs Sadie Merwede. 20 gch. 1 ggch. Imm USA to NY ae 2 with par. Clerk, foreign branch, NY PO 38 yrs. Rem to Hillside 26 yrs ago. **MEM**: UD25. **SERV**: 1st NY Vol Inf Reg. Reup 71st Cav Reg. Tue Mar 16.

VOLLMER, JOHN M, 80, native of Germany, d Wed Apr 18, 1917, at home, 157 E Jersey St, Eliz. **SURV**: w Franziska Volk Vollmer/ch Mrs E E Yess, Mrs M J Swann, Louisa, Louis, Charles G, Edward F, Frederick P, of E, and Henry J, Hammond, IN. Imm USA 60 yrs ago to NYC. Res E last 55 yrs. Conducted a shoemaker shop E Jersey St, ret 15 yrs ago. **MEM**: JK 64. Schwabischer Unterstuetzungs Verein. **CHH**: 1st German Presby.

SERV: Enl Tue Apr 23, 1861, Co H, 8th Reg, NY Vol Inf, Capt Frederick Werthers. Reuped Wed May 20, 1863, Co B, 6th Reg, US Vet Vol, Capt Louis J Sariste, to end. Thu Apr 19. (P)
VON KUMMER, OTTO, 70 + 8 mos, b Germany, d Thu noon Mar 16, 1911, Gen H, Eliz. **SURV**: w Mary/ch Henry, Fred and Mrs Charles Huften. Res 925 Magnolia Ave, and E 50 yrs. Employ oil milling dept Singer past 35 yrs. **MEM**: Oil Milling SBS. **SERV**: Lt German army. Lt 37th NY Reg.
VON KUMMER, MARIE, MRS, 75, b Hoboken, d/o late Dr Herman M & Philipine, d Sun Dec 16, 1928, at home, 925 Magnolia Ave, overcome by gas, Eliz. **SURV**: ch Henry, same address, and Frederick H, E. 2 gch, George and Elsie Huften, New Britain, CT. sib Mrs Ida Perrine, Newark, and Frederick, NYC. CW vet h d svrl yrs ago. Res Magnolia Ave 25 yrs, and E 50+ yrs. **F**: D J Leonards Home for F, 1143 Elizabeth Ave. Mon Dec 17.

W

WAGNER, LOUIS, GEN, b 1838, Germany, d early Thu Jan 15, 1914, PHL, PA. Dir of the PA RR and Pres Third Natl Bank. Obit Thu Jan 15.
WAIIL, FRANK C, 82, b Weotfield, d Tue aftn Apr 13, 1920, at home, Somerville. **SURV**: Nieces Mrs M H Stratemeyer, Roselle, and Mrs John Newsome, Eliz. bro-in-Law John Kidd, Eliz. Res Eliz for yrs. Connected with Central RR of NJ as manager of the old ferry docks. **CHH**: Fulton St ME, Eliz. **SERV**: Co I, 3rd Reg, NJ Vol. Wed Apr 14.
WALKER, THOMAS E, 79, native of England, d Mon ngt Aug 10, 1903, at home, 907 Bond St, Eliz. **SURV**: A fam. Res E 65 yrs, 30 yrs in the employ of Isaac Faulks, 134 Broad St. **SERV**: Enl otbrk Co C, 14th Reg, NJ Vol, recruited in E by Col Chauncey Harris. Fqt attendant at GAR reunions. **F**: Mon aftn Christ chh. Int Evergreen. Tue Aug 11.

WALPOLE, SAMUEL, 67, d Sun Jul 7, 1907, at his Scotch Plains hotel res. **SURV**: bro Constable Robert. w d 15 yrs ago. **SERV**: 11th NJ Vol. Mon Jul 8.

WARD, JOHN, 75, b Ireland, d Thu 1210 pm Jul 22, 1915, Alexian H, Eliz. **SURV**: ch Detective James, Frank, Florence, Mrs Walter Maise, 441 Fulton St, with whom he res, Mrs William Bellis, E, Mrs Henry Morley and Mrs William Franklin. w d some yrs ago. Imm USA ae 14, going to work for late Capt Spencer on the 3rd Ave Spencer farm. Molder by trade, resumed that work aft CW for Dravis, Eugene Munsell Co, and A & F Brown. **CHH**: Holy Rosary, one of the earliest mem. **SERV**: Enl Co K, 9th NJ Vol, Oct, 1861. Reup Nov 1863, to end. WIA Gettysburg, spent mos in a Newark H. Fri Jul 23. (P)

WARNER, JEFFERSON T, d Mon Mar 15, 1926, at home of niece Mrs Annie Lobdell, 7 Hillside Ave, Hillside. Res H 4 yrs. **MEM**: UD25, having been rcvd by transf fm Fielder Post, Plattsburg, NY. Jr V-Cmdr. **SERV**: Enl Sat Aug 9, 1862, Co K, 118th NY Vol, promo to Cpl at Harrison Landing, VA, lost left foot. Disc Fri Sep 22, 1865. **F**: Wed. Int Evergreen 230 pm. Tue Mar 16.

Serv with Co K, the "Adirondack" Reg. Res in Peru, Clinton Co, NY, at enl. Assigned to Plattsburg, and aft training, to VA, on the James Riv. A color guard, and there were 32 Pvt, 4 Sgt, 3 Cpl and 3 com officers. Aft the battle, left as the highest ranking officer, finding but 8 Pvt who were not WIA. Also at Petersburg and WIA Fort Hamilton, a 200-lb shell robbing him of his left leg. Stayed 3 wks at Gen H, Fortress Monroe, then sent by steamer to Willard's Pt, NY. Aft recovery, drove an ambulance at the Battery, NYC. Disc Wed Dec 12, 1866. He and a friend bought a grocery store in NY, which he ran abt a yr. Rem to Plattsburg, where he once lived. His w d 5 yrs ago, and he rem to Eliz. Fmrly Cmdr GAR Post West Chazy, NY. Installed as Jr V-Cmdr at the UD25 meeting Tue ngt. Res 742 Pennington St, Eliz. Tue Jan 8, 1924.

WARNOCK, JAMES ALEXANDER, native of Belfast,

Ireland, d Sat Apr 8, 1915, at home, 212 Delaware St, Eliz. SURV: w Mary J/ch Mrs Charles Warren, James A and Charles. 13 gch. 2 ggch. Imm USA to downtown section of E as a boy. Educ PS1. Chh: Grace Epis. MEM: JK64. SERV: Throughout. WIA. Mon Apr 10.

WATERBURY, CHARLES S, d Sun 9 am Jan 23, 1910, at home, 411 Lafayette St, Newark. SERV: Co C, 1st NJ Militia, "First Defenders," under the call of Lincoln for 75,000 men to defend DC, in Apr 1861. Aft campaign, enl Navy, to end. Joined Vet Z nearly 25 yrs ago. F: At home Tue 8 pm. Mon Jan 24.

WATERS, ISRAEL B, b Wed Aug 15, 1838, Irvington, d Sat Mar 17, 1900, at home, Eliz. m 1863 Miss Catherine J Laren of Plainfield. Passed the greater part of his early life in E. Carpenter by trade, worked for Thomas B Budd. For 17 yrs carried on the milk biz. MEM: WL33 F&AM, since 1868, the Natl Provident Union. CHH: 1st Bapt since Mar, 1874. SERV: 2 yrs. (Partial obit) Mon Mar 19.

WATSON, THOMAS, 75, b Brooklyn, d Mon ngt Sep 21, 1914, at home of his s William H, Henry St, Linden. SURV: w Catherine/ch L Councilman John F, George W, William H, Aldwyn and Mrs Mary T Randolph. Res Jersey City most of his life. Rem to L a few yrs ago. Gen foreman of the grain elevator of PA RR in Jersey City 30+ yrs, ret. MEM: GVH3, past Cmdr 33rd Degree Mason and past Master Jersey City Lodge 74 F&AM, one of 6 mem of the Watson fam who are Masons, the order being represented in 3 gens of the fam. F: Thu 8 pm at home, Rev A C Van Raalte, P Reformed chh. Int Belmar. Thu Sep 24.

WEAVER, JOHN W, 95, of Muldrow, OK, d at the Jul 7, 1938, 75th B&G Reunion, Gettysburg. SERV: C sol. Thu Jul 7.

WEAVER, PETER V, 70, d Mon Jul 28, 1913, at home of dau Mrs V L Frazee, Plainfield (Dateline). SURV: ch Mrs Frazee, Mrs Walter N Martin, Puerto Rico, and John W, Orange. Aft CW joined P PF, bcmg Chief. Entered PO, made Deputy in 1890. Serv as a dep sheriff in Houston Admin. SERV: Co A, 30th NJ Inf, 9 mos. Reup Co D, 4th Bat, Lgt Art, to end. Tue Jul 29.

WEBER, JOHN P, 82, b Germany, d Mon mrng Apr 15, 1918, at home, 405 Court St, Eliz. **SURV:** 2/w, Mary. 6 (partial obit). Imm USA as a boy, res E since 1875. Learned the cutter trade in the clothing business. **MEM:** UD25. **SERV:** Enl otbrk Co D, 1st NY Mounted Rifles, disb and merged into 6th US Inf. At Black Water, Bottom Bridge, Dry Neck, Carrelton Stones, Suffolk, and Zuni. WIA. Aft H at Fortress Monroe, duty at Bedloe's Island, NY, and Fort Ward, NY Harbor. Mon Apr 15.

WEBER, HENRY M, 64, b Germany, d early Tue mrng Mar 15, 1910, at home, 218 Centre St, Eliz. **SURV:** w/ch Frank, Frederick, Charles, Mrs William Manske and Mrs Frederick Freckman, all E. Res Newark bfr rem to E. Worked 26 yrs at Singer. **MEM:** Polishers and Buffers Union. **CHH:** St Michaels. **SERV:** Co A, 39th Reg, NJ Vol, mu/i at Newark. Tue Mar 15.

WELDEN, WILLIAM H, b Sat Aug 6, 1842, Belvidere, Warren Co, d Fri mrng Oct 17, 1924, at home, 87 Union St, Rahway. **SURV:** ch William H, Jr, Westfield, Frank E, Fanwood, Mrs G E Sovereign, Plainfield, Mrs C W Simpson, Boston, Mrs C Covert, Harlingen, Mrs O C Rinehart, Scotch Plains, and Mrs H E DeWees, Asbury Park. 8 gch. 1 ggch. Engaged in contracting biz all his life. Dir R Savings Bank. **MEM:** LL27 F&AM 50 yrs. **CHH:** 1st Presby, mem B of Trustees at dod. Fri Oct 17.

WELLS, W H, 98, b Bedford, VA, d Thu Jan 26, 1939, Dallas (Dateline). Refused to surrender to the Yankees at Appomattox. Enl ae 21 1861 with the Old Dominion Rifles. Fought in 20 major battles with Lee and Jackson. Aug 9th was always his private holiday. On that day at Slaughter's Mountain, a shell landed between his legs, showering him with dirt. When Lee surrendered, Bill Wells stormily refused to give in "to those Yankees," and walked 25 miles over a wrecked RR track to his home. Always attended the B&G natl R and finally made his peace with the U Vets. The war was a mistake, he said in recent yrs. Fri Jan 27.

WESTBROOK, ZERAH S, JUDGE, b Mon Apr 7, 1845, Montague, Sussex Co, found d in the Hoffman House, NY. Grad

Albany Law School. Admitted to the Bar 1867. Elected Pres Amsterdam Village 1873. Judge for Montgomery Co 1877, re-elected 1883. Appointed dep State Comptroller, serv til 1892. **SERV:** 15th Reg, NJ Vol. Mon Apr 30, 1900, Dateline Amsterdam, NY.

WESTERVELT, WILLIAM, 77, b Hackensack, d Sat Apr 21, 1917, Morristown. **SURV:** 2 dau. In Rahway abt 60 yrs, res at 227 Hamilton St. Conducted a large contracting and building biz, ret abt 15 yrs ago. An org of the R B&L Assoc. **MEM:** WFB27. **SERV:** 2nd NJ Vol. Mon Apr 23.
Jr V-Cmdr WFB27, attended the complimentary dinner for mems given by A Edward Woodruff Tue eve May 30, 1911.

WESTLAKE, SYLVANUS F, 74, d Mon ngt Jan 4, 1915, Alexian H, Eliz. Res 184 Union Ave, Roselle Park. **SERV:** Co H, 30th NJ Vol. Hon disc Sat Jun 27, 1868. F: Chapel of William Necker, 919 Elizabeth Ave, E. Int Connecticut Farms chh, Union, NJ. Tue Jan 5.

WESTON, EDWARD PAYSON, 90, d Mon May 13, 1929, Brooklyn. World famous walker, began his career as a walker while a CW spy in the U Army. Later, his ability to cover ground enabled him to beat rival reporters when he was on the NY Herald staff. A friend of Horace Greely and at the deathbed of the famous editor. His first long walk was at ae 22 when he trudged fm Boston to DC to attend Lincoln inauguration, covering the 443 miles in 208 hrs. Began his professional walking career in 1867 when he walked fm Portland, ME, to Chicago, 1326 miles in 26 days. Took part in many contests and exhibitions in America and Europe. In 1879 he won the Asiley (?) Belt in England by covering 550 miles in 141 hrs and 44 min. At age 70 walked 2895 miles fm NY to San Francisco in 104 days and 7 hrs. Spent last 2 yrs in a wheelchair, aft being hit by a taxicab. Tue May 14.

WHEELER, JOHN RICHARD, 78 and 8 mos, b in the W, d Mon mrng Jan 23, 1911, at home, 325 Williamson St, Eliz. **SURV:** s/dau. Came to E abt 35 yrs ago. A painter. Appointed to the new Central high school in 1887. 2 yrs later school moved into the Battin Bldg, and became known as the Battin High School. Held the record for the longest serv of any janitor of an E PS. Only 2 teachers remain when he first started as custodian. Ret last Dec. MEM: UD25, past Cmdr. WL35 F&AM, Washington Chap RAM KT, St Johns Commandery, and a Wrn lodge of the IOOF. SERV: Famous 74th Reg, first on the field of Chickamauga, and one of the last to leave. At Lookout Mountain and Missionary Ridge. F: Wed 230 pm Christ chh. Int Rosehill. Mon Jan 23. (P)

WHEELWRIGHT, GEORGE, 88, native of Brooklyn, NY, d Thu Jan 3, 1929, at home of dau Mrs W M Brownell, 39 Gerard St, S Manchester, CT. SURV: ch G/C Edward and Louis, Eliz, and Mrs Brownell. Res Eliz most of his life, and with dau for a yr. SERV: 13th Reg, NY Vol. F: At home of s Edward, 887 Colonia Rd. Fri Jan 4.

WHITE, NICHOLAS VAN SANT, 92, d Fri ngt Feb 8, 1935, at home, Long Branch. Built the summer residence in which U S Grant d. He built 2 homes in L B for the Grant fam, summer res for yrs. He and Grant, his wartime Cmdr, became acquainted then fast friends, spending many hrs reminiscing on war days. The first Marshal of the Boro of W L B. 3 terms on Eatontown Tp Comm. MEM: His d leaves 1 mem of the disb JBM46, Henry W Wingert. SERV: One of 2 surv of the 1,100 men of Co A, 14th NJ Vol. In 20 engage. WIA. Sat Feb 9.

WHITNEY, EBEN, CAPT, 83, d Jun 14, 1921, at his home, Flemington. SURV: w/dau Mrs P O Godown of F. Once res Jefferson Ave, Eliz. Aft CW worked 35 yrs for the Railway Mail Svc. A Repub. CHH: Central Bapt, when in Eliz. SERV: Vol officer for colored troops. Word of d rcvd Thu Jul 7.

WHITNEY, JOHN J, 77, b Perth Amboy, d Sat mrng Feb 14, 1920, at home, 84 W Jersey St, Eliz. SURV: w Emma Stringham Whitney/ch Samuel L, NY, and William H, Point Pleasant. sis Mrs Margaret Allen, Point Pleasant. Res E 55 yrs. Worked in Singer polishing dept, ret 16 yrs ago. MEM: UD25. Took great pleasure in decorating CW Vet graves on MDAY. **SERV:** Co D, 139th Inf, NY, 3 yrs. Sat Feb 14.

WILKE, HENRY, 84, b Germany, d Sat eve Feb 27, 1909, at home, 428 Elizabeth Ave, Eliz. **SURV:** ch Henry, Otto E, Frederick and Mrs Frederick Olinger. 4 gch. Res E abt 50 yrs. **SERV:** Co D, 1st Reg, NJ Vol, Wed May 22, 1861 to Thu May 21, 1863, Capt Mutchie, who d yrs ago. Hon disc. Mon Mar 1.

WILKINS, ISAAC, 77, native of NY, d Sat Jul 1, 1911, Rahway. **SURV:** ch Arthur, Delair and Everett R. A gdau. sib Mrs C R Oliver, Daytona, FL, and Alfred, Newark. Res R almost all his life. An expert carriage body builder, worked yrs for D B Dunham & Son, R, ret abt 2 yrs ago. **CHH:** 1st Presby. **SERV:** Cpl 30th MA Unattached Hvy Art. **F:** Wed 3 pm at home, 12 White St, Rev Graham Jr, P. Int Wilkins plot Rahway. Mon Jul 3.

WILKINSON, ALBERT, 64, b NYC, d Tue ngt Jan 11, 1910, at home, 710 S St, Eliz. **SURV:** A dau. Employ in auditing dept of Natl Express Co, NY. **SERV:** Troop E, 1st NY Cav. **F:** Fri eve. Int Greenwood, NY. Wed Jan 12.

WILKINSON, FRANK A, 57, b Newark, d Fri ngt Jan 25, 1901, Newark. **SURV:** w/3dau/2s. Treas of Wilkinson, Gaddis & Co. Dir Essex Natl Bank and of the Security Savings Inst. Pres Orville Milling Co of Orville, OH. Sec N Bangor Slate Co, and Dir Brooklyn Slate Mantel Co. **MEM:** B of Trade, the Essex Club, and the Soc of the AP. **CHH:** Pres B of Trustees St Lukes. **SERV:** Bat B, 1st NJ Vol Art. **F:** Tue 2 pm St Lukes. Int Evergreen. Mon Jan 28.

WILLIAMS, CHARLES T, 75, native of Newark, d Tue Apr 30, 1918, at home of s Ray F, Irvington. Super of Summer Ave Public Bath, Newark. **MEM:** Prominent in local and state GAR. **SERV:** Enl otbrk. POW 4 times, Belle Isle, Pemberton, Libby, and Andersonville. Thu May 2.

WILLIAMS, DAVID T, d Wed ngt Dec 20, 1916, S'H, Kearny. **SURV:** ch Mrs William Houfman and Frederick, Rahway, Adolphe, Baltimore, MD, Percy, Newark, and Charles, NYC.

Thu Dec 21. (Rahway Dateline)
WILLIAMS, GEORGE W, d early Thu Jun 23, 1910, PHL (Dateline), the 4th day of a torrid heat wave. Temperature at 10 am was 85 degrees and the humidity far more oppressive. d toll currently 26. **SERV:** Capt 118th Reg Vol. Thu Jun 23.

WILLIAMS, JARVIS W, b Tue Jun 24, 1834, NYC, s/o Daniel & Mary (Jarvis) Williams, d Sun Jan 6, 1929, Eliz. **SURV:** ch Mrs Ida F (Joseph) Heller, Harry W, 115 Sayre St, with whom he res aft d of w, and L D, who conducted a grocery store at 300 Westfield Ave. w was Mary Elizabeth Morris, d/o Louis, of Woodbridge, m 1857, d 1903. f, also a native of NYC, was a manu of wrought iron nails. Fam res 5 yrs on Willett St, off the ern section of Houston St, on the Lower E Side, now a crowded biz section. When he res there, there were less than 20 houses on the St, all frame cottages occupant owned. In 1839, fam rem to 5th St, NY, res in a house next to f's factory, where nails were made by a slow hand process. Fam still possesses a framed lithograph made more than 75 yrs ago showing the 5th St house and the 2 bldg factory. Aft 10 yrs on 5th St, rem to Woodbridge, taking up farming. Aft CW became a mason by trade, pursued earlier in NY, then rem to Rahway. Much of his work was in NYC, where jobs were more plentiful. Commuted on trains of the Jersey Transp Co, forerunner of the PA RR. Rem to Eliz in 1874, first at S Reid St, then Sayre St. Ret 30 yrs ago, then worked around store of s. Fam were Whigs then Repub, and he cast his 1st vote for John C Fremont, anti-slavery candidate opposing Buchanan, when Lincoln was only a struggling lawyer of Springfield, IL. Of Welsh, German and Dutch ancestry. **MEM:** UD25, 8 yrs as Cmdr. **SERV:** Enl Ford's Corner, now Fords, under Capt Bloomfield, s/o the man for whom the town of Bloomfield was named, and sent to Camp Wyman at Fort Hamilton, NY, assigned as Pvt in Co H, 48th NY Vol Reg, Col James H Perry, Cmdr. Fought in the 48 battles of the Reg, never WIA but caught smallpox, leading to a humorous but dangerous experience (See **Experiences**). At Hilton Head Island, Moultrie,

Pulaski, Port Royal SC, Port Royal Ferry, Savannah River, Bluffton, Morris Island, Fort Wagner, Shester Heights, Cold Harbor, Petersburg and Cemetery Hill. In 1864 serv as Orderly for Reg Surgeon, then mu/o Sep, 1864. **F:** Tue 2 pm at home, Rev Charles M Anderson, P Epworth ME, and Rev Allan Swift, P Trinity Pent. Mon Jan 7.
  F article Wed Jan 9. (P)
  Attended a Christmas party for CW Vets given by WRC27 Tue ngt. Wed Dec 23, 1925. (P)
  Purchases 1st poppy of MDAY, and Marshall of the parade. Wed May 23, 1928.(P)
  Attended UD25 annual Christmas party. Thu Dec 30. (P)
  Installed as Qtmstr at the UD25 meeting Tue ngt. Qtmstr-Sgt last 4 yrs. Tue Jan 8, 1924. (P)
WILLIAMS, JOHN H, 71, b Ireland, d Mon Mar 6, 1916, at home, 407 Monroe Ave, Eliz. **SURV:** w Nellie. Imm USA as a yng man. Res Brooklyn for yrs, rem to Eliz 4 yrs ago. Employ BNY, a foreman. **MEM:** Intl Assoc of Machinists, Brooklyn, and the Natl Soc of Andersonville Surv of NY. **CHH:** Immaculate Conception. HNS. **SERV:** Enl otbrk Co A, NY Vol Inf, to end. POW. Tue Mar 7.
WILLIAMS, WHITED, 80, d Fri Feb 28, 1908, found in one of the greenhouses of the S'H, Kearny. Wandered away Thu eve. **SERV:** Co G, 14th NJ Vol. **F:** Int Mon aftn Rahway. Sat Feb 29.
WILLIAMS, WILLIAM, b NY, d Thu Dec 15, 1932, at home, 580 Jackson Ave, Eliz. **SURV:** dau Mrs Gilbert Weeden, E. 2 gch. sib Luther, James and Joseph, all of Newburgh, NY, and Mrs Sarah Shay, Waldron, NY. Res some time in S River and rem to E 16 yrs ago. **MEM:** Riverside Council 33, Jr, OUAM, S River. **CHH:** S River Bapt. **SERV:** Enl Pvt Co K, 48th Inf. Also in Co I, 5th Reg Cav. Fri Dec 16.
WILLIAMS, WILLIAM H, b Sat Jun 15, 1839, NYC, d Mon mrng Jul 24, 1911, in the store of Mulford Estil, Plainfield. At an early age rem to Westfield, and at ae 22 to P. Conducted a newspaper agency for yrs. Of late, employ as a messenger for biz

men in NYC. **SERV:** Co D, 6th NJ Vol. At Bull Run. Mon Jul 24.
WILLIAMS, WILLIAM H, b Tue Nov 14, 1843, Westfield, s/o William & Phebe Seaman Williams, d Fri ngt Mar 1, 1918, at home, 19 Cherry St, Eliz. **SURV:** w frmr Anna L Vorhees, of E, m Sat Oct 20, 1866/ch Lillie, Mabel, G Henry and Clifford, E, Mrs J E Welch and Fred, Palermo. sib Mrs James O'Connor, Cranford, Seaman, Plainfield, and Joseph S, Plymouth. Except for brief absences, always Res E. Mason by trade, ret 6 yrs ago. **CHH:** 2nd Presby. **SERV:** Enl Pvt Tue Sep 17, 1861, Co A, 9th Reg, NJ Inf, Capt T B Applegate. Hon disc Tue Nov 24, 1863, Newport News. Reup next day same Co, disc Wed Jul 12, 1865, Greensboro. In many imp battles. POW 9 mos Andersonville. Sat Mar 2.

WILLIAMSON, PETER S, MAJ, b Sat Jul 20, 1844, Jersey City, d Sat mrng Apr 30, 1910, at home, Maple Ave, Rahway. **SURV:** w frmr Harriet J Hopson of Brooklyn, m 1874(?)/ch Stanley, cashier of the Menger Hotel, San Antonio, TX, and Mrs Charles Edwin Russ, R. gch Harriet and Stanley Russ. Res R 21 yrs. Desc fm an old rev fam prominent in the annals of NY. ggf was in RW, and gf in 1812. Rem to Brooklyn at an early age, where he rcvd a liberal educ. In 1871 entered the notion dept of H B Claflin & Co store in NY, working there until dod. For abt 3 yrs was confidential clerk to Judge Gildersleeve of the Supreme Court Bench. **SERV:** Enl Pvt Fri Sep 26, 1862, Co C, 150th Reg, NY Vol, 3 yrs. Garrison duty at different points for many mos. At Gettysburg, remaining some time aft at Kelly's Ford. Joined the Reg formed when the 11th and 12th Army Corps consolidated into the 20th under Gen Hooker. At Resacca, New Hope Church, Kenesaw Mountain, Pine Knob, Culp's Farm, Peach Tree Creek and Dalton, GA. Aft Reg arrived at Atlanta, GA, detailed as clerk to Gen Steedman. Joined Reg at Goldsboro, NC, in that engage. Mu/o Cpl Thu Jun 8, 1865. During the F obsequies of Gen Grant, in which GAR Post 327 bore a conspicuous part, serv on a relief guard at Albany on Aug 4, at NY on Aug 5 and 6, and on Maj Tait detail Aug 8. **F:** Tue 3 pm at home, Rev Dr C L Cooder,

Rector St Pauls Epis. Sat Apr 30.

WILLSEY, ANDREW J, 81, b NY, d Sat ngt Jan 17, 1914, at home, 416 Seton Ave, Roselle Park (Dateline). **SURV**: 2s/dau. Res R P for yrs. **MEM**: HW13. **F**: Orangetown, Rockland Co, NY, Palisade ME Chh. Int Palisade. Jan 19, 1914.

WILLSIE, HENRY, 70, d Mon ngt Nov 17, 1913, at home of s Henry E, Berkley Pl, Cranford. **SURV**: w/ch Henry E and Etta J. One of the early settlers of Fayette, IA. Worked in the contracting biz. Res C last 2 yrs. **SERV**: Co H, 9th IA Vol. WIA Pea Ridge. **F**: Tue aftn, Rev Gordon M Russell, assist Minister Presby Chh. Int Fayette. Tue Nov 18.

WILSON, JAMES A, d Mon aftn Dec 9, 1912, at home, 24 Union St, Eliz. **SURV**: w/ch Edith, Frederick and Herbert. Employ by Eliz Ice Co. **MEM**: UD25. **SERV**: Pvt Co H, 5th Reg, NJ Vol Inf. Tue Dec 10.

WILSON, JAMES HARRISON, MAJ GEN, b Sat Sep 2, 1837, Shawneetown, IL, d Mon Feb 23, 1925, at his home, Wilmington, DE. **SURV**: ch Mrs Henry B Thompson, W, and Mrs Edward Carey Willard, Hyde Park, MA. Earliest known f ancestor was in RW, and f was a Capt in the Black Hawk War (1832) and a Col in the IL Militia. Educ McKendree College, Lebanon, IL, and grad WP 1860, assigned as topographical eng. Aft military svc, built and managed RR in the MS valley and NE, notably the Cairo & Vincennes, the St Louis & SErn, and the Louisville, Evansville & St Louis Air Line. Chairman of the DE Repub State Comm for yrs, and at one time mem Repub Natl Comm. An author, writing biographies of Gens Andrew T Alexander, McCook, John A Rawlins and Grant. Also wrote *Under The Flag*, a book of reminiscences, and *China Travels and Investigations in the Middle Kingdom*, based on his travels in China where he engaged in RR work. **SERV**: Last of the Corps Cmdr of either the U or C forces and last mem Grant staff. Famous as captor of Jefferson Davis. At the head of 15,000 mounted men, conducted the campaign through AL and GA known as "Wilson's Raid." Ret 1870, returning to the Army for the S/AW and the Boxer campaign in China. In Feb, 1901, appointed a Brig Gen of the Regular Army by Act of Congress, and ret for age shortly aft. On Jan 14, 1902, Pres Roosevelt appointed him a mem of the special embassy to represent the USA at the Coronation of King Edward VII. Mon Feb 23.

WILSON, JOHN F, 77, native of MS, d Sun mrng Oct 10, 1909, at home, Plainfield. Found d by dau Mrs J P Truitt. Only s Allan also dropped d just a yr ago while touring Scotland. Res P 40 yrs. Aft CW rem to Baltimore and became head of the coal biz for Baltimore & Ohio RR, ret 17 yrs ago. A Dem, Mayor of N Plainfield 2 yrs, one of only 3 Dems ever holding that office. **SERV**: C Col. **F**: Int Baltimore. Mon Oct 11.

WILSON, JOHN WARREN, 63, b Eliz, d Mon Oct 4, 1904, at home, 62 8th Ave, Brooklyn. **SURV**: w/2s/3dau. Took up res in NY when a yng man. Head of the firm of J W Wilson & Co, exporters and importers at 52 Front St, NY. A Dir of the Atlantic Mutual Marine Ins Co. **MEM**: CoC. Montauk Club. James Monroe Post, GAR. **SERV**: 22nd NY Reg, to end. Tue Oct 4.

WILSON, MATTHEW, 60, d Sat mrng Nov 4, 1911, Eliz. **SURV**: bro and s, E, it is believed. Inmate of the S'H, Kearny, for some time. When attempts were made to have him sent back, he said, "I would rather be in jail than in the S'H." Sat Nov 4.

WINANS, ELIAS CRANE, 61, b Linden tp, s/o Nathan, gs/o Aaron, d Thu 430 am Aug 13, 1903, at home, 149 Liberty St, Eliz. **SURV**: w frmr Miss Lydia Shotwell, m soon aft CW end, Rev Dr Kempshalt/ch Frederick Shotwell, Edward P and Mrs Mary E Godfrey, NY. gch Clara F and Mabel Godfrey. dau Amie d a few yrs ago. Res E 35 yrs, last 23 yrs Liberty St. Painter by trade. **MEM**: UD25. **SERV**: Enl ae 18 Co K, 9th NJ Vol, Capt Jonathan Townley. Disc Wed Dec 7, 1864. A graphic sketch on Winans's heroism is taken fm Gen Drake's Hist of the 9th NJ Vol (See **Experiences**). Thu Aug 13.

WINTERS, WILLIAM, 86, d early Wed mrng Aug 29, 1900, at home, 16 Kearny Ave, Kearny. w d Mon Aug 27. Some yrs ago a figure in NJ politics. A cuz to VP Hobart. **F**: A double Thu at home. Wed Aug 29.

WODEY, AUGUSTUS F, 63, b Eliz, d Sun Jul 17, 1910, Alexian H, Eliz. Res 353 Elizabeth Ave. MEM: Vol FD, foreman old Engine Co 4, and assist Chief. A Mason SERV: Enl ae 14 1861 Navy as a Cabin Boy on the "Moonlight." In many battles. When "Moonlight" was defeated in an encounter with one of the C boats, he and other crew mem were captured. Taken to TX, penned in an open stockade with other naval POW, and treated as were all POW during the CW. No shelter was provided. They were given only the poorest of food and very little of that. The water was bad, and many POW were not even provided with blankets. Escaped aft 2 yrs. Being only a boy, his health was ruined for life, his final illness attributed to this. For 38 yrs an eng for Central RR, ret many yrs ago due to health. (Partial obit) Mon Jul 18.

WOLF, GEORGE, 76, b 1858, Easton, PA, d early Tue Jan 23, 1917, at home, 124 5th Ave, E, Roselle. SURV: w/ch Mrs Selden Greves, Georgette and Marguerite, all R. Started working in gen passenger dept as a clerk in 1858 for Central RR, and a traffic auditor in 1887. Completed 59 yrs of svc at dod. MEM: UD25. R Council, RA. Tue Jan 23.

WOLTERS, CHARLES HENRY, 71, b NY, d Thu Mar 18, 1920, at home, 137 Roselle Ave, Roselle Park. SURV: w Elizabeth Mesch Wolters/s Jacob. sib Julius and Henry, Eliz. Res R P 10 yrs, coming fm Eliz, where he res 22 yrs. A ret molder. SERV: Co D, 1st NY Eng, 1862 to end. Enl 19th Inf Regulars, 3 yrs. Fri Mar 19.

WOODARD, WALTON, 67, native of Oneida Co, NY, d Sat ngt Apr 30, 1904, at home, 1019 Olive St, Eliz. SURV: w/s/dau. Res E 36 yrs. Well-known expressman. MEM: ERL IOOF, and Harmony Council DL. CHH: A founder of Westminster Hope Chapel, Olive St. SERV: Co B, 4th NJ Vol. F: Tue 230 pm at Hope, Rev William B Hamilton. Int S&S' plot, Evergreen. Mems R L IOOF, of which w is a mem, invited to attend. Mon May 2.

WOODHOUSE, JOHN HENRY, 65, native and lifelong res of

Rahway, d Thu ngt Oct 26, 1911, at home of sis Mrs William Baker, 8 Elm Ave, Rahway. **SURV**: dau Mrs John Silkworth. sib Mrs Baker and Mrs William Corbin, Elm Ave. A baggage master for PA RR 30+ yrs, recently pensioned. **MEM**: GAR. Union Council 31, Jr, OUAM. **SERV**: Co G, 37th Reg, NJ Vol Inf. **F**: Sun aftn at home, Rev C L Cooder, Rector St Pauls Episc. Int fam plot R. Sat Oct 28.

Attended the complimentary dinner for Barry 27 mems given by A Edward Woodruff Tue eve May 30, 1911.

WOODRUFF, AMOS, s/o late Amos & Rachael, d Wed Apr 9, 1902, Fordham, NY. A bro/o Henry C, 461 Morris Ave, Eliz. Another bro, Valentine, frmr Eliz res, d a few days ago, Yonkers, NY. Elsie Westervelt, d Apr 2 ae 80, and who had been hired at ae 20 by Amos the f, was int in the fam vault in accordance with a clause in his will. **MEM**: Lafayette Post GAR NY. **F**: Fri 3 pm fm his Kirkside Ave home. Fri Apr 11.

WORTS, HENRY NELSON, 76, d Sun Nov 29, 1925, at Webb Inst, NY. **SURV**: s William E, Belleville. 2 gch. Res Eliz since S/AW, 11 S Spring St. Employ in the Title Searching Room at the Courthouse, where he took care of the records. **SERV**: Enl ae 15 Navy during the CW and serv until close of S/AW in 1899. Under Adm Farragut in CW. **F**: D J Leonard Home for F, 1143 Elizabeth Ave. Mon Nov 30.

WRIGHT, CHARLES F, 89, b N Adams, MA, d Tue ngt Feb 5, 1935, at home, Westfield Ave, Westfield. **SURV**: ch Capt Harold B, Vet S/AW, with whom he res for the past yr, and Charles F, Jr, Bloomfield. 5 gs. A ggd. Grand Marshall in the MDAY parade last yr. **SERV**: Enl 32nd MA Inf. Attached to Gen Butler Div, which saw svc around New Orleans. Incapacitated and spent 2 yrs in a New Orleans H. Wed Feb 6.

WRIGHT, JAMES, b Ireland, d Wed eve Jul 12, 1911, at home, 75 Livingston St, Eliz. **SURV**: w Mary/ch Mrs Louis Miller, Brooklyn, Mrs Frank Kylisch, Mrs Herbert Jones and Mrs William Davenport, all E, Albert and Wilbur. A step-s George Parsons. 14 gch. Imm USA a yng man to NYC. Rem to E 27 yrs

ago. SERV: 4th Art NY. F: Fri eve at home, Rev Joseph B Ferguson, Greystone Presby. Int fam plot Evergreen. Thu Jul 13.
WRIGHT, WILLIAM P, CAPT, b 1845, Naperville, IL, a suburb of Chicago, d Thu Jun 15, 1933, Pittsburgh, PA. Rem to Chicago just bfr the 1871 Great Chicago Fire. A yr later m, and last Oct celeb 60th m anniv. Their only s d svrl yrs ago. Conducted a real estate biz on the S side last 30 yrs. MEM: GAR, natl cmdr. In Pittsburgh to attend the annual encmp of the PA dept. Addressed a gathering of Vets and auxilliary orgs Wed ngt aft riding in the GAR Flag Day parade. Past Cmdr IL Dept GAR, elected natl cmdr last Sep, camping with his comrades of the U Army at the tomb of Lincoln in Springfield, IL. Prev chairman of the natl council of admin. SERV: Enl in teens Co D, 156th IL Inf. Thu Jun 15. (P)
WYMS, JAMES N, 83, d MDAY (Dateline Thu May 31), 1928, Marlborough, NY. When giving a MDAY speech to 500 people, he said, "I can remember at Gettysburg—" and dropped d. Led the MDAY parade at M for the last 30 yrs. Thu May 31.

Y

YOUNGLOVE, JOHN, DR, 91, b 1837, Trenton, NY, d Thu Jan 17, 1929, at home, 407 Jefferson Ave, Eliz. SURV: w frmr Miss Gertrude Langdon/ch Herbert B, Mrs H E Everett, E Orange, Mrs K W Whitehead, Ocean Grove, and Mrs W F Larned, NYC. gs Donald L Whitehead. Rem to Utica ae 13, rcvg his early educ there and in T. Went to Washington Medical College and later to St Louis Homeopathic College. Rem to Eliz 1867 and practiced medicine there ever since. Shook hands with 5 USA Pres. One of few men to hold the distinction of shaking hands with Buchanan at an 1857 New Years Day White House reception. Met Lincoln Fri Dec 26, 1862, on the battlefield of Falmouth, VA, where Gen Sickles had his HQ. First saw Grant at Spottsylvania, but formally introduced when Grant, then Pres, came to E to visit his sis, Mrs Abel Corbin, of 518 N Broad St, an aunt of William H Corbin, then of 570 N Broad. Also met Pres Theodore Roosevelt and William Howard Taft. Ancestry dates back to 1636 fm England. Ggggf was Chairman of the 1st convention in NY State to consider independence. Ggf was Col John Younglove of RW fame. **MEM:** Charter mem NJ Homeopathic Medical Soc. NY Academy of Science. UD25. Moose Lodge. Honorary mem VFW. **CHH:** 1st Presby. **SERV:** Enl 1st NY Mounted Rifles, called Cav today, and won a warrant as Cpl. Transf to 71st NY Vol Inf, AP, to near end, then transf to Regular Army as a Surgeon. At Chancellorsville, Gettysburg, Fredericksburg, the Wilderness, and Spottsylvania. Appointed 1st Lt Regular Army by Sec of War Stanton, serv at Sandy Hook, VA. Became close friend of Clara Barton. Mu/o at end, and given Brevet-Maj title by NY Gov Reuben E Fenton. **F:** Sat 2 pm at home, Rev Charles J Wood, DD, P. Fri Jan 18. (P)

In memory of Abraham Lincoln, by Linden's PS Fri aftn. They listened to an address by Dr Younglove, who had enjoyed the acquaintence of Lincoln. Capt E S E Newbury, CW Vet, also spoke. The Dr's eloquent address on "Lincoln." was listened to with ernest attention and heartily applauded. Sat Feb 11, 1905.

Aft CW res Troy, NY, then rem to E. Installed as Post Surgeon at the UD25 meeting Tue ngt. Tue Jan 8, 1924. (P)

Z

ZIMMERMAN, HENRY, 65, d Thu Oct 4, 1917, Eliz. **SURV:** w Sarah McCarnan Zimmerman/ch Frank, Asbury, Harry and Jacob, E, Mrs G A Allen, Madison, and Mrs H W Mott. Res 1032 Grove St, and E since 1871. Carpenter by trade up to 7 yrs ago. **MEM:** Treas Central Labor Union at dod. Treas of the local Carpenters Union Memorial Lodge IOOF. UD25. Capt in the frmr Vet Z. **SERV:** Enl 1863 11th Reg NY Vol, and later 3 yrs in the Lgt Art, Regular Army. Fri Oct 5. (P)

ZIMMERMAN, WILLIAM, 79, b Germany, d Fri Jan 6, 1922, NJ State Firemens Home, Boonton. **SURV:** sib Mrs Frederick

Prott, Mrs Louis Messing, Henry, Albert and Otto, all E, and Louis, Il. Imm USA ae 2 with par to E. Last res Hampton Pl. Late f William, Sr, bfr 1870 conducted an inn called Yellowstone Tavern, near the present site of the Heidritter Lumber Co plant, New Point Rd. **MEM:** E FD during the vol days. UD25. Frmr Vet Z. VVFA. **SERV:** Sgt 9th NJ Reg. Sat Jan 7.

ZIMMERMANN, WILLIAM, d Thu mrng Aug 16, 1900, Alexian H, Eliz. **SURV:** w/8ch. Res E for yrs. In the shoe biz near the city market for yrs. When PS1 was constructed on E Jersey St, appointed as a janitor. **MEM:** Frmrly with the Washington Steam Fire Engine Co. EFA. UD25, mu/i Mon Apr 21, 1879. **SERV:** 145th and 123rd NY Vol. Also in the Navy. F: Sun aftn at home, 42 Delaware St.

ZOOK, JOHN M, 94, d Wed ngt Mar 10, 1937, PHL (Dateline). Widely known as a cyclist, taking part in numerous cycling events. Among his trophies was a badge fm the Century Wheelman for the 100 mile run fm Newark, NJ, to PHL, PA. **SERV:** At Gettysburg. Thu Mar 11.

CHAPTER 2

CW VETS FROM OBITUARIES AND ARTICLES OF FAMILY MEMBERS

ARMSTRONG, ISABELLE, MRS, d Sun Jan 26, 1913, Newark. SURV: 6ch, incldg William C of Eliz. 4 gch. 3 ggch. wid/o William C, who d a few yrs ago. Res Trenton for yrs. F: Wed, Trenton, attended by mem of Bayard 8, and Dayton Camp SoV. Wed Jan 29.

BAUMAN, ELIZABETH, MRS, 62 yrs, 8 mos, 1 day, d at home, 414 Spring St, Eliz. SURV: h/ch George, Peter, Philip, Mrs Thomas McNair, Elizabeth and Barbara. An aunt of Councilman Kleinhans. Her h serv in 9th NJ Vol. Res E abt 50 yrs. **CHH:** Sacred Heart. F: Wed mrng. Obit not dated, d same day as Maj Rufus King.

BEAR, MARTHA E, MRS, 86, b Portsmouth, VA, d/o late Col Turner Wallace, a CW Srn military leader, & the late Mary Nellie, d Tue Nov 29, 1927, at home of dau Mrs Eva Vreeland, 401 3rd Ave, Newark. SURV: ch Mrs Vreeland, Mrs William H Ward, once of 242 Westfield Ave, now of 128 Murray St, with whom she res bfr rem to Newark last yr, Mrs M C Partridge, E Orange, and Mrs A C Kane, N. 28 gch. 30 ggch. 2 gggch. wid/o George, who d E Orange 14 yrs ago. Res E Orange abt 35 yrs. Par were both mem of early VA fams. h was one of the first white men to enter Japan when that nation was opened by Com Perry to the commerce of the world. Wed Nov 30.

BERRY, MARY A, MRS, b 1855, Cherryfield, ME, d Thu mrng May 30, 1918, at home of sis Mrs Charles M Bartlett, 518 Westfield Ave, Westfield (Dateline). SURV: ch Earl S, Syracuse, NY, and Stewart F, Chicago. sib Mrs Bartlett, A J Wilson, Randolph, VT, past res of W and once mem Town Council, and J A Wilson, Cherryfield, ME. wid/o Rufus W. Fri May 31.

BULL, ARCHIBALD H, 73 last Jan 14, d Fri 1 pm Feb 13,

1920, at home, 225 W Jersey St, Eliz. **SURV:** w Evelyn Van Deventer Bull/ch Mrs Willard A Kiggins, E, Mrs Louis McLean, Winnipeg, Canada, and Ernest. f, an Army officer KIA in CW, left him and svrl bro practically unprovided, for they were not given many advantages for educ. Attended NY PS, and aft grammar school, home financial conditions necessitated his going to work, securing pos as an office boy then clerk. Entered shipping biz ae 18, serv a few yrs as clerk for the Miller Shipping Co, afterwards becoming an official. Founded and became Pres Bull Steamship Co. He and w res Eliz since 1870, first at Williams St. Aft a few yrs, rem to E Grand St, and 25 yrs ago he built the home at E Jersey & Morrell St. 2-3 yrs ago erected home on W Jersey St. **MEM:** Pres Economical Homes Assoc of Eliz. **CHH:** 3rd Presby. Teacher of the mens bible class. Fri Feb 13. (See obit of James Henry Bull)

CONANT, CAROLINE MELVIN, MRS, 101, b Concord, MA, d Fri ngt Nov 26, 1937, Brookline, MA (Dateline). b when Jackson Pres. gd/o an American Minute Man. 4 bro serv in CW, 3 being KIA. **MEM:** DAR. Sat Nov 27.

DAVENPORT, FREDERICK ST JOHN, 39, b Eliz, s/o late Sgt William, d sat Aug 26, 1911, at home, Atlanta, GA. **SURV:** w/2 ch. mo, Adaline H. sib William T, George B and Daisy A, Brooklyn, and Mrs Charles D Young, of New London. f serv throughout CW, 2nd NJ Vol. Worked for Wrn Union Telegraph Co, E, then NY and NJ Telephone Co, E. Rem to Atlanta some yrs ago for the phone co. **F:** Mon aftn attended by sib. Mon Aug 28.

DAVIS, ALICE M, MRS, 93, b Tamaqua, PA, d/o William Higgins, d Sat mrng Feb 11, 1939, at home, 13 Delaware St, Eliz. **SURV:** ch William E, Catherine, R Jane and Mrs Hugh C Boyle, E, and Margaret, PHL. 17 gch. 5 ggch. wid/o Capt David Williams, 8th PA Cav. f imm USA 1826 fm Co Donegal, Ireland, to T, when it was an Indian village, building the first house there. At CW otbrk, he financed and equipped a Reg known as the Jackson Guards. s Dr George Higgins was Reg Col. 6 nephews

of Mrs Davis saw active WW svc. One, Rear-Adm William A Gill, USN, was KIA a month bfr the Armistice when the Flagship "Ticonderoga" was blown up. She was niece to the late Rev Hugh and Rev Charles O'Donnell, RC Priests of Ireland, and a cuz to the late Cardinal O'Donnell of Ireland. Margaret serv with the ARC during the WW as a medical social worker. Catherine, active in ARC charitable circle, E, is a district Deputy, Catholic Daus of America. CHH: Holy Rosary, E. HRS. Sat Feb 11.
DAVIS, SARAH, MRS, native of Linden Tp, d Mon Jul 26, 1909, Eliz Gen H, Eliz. SURV: ch Philip and Mrs Sarah Gibbs. bro George Searns, Brooklyn. 8 gch. wid/o Joseph. Res E nearly all her life. CHH: Mt Teman AME, E. Tue Jul 27. (No mention of color. AME chh specified in obit)
DEBO, JOANNA, MRS, d Sat eve Jul 24, 1909, at home, 1076 E Grand St, Eliz. SURV: s Fred S. sib Mrs Willam Strahan. 3 gch. wid/o Charles Allison. mn Green. Lifelong res E. CHH: Serv for yrs as parish visitor for Rev Dr W S Langford, Rev Dr Otis A Glazebrook, St Johns, and Rev Dr Henry Hale Sleeper, Grace Chh. F: Tue aftn at home, Rev Dr Glazebrook. Mon Jul 26.
DIMLER, CHRISTINA, MRS, 83, b Germany, d Mon Apr 11, at home of dau Mrs J P Arnold, 76 E Jersey St, with whom she res, Eliz. SURV: ch Mrs Arnold, William and David. wid/o David. Res E 61 yrs. CHH: German Luth. Ladies Aid Soc. Tue Apr 12.
DOWNEY, MARY, MRS, d Fri Apr 5, 1907, at home, 229 Marshall St, Eliz. SURV: ch Michael F and Bernard, E, Frank, Helena, MT, Mrs Farmer, NY, and Mrs Flynn, E. 12 gch. wid/o Kermon, serv 2nd NJ Cav, d 18 yrs ago. Res E 50 yrs. CHH: St Patricks. Sat Apr 6.
EWING, CHARLES, MRS, 91, b Mt Vernon, OH, wid/o a U Army Gen, and a DC Belle in post-CW days, d Thu Oct 21, 1937, Washington (Dateline). Fri Oct 22.
GREEN, CORDELIA, MRS, 75, native of New Rochelle, NY, d Fri 130 am Aug 3, 1928, at home of nephew Thomas Oliphant,

10 Henry St, Rahway. **SURV**: Nephew. sis Mrs Estelle Oliphant, Denver, CO. wid/o Franklin, d abt 7 yrs ago, Suffern, NY. Res R past 5 yrs. Bfr Suffern, res Brooklyn for yrs. In early life res Springfield, MA. **CHH**: Meth, joining at Springfield. F: Lehrers. Int Plainfield. Fri Aug 3.
HALL, MARY HALSEY, MRS, 72, d/o late Ichabod Robinson, d Sun ngt Feb 6, 1910, at home, 1170 N Broad St, Eliz. **SURV**: h, inmate of the S'H in CA. s George W. bro Preston Robinson. Res E for yrs. **CHH**: 2nd Presby. Mon Feb 7.
HALLY, MARGARET, MRS, 79, native of NY state, d Thu aftn Jun 6, 1929, St Eliz H, Eliz. **SURV**: Nephews and nieces, Timothy O'Connell, Lafayette St, Miss Josie Hally, 137 W Grand St, and others, Atlantic City and Brooklyn. sis-in-law res with her past 15 yrs. s Frank d 8 mos ago. wid/o John, d abt 35 yrs ago. Res 64 E Grand St, Rahway, and Rahway 75 yrs. **CHH**: St Marys. Altar Guild and others. Fri Jun 7.
HEADLEY, See POYSHER.
HENRY, ELLEN, MRS, 84, lifelong res Eliz, d Wed mrng Mar 18, 1931, at home, 145 Smith, Eliz. **SURV**: ch Lucian, William, Mrs Susan Bedell, and Mrs Anna V Lott. 9 gch. 9 ggch. wid/o Henry, d 25 yrs ago. **CHH**: St James ME. Mem Home Dept of the SS. Frmrly with old Fulton St ME. Wed Mar 18.
HIGGINS, JAMES WARD, b Thu Feb 21, 1839, ncar Kenilworth, abt 2 mi N of the Roselle Park Boro line, s/o David S & Margaret Searing Higgins, d Wed 330 pm Apr 1, 1914, at home, 403 Chestnut St, Roselle Park. **SURV**: w frmr Miss Adelia L Littlefield of Woburn, MA/ch J Wallace, frmr Boro eng, and Dr Spencer Littlefield, US Navy. gs J Wallace Higgins, Jr. sib Mrs Margaret A Townley, wid/o Rev H C, and Mrs Rebecca Richards, Peekskill, NY, and Mrs Phoebe N Long, Raritan. A bro, David, serv 4 yrs in CW. The Higgens fam name dates back in Union Tp to the RW, with gf James in RW. Fm gf, 4 gens were b within a radius of 2 mi in Union Tp. Attended the old Chestnut Grove school, then a student at the Suffield Literary Inst, Suffield, CT, and Clavarack Academy, Clavarack, NY. Once

one of the most successful farmers in Union Co. Rem to the Boro in 1892 and entered biz, assoc with Joseph Gordon, bro/o School Com Robert, in a feed and grain store, ret 1900. A Repub, voting for Taft and Lincoln. MEM: Union Co B of Ag, a term as trustee district school 25. CHH: He and w were constituent mem when R Bapt was inst, mem near 40 yrs, Trustee until recently. Deacon for yrs, up to dod. F: Sat 230 pm, Rev C E Goodale, 1st Bapt. Int Evergreen. Thu Apr 2.

HODGINS, MARY, MRS, 76, d Wed Apr 10, 1901, at home, 346 Bond St, Eliz. SURV: Twice m. By 1/h James Nealon, ch Mrs Chas P Davis, LI, Mrs Ahearn, E, and John J, the jeweler. By 2/h George, a dau, w/o Joseph Kelly. wid/o George, Vol 69th and 88th NY Reg, WIA Chancellorsville. CHH: A pioneer mem St Patricks. Rosary Society. Thu Apr 11.

HYDE, LORETTA E, 90, b Saugerties, NY, went to the mid W with her par as a small ch. Remembers going fm Wacon, IA, to Freeport, IL, at ae 13, in a covered wagon. wid/o B F Hyde, m 1874, res in the vcnty Chicago bfr rem to Westfield 10 yrs ago with the Bronsons. Her dau Mrs D F Bronson gave an open house Mon for mo 90th dob, at their 764 Fairacres Ave home. s Harlow res Indianapolis, and another dau, whom she has visited 5 times, Mrs J C Boyd, res Rialto, CA. 6 gch, Mrs Lawrence Everhart, Eliz, Harlow Hyde, Jr, and Barbara Boyd, Rialto, Donald and Keith Bronson, students at the Univ of MI, and their young bro Bruce. MEM: Frmr Pres of GAR Circle, Austin, IL, many yrs. CHH: 1st Meth. Dateline Westfield, Wed Mar 2, 1938.

JOHNSON, CORDELIA D, mn TOWNLEY, MRS, b Tue Jul 25, 1837, Scotch Plains, d Sat aftn Jul 23, 1938, at the 26 Beechwood Pl home of her s-in-law Richard S Earl, frmr head of the Hillside Tp Comm, Hillside. SURV: dau Emma A. bro J Hervey Townley, Westfield, ae 92 Tue. gch Marion J Earl, Beechwood Pl, Mrs Frank Wesley Smith, Waban, MA, and Frederick G Cole, Jr, E Orange. ggch, Douglas and Richard Smith, Waban, MA. Lost a bro in the CW. gmo lived to ae 102. mo, a sis, and mo-in-law all were nonagenarians. Rem to

Westfield as a child, and in 1861 m Harris L Johnson, a Broad St grocer, who brought her to Eliz as a bride. Rem with dau to H 7 yrs ago. Her h d 1898. 1st Eliz home was at 1187 E Grand St, which was unpaved. Across the St was the old 2nd Presby parsonage where Rev John H Pingry, DD, res, and who taught a few boys, thus starting the present Pingry School. Recalled the hardships of the CW period, the scarcity of staple articles, the high prices, and the "shin plasters," which were worth scarcely more than the paper on which they were printed. Housewives not only made their own bread but made their own candles and soap, "or else did without." Modern conveniences made life easier, she used to say, but she deplored the present tendency to "selfishness," "lack of neighborliness," and the ambition to "get something for nothing." Mon Jul 25. (P)

KENDALL, FLORENCE HELEN, MRS, HEROINE, d/o late Isaac Messmore, d Fri Jan 20, 1939, Palm Beach, FL. f was a Col in Gen Grant WI Vol, and a US Senator fm MI. At WW otbrk, bought 2 ambulances and took them to France, and drove one herself, despite her age. Saw much of the front lines and made many spectacular rescues of WIA men. Later maintained a H at Romavantin. Christened the first American airplane to fly in France in the conflict and given a war medal by the French govt. Mon Jan 23.

LA MOTTE, EDGAR E, 33 yrs, 5 mos, 26 days, d Thu ngt Feb 16, 1911, Gen H, Eliz. SURV: mo, Ellen. sib Walter, Arthur, Joseph, Nelson, Wilbur and Mrs Charles Holste. s/o late Walter, Co B, 30th Reg, and Co B, 35th Reg. Educ PS3. Electrician by trade. **MEM**: FD, Engine Co 2, abt 1 yr. **SERV**: S/AW, enl Wed Oct 18, 1899, Pvt Co D, 41st Reg Inf, US Vol. 2 yrs svc in Philippines, taking part in 2 expeditions under Gen Grant, one to Bulcan Province, the other to Pampanza Province. At Battle of Corona Mountains, Tue Jun 12, 1900, and in a skirmish at Zambales Mountains Feb 1901. Hon disc Wed Jul 3. Fri Feb 17.

LONGSTREET, JAMES, MRS, wid/o C Gen Longstreet, attended the 75th Gettysburg B&G R. (See **Reunion**)(P)

LUCKHURST, ELIZABETH, MRS, 75, native of Red Bank, d Sat mrng Jan 28, 1928, at home of dau Mrs J L Egan, 61 E Hazelwood Ave, Rahway. **SURV**: ch Mrs Egan, James B, with whom she res, and William J, 78 Maple Ave. 7 gch. sib Miss Julia Ennis, St Joseph Inst for Blind, NYC, Mrs Jennie Stansfield Lynnbrook, LI, Mrs Annie Egan, Mrs John Hicks, and Mrs Joseph Kelly, Long Branch. wid/o James H. Res R 50 yrs. **CHH**: St Marys. Sat Jan 28.

LUDEY, EMMA T, MRS, 83, native of Cambelwell, England, d early Fri mrng Jun 9, 1933, at home of dau Mrs Lynn E Jennison, 34 Melrose Ter, Eliz. **SURV**: dau. 5 gch. 6 ggch. wid/o Francis C, serv 4 yrs 14th NJ Vol. Imm USA 78 yrs ago. Res Bayonne most of her life, and E last 5 yrs. Fri Jun 9.

MARSH, MARTHA L, MRS, 75, d Tue eve Jun 10, 1924, Gen H, Eliz. **SURV**: ch Mrs John Lyons, 81 Elizabeth Ave, Mrs Ernest Regenthal and Mrs John DeHart, New Brunswick, and Mrs John VanHart, 561 2nd Ave, E. sib Mrs Sophie Billins, Newark, and Mrs Elizabeth King and John A VanPelt, E. 12 gch. 8 ggch. wid/o Charles. Res 83 Elizabeth Ave, and E for 60 yrs. **MEM**: Affiliated with a New Brunswick Lodge of the DAR. Elizabeth Council 10 S&D of L. SB. LRC, GAR. Camp 87 PO of A. Dames of Malta. **CHH**: East Bapt. **F**: At home of Mrs VanHart. Wed Jun 11.

MARTIN, ISABELLA M, MRS, 77, native of Eliz, d Wed 745 pm Sep 17, 1913, at home of s, 471 Walnut St, Eliz. **SURV**: ch George B, Mrs L F Neff, Sunbury, PA, and Mrs W B Ward, NYC. sib Miss Elizabeth Sparkes, Brooklyn, and George P Baker, Roselle. wid/o Capt Luther, 11th NJ Inf, KIA Gettysburg. Res E almost all her life. **CHH**: 1st Presby. Home Dept of the SS. Thu Sep 18.

MCDOWELL, JOSEPHINE TIMANUS, MRS, b Mon May 27, 1850, Columbia, SC, d/o late Col Henry & Caroline Marsh Timanus of Fernandina, FL, d late Mon ngt Mar 7, 1921, Memorial H, Newark. **SURV**: h William O, 201 Grafton Ave, N/ dau Pauline, teacher of chemistry at Battin HS. f serv in C Army.

Educ St Marys Epis Priory, Fernandina. m Mon Nov 17, 1873, and res first 7 yrs Bloomfield, and since then N. F: Thu 3 pm at home. Wed Mar 9.

MCLEOD, CATHERINE, MRS, 78, native of Nova Scotia, d Sat aftn Mar 21, 1931, at home, 1175 Chestnut St, Eliz. **SURV:** ch Neil, Co Clerk, and John V, PHL. 2 gch. wid/o Neil, Sr, Cmdr 2 yrs U/D25. Res E most of her life. **MEM:** ST, Lincoln Div. **CHH:** 2nd Presby. Mon Mar 23.

PHILLIPS, ELIZABETH BUFORD, MRS, 83, d Fri Nov 20, 1925, Bloomfield (Dateline). Honorary Pres United Dau of the Confederacy. wid/o James A, said to be the sol who fired the first gun of the CW at Fort Sumter. F: Mon. Mon Nov 23.

POYSHER, JONAH P and MARY F, celeb their 67th m anniv Mon Dec 12, 1938. He is ae 93, and b Warren Co. Res most of his early life in Rahway. She is ae 87, b in the Union house where they now live, on a section of Vauxhall Rd near the Lehigh Valley RR, which was cut off fm the present roadway when the thoroughfare was paved and straightened a couple of yrs ago. Her mn was Headley and the section where the house sits was known as Headley Town, aft her fam, who originally settled the region. When a girl the only res in the vcnty of her home were Headleys, now she is the only one. A dau res in Ocean Grove and a s just outside of Ocean Grove. Her f and a bro both d in the CW Dateline Union, Mon, Dec 12.

RIEHL, CHARLES G, b Phl, s/o late Col John S, who cmd a CW PA Reg, d Mon ngt, Dec 23, 1907, at home, 1033 Lafayette St, Eliz. **SURV:** w frmr Miss Eckman/3s/dau. Res E 27 yrs. Worked for Samuel L Moore Sons Corp as an expert machinist. **MEM:** OBL78, KP. AC25, Order United American Mechanics. **CHH:** Central Bapt. **F:** Fri at home, Rev Dr Tomlinson. Int Rosedale and Linden Park. Tue Dec 24.

ROBINSON, ELIZA E, MRS, 74, native of New Brunswick, d early Fri Feb 19, 1932, at home of s John V, 239 Hamilton St, where she res for mos, Rahway. **SURV:** ch John B/V, William, Main St, Dennis, Commerce St, all R, Oscar, Millburn, George,

Highland Park, Mrs Arthur Hamer and Sadie, N B, and Mrs Matilda Brunt, Eliz. 17 gch. 12 ggch. bro William Rubeck, W Grand St, R. wid/o James E, d 1905. Always res N B and venty until rem to R. **CHH:** Pitman Meth. **F:** Rev George A Law, N Plainfield Meth, frmly of R. Fri Feb 19.

ROWE, HANNAH, MRS, 86, d Sun Dec 4, 1910, St Elizabeth H, Eliz. wid/o Matthew, Co G, 9th Reg, NJ Vol. Had no relatives, roomed with friends Magnolia Ave. Res E 60 yrs. Mon Dec 5.

SANBORN, SARAH A, MRS, 80, d Tue Apr 12, 1932, 167 E 35th St, NYC. **SURV:** ch Ross H and Alex. 3 bro and 2 sis. All res Eliz at one time. wid/o George H, d 20+ yrs ago, auditor in the freight dept Central RR, working for 46 yrs. and past Master EL F&AM, Elizabethport Lodge 116, IOOF, and JK64. Couple res Eliz at 518 Madison Ave. School teacher bfr m. Thu Apr 14.

SEABRING, ANN, MRS, 71, d Sun May 12, 1912, Gen H, Eliz. wid/o Philip, 35th NJ Vol. **F:** M M Martin & Son. Mon May 13.

SEBRING, CATHERINE, MRS, 70, b PHL, d Sat Jan 22, 1910, at home, 558 Marshall St, Eliz. **SURV:** ch James A MacDaniel, Sexton St Johns Epis, Mrs Adelaide Strickfuss and Mrs Florence Applegate. 5 gch. wid/o William, Sr, enl fm Rahway Co E, 30th Reg, NJ Vol. Res E 40 yrs. **CHH:** Christ. **F:** Wed, Rev E P Little, DD. Mon Jan 24.

SEELY, WILLIAM HOPPING, b Sat Nov 27, 1880, Port Monmouth, s/o Col Uriah, d Thu ngt Apr 6, 1939, at home, Newark (Dateline). **SURV:** w frmr Edith Van Hook of Milan, TN/ch Anne, William H, Jr, N, and Fred C, Montclair. sib Fred L, Asheville, NC, James P, Montclair, and Uriah, Joliet, IL. f was a pharmaceutical manu. Educ E Orange PS, and a Colgate Univ grad. A newspaperman in early days, having serv on the N Eve News, the Daily Advertiser, and its successor the Morning Star, and the Eve Star, all N. Work included coverage of City Hall, the NJ Legislature and DC affairs. At dod Pres of the Osborne Co, manu of calendars at Allwood, VP of the American Color Type Co and a Dir of the Natl N and Essex Banking Co. A Repub. Chairman of the Clean Govt League of Essex Co. Fri Apr 7.

SMITH, SARAH, MRS, (NEE MILBURN), 89, b Flemington, d Wed mrng Jul 14, 1937, at home of s William J, 610 Washington St, Dunellen. SURV: ch William and Clarence, D. 6 gch. 7 ggch. wid/o William Bishop. Able to relate interesting stories concerning the CW. Res Hampton early in life. Res Eliz for yrs, D past 15 yrs. MEM: WCTU. CHH: Meth, but also attended others. Wed Jul 14.

SWEENEY, JOHN THOMAS, 74, s/o late Capt Thomas, Naval Vet, d Sun 9 pm Feb 27, 1927, Mercer H, Trenton. SURV: w Florence Patterson/ch Rev Harold J, Rector Grace Epis, Elmer E and Stella A, T, and Albert R, Pittsburgh, PA. Res 244 Tyler St, T. Desc of an old T fam. F: Calvary Bapt. Int Wed Riverview, T. Mon Feb 28.

TINGELY, KATHERINE, MRS, b Tue Jul 6, 1852, d/o James P Wescott of Newburyport, MA, d Thu Jul 11, 1929, Visingso, Sweden, fm the effects of a May 30 auto accident near Osnabrueck. f was a CW U officer. In 1889 m Philo B Tingely, an inventor. Early life was spent in NY where on the E Side she founded "The Do Good Mission," and est non-sectarian SS. Res at various times in Cuba, the USA and Europe. A leader of the Universal Brotherhood and Theosophical Soc, a worldwide movement. Founded "Lomaland" at Point Loma, near San Diego, CA, a large estate where the Intl Theosophical HQ, the Raja Yoga college, and Theosophical U are located. The bdlg incld an open-air Greek theater, one of the first erected in the USA. Thu Jul 31. (P)

TOOKER, JOANNA, MRS, 88, d Wed Nov 17, 1920, at home of dau Mrs Mary Ritter, 144 W Scott Ave, Rahway (Dateline). SURV: ch Mrs Ritter and Mrs John T Davis, 138 Whittier St. gch Mrs George H Vanderveer, Neshanic, Mrs Leo VanSant, El Mora (section of Eliz), Esther, Orrill Edith, and J Stanley Davis, Ralph F and Marion Ritter, all R, Augustus N Ritter, Suaguache, CO, James H P Ritter, Brooklyn, and Charles R Davis, New Haven. ggch Roger VanSant, Eliz, Lois Vanderveer, Neshanic, Marjorie and Virginia Ritter, Brooklyn, and Rosamond B, CO.

wid/o Sgt Sam, KIA Chancellorsville. **CHH:** First ME. **F:** Sat aftn Mrs Mary Ritter home, Rev E A Quimby, P. Thu Nov 18.

<u>TOWNLEY, SARAH W, MRS</u>, 59, lifelong res Eliz, d/o late Charles & Adeline M Walker, d Thu ngt Jun 3, 1909, at home, 1108 Elizabeth Ave, Eliz. **SURV:** ch William E, Jr, Charles L, Robert W, Mrs H H Kenyon, Pittsfield, MA, Mary E and Margaret Adeline. sib 5 sis and 3 bro. <u>wid/o William E, for yrs one of the best known and most successful dry goods merchants of E, d Wed Jul 1, 1903.</u> **CHH:** St Johns Epis. Fri Jun 4.

<u>WARNER, MARY E, MRS</u>, b Sat Feb 2, 1861, Lebanon, <u>d/o late William J</u> & Emma Bragg <u>Mitchell,</u> d Wed aftn Feb 8, 1939, Eliz Gen H, Eliz. **SURV:** sib Annie A and Charles L Mitchell. Svrl nieces, nephews, gnieces and gnephews. wid/o Silas C. Res E since ae 3, at 350 E Jersey St bfr bcmg a patient at the H 2 yrs ago. On mo side, desc of Pieterse Schuyler, imm 1650 fm Holland, and d in Albany 1683. On f side, desc of John Mitchell, imm 1749 fm England, he and w Mary int St Johns churchyard, E. Engaged in the dressmaking biz for yrs. **F:** Daniel J Leonards Home for F, 242 W Jersey St. Thu Feb 9.

<u>WHELAN, MARY MCGLYNN, MRS</u>, d abt midnight Tue/Wed Jun 3/4, 1902, at home, 141 Washington Ave, Eliz. **SURV:** ch Rev Isaac P, P St Marys Star of the Sea, Bayonne City, John W, William J, Joseph and Mary M, w/o Dr Stephen J Quinn. 2 gdau, ch/o John W. <u>wid/o Capt John, serv Co K, 3rd NJ Vol, POW, d Fri Mar 28, 1873, at home, E.</u> Res Washington Ave home last 50 yrs, and E 60 yrs. Last of a fam of 5 ch. **CHH:** An original mem St Marys. **F:** St Marys, Rev Isaac P Whelan, Rev Father O'Neill, and Rev Father Carroll. Int Bishops, near Orange, Fri mrng. Just recently had h rmvd fm St Marys to Bishops. Wed Jun 4.

<u>WILLIAMS, SUSAN JANE, MRS</u>, 80, d Tue Oct 15, 1912, at home, New Hope, PA. **SURV:** ch Mrs John M Firth and Sadie M, N H, Mrs J W Valentine, 42 W Scott Pl and Mrs D W Barton, 101 Pearl St, Eliz. <u>wid/o James H, Co A, 1st NJ Reg.</u> Frmr res Eliz, rem to N H a few yrs ago. **CHH:** Frmr mem 3rd Presby.

Wed Oct 16.

WITTEMAN, HENRIETTA ELIZABETH, MRS, 82, d Sat Apr 9, 1927, at home, 41 N Reid St, Eliz. **SURV**: ch Anna M, Principal of PS15, and Frederick, E. 3 gch. wid/o Adam, with Hawkins Z, winning many honors for heroism, and mem GAR, d 1923. Couple rem to E fm NYC at close of CW. **CHH**: St Michaels. Mon Apr 11.

WOOD, SARAH M, MRS, 79, b Eliz, d Fri aftn Feb 25, 1927, at home of Mrs Albert M Khun, with whom she res, 516 Morris Ave, Eliz. **SURV**: Foster-ch Mrs Khun and Mrs Richard Smith. sib George Anderson, E, and John Anderson, Brooklyn. 4 "gch." 6 "ggch." d/o late John & Liddy Anderson. f was b E, as were his par, and were desc of early settlers and Vets of the RW. wid/o Henry C, lifelong E res, and a desc of one of the oldest E fam. Being childless, reared 2 ch of a bro and sis, Mrs Kuhn, d/o George, and Mrs Smith, d/o her sis. **MEM**: Mystic Council 18 S&D of L. **CHH**: St James ME. **F**: Mon, Rev Chester J Hoyt. Int Evergreen. Sat Feb 26.

ZEISS, MELISSA A, MRS, 83, b Perth Amboy, d Sun Jun 11, 1933, at home of Harry Johnson, 610 Marshall St, where she boarded, Eliz. **SURV**: Svrl nieces. wid/o William N. Res E 50 yrs. **F**: Martin Mortuary, 1019 E Jersey St. Mon Jun 12.

Chapter 3

OBITUARIES OF BLACK CW VETS

CHAMPION, JOHN, native of the W Indies, d Fri Oct 26, 1906, at home, Thompson Lane, Eliz. SURV: w. A gardener and gravedigger, for many yrs digging graves in the 1st Presby Chh cem. SERV: 20th Reg, US Colored Troops, svc in SC. F: Mon aftn. Int S&S' plot Evergreen. Sat Oct 27.

CONYARD, JASPER, 75, native of Greensboro, NC, b a slave, d early Thu mrng Mar 29, 1906, at home, 232 Harrison St, Eliz. Vet never m. A porter for the Central RR for yrs. Abt a yr ago went to NC to visit his old home and returned Sat eve in poor health. Wanted to spend his last days in E, where he was well known among colored people. MEM: LL7 F&AM. SERV: C Army. Thu Mar 29.

COSTER, WILLIAM BENJAMIN GRIFFIN, REV, nearly 78, b Hempstead, LI, s/o Rev & Mrs Peter C, d Thu Feb 3, 1927, at home, 26 Newton St, Rahway. SURV: w Mary Louise/ch Evangelist Mrs Evelyn Miller, NY Conf, and Mrs Ward Lawrence, Newark. gch Alfred Coster, Long Branch, William Benson and Ethel Benson, Newark, Mrs Louisa Harris, Asbury Park, Mrs Madeline Haymer, Comet, LI, and Mrs Edna Treadwell, Huntington, LI. 7 ggch. Par for yrs were well known throughout the NY Conf. 46 yrs of active evangelistic and ministerial duties, res R last 4 yrs, and the past 7 yrs had been a traveling evangelist. Bfr that, serv in some of the most prominent and influential AME Chh of the NY and NJ Conf. Last charge was at Stroudsburg, PA. Prior to there at Scranton, PA, Binghamton, NY, Camden, Hightstown, Metuchen and Eliz, as well as other NJ locations. Retained mem in St James Zion AME, Newark. MEM: William Lloyd Garrison Post 207, GAR, Brooklyn. Frmly with colored Masons and Odd Fellows. Silver Leaf Club Ebenezer AME, R, at dod. A JP, Eliz. SERV: With

Fed forces 2 ½ yrs in Capt Spink 14th RI Bat of Heavy Art. WIA. Returned to svc, to end. F: Rev J W P Collier, Ebenezer AME, will officiate at R, and Rev J F Vanderhorst, R, presiding Elder Newark District, and Rev R B Smith, presiding Elder Camden District, who m Rev and Mrs Coster, will officiate at St James Zion AME, Newark. Sat Feb 5.

DAVIS, JOSEPH, h/o Sarah.

DAVIS, SARAH, MRS, native of Linden Tp, d Mon Jul 26, 1909, Eliz Gen H, Eliz. SURV: ch Philip and Mrs Sarah Gibbs. bro George Searns, Brooklyn. 8 gch. wid/o Joseph. Res E nearly all her life. CHH: Mt Teman AME, E. Tue Jul 27. (No mention of color. AME specified in obit)

EDGAR, MAHLON, 75, d Sun Oct 17, 1915, Matawan. SURV: ch Samuel, Linden, John, Rahway, and 3 m dau. Res Rahway for yrs and went to M for his health. Tue Oct 19.

FRANCIS, ELIAS, d Wed Mar 21, 1917, at home, 214 8th Ave, E, Roselle. SURV: dau Mrs Solomon Walker. A s, Leonard, d just last wk. CHH: Union Bapt. SERV: Co D, 20th Reg, US Colored Vol Inf. Thu Mar 22.

GARLAND, PRESTON, 107, b on the plantation of Paul Calvary, Lynchburg, VA, s/o Fannie Garland, d announced Fri Mar 30, 1906, Morristown. When he was b, he had 19 sib. Always claimed there was no doubt of his age because his master, Paul Calvary, kept a record of the b and d of all slaves. When a ch was b on the plantation the fact was recorded in the book. Aft the ch was named, that name was put opposite the dob, and that way, he said, he came to know his age to a fraction. Res first 19 yrs on the plantation, then sent to the New Orleans slave market. Bought by a Negro named Bon Lewis for whom he worked until Lewis d in 1856, then given the privilege of working for wages. Worked as a cook in one of the principal hotels to the beginning of the CW. Aft CW went to Cuba for 3 yrs. Rem to M, living in the same house all that time. Oldest res Morris Co. SERV: Shouldered a musket on the call of Gen Butler for colored troops and became a Fed sol under Col Kyles, the Cmdr of his Div being Gen Banks. Serv in Army 5 ½ yrs. Fri Mar 30.

GREEN, JOHN H, 57, b VA, d Tue eve Mar 24, 1903, Eliz Gen H, Eliz. Res 110 Catherine St, and E for yrs. Janitor of the old Arcade bldg on Broad St for yrs. **MEM:** L11. **SERV:** Cpl, Co G, 29th CT Vol. The Reg was the first colored Reg that entered Richmond aft its fall. Wed Mar 25.

F: Took place Fri aft Mt Teman AME, of which he was mem and trustee for 25 yrs, at one time chorister. Officiating were Rev Dr Stewart, P; Rev J S Stark, Siloam Presby; Rev W H Taylor, Shiloh Bapt; Rev W P Lawrence, Union Bapt; Rev W H Bailey, NY; Rev J H Bailey, Lambertville; and Rev William H Cheek, Camden, frmr P of his chh. Rev Lawrence and J H Bailey eulogized his sol qualities and his bravery on the field of battle. Dr Bailey related the charge of the Reg at Deep Bottom, VA, 1864, and how, when Cpl Green's bro was shot down, the Cpl, with shot and shells falling all abt him, rushed to his fallen bro, placed him on his shoulder and carried his body to the rear, and then resumed his place in the ranks. Int Evergreen. Sat Mar 28, 1903.

HAWKINS, CHARLES R H, b Sun Dec 9, 1849, Medina, NY, d Wed Aug 20, 1924, at home, 134 W 134th St, NY. **SURV:** ch Frederick, PHL, PA, and Mrs Elizabeth H Davis, NY. 2 gch Sgt Ralph F Hawkins, NY, 15th Inf, and Harold Montague, Newark. 3 ggch. sis Mrs Frances E Leigh, NY, with whom he lived. Res Eliz 1878 to 1912, his last res 57 Broad St. A newspaper reporter. Rem to S'H, Kearny, for a yr, then to NY, where he wrote for svrl of the NY papers. **SERV:** Sgt, a scout under Col William M Cody, better known as "Buffalo Bill." Aft CW reup in regular Army and for some time scout for the Indian Commission. Fri Aug 22.

JACKSON, HENRY L, d Thu Feb 18, 1926, at home, Roselle. F was Sat aftn fm Mt Teman AME, Rev J O Vick, Asbury Park ME, Rev H M Kemp, St Lukes, Newark. UD25 attended in a body and conducted int svc at sol plot, Evergreen. Mon Feb 22.

LAMB, JEREMIAH, 72, b a slave in the S, d Sat Jan 28, 1905, at home, 25 Greenville Ave, Jersey City. Employ 40+ yrs Singer til last Oct 27, when stricken ill. Came N in 1864 with a Capt of the 10th NJ Vol. Mon Jan 30.

LEWIS, ANDERSON, 75, b Putnam Co, TN, d Sun Mar 21, 1915, at home, Haydock St, Rahway. **SURV:** w/3 nieces, Mrs Margaret Ferris, Mrs Viola Bailey and Gertrude Washington. Nephew George Washington, R. Res R past 25 yrs. Up to CW a slave on a Srn plantation. Employ by the city St Dept for yrs. **SERV:** Fought for the U. **F:** Wed aftn Ebenezer AME, Central Ave, Rev O F Flipper. Int R. Mon Mar 22.

MORRIS, THOMAS JEFFERSON, 97, b free in VA, d Mon Sep 14, 1908, Morris Plains H. **SURV:** w/2dau/2s, being the pugilists "Shadow" and "Ninna" Morris. Half-bro Richard Jordan, a painter, res on 2nd Ave. For yrs "Uncle Jeff" followed the calling of an oysterman on SI Sound. Later, became a St peddler of ice cream in the Summer and oysters during the Winter, his cry of "ice cream" and "oh, you, oyst'" are well remembered. **SERV:** 11th US Colored Hvt Art, which was raised in Providence, RI, 1863-65, pens. During the first Cleveland admin applied for an increase, it was then asserted that he did not have an hon disc, and pens was revoked. He had his papers of hon disc, so the Overseer of the Poor Eckerson, Congressman Fowler and Senator Kean became interested, with bills offered in Congress to restore his pens. The bills failed. Vet was deeply affected, and entered H 3 yrs ago. **F:** Int sol plot, Orange, Wed. Thu Sep 17.

PARKER, JAMES A, native of Pottstown, near Baton Rouge, LA, d Mon aftn Jun 17, 1929, at home, 28 Newton St, Rahway. **SURV:** w Amy T. Came to R 50 yrs ago. A mason by trade. **MEM:** Connected with a Brooklyn GAR Post. **CHH:** Silver Leaf Club of Ebenezer AME, Pres B of Trustees for yrs, a class leader. Hon mem Ruth Missionary Circle, 2nd Bapt. **SERV:** Enl U as a messenger boy 1862, to end. While aboard a naval vessel, lost an eye by the premature explosion of a shell. **F:** Ebenezer. Tue Jun

18. (No mention of color. Obit specifies chh as AME.)

ROBINSON, JOHN BENJAMIN, 71, d Wed ngt Aug 20, 1919, at home, 191 Elm Ave, Rahway. **SURV**: dau Mrs Rosa E Van Cline, R. **SERV**: Hon disc. Fri Aug 22.

SAYERS, GEORGE A. COL, 68, d Wed ngt Feb 24, 1908, Gen H, Eliz. **SURV**: s and dau in NY, and a dau, Mrs Milton Kane, E. Aft CW, returned to E and employ by Joseph Davis, a mason and builder. Once conducted a saloon at Division & Martin St, then aft employ by the frmr Elizabethport Cordage Co. In 1873, found a lady nearly murdered, near Division St in the venty of Schardien's Woods, where Vet had his home, he being an expressman at the time, and reported the facts to the police. Her assailant was arrested in PHL and returned to E, where there was a sensational trial, and the criminal was sentenced to state prison for a long time. A pens, able to ret svrl yrs ago. Res Public Lane last few yrs. **SERV**: Pvt Co D, 11th US Colored Hvy Art 1863-65, svc in TX and LA. On Sat Nov 23, 1872, appointed as Lt Col in the NJNG by Gov Joel Parker. The only colored man in NJ ever to hold a field com in the NG. His Reg had been org abt 2 yrs ago, composed of Cos fm E, Newark, Jersey City, Camden, Rahway and New Brunswick. Cmdr Co A, E, for a long time, until disb by Gov Joseph D Bedle, due to lack of interest among the Cos of colored sol. **F**: Sat 2 pm at home of dau Mrs Araminta Cain, 646 Grove St. Int Evergreen. Thu Feb 25. (Note: Dif in dau last name is as reported.) (P)

SIMMONS, JOHN H, d Mon mrng Jul 16, 1906, at home, 1087 Lafayette St, Eliz. **SURV**: w/3dau/s. **MEM**: LL of Free Masons. **SERV**: Co F, 37th Reg of Colored Vol, NC. **F**: Wed aftn. Mon Jul 16.

SMITH, ANDREW JACKSON, 89, s/o an African slave & her white master, d 1932. A runaway slave, enl 55th MA Vol Colored. In an unsuccessful assault by his Reg on a C position in SC called Honey Hill, the Color Bearer was killed by an exploding shell. He picked up the fallen flag and Reg banner and carried the Colors through the rest of the battle, helping direct his Reg art while making himself a prominent target of C fire. Woodrow Wilson initially denied recognition for a medal, stating there was no record of his action. The records were eventually found by his gs, Andrew Bowman, in the National Archives. **The Medal of Honor** was presented to his dau, Caruth Smith Washington, ae 93, in recognition of her f's heroic act of gallantry, by Pres Clinton at the White House, Tue Jan 16, 2001, 8 fam mem, including Bowman, present. "As long as they saw the flag waving, they would continue to fight," Washington pointed out. Star-Ledger (NJ): Tue Jan 23, 2001, Rebecca Goldsmith, Star-Ledger reporter.

STILL, CHARLES R, lifelong res Eliz, d Sat mrng Jul 29, 1905, at 194 Public Lane, Eliz. A wid. **SERV:** Co C, 14th US Colored Vol. **F:** Int sol lot, Evergreen. Sat Jul 29. (No mention of rank/color)

TAYLOR, THOMAS. See **Monitor**.

TURNER, EDWARD A, 81, d Sun 610 pm Jan 14, 1917, at home of dau Mrs John D Myers, 18 Grove St, Cranford. **SURV:** w. Res C 20 yrs. Desc of Nathaniel Turner, who was put to d in Richmond, VA, on account of his views on slavery. **CHH:** Elder many yrs 2nd Bapt, Roselle. Past Chapl and mem of the Seven Wise Men of Baltimore and mem True Reformers, C. A licentiate preacher 50+ yrs, called the Bishop of the Bapt Conf in Newark, life mem. **SERV:** Aft 4 unsuccessful attempts, got his fam out of VA and into OH, then enl 34th OH Art, to end. Mon Jan 15.

WOOD, HENRY, b Rahway, d Wed mrng May 26, 1909, at home, 315 John St, Eliz. **SURV:** w/ch Charles and William. 6 gch. 2 ggch. Res E since 1862. Through thrift and economy, succeeded in owning his own home and saving enough to make his latter days comfortable. **CHH:** Long a mem and officer Mt Teman AME. Past Master Ark of Safety Lodge, Order of Good Samaritans. **SERV:** Enl 1863 Pvt 29th CT Vol Inf, to end. **F:** Sat, bearers the only 4 surv colored Vets in E. Wed May 26.

CHAPTER 4

LIVING CW VETS

AMES, ALONSO H, 93, and Maria, 91, marked their 75th m anniv today. Pres Roosevelt sent his greetings. Vet recalls shaking hands with Lincoln in the White House. NY, Sat Feb 23, 1935.

APPLEGATE, ADRIAN S, of Trenton, one of 3 candidates for dept Cmdr to be elected during the 44th annual encmp of the dept of NJ GAR at Trenton, to the natl encmp. Fri May 19, 1911.

AVERBECK, FRED, in the Wed tribute paid to CW Vets, with 27 other NJ Vets and one NY Vet. GAR R with colorful parade and amory fete in Eliz. Mem-at-Large, represented Newark. Thu Mar 30, 1933.

BARNES, H S, attended the complimentary dinner for WFB27 mems given by A Edward Woodruff Tue eve May 30, 1911. Rahway, Wed May 31.

BAUER, JOSEPH, flies at ae 92. "Why, there's nothing much to it," he said, as he relinquished the controls of the Stinson airplane in midair. A few moments later he was stepping from the plane and thanking the pilot for "the best birthday anniv I've had in 92 yrs." Rochester, NY, Thu May 6, 1937.

BEECHLER, JOSEPH, attended the complimentary dinner for WFB27 mems given by A Edward Woodruff Tue eve May 30, 1911. Rahway, Wed May 31.

BENTLEY, C L, 94, of Fenton, MI, attended the 75th Gettysburg B&G R. (See **B&G**)

BILBEE, W H, in the Wed tribute paid to CW Vets, with 27 other NJ Vets and one NY Vet. GAR R with colorful parade and amory fete in Eliz. Mem-at-Large, represented Trenton. Thu Mar 30, 1933.

BISHOP, FRANCIS A, 92. (See **Experiences**)

BLORE, JOHN C, Cmdr WFB27, attended the complimentary

dinner for WFB27 mems given by A Edward Woodruff Tue eve May 30, 1911. Rahway, Wed May 31.

BOUCHER, J W, PVT, 73, 257th Canadian Railway Btln, was sent home fm France because he is "too old to fight." He faced the German lines for 8 mos and endured all the hardships. Then his age was discovered and he was disc. King George heard of the case, and thanked him at a Buckingham Palace audience. CW Vet, 23rd MI Vol. Kingston, Ont, Tue Feb 19, 1918.

BOWMAN, JOHN, C CAPT, celebrated his 102nd dob. Rem to ID shortly aft CW and now lives among 5 gens of his fam. Caldwell, ID, Thu Apr 2, 1936.

BROW, BENJAMIN, in the Wed tribute paid to CW Vets, with 27 other NJ Vets and one NY Vet. GAR R with colorful parade and amory fete in Eliz. Mem-at-Large, represented Trenton. Thu Mar 30, 1933.

BROWER, ROBERT, of Milburn, one of 3 candidates for Jr V-Cmdr during the 44th annual encmp of the dept of NJ GAR at Trenton, to the natl encmp. Fri May 19, 1911.

BROWN, J T, Garfield Post 4, oldest Vet present, in the Wed tribute paid to CW Vets, with 27 other NJ Vets and one NY Vet. GAR R with colorful parade and amory fete in Eliz. Mem-at-Large, represented Newark. Thu Mar 30, 1933.(P-lists initials as J J)

BRUBAKER, HATTIE, MRS, NURSE. (See Experiences - Nurses)

BRYSON, W F, one of 11 candidates for 9 delegates, to be elected during the 44th annual encmp of the dept of NJ GAR at Trenton, to the natl encmp. Fri May 19, 1911.

BUCHANAN, WILLIAM, in the Wed tribute paid to CW Vets, with 27 other NJ Vets and one NY Vet. GAR R with colorful parade and amory fete in Eliz. Mem-at-Large, represented Irvington. Thu Mar 30, 1933.

BURROWS, CHARLES, frmr Natl Cmdr, in the Wed tribute paid to CW Vets, with 27 other NJ Vets and one NY Vet. GAR R with colorful parade and amory fete in Eliz. Mem-at-Large, represented Paterson. Thu Mar 30, 1933. (P)

BUSH, W J, of Fitzgerald, GA, attended the 75th Gettysburg B&G R. (See **B&G**) (P)

CANNON, JOSEPH. Memories of '61 recalled. Mon Jun 1, 1931. (P)

In the Wed tribute paid to CW Vets, with 27 other NJ Vets and 1 NY Vet. GAR R with colorful parade and armory fete in Eliz. 3 GAR mem-at-large represented Eliz. Thu Mar 30, 1933.

Article on dob party for Cannon and McCandless. Mon Jan 6, 1936. Res Eliz since 1867 and at 533 Marshall St 17 yrs. Fam: ch Robert and Joseph, Eliz, and Mrs Frederick H Davis. 14 gch. 8 ggch. MEM: PL78, KP. TL134 F&AM. SERV: WIA aft 1 ½ yrs of svc and taken to the Army H, Alexandria, VA. Disc aft release.

Article on forthcoming dob party. b Travis, LI. Enl with NY troops. Aft CW rem to Perth Amboy, then Eliz. Conducted an oyster business, ret yrs ago. Dec 29, 1936.

Article on Eliz MDAY celebrations. Of 533 Marshall St. At ae 91 will ride at head of parade. Sat May 29, 1937.

dob gifts for CW pair Cannon and McCandless. Mon Jan 10, 1938. (P)

CW Vets vote. Wed, Nov 9, 1938. (P)

Honored at MDAY parade. Wed May 31, 1939. (P)

CASNER, MR & MRS WILLIAM H, 75 1st St, Eliz, celeb their 50th m anniv at 535 Livingston St Sat ngt. Res on 1st St entire m life. He was b near Spottswood, Middlesex Co, and res Eliz since 1855. She was b England as Mary Hague, and res Eliz since 1853. He conducts a wholesale and retail tobacco biz on 1st St, and is a carpenter by trade. MEM: JK64. Presented with an armchair by Joseph E Cannon on behalf of the Post. SERV: Enl otbrk, to end. m shortly aft disc. They have 5 ch, Mrs Max Miller, Mrs Joseph E Cannon, Frederick, Henry and Charles, all present except Frederick, who res MD. Among those attending were Alfred B Casner, Brooklyn, Mr & Mrs Joseph E Cannon, Mr & Mrs Joseph E Cannon, Jr, Mr & Mrs J C Cannon, Mr & Mrs Max Miller, Mr & Mrs Henry Casner and Mr & Mrs Charles Casner,

Eliz. Mon Jan 4, 1915.

CLAYPOOL, JOHN M, GEN, of St Louis, MO, Cmdr of Vets in all probability what will be the last encmp of the C Army, was honored at pre-reunion receptions Mon ngt. Also honored were Mrs A McD Wilson, Pres-Gen of the CSMA and Gen J W Harris, Adj-Gen and Chief of Staff of the UCV, and the SOCV. Officials est abt 500 Vets would attend. The conventions of the CSMA and SOCV are being held at the same time. Columbia, SC,Tue Aug 30, 1938.

Attended the 75th Gettysburg B&G R. (See **B&G**)

COLE, FRANK O, of Jersey City, attending the 1927 61st GAR natl encmp, has NJ delegation support for natl Cmdr-in-Chief. Long active in civic affairs of Hudson Co, and in 1883 and 1884 represented the co in the state legislature. SERV: Enl 1861 13th MA Vet Vol, to end. Tue Sep 6, 1927.

CONGER, J H, in the Wed tribute paid to CW Vets, with 27 other NJ Vets and one NY Vet. GAR R with colorful parade and armory fete in Eliz. Mem-at-Large, represented New Brunswick. Thu Mar 30, 1933.

CONNETT, ISAAC S. See **Experiences**.

COOPER, JOHN W, 91, of Largo, FL, attended the 75th Gettysburg B&G R. (See **B&G**)

CORSON, WILLIAM A, attended the complimentary dinner for WFB27 mems given by A Edward Woodruff Tue eve May 30, 1911. Rahway, Wed May 31.

COURTNEY, H E, 92, claims to be the only one of 381 remaining AL C Vets to have fought directly under Lee. "Gen Lee was a fine man...He was a fighter and a smart one. He'd never have lost a battle if he hadn't been outnumbered more than 2 to 1." The oldest man, and Cmdr of the local chap of the C Vets. Fm his watch dangles a locket containing a picture of his beloved Cmdr Lee. SERV: Left f's home ae 18 to enl. At Seven Pines, Malvern Hill, Manasses Junction, Snigger's Gap, South Mountain and Gettysburg. Mobile, AL, Fri Apr 19, 1935.

CRANE, STEPHEN S, 65, began suit for divorce against his yng w whom he m last Nov in Passaic under the name Helen Kirkman. He declares he has since learned she is Henrietta de Kerguelan, who has a h and 3 ch in Bayonne. Newark, Fri Jan 14, 1910.

CROSBY, M B, one of 11 candidates for 9 delegates, to be elected during the 44th annual encmp of the dept of NJ GAR at Trenton, to the natl encmp. Fri May 19, 1911.

CYESTER, LOUIS, in the Wed tribute paid to CW Vets, with 27 other NJ Vets and one NY Vet. GAR R with colorful parade and amory fete in Eliz. Mem-at-Large, represented Jersey City. Thu Mar 30, 1933.

DANA, ROBERT S, DR, of Morrisville, claims the distinction of being the last man to leave the battlefield at Gettysburg. An enthusiastic GAR mem, his home, nestling close to the banks of the Delaware Riv, is filled with CW relics. One is a B flat cornet that he played in the 9th Cav band. It was twisted by striking against a tree while his Reg was in pursuit, but he straightened it with a broom handle. Congress passed an act in 1862 mu/o military bands, and he returned to Wilkes Barre. 6 days aft arriving home the invasion of MD demanded more men, so he reuped and serv to end. He then came to his present home, which was the res of his f, Sylvester. Yardley, PA, Fri Jan 28, 1910.

DAVIS, MOSES, 86, of Moscow, PA, b in Wayne Co, PA, on Mar 17, still works in a factory. 6 relatives of a large fam remain. SERV: Co G, 187th PA Vol. Believed to be last mem of Lincoln bodyguard. When Pres Lincoln was rem fm Washington to Springfield, IL, his Co met the F train at PHL. He had often seen Lincoln while in the U Army. Mon Apr 1, 1929. (P) (Article creased on one side. Has fam names, and description of events in PHL)

DEY, GEORGE, in the Wed tribute paid to CW Vets, with 27 other NJ Vets and one NY Vet. GAR R with colorful parade and amory fete in Eliz. Mem-at-Large, represented Newark. Thu Mar 30, 1933.

DINKINS, JAMES, CAPT, one of those who accepted a flag fm

Ira R Wildman in 1924 of the 10th New Orleans Cav. The flag, captured at Cold Harbor, was authorized to be returned by the CT Legislature. (See **B&G**)

ELLWOOD, JAMES, Co A, 1st Reg, on the honor roll for bravery. 50th anniv of 1st Brig article, Tue Jul 18, 1911.

FAGAN, JOHN B, one of 11 candidates for 9 delegates, to be elected during the 44th annual encmp of the dept of NJ GAR at Trenton, to the natl encmp. Fri May 19, 1911.

FOWLER, CHARLES B, 70, Pvt Co B, 1st NJ Cav, listed as d for 50 yrs, has obtained a pens, with the help of Adj-Gen Wilbur F Sadler. Had been fighting for svrl yrs to get it, but the govt always replied that he had been KIA. When he inquired abt entering one of the NJ S'H, Sadler heard the story and took up the case. The Vet rcvd $168 back pens and a warrant for $21/mos for as long as he lives. Had been needy with practically no relatives, but now is happy that he will not become an object of charity, but instead will be repaid for fighting in defense of his country. Trenton, Tue Dec 24, 1912.

FOWLER, CHARLES B, Co E, the man who was actually KIA on one of the Srn battle grounds, and not the Charles B Fowler, of Co B, 1st NJ Cav, listed as d for 50 yrs. Trenton, Tue Dec 24, 1912.

GERHART, LEROY H, 16, s/o Mrs E J Gerhart, 444 E Jersey St, Eliz, gs/o CW Vet Joseph A Backert, is at Camp McClennan, in Co G, 113th Inf. Enl Jun 14, 1917. Wed Apr 3, 1918. (P)

GOFF, JOHN S, ST Paul, MN. See obit Graff, Emil.

GOGGINS, WILLIAM T, b Ireland, imm USA 1864, and in a few mos was working for Singer, NY. Aft CW went back to Singer as a foreman and worked in spring dept for 49 yrs (See **Experiences**). Res 309 S Park St. **MEM**: SVA and of Court Columbus IOF. Excelsior B&L Assoc, Pres 27 yrs, since it was org. **SERV**: Enl 1865 Fed Navy, assigned to the steamer "Shenango." "I'll never forget the days which followed," he said (See **Experiences**). Fri Feb 28, 1913. (P)

GOODRICH, J A, in the Wed tribute paid to CW Vets, with 27 other NJ Vets and one NY Vet. GAR R with colorful parade and amory fete in Eliz. Mem-at-Large, represented Jersey City. Thu Mar 30, 1933.

Goodrich, John, Dept Cmdr, attended annual UD25 Christmas party Wed. Thu Dec 30, 1926. (P)

GORDON, JAMES F, one of 11 candidates for 9 delegates, to be elected during the 44th annual encmp of the dept of NJ GAR at Trenton, to the natl encmp. Fri May 19, 1911.

GREYSTONE, DANIEL, in the Wed tribute paid to CW Vets, with 27 other NJ Vets and one NY Vet. GAR R with colorful parade and amory fete in Eliz. Mem-at-Large, represented New York. Thu Mar 30, 1933.

GRIFFIN, ALEXANDER, 82, of Hampton, TX, and his bro Jacob, 79, of Stone Mountain, GA, met for the first time in 62 yrs. They were 2 of 5 bro who left their home in Brunswick, GA, in 1861 to enl. 2 were KIA. Alexander, heartsick ovr the defeat and devastation of the C, wandered off to TX aft CW. Had heard nothing of fam since. The 2 bro had been at a C Reunion at Birmingham last yr not knowing the other still lived. They left last ngt for Macon, GA, to visit the other bro. Tampa, FL, Apr 8, 1927.

GUNNERSON, GEORGE M, res S'H, Kearny. Found wandering along PA RR tracks at Trinity Pl, Eliz, Mon aftn, was taken aboard the train and brought to Broad St station. Sent to Newark on next train. Tue Feb 13, 1906.

HALL, PETER, Atwater, MN. See obit Graff, Emil.

HAM(M)ACKER, JAMES P, 94, of Aledo, Parker Co, TX, attended the 75th Gettysburg B&G R. (See **B&G**)

HANDCOCK, JAMES, 104, AWOL! Slipped away fm the Gettysburg R to go sightseeing. Turned up in PHL where a cop found him alternately watching a ball game and taking a nap. Police made arrangements to return him to the C S'H at New Orleans. Fri Jul 15, 1938. (P)

HARKINS/HAWKINS, THOMAS R. See Pollard, Robert M.

HARRIS, J W, GEN, of Oklahoma City, OK, attended the 75th

Gettysburg B&G R. (See **B&G**) (P)

HARTUNG, JOHN, 97, one of just 2 mem left of the "1841 Club," est here a n/o yrs ago for CW Vets b 1841. The other is W W Thomas. They have observed the club custom this yr of jointly celeb each other's dob and count on doing the same thing next yr. Pasedena, CA, Mon Aug 29, 1938.

HATCH, DURANT, of Oklahoma City, OK, attended the 75th Gettysburg B&G R. (See **B&G**) (P)

HETFIELD, D B, attended the complimentary dinner for WFB27 mems given by A Edward Woodruff Tue eve May 30, 1911. Rahway, Wed May 31.

HOLT, CHARLES H, (See **Monitor**). Sat Feb 20, 1926.

HOPKINS, CHARLES F, one of 11 candidates for 9 delegates, to be elected during the 44th annual encmp of the dept of NJ GAR at Trenton, to the natl encmp. Fri May 19, 1911.

HOWELL, HENRY C, attended the complimentary dinner for WFB27 mems given by A Edward Woodruff Tue eve May 30, 1911. Rahway, Wed May 31.

HUGHES, BENJAMIN W, attended the complimentary dinner for WFB27 mems given by A Edward Woodruff Tue eve May 30, 1911. Rahway, Wed May 31.

INGLIS, JAMES, JR, departing Cmdr of the dept of NJ GAR, during the 44th annual encmp of the dept of NJ GAR. Fri May 19, 1911

JACKSON, JOHN S. See **Experiences**.

JOHNSON, ISAAC, 87, New Martinsville, WV, triumphantly pulled up past the reviewing stand in the Washington GAR parade to get a kiss and hug fm gd Sue Conrad. Fri Sep 25, 1936. (P)

JONES, CHARLES D, in the Wed tribute paid to CW Vets, with 27 other NJ Vets and one NY Vet. GAR R with colorful parade and amory fete in Eliz. Mem-at-Large, represented Trenton. Thu Mar 30, 1933.

JONES, OBADIAH F, attended the complimentary dinner for WFB27 mems given by A Edward Woodruff Tue eve May 30,

1911. Rahway, Wed May 31.

JUDD, BENJAMIN F, who says he witnessed the assassination of Lincoln, observed his 103rd dob recently. Helping the Vet celeb were 5 gens, fm his ae 2 gggdau to his s Frederick, ae 71. New London, CT, Fri Jul 9, 1937.

KENNEDY, JENNIE, NURSE. (See Experiences - Nurses.)

KNOBEL, CASPAR, 70, the last of a band of 14 Cav men who captured Jefferson Davis, was found unconscious today, with a Gold Medal awarded him by Congress clasped in his hands. Last Sat he was the central figure in the 48th anniv of the day he personally called on the C Pres to surrender. PHL, May 16, 1913.

JOHNSTON, JANE SEIGMUND, MRS, 80, who, as a girl in GA figured in the capture of Jefferson Davis, Pres of the C, d here Sun Aug 19, 1933. When ae 12, res with par near Irwinville, GA. On Wed May 10, 1865, aft the C had collapsed, the little girl noticed a stranger in the vcnty. U soldiers were encmp nearby and she told them abt it. The stranger soon was in custody and was identified as Jefferson Davis. The child became widely known as "the barefoot girl." NYT: Tue Aug 22.

LANG, NOAH S, attended the complimentary dinner for WFB27 mems given by A Edward Woodruff Tue eve May 30, 1911. Rahway, Wed May 31.

LEE, HARRY RENE, LT GEN, 86, of Nashville, TN, said on a visit to Hot Springs, AR, that there are only abt 11,000 C Vets left, abt 7,500 pens by their respective states. Adj-Gen to the Cmdr-in-Chief of the UCV, he has many distinctions: serv as Adj-Gen under 12 Cmdr; one of the 2 men rcvd at the White House in C uniform; and a shipmate of King George V of England while the latter was serv in the British Navy. His concern now is with arrangements for the 1935 C R at St Petersburg, FL, in April. Hot Springs, AR, Fri Oct 19, 1934.

LENOX, A G, one of 3 candidates for Jr V-Cmdr during the 44th annual encmp of the dept of NJ GAR at Trenton, to the natl encmp. Fri May 19, 1911.

LEONARD, CHARLES H, Qtmstr, attended the complimentary

dinner for WFB27 mems given by A Edward Woodruff Tue eve May 30, 1911. Rahway, Wed May 31.

LILLY, THOMAS. When a POW in a C prison camp, mailed a letter to a relative, Mrs Julia Waller, in Evansville, IN, 60 yrs ago. The letter was recently found in a lost bag of mail at Cleveland and forwarded. Vet d 50 yrs ago. Evansville, IN, Tue Dec 31, 1929.

LINDSEY, NATHANIEL W, 97, believed by MO CW Vets to psbly be the only living surv of the thousands of Fed sol held at Andersonville. "I'll be 98 in Dec, but I hope to round out a hundred bfr I die. I've lived to see our country recover fm the bitter hatreds of the CW, fight other wars, and now I want to live to see the country win out in the fight against the Depression," he said recently. He has a large steel etching of the old prison and is pleased to point out to visitors the various parts of the picture that were impressed upon his mind forever in the terrible days when sol d of hunger, lost their minds, or were shot. Eldorado Springs, MO, Fri Oct 26, 1934.

LOCKWOOD, CHARLES, Chamberlaid, SD. See obit Graff, Emil.

LOGUE, DANIEL C, DR, (See Monitor). NYT Tue Jan 16, 1900 and EDJ Fri Jul 16, 1909.

LOOP, MARTIN E, of Sacramento, CA, attended the 75th Gettysburg B&G R. (See **B&G**) (P)

LOTZ, JACOB, 93, of Clifton, was named a Maj in the NJNG tdy by Gov Moore. The oldest CW Vet in Passaic Co. Enl Aug 1863 Co M, 2nd Reg. Trenton, Tue Nov 22, 1938.

LUCAS, FIELDING, 86 next Nov 20, believed to be the only C soldier living in NJ. Res NJ 63 yrs, "so I guess I'm 7/8th Jersey Blue," he said with vigor. His ggf was in RW, his gf in 1812, and a s and gs in the WW. Rcvd his annual invite to parade Sat with the 8 surv mem of BJ67 on MDAY. Nothing pleases him more. Has been parading yr in and yr out, but he gets a new thrill every time he rides with the GAR. "And aft all, what's so unusual about it?" he asked. "Didn't we fight like men and like men made peace." Says he would go to war again if his country needed him and he was capable of svc. He will wear no uniform. "We didn't have much in the way of uniforms," he explained. "A lot of us wore what we could get. What was left of mine aft the war has been eaten by moths." New Brunswick, Fri May 29, 1931.

LYDECKER, A J, of Paterson, one of 3 candidates for Jr V-Cmdr during the 44th annual encmp of the dept of NJ GAR at Trenton, to the natl encmp. Fri May 19, 1911.

MACDONALD, TERRENCE, of Jersey City, one of 3 candidates for Dept Cmdr to be elected during the 44th annual encmp of the dept of NJ GAR at Trenton, to the natl encmp. Fri May 19, 1911.

MANSON, GEORGE, Roselle's oldest citizen, turned 90 today. B in Scotland, in a little hamlet on the N coast near Wick in 1827, imm USA 1854. Res of the Roselles 12 yrs and, when the boro ARC branch org last May, had his name read fm the stage as the oldest mem of the new org. Res with dau Mrs A W Burt, 4th Ave, E. SERV: 9th Reg, Col Fisk. Roselle, Mon Oct 29, 1917.

MARCUM, "AUNT JULIA," recently ae 91, of Williamsburg, KY, is the only woman in the US rcvg a CW pens as a combatant. In an 1861 raid on her TN home, she killed a C sol with an axe. Wed Apr 1, 1936. (P)

MARINUS, L H, one of 11 candidates for 9 delegates, to be elected during the 44th annual encmp of the dept of NJ GAR at Trenton, to the natl encmp. Fri May 19, 1911.

MARTIN, JOHN W, Chapl, attended the complimentary dinner for WFB27 mems given by A Edward Woodruff Tue eve May 30, 1911. Rahway, Wed May 31.

MASSIE, WILLIAM, attended the 75th Gettysburg B&G R. (See **B&G**)

MCCANDLESS, ROBERT. Attended a Christmas party for CW Vets given by WRC27 Tue ngt in Eliz. Wed Dec 23, 1925. (P)

Honored at MDAY svc. Sat May 31, 1930. (P)
Memories of '61 recalled. Mon Jun 1, 1931. (P)

Article on dob party for McCandless and Joseph Cannon. Mon Jan 6, 1936. McCandless b Mon Jan 4, 1847, Eliz. Res 1081 Lafayette St. Fam: ch Albert, David, John, William, George, Mrs Clara Sheedy, Mrs William Emmett and Mrs Louis Finnerty, all Eliz. 20 gch and 16 ggch, who res in Eliz, Brooklyn, Carteret, Newark and Bayonne. 2 sis, Mrs Elizabeth Lane and Mrs Jane Fulton, attended the party. His f d ae 95, Eliz. MEM: UD25, as was his f. SERV: Enl ae 16. His f enl ae 50. (See Experiences) (4-gens P: L-R, Mrs William Emmett, dau; David Nesbitt, gs, holding John David Nesbitt, ggs; Mr McCandless; David McCandless, s; and Mrs Robert McCandless, the Vet's 2/w.

Article on Eliz MDAY celebrations. Fri May 29, 1936. (P, holding the flag)

Article on forthcoming dob party. Dec 29, 1936.

Article on Eliz MDAY celebrations. Of 40 Orchard St At ae 90 will ride at head of parade. Sat May 29, 1937. (P)

dob gifts for CW pair McCandless and Cannon. Mon Jan 10, 1938. (P)

Receives homage MDAY svc. Tue May 31, 1938. (P)

CW Vets vote. Wed Nov 9, 1938.

Honored at MDAY parade. Wed May 31, 1939. (P)

MCCOY, W H, in the Wed tribute paid to CW Vets, with 27 other NJ Vets and one NY Vet GAR R with colorful parade and amory fete in Eliz. Mem-at-Large, represented Trenton. Thu Mar 30, 1933.

MCKENZIE, JAMES H (See Monitor). Sat Feb 20, 1926.

MELICK, WILLIAM R, attended the complimentary dinner for WFB27 mems given by A Edward Woodruff Tue eve May 30, 1911. Rahway, Wed May 31.

MENDELL, W W, JUDGE, celeb his 84th dob at his Walnut St home, Cranford, Fri. b Tue Jul 5, 1836, in that part of Eliz then known as the Black Horse Tavern, Rahway Ave, m Tue May 4, 1858, Miss Mary F Randolph of Eliz, b Thu Sep 20, 1838. They have 2 ch living, Mrs Warren V Kirkman and Miss Lillie B, and a gs Randolph Mendell Kirkman, all C. Rcvd early educ in the little schoolhouse which had stood on Lincoln Ave, and Miss Martha Garthwaite's school, located in present Normandy Park. Worked for his f on a farm in C, then ae 17 began to learn the carpenter trade in Eliz, and is still engaged in the building biz, having erected more than 100 C houses. A Repub. Comm of Deeds 30+ yrs. JP since 1878, and C Police Court Judge 14 yrs ago. MEM: Rolla Engine Co 2, 1856-67, and is an Eliz EF. Charter mem C FD, the first foreman of Hose Co 1. UD25, past Cmdr. SERV: Enl Aug 1862 30th NJ Vol, into part of 1863. C Jul 5, 1919. (P)

Attended a Christmas party for CW vets given by the WRC27 Tue ngt in Eliz. Wed Dec 23, 1925.

Attended annual UD25 Christmas party Wed. B Rahway Ave, but res C many yrs. Thu Dec 30, 1926. (P)

MENNET, OVERTON H, DR, 89, of Los Angeles, CA, attended the 75th Gettysburg B&G R. (See **B&G**) (P)

MILLER, MARY E, NURSE. (See Experiences - Nurses)

MITCHELL, MR & MRS WILLIAM J, of 653 Adams Ave, Eliz, celeb their 50th m anniv last ngt, with 4 fam mem celeb their dob. They were m 1860, she the frmr Emma Bragg, in Ollertown, near Clinton, by Rev D Van Horn, and 5 yrs later rem to Eliz. He turned 72 ystdy, s John B was b Feb 13, gd Miss Marguerite was ae 11 on the 13th, and dob of dau Miss Mary E was Feb 2. Res in the vcnty of Adams Ave 35 yrs, 19 yrs in their present home. 4 ch were present, Mary E, Anna A, Charles L and John B, all of Eliz. Carpenter by trade. He was b Liberty Corners, and she at Lebanon. MEM: UD25. SERV: 31st NJ Vol Inf, Co A, enl 1864 for 9 mos, but was confined to a H for most of his svc. Tue Feb 15, 1910. (P) (Other attendees mentioned)

Charles L, whose home adjoins his par, and John B, E Liverpool, OH. They have 10 gch. Mrs Fannie Bragg, Lebanon, John Bragg, Chester, and Mr & Mrs C S Mitchell, Highbride, are 4 relatives who attended their m.

MORTON, HOSEA QUIMBY, 97, who "voted twice for Lincoln and fought at Gettysburg," as he sits in Los Angeles court and hears 71 yr old w in alimony squabble. Court postponed his case for 3 wks. Fri Feb 26, 1937. (P)

MURPHY, BERNARD, in the Wed tribute paid to CW Vets, with 27 other NJ Vets and one NY Vet. GAR R with colorful parade and amory fete in Eliz. Mem-at-Large, represented Jersey City. Thu Mar 30, 1933.

MURPHY, BRIDGET, NURSE. (See Experiences - Nurses)

MURPHY, FRANCIS, of Trenton, gave affidavit that Charles B Fowler was the man who serv with him in Co B, 1st NJ Cav in the CW, and that this Fowler is still alive. Trenton, Tue Dec 24, 1912.

NEGLEY, WILLIAM, attended the complimentary dinner for WFB27 mems given by A Edward Woodruff Tue eve May 30, 1911. Rahway, Wed May 31.

NELSON, OLEY, Cmdr-in Chief GAR, gives a last salute at the last parade up Pennsylvania Ave, DC, as the final GAR encmp ends. The closing scene to the GAR triumphant history. Fri Sep 25, 1936. (P)

NEWBURY, E S E, CAPT, res Eliz, frmrly of Linden, addressed the pupils of Linden PS Fri on Abraham Lincoln. Also speaking was Dr Younglove, CW Vet. Sat Feb 11, 1905.

NEWLIN, ALFRED E, 92, of Graham, NC, reported in serious condition while attending the B&G R at Gettysburg battlefield. Thu Jul 7, 1938.

NORTON, MR & MRS HENRY L, 42 Union Ave, Jamaica, LI, celeb their 50th m anniv last Tue eve. He was b 1838, Salisbury, CT, and she, mn Adams, in 1840, Saugerties, NY, m Eliz by Rev Dr John F Hurst, P Fulton St Meth, who aft became a Bishop, at the home of the bride, 1st St near Broadway. They have 3 ch, Mrs Helen Adams Bronson, Waterbury, Ct, Herbert Lincoln Norton, Brooklyn and Ralph, Jamaica. 3 gch, all in attendence. Among those also attending, fm Eliz, were Mrs William H Adams, and Mr & Mrs James B Adams and their dau Sue. James is b/o Mrs Norton. Also, Mr & Mrs James E Febrey, their s Harold and dau Ethel. Another bro, Jeremiah E, could not attend. He was best man at their m. A clerk for PHL & Reading Coal & Iron Co while res Eliz. Rem to Brooklyn 1872, and is now Treas Jamaica Water Supply Co. **SERV**: Enl otbrk Eliz 13th Brooklyn Reg, aft listening to a patriotic sermon by Hurst. Others who enl at the same time were his bro-in-law Jeremiah E Adams (See obit), Edward L Tillou and George H Ropes, who aft became City Attorney. Mr Ropes is deceased. Tue Dec 10, 1912.

OAKLEY, MR & MRS JOHN B, 40 Caldwell Pl, Eliz, celeb their dob Fri, he 71 and she 67. He was b Ellenville, Ulster Co, NY, Tue Mar 24, 1840, s/o Meth Rev Bronson K, and she on a Sun in 1844, also Ellenville. They m Thu Feb 6, 1862. His name was given to him by Mrs John L Bloomer, Ellenville, who lived to ae 102. Returning to Ellenville aft CW, took charge of a pattern maker dept in a large concern. Rem to Sullivan Co and started in biz as a wagon maker. His shop burned twice, and once he was held up and stabbed, a notebook in his pocket saving his life. Rem to Catskill, NY. His wagon shop burned here. Rem to Eliz 1891 and purchased the wagon biz of John V Bavokel, E Grand St, then moved to present 84 Union St location. **CHH**: Meth. **MEM**: Past Cmdr J W Matson Post GAR Sullivan Co. Org UD25 WRC. Pres 156th Reg, NY Vol, 5 yrs, forced to resign when rem to Eliz. Honorary mem Plainfield Council 293, Jr, OUAM, also of Washington Camp 78 Post of A, Eliz. **SERV**: Enl on call for Vol, Sun Aug 24, 1862, 156th Reg, NY Vol, gen rank. With his Reg, the 19th Army Corps, defending DC in 1864. With Phil Sheridan in Shenandoah Valley, in every battle of the campaign. At Cedar Creek Wed Oct 19, 1864, taken prisoner. POW Libby, then Salisbury, the "Hell Pen." Paroled Wed Feb 22, 1865, reaching home nearly a skeleton. Rejoined Reg at Savannah, GA, and on Thu Jul 27, 1865, disc as POW by order War Dept. Fri Mar 24, 1911. (P)

O'BRIEN, BURKE, GEN, 90, of Pierre, SD, attended the 75th Gettysburg B&G R. (See **B&G**)

PALMER, A J, REV. See **Experiences**.

PARSONS, CHARLES B, of Red Bank, one of 3 candidates for

Dept Cmdr to be elected during the 44th annual encmp of the dept of NJ GAR at Trenton, to the natl encmp. Fri May 19, 1911.

PAUL, JAMES ROBERT, 105, of Charlotte, NC, attended the 75th Gettysburg B&G R. (See **B&G**) (P)

PHILLIPS, WILLIAM R, 90, of Crescent City, FL, attended the 75th Gettysburg B&G R. (See **B&G**)

POLLARD, ROBERT M, past RI GAR Cmdr, was reunited with Thomas R Harkins aft 64 yrs. Serv in CW together. Hawkins left Pawtucket for Omaha, NE, and was back visiting his s. Tue Jun 11, 1929. (P - Mrs Harkins in center)

PORTER, JOHN W, 92, became a Col in the C Army 75 yrs ago, but didn't know it until the B&G R at Gettysburg last Jul. Pres Davis made the appointment, but Vet was WIA Battle of Atlanta bfr being notified. C lost him aft that, until someone dug into old records at R. Memphis, TN, Fri Jun 23, 1939.

PYLE, ELIZA, NURSE. (See **Experiences - Nurses**)

RAMSEY, R S, 94, of Monticello, KY, attended the 75th Gettysburg B&G R. (See **B&G**)

RATH, CHARLES, in the Wed tribute paid to CW Vets, with 27 other NJ Vets and one NY Vet. GAR R with colorful parade and amory fete in Eliz. Mem-at-Large, represented Newark. Thu Mar 30, 1933.

REYNOLDS, F J, one of 11 candidates for 9 delegates, to be elected during the 44th annual encmp of the dept of NJ GAR at Trenton, to the natl encmp. Fri May 19, 1911.

ROBINSON, BENJAMIN D, in the Wed tribute paid to CW Vets, with 27 other NJ Vets and one NY Vet. GAR R with colorful parade and amory fete in Eliz. Mem-at-Large, represented Newark. Thu Mar 30, 1933.

RORAY, LOUIS, in the Wed tribute paid to CW Vets, with 27 other NJ Vets and one NY Vet. GAR R with colorful parade and amory fete in Eliz. Mem-at-Large, represented Camden. Thu Mar 30, 1933.

ROSE, CHARLES J, 95, of Miami, FL, attended the 75th Gettysburg B&G R. (See **B&G**)

RUHE, C H WILLIAM, of PA, who ran away fm home ae 15 to enl in U Army, has been accorded the highest honor the GAR Vets can pay - election as Cmdr-in-Chief. He succeeds Oley Nelson of Slater, IA. Tue Sep 29, 1936. (P)

RUSH, JACOB, Orange, CA, attended the 75th Gettysburg B&G R. (See **B&G**)

RUSSELL, WASHINGTON, in the Wed tribute paid to CW Vets, with 27 other NJ Vets and one NY Vet. GAR R with colorful parade and amory fete in Eliz. Mem-at-Large, represented Jersey City. Thu Mar 30, 1933.

RUTHERFORD, PETER, 85. To him, desertion is a crime that should be punished even aft 50+ yrs. He told the CO of nearby Fort George Wright that aft serv one enl in the CW, he reuped, but deserted 2 yrs later. "My life since then has been one of regrets. I have always been ashamed of the thing I did. I am here to pay the penalty," he told the CO. Told by the CO that an old law provided that if a deserter remained in the US for 18 mos aft the desertion his crime was outlawed, he replied "I want my record cleared. I shall take it up with the Washington Adj-Gen." Spokane, WA, Tue Aug 6, 1929.

RYERSON, ABRAHAM, in the Wed tribute paid to CW Vets, with 27 other NJ Vets and one NY Vet. GAR R with colorful parade and amory fete in Eliz. Mem-at-Large, represented Paterson. Thu Mar 30, 1933.

SEELY, URIAH, one of 11 candidates for 9 delegates, to be elected during the 44th annual encmp of the dept of NJ GAR at Trenton, to the natl encmp. Fri May 19, 1911.

SEWARD, GEORGE H, attended the complimentary dinner for WFB27 mems given by A Edward Woodruff Tue eve May 30, 1911. Rahway, Wed May 31.

SHARP, CHRISTIAN L "UNCLE CHRIS," 96, has a different idea regarding what's wrong with the yngr gen. "The yng people of tdy are no worse than the yng folks of my day. Their only trouble is that they don't get enough sleep," he said. He doesn't object to a woman taking an occasional highball, but he dislikes their smoking. He recalled visiting a yng girl in his youth and seeing her mo walk into the room smoking a corn cob pipe. Takes out a hunting license every yr. Lost an eye at Fredericksburg. Williamstown, Fri Nov 11, 1938.

SIMONS, SAMPSON S, GEN, of Los Angeles, CA, attended the 75th Gettysburg B&G R. (See **B&G**) (P)

SMITH, SPENCER, of Paterson, one of the CW Vets marching in that city's MDAY parade. Few GAR men left to march. A frmr GAR Cmdr. Fri May 29, 1931.

Smith, Spencer, in the Wed tribute paid to CW Vets, with 27 other NJ Vets and one NY Vet. GAR R with colorful parade and amory fete in Eliz. Mem-at-Large, represented Paterson. Thu Mar 30, 1933.

SNOW, CLARK. See Experiences.

SOLDEN, JONATHAN, in the Wed tribute paid to CW Vets, with 27 other NJ Vets and one NY Vet. GAR R with colorful parade and amory fete in Eliz. Mem-at-Large, represented Trenton. Thu Mar 30, 1933.

SPANGER, JOHN, the only CW Vet in Atlantic City. Moved fm PHL a few yrs ago. Obit of John C Allen, Thu Nov 18, 1937.

STAMETS, CYRUS, of Richwood, OH, attended the 75th Gettysburg B&G R. (See **B&G**) (P)

STEELE, W A, in the Wed tribute paid to CW Vets, with 27 other NJ Vets and one NY Vet. GAR R with colorful parade and amory fete in Eliz. Mem-at-Large, represented Trenton. Thu Mar 30, 1933.

STEPHANS, RICHARD, attended the complimentary dinner for WFB27 mems given by A Edward Woodruff Tue eve May 30, 1911. Rahway, Wed May 31.

STIMERS, A C, (See **Monitor**).

STINSON, GEORGE B, one of 11 candidates for 9 delegates, to be elected during the 44th annual encmp of the dept of NJ GAR at Trenton, to the natl encmp. Fri May 19, 1911.

STODDER, LOUIS N, CAPT, (See **Monitor**).

SWEET, GEORGE H, COL, b Nov 28, 1830, Oswego, NY, celebrated his dob Mon at home, "The Maples" in Linden, where he has res for 30 yrs. At one time the Tax Collector, and owned much valuable land in Linden. A Dem until the McKinley campaign, now addresses Repub meetings. Serv on Grand Jury a few yrs ago when excise conditions were brought out. He m his 3/w a few yrs ago. Aft MW settled in San Antonio, TX, where he edited and pub a newspaper, put up the first steam printing press west of the Mississippi Riv, and aft CW rem to Laporte, IN. At the request of many citizens, org a military Co, the Cmdr for yrs. Presented with a silver-headed cane, which he carried in all his journeys, when he rem fm Laporte. CHH: Meth. MEM: A Mason 50 yrs, mem of a San Antonio Lodge. An incorporator of the Winfield Scott Memorial Assoc. SERV: Soon aft leaving school ae 17, enl First Regulars at Rochester, NY, and went to Mexico, seeing much svc with Gen Winfield Scott. The Reg went fm Governor's Island, and during the S/AW, the Reg sailed fm NY for Manila; but he was too old to go. At CW otbrk enl Pvt 15th TX Cav, C Army, and aft became its Col, at one time Cmdr of a Brig. In svrl imp battles, having 2 horses shot out fm under him. Became acquainted with Gen Sam Houston, who had at dod an autographed letter fm Gen Robert E Lee. Vet is a MW pens, and the only MW sol res in the co. Tue Nov 29, 1910. (P)

TAYLOR, JOHNSON, 93, doesn't mind reminiscing. "Why, man, I was shot at more times close up than I got fingers and toes, and yet I escaped with only a bullet hole in the arm and a little scalp wound. I often wondered how they missed me so often when they 'had a bead' on me. It must have been providence." He can rattle off names, dates, Gens, and minute details of every major engage he participated in as if they happened ystdy. He fought in KY, TN and GA. Galion, OH, Wed Mar 27, 1935.

TENCH, ARTHUR W, in the Wed tribute paid to CW Vets, with 27 other NJ Vets and one NY Vet. GAR R with colorful parade and amory fete in Eliz. Mem-at-Large, represented Newark. Thu Mar 30, 1933.

TILLOU, EDWARD L, enl otbrk. (See Norton, Henry L)
TODD, L W, CAPT, Owosso, MI, has a prized possession, a letter yellowed with age, to Col Evernezer Gould, Owosso CW hero, fm Gen George H Custer, when they were officers in the U forces. The letter is dated (Sun) Oct 4, 1863, and expresses Custer's regret not to visit the Gould home because of war duties. Owosso, MI, Tue Sep 15, 1936.
TULLY, WALTER S, Hillside, attending the 1927 61st GAR natl encmp with G Dwight Stone, is assist Adj-Gen for the State Dept, mem GVH3, and on the natl encmp credentials. Tue Sep 6, 1927. (See obit G Dwight Stone)
    Attended annual UD25 Christmas party Wed. Thu Dec 30, 1926. (P)
    In the Wed tribute paid to CW Vets, with 27 other NJ Vets and one NY Vet. GAR R with colorful parade and amory fete in Eliz. Mem-at-Large, represented Hillside. Thu Mar 30, 1933.
UPTON, MARY C. See Experiences - Nurses.
VAN KIRK, PETER, in the Wed tribute paid to CW Vets, with 27 other NJ Vets and one NY Vet. GAR R with colorful parade and amory fete in Eliz. Mem-at-Large, represented Trenton. Thu Mar 30, 1933.
WASHINGTON, W N, of Atlantic City, only candidate for Senior V-Cmdr during the 44th annual encmp of the dept of NJ GAR at Trenton, to the natl encmp. Fri May 19, 1911.
WATSON, MARY M, NURSE. (See Experiences - Nurses)
WEDDELL, WILLIAM, one of 11 candidates for 9 delegates, to be elected during the 44th annual encmp of the dept of NJ GAR at Trenton, to the natl encmp. Fri May 19, 1911.
WESTCOTT, S E, one of 11 candidates for 9 delegates, to be elected during the 44th annual encmp of the dept of NJ GAR at Trenton, to the natl encmp. Fri May 19, 1911.
WILDMAN, IRA R, 88, of CT, attended the 75th Gettysburg B&G R. (See B&G)
WILLIAMS, JAMES. See Young, Ferdinand.
WINGROVE, CHARLES, of Clay City, KS, attended the 75th

Gettysburg B&G R. (See **B&G**) (P)

WINSLOW, JACOB, 94, of Los Angeles, CA, attended the 75th Gettysburg B&G R. (See **B&G**)

WOLF, GEORGE, of Los Angeles, CA, attended the 75th Gettysburg B&G R. (See **B&G**) (P)

WOOD, LORENZO D C, 87, and Miss Bertha C Beck, 65, of Eliz, were secretly m in Newark last wk, looking forward to many yrs at their 95 Woodland Ave, Kearny, home. His l/w d some time ago. 2 ch opposed the m. License was issued in Eliz, since she res there 23 yrs. She res 653 Montgomery Ave, and lived Irvington bfr. Wed Sep 22, 1926. (P)

WOODRUFF, A EDWARD, gave a complimentary dinner Tue eve at "The Elm," Sidney Hulsizer's new hotel at Irving St, Rahway, for mems of WFB27. An inspiring letter was rcvd fm Maj-Gen D E Sickles relative to the record of Gen William F Barry, Chief of Art of the AP, aft whom the local GAR Post was named. Jack Dunn, the bright little mascot of the Vets, when called upon by Toastmaster Woodruff, gave a pleasing recitation, "I want to go home," which elicited great applause. Rahway, Wed May 31, 1911.

WOODRUFF, NOAH OGDEN, oldest Eliz CW Vet, celebrated his 94th dob in Miami. Res with a sis Mrs Charles Moore at 820 Stanton Ave, and has been going to FL in recent yrs to escape Winter. His cuz Mrs Bertha Berriman and Miss Elizabeth Ball, with whom he stays at 1650 SW 11th St, Miami, made the birthday cake. His peaceful and beautiful surroundings were a sharp contrast to the "terrible fighting" on Seminary Ridge, witnessing the "wholesale murder" of Pickett's charge, and escaping fm that "despicable pit" of Andersonville. One of the "Boys in Blue" who mingled with the "Boys in Gray" on the 75th anniv of Gettysburg. "It was a wonderful occasion and a wonderful trip," he said upon returning. "It was the greatest thing of its kind that has happened in this country." Fri Feb 17, 1939. (See **B&G**)

Woodruff, Noah, 93, of 820 Stanton Ave, Eliz. Wed Nov 9,

1938.

WRIGHTSTONE, G D, attended a Christmas party for CW vets given by the WRC27 Tue ngt in Eliz. Wed Dec 23, 1925.

YOUNG, FERDINAND, 80, of Cranford, having a technical charge of dissertion against him, is now asking for an hon disc so his w, if she outlives him, may secure a pens, and his ch may preserve the corrected record. A bill is pending in the House of Reps. **SERV:** Enl otbrk ae 17 Co K, 14th NY Militia, aft changed to 84th NY Inf. At 2nd Bull Run, South Mountain, Antietam and Fredericksburg. Serv 2 out of 3 yrs enl, then given a furlough and went to his Rockaway Neck, Pine Brook, Morris Co, home. Overstayed leave and remained home svrl mos. Reup, under the name James Williams, Co B, 11th MD Inf. At Monocasy. A short time enl, aft hon disc, reup with the Civilian Corps of the Qtmstr-Gen, at Edgefield, TN. Drove an ambulance, and in charge of smallpox patients at the smallpox camp near Nashville. Hon disc at end as James Williams. Rcvd no bounty or other reward for 2nd and 3rd enl. Could have applied for a pens under Williams, but chose not to do so. Washington, Fri Apr 4, 1924.

CHAPTER 5

LIVING BLACK CW VETS

CHASE, ALEXANDER, 69, chef on the 3-masted schooner "Mary L Crosby," now at Heidritter's Lumber Dock in S Front St, with a load of timber fm Bangor, ME. The Vet has followed the sea for 50 yrs and was in San Francisco during the 1864 and 1907 earthquakes. Visited all parts of the world, having first shipped to sea on a sailing vessel at ae 12 as a cabin boy. "I have been in every part of the world," he said, "with the exception of the far N and I believe I will sail there bfr I d. In all my career I have never been arrested. Wherever I have gone I have been respected because I respect myself. I was b in Newark, NJ. That's my native town and I'm going back there for a few days." Wed Sep 1, 1909.

JOHNSON, SAMUEL, 103 on Sep 26, 1939. "I'm going to live to be the last CW Vet," said Johnson, who missed his first MDAY parade this yr because of a sore foot. "My foot's better now and I walk the half mile fm my home to town any time I feel like it." (A- Study Two Over 100, Seek Longevity Data), Norwalk, OH, Fri Dec 15, 1939.

MILLS, WASHINGTON, b 1848 into slavery, Murfreesboro, NC. Had an uneventful life until Nov 1862. (See **Experiences**)

PAIGE, R H, 109. Everything is changed but himself, he commented when arriving in Athens, TX, fm New Orleans for a visit. He is f of 22 ch, his oldest boy 83. He told how he was "tired of being a slave" when the CW opened, so he joined the U forces. At Shiloh in the 111th Field Art. Now lives on a $100/mos pens. "I'll live to a ripe old age," he predicted. Athens, TX, Fri Apr 15, 1938.

RUSSELL, ROSE. See Experiences -Nurses.

THOMPSON, EDWARD, ex-slave, octogenarian, b 1821, New Brunswick, an inmate of the S'H, Kearny. Had res at the home of his s, Abram, 706 Fay Ave, Eliz, bfr S'H. "Uncle Ed" claims to be the last person who was held a slave in NJ. His first master was Peter C Majorau. When very small he was sold to John Thompson, fm whom he took his name. He later became the property of Dr Ferdinand Schenck of Somerset Co. At ae 25 he obtained his freedom and went to live in Millstone, Somerset Co. Rem to Flemington with his fam, having m some 5 yrs bfr rcvg his freedom. She d 12 yrs ago, and he entered S'H 2 yrs later, taking ocnl visits to his ch. **SERV**: Enl 1863 at the first call for colored troops, sent to Camp William Penn, PHL, and assigned to the 22nd US Colored Troops. His Reg serv in the AP until aft Lee's surrender in Apr 1865, when it and other colored Reg were sent to TX, as that country at the time expected trouble with France ovr Mexico. His Reg was mu/o Oct 1865 and disc at Camp Caldwaller in Dec. Fri Dec 8, 1905.

WILLIAMS, CHARLES J, 97, serv throughout CW, and at one time was a bodyguard for Lincoln. Possesses a "Strad" violin, in the fam since his ggf. The box is the original container, although he has painted it a couple of times and made other repairs. Inside near the bridge can be plainly seen the name Antonius Stradivarius together with 3 Roman words and the numerals 1736. At one time he used to lead an orchestra and used the violin. Once was offered a large sum of money for the violin. Res with his w in an old house on Bachellor Ave and only uses it occasionally to play some of the old songs popular in his yngr days and marches, to the tune of which he and other sol of the CW went into battle. Sat Feb 12, 1927. (P)

CHAPTER 6

EXPERIENCES OF

Francis A Bishop

CW Hero Honored By USA.
Vet, 92, Gets Bid to Roosevelt Inauguration.

"It was early the mrng of May 12, 1864, and Lee's Johnny Rebs had licked Grant almost to a standstill at Spottsylvania Courthouse when Frank Bishop did his bit toward saving the U. The Nation never forgot it and today Francis A Bishop, 92, oldest living holder of the **Congressional Medal of Honor**, was polishing his decoration proudly and telling why his govt invited him to attend the inauguration of the U's 32nd Pres, Franklin D Roosevelt. 'It was Hancock's charge at Spottsylvania,' he said, eyes gleaming 'and the Johnnies were in a thicket...'

"Early fog was lifting from the forest, revealing an ugly line of trenches along the edge of the thicket, spiked with C bayonets - weapons that had taken cruel toll of the Feds as Grant hurled his men against Lee. The ragged Stars and Bars of the C fluttered faintly over the lines Grant had not been able to break. Bishop knew Grant had passed the word to Gen Hancock to charge, and there he was, peering at those trenches, while the ground shook with the crash of mortars, and minie-balls whined overhead. 'Our men struck,' said Bishop. 'The C flags were in front. I grabbed one. There were men all around me, but I was lucky.'

"He winked slyly. 'At that I guess I was pretty close to the front ranks to have taken a flag.' Hancock's men, holding the captured Stars and Bars, swept those trenches while Lee flung five attacks at them, and the musket balls were so thick they cut down half the trees. But Grant had won, and as Lee retreated Bishop received acclaim for his part in cracking that gray line and taking the Reg colors. 'For most distinguished gallantry in action in the capture of a flag at Spottsylvania, VA,' the War Dept citation said.

"Bishop enlisted Sep 15, 1861, in the Vol Co C, 57th PA Inf, from Bradford Co. Despite a gunshot wound, he is active today. When the Pres-elect sent his invitation, Bishop turned to his w and said: 'Pack your bags, mother, we'll leave right away.'" (A) by the AP, Retsil, Washington, Jan 27, 1933.

CHAPLAINS

Union Chaplains did much more than preach to the troops.

"Their duties often included offering comfort to the sick or dying, securing supplies from home congregations, serving as correspondents to home newspapers, burying the dead, writing letters for the disabled or illiterate, distributing mail, carrying men's pay home to their fam, and even acting as Reg hist. Since most chapl serv in Reg from their own communities, they often provided the only sol and fam link.

"Despite the difficult serv, however, many still had trouble wielding influence and gaining respect among the men. One Cav man said that his chapl was 'not at all fitted for the hardships and exposure, and it was as much as he could do to look aft his own physical well-being, and the spiritual condition of his flock was sadly neglected.'

"By 1863, half of the U Reg lacked Chapl. By the end of the war, at least 2,300 Chapl serv the U Army, at least 66 d in the svc, and 3 rcvd the **Congressional Medal of Honor.**

"As the war continued to drag on, the phrase 'fighting parson' became a rarity, but that was not the case of Rev Ashton. He remained a diehard Unionist to the end" (A) Times News (PA): Sat, Apr 6, 2002, quoted from "Early Times capsule," Jim Zbick, Times News reporter.

Isaac S Connett

Recounts Drowning Story Connected With CW. Sgt Isaac S Connett, Vet Z of this city, on Eliz Birthday Anniv, Tells How 33 Sol met Death Crossing Cumberland Riv.

"Time had dealt gently with Sgt Isaac S Connett, of Madison Ave, this city, for more than 40 yrs an active mem of the Vet Z, and still robust and in the enjoyment of all his faculties. Sgt Connett Wed attained the age of four-score yrs, and in entertaining some of his comrades of the long ago, in honor of the event, he gave the following graphic description of one of the spectacles of the CW, when 33 officers and enl men belonging to Cos A, B, C and L of the 27th NJ Vol, out of a total of 50 on a flatboat, while crossing the Cumberland Riv in KY, May 6, 1863, were drowned in the flood by the upsetting of the unwieldy craft, in which they were transporting themselves across the swift-flowing stream. Sgt Connett told of the event as follows:

'Our Reg, with 3 others and a Bat of Lgt Art, aft a raid in the latter part of Apr, 1863, and a pretty stiff fight at Monticello, KY, on our return, reached Stigold's Ferry, on the Cumberland Riv, where we expected to find small boats in which to cross the riv, but instead discovered two large open flat-boats, whose only means of propulsion were by means of heavy rope cables, attached to trees and stretched from shore to shore, worked hand over hand by human power. The 2nd TN and 104th OH Reg, a portion of the Bat and 8 Co of the 27th, had successfully effected a crossing in the 2 boats, when the remainder of the Art embarked in the larger flat, and 3 Co of our Reg, in the smaller boat started to cross. All were in joyous spirits, as the term for which we had enl was on the eve of expiration and our hearts rejoiced at the early prospect of reaching home.

'We had been kept busy since joining Burnside's 9th Corps, just previous to his attack on Fredericksburg in Dec, 1862, and aft chasing Longstreet from Suffolk, accompanied Burnside to KY, to clear that country of infesting bands of guerrillas. Most of those who had already crossed the riv and lined the high bank to witness the movements of the two boats were giving exuberance to their feelings by indulging in patriotic songs little dreaming of the terrible calamity that was soon to overtake the voyagers and throw the entire Com into a state of excitement, and fill all hearts with the deepest sorrow.

'Perhaps I ought to explain that the flat-boats were pulled across the stream, which had a current of 6 mph, by 4 men standing in the bow of each craft, who in its manipulation passed one hand over another on the rope. They had been cautioned not to loosen the grasp of one hand until the other firmly grasped the cable. When the flat containing the 50 men of our Reg had reached the middle of the riv, the men who manned the cable suddenly and unaccountably released their hold, and the lumbering craft instantly swinging around with its broadside to the rapid current drifted swiftly down the stream toward the larger and lower boat in which the Art had taken passage.

'When those of us on shore realized the situation of our comrades in the ungovernable boat as extremely perilous, all gaiety was instinctively hushed, and brave men held their breath lest the dangers of the imperiled be increased. Had the men in charge of the rope maintained their composure and raised the lower rope over their heads, enabling the craft to drift underneath, danger might have been averted, but many of the men became instantly excited, and as the flat neared the lower rope, they leaped up and attempted to seize it hoping thereby to stay the progress of their craft. This sudden movement caused the boat to careen, fill with water and precipitate the passengers into the flood. It was a moment fraught with the utmost peril, and the scene that followed beggars description, I never before, nor since, saw such an exciting, painful and heartrending spectacle, nor heard wilder, more agonizing cries, nor may I ever again have my soul wretched by the sight of such a horror.

'The wild shrieks on land, as well as in the engulfing waters, which at that instant arose, still rings in my ears. Strong, bravehearted men, inured to dangers, wrung their hands in passionate grief as they stood helplessly by and saw their comrades, one aft another, disappear under the cruel waters, utterly unable to render the slightest assistance. The men struggling in the stream, heavily laden with accoutrements, overcoat and blankets, were unable to swim, even though they understood the natatory art, while their perils were increased by many in their wild efforts to escape a watery grave instinctively grasping their comrades for support, thus carrying down supporters and supported.

'Those of us on shore who were compelled to behold the sad and sickening scene, were utterly powerless to render aid to our drowning companions. No means were at hand to reach any who were struggling fiercely in the waters which finally entombed 33 out of the 50 gallant fellows who had embarked. 19 of those who thus miserably perished, belonging to Co L, were fm Morris Co. Among those who that day in that manner, laid their lives upon their country's altar, were <u>Capt John T Alexander of Co B, and his 1st Sgt Albert D Wiggons,</u> of Morris Co. It was only aft the waters had closed over the mortality of my comrades, that we resumed our wonted calmness, that with sorrowful and meditative hearts, late that beautiful aftn in May, we took up our line of march for camp at Somerset. Some few of the bodies were subsequently recovered, but most of them never found an earthly resting place, their bodies finally being buried in the depths of unknown seas.

'My brave companions thus d, not as they could have wished, in the red heat of battle, but none the less they sacrificed themselves for the Nation's cause, and left a martyr's heritage to all who love our starry banner and cherish the priceless inst bequeathed by our forefathers, and preserved by the valor of the Vol army of 1861-1865. Today, boys, the sun shines clear in the woods, hills and riv of old KY, where I, with a thousand other Jerseymen, during the war, passed pleasant as well as saddened days, and the beautiful blue-grass region, through which the Z toured in 1891, en route to New Orleans, now a scene of peace and plenty, is as lovely as ever few, if any, of the industrious and quiet denizens of the charming valley having recollection of the appalling horror myself and thousands of comrades witnessed, there in those troublous times half a century ago.'" Fri Oct 13, 1911.

William T Goggins

Singer Company

"Mr G had started in the spring dept of the Singer plant. This was located in the Mott St factory. On his return fm the war, he went back into that dept, taking the pos of foreman, and he has held the same job ever since. He was first employ by a man named Fischer, who had the contract for turning out the springs. Of course, the entire plant at that time was operated under the contract system under which each branch of the industry was in the hands of private individuals who rcvd their pay from the co in lump sums. These contractors had to pay their own men, taking their profits from the difference btwn their pay rolls and the money they rcvd from the Singer Co.

"Aft the contract system was abolished, Mr G retained his pos. He recalls the circumstances of the Singer strike, but his story differs considerably from the tales told by other Singer veterans. He says that the trouble started in a sewing machine factory operated by a man named Howe, located at 3rd Ave & 33rd St. Howe's employees, who were dissatisfied with their hours and the gen conditions under which they worked, induced many of the employees in the Delaney St & Spring St plants of the Singer concern to strike in sympathy with them, and many of the workers in the Mott St factory followed their lead. Mr G did not take part in the strike, he says, but work in the entire plant was suspended until order was restored.

"He remembers, hearing some of the workers who had started

with the Singer Co when it was org, tell of the early days of the concern. The first workrooms of the co were located over an old car shop in Spring St. The co at that time employ only a few hands, and practically only one machine was made at a time. When a machine was completed it was placed on a handcart and taken to the salesrooms of the co in another part of the city, where it was finally disposed of. For many yrs after the Singer Co est its local plant the old handcart was on exhibition in the shop where it could be seen by the workmen.

"Mr G came here in 1873, when the Singer Co opened its downtown factory. In fact, he helped to get the factory ready for the opening. He worked here many wks in advance of the arrival of the small army of employees."

Military

"The Shenango was sent to aid in an attack on the city of Savannah, GA. We streamed up the Black Riv and reached the wharves in Savannah 3 days aft the city had been evacuated. Then we rvcd orders to go on up the riv and chase back the bushwhackers who were giving considerable trouble to the Fed troops. It was an awful trip. The bushwhackers were bad enough, but the difficulties of sailing up that riv were worse.

"The stream was so narrow and the channel so devious that the rigging of the boat was fqtly caught in the trees that lined the banks. Svrl times we nearly ran aground. When we finally completed our trip, although we had taken part in no naval engage, the ship looked as if it had been through a battle and had to be laid up for repairs. The masts and rigging were wrecked by the trees along the Black Riv. We only lost 1 man on the trip. He was shot by bushwhackers while doing duty in the crow's nest."

John Jackson

"Marine torpedoes have changed mightily since the CW. A

pens has recently been granted to John Jackson, who was a sailor on the Fed man-of-war, the 'Miantonomoh.' During the blockade of Charleston, when the C launched 3 torpedoes in the harbor, Mr Jackson swam from his ship and unscrewed the caps to prevent explosion. The pens comes late only because it was not necessary before. The govt recognized the deed at the time, and gave Mr Jackson a medal." The Youth's Companion - NE Edition, Thu Jul 7, 1904.

Benjamin Lawrence

"On a wide field at Belle Plains near DC one day, Lincoln and his cabinet adjourned to review the army. As Lincoln marched btwn the lines he approached Col Lawrence. 'Greenbacks,' suddenly shouted Lawrence, reminding Lincoln of the arrearage in pay. The entire army took up the chant as Lincoln continued his review. 'All right, boys,' said Lincoln smiling sadly, 'You'll get it.' Svrl letters mailed to his fam bear this legend on the envelope, 'Dear Uncle Sam, please put this through. We haven't a cent. Three months due.' All mail bearing that plea was delivered."

Robert McCandless

"Stirring incidents during the 3 yrs he serv as an 'unofficial sol' of the U forces stand out in the memory of Robert McCandless, 89, of 1081 Lafayette St, one of the city's 2 remaining CW Vets. Mr M saw much action as one of the yngst mem of the U Army. For 3 yrs he fought in his f's Co without having been formally enl. It wasn't until the last yr of the conflict that he officially became a sol. Mr M came to Eliz fm Ireland when ae 3. His f David was a carpenter. <u>David</u> formed a Co of Vol shortly aft the war started and it became Co F of the 14th Inf. Mr M went along with the group to Trenton where the mem were sworn in without examination. He wanted to be a drummer boy but he was not present when the others were accepted. He was only ae 13 at the time and was 5' 3" tall.

"The youth was with the Co in numerous engage, serv as aid to the Co physician, <u>Dr Brown</u>, who came fm the downtown section. The Co sailed around Cape Hatteras in a brig and later participated in an attack on C Bat massed in a swamp on Roanoke Island. It was this engage, Mr M recalled, that flag bearers who had covered the colors in a train, neglected to remove the covers with the result that mem of a NY Reg, mistaking the NJ group for the enemy, fired into their ranks, wounding a number.

"Mr M came home with his f after the latter had serv 3 yrs. The youth then wanted to enl but his par refused permission. Finally he went to CT, where he evaded his f's consistent opposition by enl at Fort Trumbull. Mr M declares he actually saw more action in the 3-yr period before he enl than during his official svc. He fought at Kingston, NC, where the C forces attempted to burn a RR bridge, and in other NC engage. The war ended when Mr M was 17. He was stationed at Burkesville Station, VA, at the time. Mem of the Co, believing they would be permitted to go home at once, celeb when they heard of the surrender of Lee at Appomattox Court House. Their enthusiasm was short lived, however, for their CO reminded them they had enl for 3 yrs and would have to serv the full time.

"The Co was sent to Richmond where civilians had been firing factories and looting warehouses. Aft 3 mos there the sol were transf to NYC, then to CA. Later they moved to Fort Vancouver on the Columbia Riv, and finally to Fort Watson, OR, where they remained for many mos. Here barracks were built. Fqt expeditions were made in pursuit of small groups of Indians who stole the Co horses. The Co was disc in Jan 1868 and arrived in NY abt 7 wks later.

"Sol in those days were paid $13/mos, Mr M stated. However, he said, they were able to purchase far more with that sum than is possible tdy. While at Fort Watson they were paid every 4 mos.

Mr M said that Srn POW were treated far better during the war than the C treated their captives. During the conflict the S was hard-pressed for food and consequently the POW were given last consideration. Many POW d of starvation at Andersonville, he said."

Washington Mills

This Man Was Once A Slave. Boston Janitor Had Lively Experience as Fugitive. Story Of How He Fled Into The U Lines. Attached Himself to a MA Reg.

"Washington Mills, b into slavery in Murfreesboro, NC in 1848, was destined to pass through many and varied experiences bfr he attained his present pleasant pos as janitor and eng at the American Unitarian Assoc bldg in Boston, says the NY Herald. As a boy his life was uneventful until Nov 1862 when the rumor spread that the 'Yanks' were near by, in Winston, NC. A little co of 12 slaves, 2 of whom besides yng Mills were boys, decided to run away to the Yankee lines.

So one dark Sun ngt they met and set out upon this desperate venture. They traveled through a dense wood until 2 am, when they reaches the house of the mo of one of the men. Here they rested a short time, then went on to the banks of the Clowan Riv. They waited a week, hoping that a gunboat would pass which would put them across. None came, however, but at sunset, just a week from the time they started, they procured a boat which landed them on the other side. They traveled on and on through the deserted C country til they were halted by a Yankee picket. Their leader stepped forward and replied "Friends."

"The little band was at last within the Nrn lines and under the protection of the Fed govt and then for the first time in his life, Mr M says, he 'breathed free air.' This camp which the co had reached was at Trenton, NC, and they with svrl other fugitive slaves, were placed upon an old schooner, which in a wk's time landed them in Newberne, NC. There they separated and little 'Washy,' with another boy, set out to look for employ, which they soon found with the 43rd MA Reg, 'Washy' working for the cook and the other boy for an officer. In the middle of Dec the Reg went on a short expedition, and engaged in svrl skirmishes. The little colored boys tramped in advance of the Reg. One day as they were on the march little Mills happened to walk beside Adj James M Whitney, of Boston, who was riding in front. 'Hello! Where are you going?' Mr Whitney asked the boy.

"Mr Whitney said he had promised his mo to bring her a little black boy from the S, and suggested to the boy that he enter svc and go home with him. It was satisfactorily arranged and yng Mills entered upon the fourth great event of his life. When the Reg was ordered home a train fm Baltimore was boarded. All the cars were flat except one, a box car, into which 'Washy' climbed, and fell asleep. When he awoke he was amazed to find that the train was wholly made up of box cars. Upon inquiry he learned that his car had been switched off. Within a few hrs he arrived in DC friendless and alone. He tried to board a train, but was knocked off. At last he climbed onto a train, which he told was bound for PHL.

"He had no idea of either the route or the destination, but as luck would have it he rode to Baltimore. At that time the railroad passed through the main streets of the city, so the train was obliged to slow down. The boy, tired of the long ride, got off and ran along beside the cars. He happened to glance across the street and there stood Adj Whitney, who had given him up for d. This completes the story of the more exciting adventures which Mr M has passed through. He reached Boston on Jul 21, 1863, and went to live in Adj Whitney's home. Miss Whitney, his benefactor's sis, undertook to teach him the "three Rs,' as he did not know A fm B. He learned quickly and attended the PS for 2 ½ yrs." Fri Oct 16, 1908.

Nurses

8 CW Nurses Living. All Are on Pension Rolls of Govt.

" 8 aging women who remember the dawn of mercy on the battlefield remain on the pens rolls of the US govt. They are the last of the CW nurses, who saw with their own eyes the beginnings of the profession of nursing as it was so splendidly launched by Florence Nightingale in the Crimea and by Clara Barton in the US. Continuing even today, 70 yrs and more aft their svc with the armies of '63, to live lives of svc and helpfulness, all these women have proved themselves an inspiration to the communities in which they dwell. They were pioneers in a field which tdy gives opportunity for svc to thousands of women. For CW nurses were almost all men, as anyone will recall from Walt Whitman's poems which he wrote as 'The Wound Dresser.'

"Male nurses in that conflict totaled 10,252 as against the 491 women who dared to enter boldly into that field. There may have been, and probably were, more women nurses than 491 during the CW, but many were employ by pvt org which kept no permanent records. This 491 counts only those directly employ by the govt. And of these, only 8 remain tdy on the govt pens lists. They are Hattie Brubaker, St Paris, OH; Jennie Kennedy, Bagdad, FL; Bridget Murphy, Ashland, KY; Mary E Miller, Logansport, IN; Eliza Pyle, Norris City, IL; Rose Russell, Vicksburg, MS; Mary C Upton, Clinton, IL; and Mary M Watson, Lockwood, MO.

"Memories of the war and of the early days of nursing crowd upon these aging women as they look back across the yrs. Mrs Brubaker, for instance, at 92, looks back on the day when she was 18. As Miss Harriet Manning, she accompanied a friend to an army H. She was so stirred by what she saw there that she vol to remain, though entirely without nursing experience. For 2 yrs she fought typhus and fever, and then she herself had to be sent home for a rest. Tdy she does her own shopping and marketing, keeps the garden of her small house, and takes an active interest in the passing show of world affairs. And the habit of svc has never left her. Even today villagers often call upon her when they are ill, and she never fails them.

"Mrs Miller is known as 'Aunt Mary' to the people in her home town of Logansport, IN. Though she is 93, she still is active, carrying on her housework and caring for an invalid s. <u>Her h, Assalon Miller, had been a Cpl in the U army,</u> and she followed him as well as she could, in the nursing svc. Once, returning from Vicksburg by boat, she was wounded in the arm by a shell fired from a shore battery.

"Rose Russell doesn't know for sure just how old she is, but she must be around 100, for she was b a slave near Vicksburg. During the siege of that city, she offered her svc to the U army as a nurse, and later continued in the svc in New Orleans. In these memories and those of the other surv nurses lies the whole history of military and to a large extent of civilian nursing. Clara Barton, most famous of the CW nurses, was founder of the ARC, and helped to advance its work in many other countries. Not for these heroic women, however, were the splendid equipment and modern technique of today. A hastily improvised ward in a Sibley tent with straw strewn about the floor, ghastly operations without benefit of anaesthetic by the light of oil lamps, crowded wooden wards without adequate sanitary arrangements - all these things can be recalled by such pioneers of a noble profession." Thu Jun 18, 1936.

Rev A J Palmer

"The Rev A J Palmer, Meth minister, res in Yonkers, NY, was in town on Tue, on biz with Dr J L Mulford and O A Kibbe. <u>Mr Palmer was a Pvt of Co D, 48th NY Vol</u> in the late war, and a POW 9 mos. <u>Dr Mulford was the Surgeon of the 48th Reg</u> and well acquainted with Mr Palmer in the svc and since. The visit of the latter recalled an incident that took place at the GAR Reunion yrs ago, of which many of the GAR hereabouts well remember. Gen Grant was at the reunion in Paterson, and sat on the platform during the speeches. As usual he sat passively, and apparently unmoved and indifferent, until one of the speakers, in a burst of eloquent and patriotic allusions to battle scenes, mentioned the Cmdr-in-Chief by name.

"Gen Grant suddenly turned his head to the right, and with crimsoned cheeks, eyed the speaker, and listened with rapt attention. The mention of the name of Grant was like an electric shock, and the vast audience cheered to the echo. As soon as the meeting broke up Gen Grant sought an introduction to Mr Palmer, took him to his own home, and a close intimacy continued to d. Mr Palmer was invited and expected to preach the F sermon of the great Cmdr but a sudden attack of nervous prostration, to which he has been subject since the war prevented." Daily Fredonia, Wed Dec 22, 1886.

George H Sanborn

"Had an experience never forgotten giving much concern to his f. Had 2 memorandum books, each with his name on them, and gave one to a companion who d a few days aft. The next day, NY papers announced the d of Sanborn. His f, reading this, hastened to the battlefield, securing a pass fm his friend Gen Butler, and had the body disinterred. Intending to send him home for int, was unable to make a positive ID. While gazing at the body, a nearby orderly noticed his dilemma and informed him that the Reg, which had stacked arms a short distance away, would soon arrive. Bfr they arrived, he met Thomas Flynn, a frmr E downtown res, who said he just saw his s. F and s met a little later, in a most affecting scene."

Clark Snow

Vet of '61 Guest of Camp / C Soldier Praises Men and Work at Anniston.

"Pvt Clark Snow of the AL 'Yellow Hammers' limped into Camp McClellan to give the boys of the B&G a few pointers on how to lick the Huns. 'I ain't had no experiences with Mr Kaiser, but I reckon what me and Col Johnson went through a few yrs back was a fair sample of what you youngsters are due to stack up against over yonder,' he declared. 'We didn't have some of those new fangled smelling gases but we had to battle against the effects of some of the rottenest corn whiskey that ever came from a still and I reckon that's just as bad. Take it from me, youngsters, it's a good thing for Uncle Sam that these here mountain moonshiners have been skeert into burying themselves away for the winter.' Pvt Snow, in his gray uniform made fm remnants of the one he had worn, was standing on a modern sol city of 30,000 men and nearly as many canopies.

"Watching bayonet practice, he gasped 'B'gosh, I thought I knew a thing or two about using those hedge trimmers, but that there Irishman (instructor) could lick a whole German army all by himself. If you youngsters ever get worked up to the same state of mind he's in there'll be a lot of the Kaiser's gang snoozing with their toes pointed toward the sky this time next yr.' At mess time he had soup, roast beef, mashed potatoes, vegetables, coffee and rice pudding, which he preferred eating with a knife. Aft eating, Snow told the boys of 1918, 'And us fellers used to think we were kings when we had bread puddin' once a wk. And roast beef - well, that was just as scarce as booze was plentiful in the old-time army. No wonder you youngsters look hale and hearty. You're just as well off in the army these days, and probably better, than back to civil life.' Next the Vet was shown the post exchange. Soft drinks of every description were on sale, candy, and crackers instead of the old-time 'chaw of tobaccy.' Nearly everyone was puffing on a 'butt.' Snow summed it up in a few words, 'They'll have a hard time smoking themselves to d, and I'd be a better man tdy if they sold more cigarettes and less booze in the old Gray boys' canteen.'

" Giant-like motor trucks hummed around instead of the old-time army mule. Peculiar to Snow was that everybody seemed to be busy performing some imp task. He summarized his inspection tour. 'If our boys had all the good things you have tdy there would be a lot more of us alive to tell the story. Conditions are not like they were back in the 60s, and since seeing your camp I'm convinced that Kaiser Bill is in for the trimming of his life. Go to it, youngsters. They won't take me back in the ranks, but I'll watch the B&G from the sidelines.'" Camp McClellan, Anniston, AL, Tue Jan 22, 1918.

Theodore Eugene Squier

"Narrowly escaped burial at sea while in a coma. Suffering fm typhoid fever on board a transport returning sick sol to the N, was thought to have d, and, wrapped in a blanket, was placed on deck with a n/o bodies awaiting burial. Fortunately his moans attracted attention and his life was saved."

G Dwight Stone

"His Co pitched its tents on the village green at Litchfield, CT, Jul 26, 1862, the grounds being named Camp Dutton. On Sep 15 the entire Reg broke camp and marched to East Litchfield, boarding 23 RR cars for the scene of battle. On the way to Burlington, NJ, the engine and 3 forward cars left the track, preventing the Reg from participating at Antietam. A Reg on the train ahead was rushed to the battlefield. Mr Stone was elected color guard in the defense of Washington. He described his experiences as follows:

'One afternoon a shell exploded near my tent, followed by 5

others, and they seemed like 1,000 thunderbolts bursting at one time. One of the magazines rose 100 ft in the air, pieces of shell flying in all directions. I counted 10 bodies on the ground, and 14 others had been hurled about in every direction. During this skirmish a train of 700 horses was captured by the C. The horses broke loose. I was sent out with a detachment to capture them. It was an exciting experience. Reports of whisky being sold to the sol caused the arrest of a citizen. As a mem of the provost guard I was ordered to search houses in the vcnty of where my Reg was quartered. We found 3 bottles of whisky in a house, and 27 bottles in a barrel in which straw had been piled and a hen setting on a nest of eggs.'

"When he was made a Sgt-Maj he was ordered to make an immediate report on the dimensions of a fort, with a drawing showing its form and location. It took from 10 pm one night until nearly daybreak to complete the task. Mud was knee deep around the fort. 'On Apr 28, 1863, I was ordered to join the AP, Gen U S Grant being in cmd. We had hoped we were bound for James Riv, but found we were attached to Gen Grant's cmd. Nearly every man threw his dress coat, shoulder scales and other useless trappings into the riv. On May 20 we resumed our march, passing over Mary's Heights, some 15 miles from the front. Before sunset we reached the 6th Army Corps, Gen Sedgwick in cmd. On May 21 we witnessed one of Gen Grant's flank movements in the direction of Richmond, VA. We were at the extreme left of Spottsylvania Courthouse. The next day Gen Grant and staff passed. Pieces of artillery poured shot and shell. The engs swung a pontoon bridge across the riv and the army crossed over and lay for the ngt. May 27 we recrossed Jericho Ford.

'We started at 8 pm. Not a work was spoken, canteens tied so they wouldn't rattle. The road was dusty and dead horses lay in it from the day before. We reaches the Pamunky Riv at Hanover Town, marching 35 miles in 10 hours. Jun 20 was a terrible day. The ngt before we threw up a breastwork at Petersburg. Pickets were sent out in front digging holes, remaining in them.

Sharpshooters were on the roofs of houses and it was dangerous to expose even a hand above our works. Two men were KIA and 11 WIA. A body of colored troops was repulsed 3 times in charging the enemy lines. Jun 22 we moved abt 3 miles s of Petersburg. We lost connection with the 2nd Corps on our right and the Johnnies poured in through the gap. It took ½ hour to est the line again. We were relieved at ngt by another Reg and moved back. We were ordered to throw up breastworks and in bringing up a stick of wood it was hit by a bullet and knocked off my shoulder.

'Jul 12 we reached Washington. I asked Joseph Vail, of Litchfield, if Harper's Ferry had been captured. 'Thunder' said he, 'they are fighting on 7th St now.' We went through the saloons and gathered up quite a number. On 7th St women were in front of the houses with pails of lemonade. One of them asked me if I wanted anything. I told her I wanted a handkerchief and she took one from her belt and gave it to me. Sep 19 at the battle of Winchester, Capt Shumay fell in my arms, shot through the leg. On our right the enemy had pushed the 2nd and 3rd Div back and Gen Russell rushed the 1st Div into action. He was KIA. Gen Upton was also severely WIA. For 4 hrs we were under fire, advancing and lying down. Late in the aftn a gen advance was made and the army of Gen Early sent whirling through Winchester. The loss was 136 K/WIA.

'Starting the next mrng I crossed the battlefield and saw women peering into the faces of the d to see if some one they knew was there. It was a most pathetic sight and one I can never forget. During the day's tramp I knew of a cucumber pump in a side st and going there to fill my canteen, found a few of the DeEpinuel Z at the well talking with 3 VA girls, all of them 6' tall. An older woman came to the door of the house and cried out, 'Gals come in away from them Z. First you know they will kiss you.' Sep 26 we moved into camp on the s end of the Massanutten Mountain, resting there for 10 days. During that time Gen Sherman's chief of staff was KIA by a guerilla. Gen Sheridan sent word to Gen

Early to surrender or he would leave the valley so a crow would not fly over it. Oct 6 Gen Sheridan executed his threat and the valley was lighted by burning barns, hay and grain stacks. We could see the advance of the Cav.

' Oct 10 at Cedar Creek, order came for the 6th Corps to rejoin Grant's Army at Petersburg, and on Oct 19 the battle of Cedar Creek took place. Gen Early's Army had been reinforced after the severe defeats at Winchester and Fisher's Hill and lay near Strasburg. We could see he had a Signal Station on tcp of Massanutten Mountain 800' high. At daybreak we heard brisk firing, followed by the roar of art which came nearer as the 19th Corps was engaged. Gen Early had captured the picket line of the 8th Corps and was in its camp before it had time to oppose him. The 19th Corps was already in retreat and Early's men were advancing towards our position. We lay down and replied to their shouts, but still they came on. Col McKensie's horse had been KIA and he took the horse the Adj was riding. The Col had been wounded in the foot. The troops on our left were in retreat and we were left alone.

'It was useless to try to hold our own and we were ordered to fall back. The whole army retreated about 2 miles. The enemy not pressing us too closely, the line was reorg and we waited for orders. Gen Sheridan had been in DC and had returned as far as Winchester. Hearing the roar of the battle 20 miles away, he made the ride celeb both in history and in verse. I was within 10' of him as he came up on his noble horse, Renzi. He rode along the whole line taking in the situation and, to inspire confidence in the men, told them, they would put up their tents on the 'old ground tonight.' About 4 o'clock an advance of the whole line was made. Early's Army was driven across Cedar Creek. 8 officers were left and the n/o men sadly depleted. Gen Custer rode through our camp with a squadron of his men bearing 22 captured flags.

'Nov 13 the weather was cold and I missed the overcoat I loaned to Capt Shumway. Early in Feb I was promo as Brig Sgt

Maj. It was a pos not held by anyone before. Afterward I learned I had been promo by Gen Buckingham as 2nd Lt. I was with Co C 3 days when I was ordered to act as Lt in place of Lt Munson, sent to the H. With my new uniform the men did not know me. Apr 9 word came that a flag of truce had been hung and the result would be known by 4 o'clock. About 3 o'clock I climbed a tree where I could see up the rd toward Appomattox. I saw a n/o mounted officers coming with Gen Meade leading, waving his hat and shouting 'The Army of Northern VA has surrendered.' Batteries commenced firing and the whole army sent up rousing cheers. We now felt our work had been accomplished and we could go home. Apr 18 the whole of Gen Grant's Army excepting the 6th Corps was started for DC to be mu/o. Aug 10 orders were issued from the War Dept for the mu/o of the entire Reg.'"

Henry H Todd

"POW Richmond, Macon, Savannah and Charleston. At Macon joined Gen J Madison Drake (then Lt in 9th NJ Vol) in unsuccessful tunneling operations. When in transit fm Charleston to Columbia, he, Drake, and others jumped train. They endured 47 days of terrible hardships, tramping 1,000 miles thru the Carolinas and ern TN, reaching Knoxville. During a hot fight with guerillas in the mountains, he and Drake became separated. Drake entered Union lines a wk later, but he did not gain safety until svrl wks later."

Jarvis W Williams

"Fought in the 48 battles of the Reg, never WIA but caught smallpox, which led to one of his most humerous albeit dangerous experiences of his fighting career. He and another were isolated in a tent in the middle of a forest. Their illness ran a couple of days, partial recovery brought a desire for food, and they went foraging. Bfr they knew it they found themselves confronted with a party of C and were forced to flee, which led them to a deep ditch. Both jumped, he making it, but his companion missed his footing and toppled. He retraced his steps, extricated his buddy, and successfully made their escape. He also recalled with a great deal of mirth that while he enl a Sgt, he left a Pvt. Shortly aft attaching to the 48th, made a duty Sgt. Someone was seen smoking in a powder magazine. He protested his innocence, was not believed, and demoted, but had no regrets."

Elias Crane Winans, as relayed in Gen Drake's hist of the 9th NJ Vol.

"In Dec 1862, while the 9th was in NC, it halted near Goldsboro. When descending a RR embankment, and a long wooden-covered bridge 3/4 of a mile away to their left and front, Col Heckman ordered the Reg to change direction to the left and march along under cover and set fire to the bridge, which crossed the Neuse Riv. The bridge was strongly defended by a RR 'monitor,' a n/o Bat and Art.

"Nearly every mem of the Reg within hearing of Col Heckman's voice begged to be selected for the duty, but as a few could perform the dangerous task as well, if not better, than many, the following were chosen: The Adj and one man of the 17th MA, Lt Graham, vol aide to Col Heckman, Cpl James W Green, Pvt Elias C Winans of Co K, and Pvt William Lemon of Co E, of the 9th.

"These brave men, supplied with fuses, set out on their perilous enterprise, with their lives in their hands. The C on the bridge, and near by, plainly seeing the object upon which Winans and his companions were bent, directed their fire upon them with terrible fury, and those who watched them believed it would be impossible for either of them to reach the structure and live. The Adj was fatally wounded. Green and Winans, despite the storm of leaden hail, were first to reach the bridge, and attempted to ignite the fuses, but they would not burn.

"Winans, determined to accomplish his mission or d, closely watched his opportunity and crept down the embankment into the edge of the woods, and, gathering up an armful of dried leaves and light wood, scampered back to his companion, who had screened himself from the enemy's fire by standing against a heavy timber on the side of the structure.

"Winans, while clambering up the embankment on his return, was discovered by a party of C under the bridge, who, with curses, sent their compliments in the shape of a shower of bullets and buckshot, one passing through his canteen, one through his tin cup, another through his coat, and still another through his old cap.

"Placing the leaves, with the fuses, upon a beam, against the side of the bridge, he set them on fire, and in a moment the interior was enveloped in flames.

"While preparing to escape, their breath was fairly taken from them by a fusillade which swept through the doomed structure, and looking out, they saw Lt Graham of the Cav, and William Lemon of Co E, entering the bridge, bearing fuses. This supply having been added as fuel, all dashed back to the U lines, where they were heartily cheered for their successful and imp act. Col Heckman congratulated them in special orders."

CHAPTER 7

THE LAST SURVIVOR OF THE USS MONITOR CONTROVERSY

DISCUSSION

The famous battle between the Monitor and the Merrimac occurred on Mar 9, 1862. She sank off Hatteras the ngt of Dec 31, 1862. Almost 40 years later, a Lt Howard, pilot of the Monitor, d in Washington. Evidently his obit related that he was the sole Monitor surv. Not so, according to a 1900 NYT article. Still alive was a Capt Stodder, who had been a masters mate of the Monitor. This was not the only time that the "last surv" d, only to have the living step forward to say "not so." The very last time that the "last surv" d, and there was no noticed article with the living stepping forward was in 1932. Could this Vet who d in 1932 be the "Last Surv?" The EDJ investigated this controversy in 1909, since a still-alive was the f-in-law of the then current Mayor of Eliz. The paper's "inquiry at the Navy Dept at DC, proved that even the govt does not know the names of the surv of the Monitor officers."

The Navy Dept does have lists of crew members which includes others besides officers. (1) Of those appearing in the newspaper, most are not listed on these lists. Perhaps they are on other rosters that the Navy Dept might possess. This long-term public controversy is interesting in itself, and also gives first-hand experiences from some of the Vets on this hist battle, as well as discussions about some of the Vets themselves. Perhaps this information just might add some Monitor Vets, who might have been left off, onto official govt rosters. A notation will be made, using the footnote A B C or D, for these govt rosters, when a Vet is on one of these lists. The Controversy begins with the d of Lt Howard.

THE CONTROVERSY

<u>TUE JAN 16, 1900</u> - A Survivor of the Monitor

"Lt Howard, just d in Washington, pilot of the Monitor, was not the sole surv of the Co of that vessel of war. There is still in the active svc of the Revenue Marine a frmr officer of higher rank, Capt Louis N Stodder (D) of the Revenue Cutter Svc, who was Master's Mate of the Monitor when she sank of Hatteras on the night of Dec 31, 1862. He is now in cmd of the anchorage svc in NY Harbor."
Special to the NYT: Tue Jan 16, 1900, Dateline Washington, Jan 15.
(D) Stodder, b NY 1838, d Oct 8, 1911. Int Greenwood, Brooklyn, NY.

<u>FRI APR 23, 1909</u> - Last Of Famous Crew Of The Monitor Dies

ANDERSON, HANS, (C) (D), 85, b Gothenberg, Sweden, d Tue Apr 20, 1909, at home, 93 Hall St, Brooklyn. S Edward d suddenly abt 2 yrs ago. Imm USA 1847. Worked at NY Navy Yard until enfeebled by age. Said to be the last surv of the Monitor, remembered for its participation in the memorable battle against the Merrimac. Never tired of relating the incidents of the famous battle. For yrs a feature at patriotic meetings in the Ern States and often called upon to make addresses at them. **SERV:** A sailor. When vol were called for the Monitor he vol. Had seen duty on the frigates "Falmouth" and "Congress," but, on account of the peculiar construction of the Monitor, it was difficult to get a crew for the little ironclad. Often said that on the mrng of the day of the hist battle, Mar 9, 1862, he, acting as Qtmstr, was the first man to sight the Merrimac. He notified Capt John Lorimer Worden (A), later Adm, and described the Merrimac as 'a roof of a house on a float." Often said that there was not a man on board the Monitor that had much hope of

235

getting out of the battle alive, but when the firing began confidence grew in the crew and finally the Merrimac was put out of commission. F: Thu ngt. Fri Apr 23, Dateline NY, Apr 23.

WED APR 28, 1909 - Monitor Surv Lives In Eliz

W S Drake Denies That Brooklyn Man's Death Wiped Out Famous Ironclad's Crew - - Story of Life as Orphan, Naval and Merchant Sailor.

"Disputing that Hans Anderson, sailor, who d in Brooklyn a week ago was the last surv of the famous CW ironclad Monitor, W S Drake, a house mover, of 407 Livingston St, this city, entered the EDJ office ystdy aftn and told a story of life and adventure that might have come from the pen of 'Henty' of Richard Harding Davis. Drake, who is ae 64, f/o 17 ch, 10 still living, surv of 2 shipwrecks and frmr ward of the US govt, says that he was one of the crew of that noted little vessel and an active participant in the great battle with the Merrimac. He also declared that there is res in Plainfield Grant Martin, another mem of the Monitor's crew. Drake makes the astonishing statement that the Monitor did not sink the Merrimac. 'Historians are all wrong,' he declared, 'when they say that we sank the rebel ship. The true version of that fight from my own observation and that afterward told by the pilot of the Merrimac to me, is that the crew of the ironclad, with machinery arranged for that purpose, sank the vessel of their own accord rather than have it fall into the hands of the enemy.'

"Mr D is as hearty and strong as a man 20 yrs his jr and credits all his miraculous escapes fm d by exposure and his strong constitution to the keeping of a promise he made his mo on her d-bed when he was but ae 6. With his mo hand in his, he said, he swore he would never swear, drink a drop of liquor, use tobacco in any form or gamble. This promise he has kept to a letter, he declares.

Thrilling Life Story

b in Barnegat, par of German birth and his German name "Dreck." When he was ae 2, his f d when thrown fm a horse, and mo d 4 yrs later. She had 6 bro, all d. He was left without friends and relatives, and adopted by US govt. "His career as a sailor began. He was placed on the school ship 'St Mary,' where he spent his childhood. At the otbrk of the CW, he was still aboard this famous ship, and when but ae 16 was trans to the gunboat 'Varuna,' on which he went to Hampton Roads. When the Monitor went into com he was detailed as one of her crew and on the ngt that little vessel sailed out in quest of the ironclad Merrimac he, then just ae 17, was in place as a 2nd gunner. The description of this battle, as told by the ex-sailor, is wonderful.

"On the day previous to the battle he said the Merrimac had destroyed all the wooden vessels in the harbor and sailed in the next day bent on more destruction. The Monitor, built like a cheese box with its 2 big guns in the turret, advanced on its foe. The Merrimac Drake described as an almost indestructible vessel. Her construction was such, he said, that cannon balls fired into her fm the Monitor's guns had no effect but would bounce off at various angles. 'When she came up,' he said, 'she gave us a nice salute with her guns. We responded pluckily. Our crew was the bravest one that ever went afloat, but I will tell you now that there wasn't a man aboard the Monitor that day who wouldn't have given his boots to be safe and secure on land.'

WIA

"'The noise in the turret was deafening. Our brave Capt, John Lorimer (Worden) (A), was in the turret during most of the engage, and whether it was the noise or what it was his eyes were injured in the engage so that soon aft he became blind.' Drake himself was injured. One of the 2 guns he was operating sprang back aft the disc of a shot and struck him, inflicting injuries he has never recovered fm. In describing the fiercest part of the fight Drake said that the crew of the Merrimac, seeing that her shots were not taking effect, rammed the Monitor. 'The shock was terrific,' he said, 'and there wasn't a man in the crew who didn't know that if she rammed us again in the same way we would not surv. But, luckily, the climax of the fight arrived at this point. We tried shot aft shot into the broadside of the vessel and I saw with my own eyes that they did not take effect, but rolled like water from a duck's back from the sides of the ironclad. In drawing back to prepare for another try at us with her ram, the ironclad met her doom. She struck on a bar and broke her shaft. This did not hinder her fm proceeding under steam, and immediately seeing that she must withdraw or lose the fight she started down stream, away fm us.

"'We pursued in a useless chase, for the big vessel could go 3 times as fast as we. The Merrimac sank later, but fm no injuries rcvd fm us. She was in a perilous pos, and being equipped with machinery meant to blow her up, or sink her, her crew, following instructions, set it in motion. The vessel slowly sank beneath the waves, having never been conquered.' Drake said he afterward carried, fm the spot where she sank, some of the wreckage of the Merrimac to the BNY.

In The Marine Svc

"5 days aft this battle Drake rcvd his disc fm the navy. Although only ae 17, he entered the merchant marine svc and secured a berth on the schooner 'Napoleon' as mate and navigator. The Napoleon was bound S with a cargo of provisions for the sol. The Capt was a 'coaster,' Drake said, and did not know anything abt navigation. 'Picture me,' he said, 'only 17 and a navigator. When the vessel got way out in the ocean, would you blame me when I straightened my shoulders and threw back my head, knowing that I was the whole thing and the only man of the crew that could take the vessel to safety?' Drake stayed with the Napoleon until his Capt became prosperous and wanted a newer vessel. From this time on Drake was fortunate, and not unlike the great seaman of the Spanish Main whose name he bears he became rich, owned shares in svrl vessels and was master of his own. He was worth abt $45,000 when he experienced his first shipwreck. For 4 days with the ice caked all ovr him, he stood lashed to the rigging of a ship. When rescued he claims that he was the only man that did not suffer by the exposure. Nearly every other mem of the crew had his feet or fingers frozen to such a degree that amputation was necessary. Drake attributes his good fortune to his good habits.

"The loss of his fortune and the end of his prosperous seafaring life came with a storm. At that time he was cmd his own vessel, the 'W S Drake.' He was carrying as passengers svrl men and women and their ch. The vessel was off Cape Hatteras. So violent was the storm that all hands were compelled to take to the life boats. 17 crowded into 1 boat. For 8 days this little craft with its shipwrecked cargo of human beings floated abt. The story of the horrors of those days, as told by Drake, is terrible. Only 5 of the 17 surv the 8 days. They were picked up by a passing vessel. The d of the other 12 was caused by starvation and exposure. In the same storm he lost another of his vessels and, as he puts it, his money went to 'Davy Jones's locker.'" Wed Apr 28, 1909.

FRI JUL 16, 1909 - Surv Of The Monitor Mayor's Father-In-Law

Was Paymaster on Famous Ironclad - Other Surv Found Since Journal's Narrative of W. S. Drake's Exp - Elizabethan Familiar With All the Boat's Officers

"Some time ago a story appeared in the EDJ about Willis S Drake, of this city, being a surv of the Ironclad Monitor. Since that time svrl stories have appeared in papers throughout the country about the surv of the Monitor. It would seem that the records of the crew are incomplete. Dr Daniel C Logue (A), assist surgeon during the engage with the Merrimac, is one of the two known surv. Following a widely published report that the last surv of the Monitor d in NY Apr 20 last, a communication was rcvd by the EDJ from Mr Drake to the effect that certain statements in the report were incorrect. He emphatically stated that he was one of the surv.

"Communications were also rcvd by a NY newspaper with reference to 2 officers of the famous boat - Daniel C Logue (A), of Belleport, LI, and Louis N Stodder (A) (D), of 284 Kingston Ave, Brooklyn. These 2 are still living. The EDJ recently obtained a list of the officers of the Monitor. Inquiries made disclosed the fact that A C Stimers (A) (D), paymaster of the ironclad, is Mayor Mravlag's f-in-law, and is still living. Mr Drake's name is not, of course, given as one of the officers, as he was not more than ae 17 when on board the famous boat. Shown the names of the officers he recognized all of them and recounted interesting incidents in connection with the svc of each as a mem of the crew.

"Inquiry at the Navy Dept at Washington, proved that even the govt does not know the names of the surv of the Monitor's officers. There is no possible way at this time to make a correct list, it was said. Of the 16 officers the records contain the names of 2, Lt John L Worden (A), Cmd officer; and Lt Samuel Dana Green(e) (A) (D), executive officer, who are known to have d. Besides the two named, the records show that John J N Webber (A), master; Daniel C Logue (A), assist surgeon; W F Keeler (A), paymaster; Isaac N Newton (A), 1st assist eng; and Albert B Campbell (A) (D), 2nd assist eng, all left the navy bfr 1865 and there are no remarks contained in the book which were written aft "hon disc."

"Hans Anderson, whose d caused the recent inquiries, was employed at the NY Navy Yard for many yrs aft he left the active svc aboard ship. To his friends he was known as Capt Anderson. Anderson was ae 85 when he d, and was b in Gothenberg, having passed most of his life on the water or around shipbuilding yards. He was one of the 10 seamen aboard the Monitor on the mrng when the Merrimac was sighted. Dr Logue (A), one of the living surv, enl as a surgeon when the CW began, and was assigned as assist surgeon on the Monitor. During the famous encounter with the Merrimac, according to Dr Logue's s, Lt John L Worden, cmd officer, was wounded and treated by his f. Fri Jul 16, 1909."

(D) Stodder - b NY 1838, d Oct 8, 1911. Int Greenwood, Brooklyn, NY
Stimers - b Southfield, Madison Co, NY, Jun 5, 1827, resigned Aug 3, 1865.
Green(e) - b MD 1839, d Dec 11, 1884, Portsmouth, NH.

FRI DEC 26, 1924 - CW Naval Fighter Is Dead

Daniel K Lester on Monitor in Merrimac Battle

LESTER, DANIEL K, b Fri Apr 6, 1838, Milton, NY, d early Thu mrng Dec 25, 1924, Alexian Bros H, Eliz. **SURV**: ch John, Los Angeles, CA, Edward, Radcliff, NY and Gray B, Irvington. 7 gch. 3 ggch. Chief eng on SI Ferry 20 yrs. At ae 16 began work on the ferry crossing the Hudson Riv fm Milton to New Hamburg. Aft CW settled in LI City, becoming eng for the Vol FD 14 yrs. 45 yrs ago became chief eng on the Bergen Point Ferry btwn Bayonne and Port Richmond. Rem to E 30 yrs ago, became chief eng on the "Uncas," "Arthur Kill" and "Aquehonga," the ferry boats operating btwn E and SI. Ret 1914, res with s Gray for awhile. Returned to E, res 78 E Jersey St, to be near old friends and the waterfront. Thought to be the oldest licensed pilot in the NY district. **MEM**: Natl Assoc of Steam Eng. Life mem Island City Lodge 583 F&AM, LI City. **SERV**: Enl otbrk Navy. In addition to being Chief Eng on the Monitor, he was Chief Eng on Mississippi Riv transports and in svl naval engage. **F**: Masonic svc, per request, Fri ngt, by Essex Lodge 49, E, at J S Stiner's Home for Svc, 97 W Grand St. Int Moravian, SI. Fri Dec 26.

MON FEB 8, 1926 - Last Of Monitor's Crew Is Dead Here

Willis S Drake, 83, Was Wounded During CW Engage With Merrimac - Had Adventurous Career at Sea

DRAKE, WILLIS SANFORD, 83, b Barnegat, d Sun mrng Feb 7, 1926, Alexian Bros H, Eliz. **SURV:** w, Elizabeth M. ch Mrs Blanche Erxleben, E, George W, Ralph P, Clarence B and Kenneth I. 7 gch. mo d when he was ae 6, and extracted from him a promise that he would never swear, drink liquor, use tobacco in any form or gamble. He kept his promise to the letter. For career and **SERV:** See Wed Apr 28, 1909, EDJ article above. Mon Feb 8, 1926

SAT FEB 20, 1926 - Another Monitor Surv Appears

Nebraskan Says Elizabethan Was Not last of Crew

"Hist's pages are crowded with the chronicles of surv of great military exploits, Grant bfr Richmond, the pursuit of Aquinaldo, the Lost Btln, the Princess Pats, and now the famous iron-clad USS Monitor. Since the d here Feb 7 of Willis Sanford Drake, who believed that he was the last of the crew, 2 other men have challenged his claim. The latest is James H McKenzie of Ponca, NE. Soon aft the d of Mr D, who was injured by the recoil of one of the 2 guns in the Monitor's turret, Charles H Holt, of Portland, ME, broke into the public prints to acclaim himself a surv of the world's first battle btwn armored men-o'-war. He further declared that he enl in the U Navy for the express purpose of serv on board the famous "Yankee cheese box on a raft" and that he remained a mem of the crew until the close of the war.

"The newest contender for surv honors, Mr McKenzie, of Ponca, drapes his claim in the trappings of a com officer. He proclaims that he was a 2nd gun Capt and his duty was the pulling of the trigger cord on one of the 2 guns. Unfortunately he does not rcv a pens for this meritorious svc, for his disc papers were destroyed in a hotel fire in Elmira, NY, many yrs ago. His lifetime, he explains, has been passed as a sailor, hunter, and adventurer. What a man of these proclivities could have been doing in Elmira he does not report.

"Despite the others' sturdily-advanced claims to svc on the Monitor, neither has advanced the details of its construction nor of the battle with the C Merrimac that Mr D was able to give. He always contended that the Merrimac, unable to subdue the "cheese box," withdrew from the battle and eventually was sunk by her own crew to prevent capture by the U forces." Sat Feb 20, 1926. (P of Mckenzie)

<u>MON MAR 7, 1932</u> - Vet Of Monitor Crew Dies, Aged 85

"**Thomas Taylor**, 85, who was b a slave and serv as 'powder monkey' on the iron-clad Monitor in its hist engage with the C vessel Merrimac, d today. His d was indirectly due to a beating he rcvd in Worcester, MA, on Christmas ngt, when 2 men robbed him of $90. Taylor is believed to have been the last surv of the Merrimac-Monitor engage. He was b in Currituck Co, NC." UP, Putnah, CT, Mar 7, 1932. EDJ Mon Mar 7, 1932, Front Page.

CONCLUSION

According to newspaper articles and obits, the passing of the "last surv" of the Monitor took place over a period of at least 32 yrs. The last surv from gathered material was Thomas Taylor, b a slave in NC. No noticed "I'm still here!" article appeared aft he d. He would have been abt ae 15 when serv on the Monitor, and very likely was a slave at that time. He d a victim of violent crime 2 days short of the 70th anniv of the hist battle.

ADDENDUM

Three supplemental articles complete this chapter. 1st is a Letter to the NYT Editor giving credit to the developer of the engine of the Monitor, 2nd is an additional first hand report on the battle by a crew mem, and the 3rd on the raising of the Monitor turret.

AUG 2, 1924 - Credit For The Monitor

Part is Claimed for George Reynolds, Engine Builder

"The Times ystdy mrng had an interesting article on the anniv commemoration of Capt John Ericsson. Now, there is no doubt that Ericsson deserves all the credit for having built the Monitor, but the credit for having produced the Monitor at the psychological moment in Hampton Roads is not to be credited to the Capt, but rather to my old friend and partner, George Reynolds of CT, the greatest mechanical eng America ever produced, the head of the Delemater Iron Works during the period of its great prosperity 50 yrs ago, a man whose inventions recorded a distinct step forward in engineering.

"In the '50s George Reynolds invented an engine that was a great improvement over anything that then existed. One of these engines was placed in a famous Sound steamer, which thereupon ran away from its nearest rival and for a long time caused the boat in which it was placed to remain the champion speedster of our great inland waterway. While Ericsson was rushing work on the Monitor he was also trying to complete an engine of his own device. The govt was pushing him to the extent of the speed limit in getting the Monitor under steam. He finished the boat in time, but not the engine. His friend Reynolds had one of his own engines at the Delemater works and finally induced Ericcson to permit the Monitor to be equipped with it. This was done, and the Monitor proceeded on her way to victory.

"If Ericcson had held out, as he stubbornly did for a long time, the Monitor would not have reached Hampton Roads in time to interrupt the leisurely destructiveness of the Merrimac: nor, perhaps, to have prevented her from bombarding Nrn coast cities. Ericsson deserves the greater credit - he built the Monitor; but George Reynolds should be remembered at the same time, for it was an engine of his invention that he himself put into the little insides of the Monitor which gave her the life impulse that enabled her to be on the job at a critical time in the hist of the US. George Reynolds d abt 10 yrs ago, full of yrs and honors. He lived for many decades on a beautiful farm not very far from Bridgeport. I think that one of his s is still living, and on the old place. He was a very remarkable man, a pioneer eng of very great distinction, who conferred honor upon the land of his birth. While we are celeb the anniv of our great Swedish-American eng, we should not forget his friend, George Reynolds. J. A. S. New York, Aug 2, 1924"

THU MAR 9, 1939 - Letter Pictures Hist Battle

Monitor-Merrimac Clash 77 Yrs Ago Tdy Vividly Described By Mrs. Mravlag's Father, Who Serv on Yankee Ship

"One of the most imp battles in naval history - that btwn the Merrimac and the Monitor - took place 77 yrs ago today. It was on Mar 9, 1862, in the 2nd yr of the CW, that the N's 'Yankee cheese box on a raft' met and repelled the C ironclad which had threatened all U shipping and which was to usher in a new era of the steel ships. Recollections of the event may be of particular interest to Elizabethans in that Alban Crocker Stimers, chief eng, USN, who serv on the Monitor, was the f/o Mrs Cordelia B Mravlag, wid/o Dr Victor Mravlag, Mayor for 10 yrs and one of Eliz's leading citizens for svrl decades. Stimers had super the construction of the Monitor and gave his svc in the battle at the request of the Capt of the U ship. 2 days aft the engage he wrote his f in detail abt the great battle off Hampton Roads, VA. The letter is still in Mrs Mravlag's possession. Stimers' letter vividly shows the terror a new military weapon - like the steel tanks and poison gas of the WW - can cause, until, as invariably has been the case, means are devised of combating it. The letter follows:

"Ironclad Monitor, Hampton Roads, March 11, 1862.
'My Dear f:
'Aft having been 13 yrs in the Naval Svc without ever having witnessed a naval fight, I have at last been an actor in a long and hotly contested engage, one that is now considered the most imp and the most brilliant that ever occurred in American waters. Moreover, it was the 1st of its kind which ever occurred in hist. It was iron-clad against iron-clad. The rebel ironclad frigate Merrimac against the little Ericsson battery, and I am proud to tell you that we drove the monster back to her den in a sinking condition. She had been out the day bfr and destroyed 2 of our frigates, the Congress and the Cumberland, and when we arrived at 9 pm - having seen the firing fm a distance as we approached - the whole army and naval forces were perfectly panic-stricken. It was not believed that a power existed which could prevent her fm destroying every ship in the harbor, shelling out the entire army encmp outside of Fortress Monroe - which is not large enough to hold them - and then proceed to NY and utterly laying it waste.

'Our arrival was hailed with joy by the few who were cognizant of it, but at the same time we gave them but slight hopes, as we were new and untried, whereas she had proven herself to not only possess tremendous offensive powers but to be entirely impregnable to the heaviest ordnance carried by our largest ships. The Capt of the frigate Minnesota told me that his 10-inch solid shot weighing 124 lbs had no more effect upon her than as if he had tossed so many pebbles against her side. When, therefore, the 15 or 20 thousand deeply interested spectators saw us the next mrng btwn the Minnesota - which had grounded the day bfr - and her fearful antagonist bearing directly for what she supposed would be an easy prey, they looked upon us as a pygmy about to attack a giant: as one officer expressed it, we looked "like a hat set on a shingle."

'The chief eng if the Minnesota, an old shipmate and great personal friend of mine, was probably the only man who believed we could whip her and his confidence was based entirely upon his favorite opinion of my judgment. He told his doubting shipmates that "Stimers had told him she could whip the Merrimac and that Stimers never made mistakes." The Merrimac came there with 2 other steamers, also partially clad in iron, and commenced the attack upon the Minnesota bfr we could get our anchor, never appearing to have even suspected our existence. As soon as possible, however, we were directly at her, fm which moment she paid us her entire attention. Sometimes we were touching, but the favorite distance was 20 yds. Once she came head on to our broadside, expecting to run the iron plow which extends forward fm her keel through our side below the armor plates, but our peculiar form protected us fm it, and she brought instead her vulnerable stern against the sharp corner of our strong armor and went off with an injury, while we are now hardly able to find a dent where she struck.

'For 3 hrs and ½ she pelted us and we pelted her. She left the marks of 23 shots upon us, 9 of which struck the revolving turret which contains our guns, and within which I was stationed, until our Capt was disabled by a shell exploding against the peephole exactly opposite his eyes, filling them with little particles of iron. We thought at first he would lose the sight of one eye, but it proved not so bad. My duty was to turn the turret to bring the guns to bear upon the enemy, the Lt of the ship sighting them. Aft the Capt was wounded I had to fight the turret all alone and turn it too. (That is, you understand, there were 8 men to each gun to load them.)

'The crash against the turret was tremendous when their heavy shot struck it, and if a man happened to lean against the inside of where a shot struck it knocked him down and stunned him for a couple of hrs. I was myself knocked down, but as the shot struck

a little one side I was not disabled. The iron of our sides is indented 4 inches in some places, but we are ready for her if she ever comes out again. The Pres himself has sent us strict orders to not risk ourselves to act on the offensive for fear something may happen to us, but to defend the pos against her attacks. If she comes out again we are to go after her and destroy her.
'I am in excellent health. Give my love to all. Your affectionate son,
"Alban"'

RAISING OF THE MONITOR TURRET

On Mon Aug 5, 2002, the 120 ton turret of the Monitor saw sunlight for the first time in nearly 140 yrs as it was raised fm the sea floor 16 miles off Cape Hatteras, NC. The Navy and the National Oceanic and Atmospheric Administration (NOAA) were in charge of the salvage operation. As stated in Assoc Press articles (2), a huge crane on a 300 ft barge lifted the turret out of the water as a CW era American flag fluttered in the breeze. Silt colored water poured out of the turret before the wreckage was swung aboard the barge. The turret was rusty, coral-covered and pocked with dents. However, according to Navy dive chief Cmdr Bobbie Scholley, "She came cleanly to the surface. She's all there. She's beautiful."

The turret is the biggest and most imp piece of the Monitor recovered during the multi-yr operation, the articles continue, because it was the world's 1st revolving gun turret, which changed naval warfare and architecture. Before the turret, an entire ship with conventional banks of guns had to be turned to maintain the best line of fire. With the turret, guns could be moved independently fm the ship. The Monitor turret's 7 dints were caused by cannonballs fm the CSS Virginia aka Merrimac during the 1862 battle.

Another newspaper columnists (3) stated that even though the Monitor fought only one battle, it revolutionized naval warfare, dominating naval strategy until WWII. When the British navy, the most powerful in the world, learned of the battle, it canceled all outstanding orders for wooden ships. The raised turret will end up in the Mariners' Museum, Newport News, VA. With the price tag for the salvage standing at $6.5 million just for the last yr of the 5 yr operation, there are no plans to retrieve any of the larger parts of the Monitor, such as the iron pilothouse, the cookstove and boilers.

(1)
A - List of Officers of the U. S. S. Monitor, March 6, 1862.
B - List of the Surv of the Original Crew of the U. S. S. Monitor.
C - U. S. S. Monitor - List of Men When This Vessel Left the Navy Yard, New York, March 6, 1862.
D - Some of the Members of the Crew of the Monitor, taken from a letter of Victor M. Drake, 175 New Milford Avenue, Dumont, NJ, dated June 27, 1954, with the letter stating that the records were made by David Cuddeback (1840-69) of Port Jervis, Orange Co, NY, who remained a seaman and was killed on board a sloop in 1869. In addition, 5 deaths noted in newspapers 1892-1920; and the records of William F Keeler, Asst. Paymaster, USN, and Peter Truscott of Washington Co, ME, who serv on the Monitor and later wounded on board the Catskill.

(2) Tue Aug 6, 2002, Sonya Barisic, Assoc Press

(3) Fri Aug 9, 2002, Dale McFeatters, Scripps Howard News Service

CHAPTER 8

75th Blue and Gray Reunions

GETTYSBURG

"...THE THINNING BAND OF BUTTERNUT AND BLUE WILL TURN HOMEWARD, TO THE WHISPERING OF LONG SUMMER WINDS AND FADING MEMORIES. IT IS THE LAST GETTYSBURG REUNION."

<u>WED MAR 16, 1938</u> - CW Vet, 90, Will Fly To Meeting

"Gen Burke O'Brien, 90, will fly to the reunion (henceforth R) of the B&G at Gettysburg (henceforth G) battlefield Jun 26. 'I think it'll be quite a thrill,' the aged statehouse guide said, 'to fly back to the old battlefield 75 yrs aft the battle.' He has nursed no grudge against the 'boys in gray' and looks forward with pleasure to the opportunity to shake hands with those who spilled the blood of the U soldiers. 'The issue over which we fought is dead now,' he says. 'The N and S are united in one nation with the same objectives and ideals.'" UP, Pierre, SD, Wed Mar 16.

<u>TUE MAY 17, 1938</u> - CW Vets On Equal Terms

No "Mason-Dixon-Line" Division at G R

"There will be no 'Mason and Dixon Line' to divide the Blues and Grays at their final R on the battlefield of G. 'There will be no embarrassing moments for any Vet,' proclaimed Chairman John S Rice of the anniv comm tdy. 'Our sole objective is peace and harmony within the US. There shall never again be a Mason and Dixon Line.' Rice expained his statement was prompted by queries fm svrl hundreds of Vets - Nrn and Srn - abt 'equalization and treatment of Vets.' Approximately 2,500 Vets are expected to attend the 75th anniv of the CW battle, Jun 29-Jul 4. A bill authorizing appropriation of money for expenses of the celeb was signed ystdy by Pres Roosevelt. Dr Overton H Mennet of Los Angeles, natl Cmdr of the GAR, and Gen James M Claypool of St Louis, Cmdr-in-Chief of the UCV, have both accepted the 'last roundup call.'

Arrangements are being made for them to speak ovr a nation-wide hookup. While the camp-homes for the Vets neared completion, Fed officials assigned to aid PA in the observance dispatched more than 8,000 invitations to B&G surv throughout the nation. Traveling expenses and food and housing costs during the wk encmp will be paid by the govt. Approximately 400 state police and 500 NG have been detailed to duty at the hist battle site during the celeb." Assoc P, G, PA, Tue May 17.

TUE MAY 24, 1938 - CW Vets Yield Hist Task

"Old sol who for yrs have decorated the graves of those who fell on the nation's most famous battlefield called tdy for younger men to carry on the duty grown to strenuous for them. Disdainful of advancing age, the handful of surv, Vets who shouldered muskets here 75 yrs ago have proudly handled the work of keeping forever green the graves of the fallen comrades. This yr, however, the gray-haired and enfeebled Vets were obliged to delegate the task to younger and sturdier hands. Holding to tradition, they called upon s and gs to take up preservation of the 3,000 graves. Nevertheless the Vets still will have a part in the MDAY celeb next Mon. Donning again their faded blue uniforms they will motor in the annual parade that attracts thousands to this hist observance.

"Judge W C Sheely of the Common Pleas Court of Adams and Fulton Co will recite Lincoln's G address at the ceremony in the natl cem. Another speaker will be Senator Arthur H Vandenburg of MI. The exercises have aroused unusual interest this yr because of the 75th anniv celeb of the battle of G next mos. Pres

Roosevelt will dedicate a sol memorial at the anniv observance."
Assoc P, G, PA, Tue May 24.

WED JUN 29, 1938 - Warriors of '63 In Final Rally
Vets of Both Armies Converge on G

" 2 aged armies came back to the G battlefield for the last time tdy with the sound of dusty drums in their ears but with peace in their hearts. They came - Vets of the GAR and the men of Robert E Lee - for a final R in the little Blue Ridge foothills town to which weary sol trudged 75 yrs ago in search of shoes and where they found instead the bloodiest battle of the CW. Many of them had been here bfr. Some clanked through this little diamond-shaped biz district in dusty blue or gray uniforms long ago as the ripe peaches which they saw shaken to the ground by the rumble of art Hundreds more visited the battlefield in 1913 on the 50th anniv of Lee's last vain bid for victory. Tdy there were less than 2,000 converging on the spot where James Gettys stopped his ox cart in 1780 at the end of his search for a fertile, peaceful farm.

"They will not come again. This 75th anniv R is the last, and G - which once trembled to the clump of sol boots along her dust-white pikes - welcomed C and U Vets with a sunburst of flags in which the stars and bars shook in the sunlight beside Old Glory. All of ystdy the advance guard drifted in fm the w, the s, the ne, and soon aft dawn this mrng they were coming in full strength by special train by bus and by auto. Knotty fingers fumbled at the brims of black campaign hats as they saluted. Grey hats came off to the weak cackle of a rebel yell. All day the flags in the sts frmd an unending row of striped sentinels and at ngt the white threads of searchlights circled the sky. Hot dog stands studded the roadsides and overshadowed the little shack, marked by a C flag, where Longstreet had his HQ.

"Still further along Seminary Ridge, beyond Lee's HQ, the tent city housing the Vets spread out ovr the fields. There the Vets faced each other across a narrow rd as Lee and Meade once faced each other across the broad valley at the foot of Round Top Hill. Then the future of a nation was hidden by the smoke of cannon and the screech of shells. But peace and friendship replaced the conflict of 75 yrs ago when the Vets gathered tdy. Charles J Rose, 95, of Miami, danced a jig on the board walk bfr his tent. J Robert Paul, a new straw hat balanced on his head, wearing a gray suit he had had to hunt over 4 co to find, came in fm Charlotte, NC, with his ae 19 gs. 'My oldest ch is 72,' he chuckled. 'Me? I'm 103.'

"Ira R Wildman, 88, and his bride of 3 yrs, strolled through the 'diamond' looking for Capt James Dinkins, of New Orleans. '14 yrs ago I returned the flag of the 10th New Orleans Cav which was captured at Cold Harbor," Wildman, the yngst Vet in the GAR explained. 'I was authorized to return it by the CT Legislature and Capt Dinkins was one of those who rcvd it. I thought I'd find him here.' R S Ramsey, 94, of Monticello, KY, displayed a photograph taken last fall which showed him jumping his horse ovr a rail fence. 'You must have been a great Cav man,' a bystander suggested. 'I was in the 30th KY Inf, suh,' Ramsey replied.

"C L Bentley, 94, of Fenton, MI, reported that he appeared to be approximately 75 yrs late in reaching the battlefield. A mem of the regular eng in the AP, his brig built the bridges on which the U army advanced and was later ordered to the battle field but failed to arrive until it was all ovr. They were then ordered into VA without reaching G and he had never seen the town until last ngt. Dr Overton H Mennet, 89, of Los Angeles, natl Cmdr of the GAR, was on the field early to see that the gray-clad vets did not outshine his men. Svrl who arrived without their uniforms were sharply reprimanded.

"Gen John M Claypool of St Louis, cmds the UCV. The program, opening officially on Fri with ceremonies in the G College stadium, will be climaxed by an address by Pres Roosevelt when he unveils the new $60,000 eternal light peace memorial on a hillside overlooking the battlefield." UP, G, PA,

Wed Jun 29.

(P): Leading the march of CW Vets to the battlefield of G, PA, for the 75th anniv observance of the famous struggle, Dr Overton H Mennet (left) 89-yr-old Cmdr of the GAR, and James R Paul, 105-yr-old Vet of the C army, look ovr a map of the area with Capt W J Baird (right) of the regular army.

THU JUN 30, 1938 - Vets Recall Their '63 Deeds Swap Yarns at G in Final Bivouac

"2,000 CW Vets, tenting for the last time on the old camp ground, turned back the pages of the nation's hist 75 yrs tdy to the stirring events of the great conflict btwn the N and the S. Across the same dusty PA road that once divided the armies, the remnants of 2 mighty fighting forces faced each other again as they did nearly 4 score yrs ago in the battle that marked the turning point of the war in which many of them fought. But it was not as the boys in blue and the striplings in gray that the old sol met - on this 75th anniv of the Battle of G - but as comrades, without regard for blue or gray, without heed for stars and stripes, or stars and bars.

"They hobbled together ovr the battlefield which once had been dampened by the blood of 43,000 fallen comrades, and they pointed out Oak Hill, the Bloody Angle and Seminary Ridge, where much of the fighting took place. Once again they hailed one another as 'Johnny Reb' and 'Damyankee,' but there was no rancor in their quavering words. Together they sat on the tented verandas of their tented city, swapping yarns about Early and Sheridan and Lee, or joking with the thousands of visitors. Except for a few late comers, the last bivouac of the GAR and of the men of Robert E Lee was completed tdy. Most of them checked in to camp ystdy, where 2,000 tents have been pitched in the semblance of a small city - a city of R and memories.

"Ystdy and tdy were set aside for the Vets to renew old

friendships. Carefully attended by traveling companions, aided by NG and boy scouts, they will be feted for the next 4 days with parades, band concerts, military displays and tours of the battlefield and its natl Cem. No camp fires will burn in the tented city, guarded by army troops and state police. No re-enactment of any battle scene will take place during the peaceful observance. And no Vet will be called upon to ride or march in any parade. 6 H cases were reported on the 1st day of the encmp but all but one were classed as minor. James Hammaker, 94, retired rancher fm Parker Co, TX, fell fm his lower berth and fractured his shoulder. Physicians said his condition was 'as good as could be expected.'

"A top-Sgt, with a squad of NG detailed to meet Vets on incoming trains, felt his charges had not been sufficiently well-grounded in hist. "Put their luggage in 2 separate places,' he said, the C on the right, and the U on the left. Is there anyone here who doesn't understand which was which?' he blandly inquired. 'The C were the S and the U was the N.' It may be 'Marching Through GA' to the vizened Boys in Blue who tramped with Gen Sherman long ago, but to 4 little girls on a G lawn, it's just another 'swing' tune. When the military band struck up the march, the youngsters, each less than ae 6, amused an audience of passers-by with their 'truckin,' while the U Vets were arriving at their tent city.

"Wheel chairs - 400 of them - are being used to save the old sol fm becoming too weary when they wish to visit comrades in a distant section of the camp. Boy scouts await their beck and call, to wheel them about in the sun on the boardwalks, to carry luggage, or do any menial chores. 3 kitchens serve the camps of the old sol, each capable of feeding 1,500 at a sitting. Their food is carefully prepared in huge aluminum urns, with electric choppers and mixers, under supervision of accomplished army chefs. For their 1st meal in camp, the Vets were given: Cream of mushroom soup, chicken a la king, or baked ham and cold meats, saute potatoes, green peas, cantaloupe, rolls, iced tea, coffee or milk, and ice cream." Assoc P, G, PA, Thu, June 30.

(P): Vets Move Into "Tent City" - Beside the pitched tents which will house them during their R on the G battlefield sit Vets of the B&G, encmp for their last get-together. Some 2,000 men who fought in the War Btwn the States were expected to take part in ceremonies at the spot where the tide of conflict turned against the C.

(P): Oldest C at G Event - James R Paul, who gave age as 105, shown arriving at 75th anniv celeb.

FRI JUL 1, 1938 (P) - The B&G Celeb Anniv of G

(P) While Martin E Loop, left above, and Gen John Harris visit the natl cem at G, PA, on the 75th anniv of the CW battle there, William Massie, left, discusses war days at Waynesville, NC, scene of the last encounter of the war.

B&G Join In Peace Echo
G R Opens - Woodring to Speak
Vets Of Meade, Lee Relive '63 Scenes

"The whisper of ancient battles rustled the young corn of PA midlands tdy, stirring rusty memories among a gallant but feeble band of old 'fighters, B&G. It was the whisper of the bloodiest conflict this continent ever saw and 3/4 of a century has not stilled the answering echoes. Tdy in this G countryside, where a crackle of musketry spurted through the dawn of Jul 1, 1863, a great spectacle was in the making. But it was a spectacle, planned and guided by a nation in peace and unity and of that Homeric clamoring of a past century there remained but the thin whispering of breezes blowing ovr fat fields and the memories of old men. To those old men, a scant 2,000 of the legions once garbed in blue and butternut, the first act in the panoply by which their nation does them homage was symbolic - of time, of the fading old passions and the coming of a new way of life.

"For tdy was R day in G. 75 yrs ago tdy G kept R with d and

destiny. This R was of a different order, a R in which U and C AP and ANVA gathered in a common stadium of G College and spoke from a common platform a common pledge of fellowship. Against this background was presented a drama which told as well as did the address of Cmdr-in-Chief Overton H Mennet of the GAR and Cmdr-in-Chief John M Claypool of the UCV, of the passing yrs since contending armies of N and S blundered into battle here. For war has changed as well as men with the passage of the yrs. And signaling the change was the first display of US Army forces encmp tdy on the G battlefield itself.

"Sec of War Harry H Woodring comes up fm Washington tdy to pay tribute to the aging Vets. But where spanking Cav charged, prancing in shimmering escort to the cmdrs of '63, tdy's honor guard typified mechanical warfare. Woodring's route by motor car lay ovr that which the Btlns of U Cmdr Meade marched in dusty order coming up toward G on that long ago Jul. ... Army tanks warmed up to escort the Sec up the battlefield along the pos of the U troops on the 3rd day of G - a lumbering mechanical procession - to the HQ tent of Maj Gen James K Parsons, of the 3rd Corps area, pitched within pistol shot of that bloody angle where Pickett's men notched the extreme advance of the battle.

"From a gun park of the 16th Field Art, armed with quick-firing weapons able to dispatch almost as many shells in an hr as sweating gunners of Alexander's crack C Bats could ram home in a day, a 19 gun salute will roar. The tempo of G was quickening tdy as the formal program of ceremonies started. Woodring's arrival is but one of svrl. Gov George H Earle of PA was due by air. Woodring, Earle and the GAR and UCV Cmdrs are principal speakers of the R day programs. Throngs of sightseers, NG, state police, and regular army men and now and then a sprightly U or C Vet crowded the streets and sidewalks of G as they had been crowded only once bfr - 25 yrs ago when the 50th anniv of the great battle was marked in a ceremony similar to this.

Pace Telling On Vets

"The pace was telling upon the aged Vets but medical officers in the tent camps where the remnants of the 2 forces bivouaced side-by-side were amazed by the resiliency of their feeble frames. 20 Vets were H tdy, and 10 others had been in the H for brief periods. The recod of illness thus far, physicians said, is better than would be normally expected among a similar group of men of ae 90 or more, living quietly in their homes. But strenuous days lay ahead - days almost as strenuous for enfeebled bodies as were those of their youthful fighting days. No physician would predict that d would not claim victims anew on the field of G. Ahead lay a day of parades and military reviews marking the 2nd day of G - the day when the full power of the U army was brought into battle and the contending armies fought desperately to a standstill. And following that a day marked by a visit and speech by Pres Roosevelt, dedicating an eternal light which will burn in memory of peace - the day 75 yrs ago aft Pickett's bright Brig crumpled in bloody heaps bfr U fire. Aft that the thinning band of butternut and blue will turn homeward to the whispering of long summer winds and fading memories. It is the last G R." UP, G, PA.

<u>TUE JUL 5, 1938</u> - B&G Voice Last Farewells

<u>Touching Scenes at G as Vets Bid Goodbye After 75th Anniv Celeb -
Leave for Homes Tdy</u>

"Armies of the N and S turned away fm the G battlefield for the last time tdy and there was a note of sadness in their friendly farewells. Many of the aged men of the GAR and the UCV had clung tenaciously to their fading health that they might see this final R of the 75th anniv of the biggest battle of the CW. They have seen it now - an incomparable R in the history of wars and the peace that follow them. Their knotted fingers have clasped the hands of other old men they once fought. They have heard Pres Roosevelt call upon the nation to struggle eternally for peace through democracy and have seen the most modern military machines. But perhaps most impressive to the men in faded blue and gray was the unveiling of a new monument on Oak Hill where henceforth a flame will burn above the battlefield as a symbol of the nation's peace and unity.

"There was much of that spirit of friendship and peace in the farewells that were said tdy by men who knew they have small chance to see each other again. 'God bless you' and 'good bye' were spoken in the same breath time and again as the armies parted with sorrow as sincere, if not as tragic, as one that day 3/4 of a century ago when the ANVA, beaten back on Cemetery Ridge, turned twd Haggerstown, leaving the AP so battered it could not pursue. 'This has been a glorious occasion,' Gen John P Claypool, Cmdr of the UCV, said as he and Dr Overton Mennet, Cmdr of the GAR, strode arm in arm to the HQ of the PA state com and of the army forces to say goodbyes. 'We of the C Army warmly thank every person who has had a part in providing this great R and congratulate them on the manner in which it has been handled.' 'I want to echo Gen Claypool's sentiments,' Mennet said. 'We have been given every courtesy and consideration. There has never bfr been an occasion like this - and there may never be another.'

"The town of G began returning to normal as the first of the Vets moved out, with the main force scheduled to leave late this aftn. Outstanding triumph of the R of 1,800 men of an average ae 94 went to the 1st Regular Army Medical Reg under Lt Col Paul R Hawley. 'I have been amazed by the manner in which these men have stood up under the excitement of the R,' Hawley said in commenting on the fact that none had died. The 1913 R was marked by 9 d. Even James P Hamacker, ae 95, of Aledo, TX, who suffered a fractured shoulder as his train neared G was able to see the battlefield fm a stretcher car Mon aftn. There has been an average of only abt 30 Vets in the H and probably 34 have been sent home because of their weakened condition. One Vet was taken to the H with his blood pressure at 80. He was given a blood transfusion and released 2 days later with the count at 114.

"Tremendous advance preparation and favorable weather was partly responsible for the record. Special diets were prepared for many of the Vets. Army doctors made abt 50 calls a day in the camps. But there was an additional factor involved that surprised the medical officers. They had on hand 5 cases of whisky with which they mixed toddies of water and sugar for such Vets as appeared to require them. The 5 cases were exhausted in 2 days and an airplane had to be sent to bring in an additional 22 cases of whiskey, and 5 cases of sherry. The usual ration of whiskey was one dram or abt a teaspoonful in a glass of water with a little sugar added. One 104 year old patient asked for a double ration. A doctor poured 2 drams into his glass. He picked it up and squinted at it. 'I can't take a little drink like that,' he muttered. The official records show one case of alcoholism among the Vets, name undisclosed." UP, G, PA, Jul 5.

WED JUL 6, 1938 - 1st Vet Dies At G
IN Man Only Anniv Fatality So Far

"The 1st fatality among the 2,000 CW Vets who attended the last R of the B&G occurred tdy with the d of Daniel Price, 90, of Marion, IN. He d at the Carlisle, PA, H of bronchial pneumonia contracted at the R on G battlefield. Another Vet was "dangerously ill" at Annie Warner Memorial H here. He is John W Cooper, 91, of Largo, FL. Oxygen treatments were administered aft he had a heart attack. Col Paul R Hawley, Cmdr of the US Army Medical Reg fm Carlisle barracks, reported his physicians were treating 23 frmr U and C sol at the H camp on G battlefield but expected 10 would be able to start for their homes tdy.

"Hawley said 3 others, Jacob Rush, Orange, CA, Jacob

Winslow, 94, Los Angeles, and William R Phillips, 90, of Crescent City, FL, were convalescing fm exhaustion at Carlisle H and 3 were undergoing treatment at the G H. Price's attendant, Robert Butler, of Marion, IN, was making arrangements to remove the body to the IN city for burial." UP, G, Pa, Jul 6.

<u>Fri Jul 8, 1938</u> - Tells Of Rally At G
Elizabethan, 94, Lauds Battle Anniv Program

"The fields of G lay bright beneath the sun and the ever-toiling grass covered the once war-scarred earth as it did at Austerlitz at Verdun and on battlefields the world ovr. The scene of the most decisive conflict of the CW looked quite different seen through the ae 94 eyes of Noah Ogden Woodruff, Eliz Vet, who returned here Wed aft attending the celeb at G, fm what it did 3/4s of a century ago, when as a youth serv with the U army. He saw the tide of C ebb and flow in the Peach Orchard, at Bloody Angle and on Seminary Ridge. Mr W appeared in excellent health and spirits this mmg, his wk sojourn in G and all the festivities surrounding the 75th anniv celeb of the battle seemingly having no ill effects on him. The Eliz Vet left Eliz on Wed last wk, accompanied by a personal friend, Frank M Lawrence, of 525 Walnut St. He makes his home at 320 Stanton Ave, where he lives with his sis, Mrs Charles Moore.

Occasions Contrasted

"Memories, instead of conquering armies rode the fields at G last wk...memories of Johnny Reb and Damn-Yankee...of Seminary Ridge and of Cemetery Ridge where Pickett and his men rode to immortality in the most glorious gesture of the Lost Cause...Instead of hoarse war cries there were the high-pitched voices of old men...instead of the thud of marching feet, the soft and sometimes faltering gate of nonagenarians...instead of youth marching to d in war, there were old men coming to reminisce in peace...

"'It was a wonderful occasion and a wonderful trip,' Mr W

said. 'It was the greatest thing of its kind that has happened in this country. I have been to G many times bfr, but this was by far the greatest celeb I ever attended. Everything went off nicely and even nature was in our favor, for the days and ngts were both quite cool and clear.' Praise for the US govt and the State of PA for the 'fine and systematic' camp arrangements was offered by Mr W who declared that 'every detail was looked aft and provided to' and that 'food and equipment were excellent.' Converging on the tent city on the battlefield with abt 2,000 Vets of both the U and C armies, Mr W renewed svrl old acquaintances and made many new friends during his visit.

Praises "Boys in Gray"

"'The boys in gray are a fine lot of men,' he said, and emphasized the feeling of friendliness and camaraderie which pervaded the atmosphere of the 2 encamp, meeting for the swapping of yarns and the exchange of pleasantries rather than for the fierce fighting of 3/4s of a century ago. There was loneliness for this Eliz Vet despite the large n/o friends and acquaintances in G. As he walked around the battlefield, its grim significance softened by the passage of 75 yrs, he was alone in his recollections of the deeds of Clarks Battery B of the 1st NJ Lgt Art, for he is the only surv of this brave unit of the AP which fought so magnificently at Bloody Angle in the Peach Orchard in one of the fiercest struggles of the 3-day battle.

"He alone could recall the events on the left of the line extending fm Emmettsburg Rd to Little Round Top where the Bat, which was a part of the Art Brig of the 3rd Army Corps was stationed. Only he remembered the terrible fighting of that 2nd day when 2 guns burned out and the others were too hot to fire, and the amazing (for the 1860s) total of 1,300 rounds were fired btwn 2 and 7 o'clock. The other Vets present were occupied with their own recollections, and the other mem of Bat B, who held the left side of the line, have all answered the final role call.

Pickett's Charge Recalled

"Memories of Picketts charge, the highlight of the battle, and one of the bravest military exploits in hist, were vivid in Mr W's mind. 'Everthing in the battle's hist centers on Picketts charge,' he said, 'although it lasted for only abt an hour and took place on the final aftn. It was nothing more than wholesale murder, for almost the entire Div was wiped out. It was a famous forlorn hope and nothing more.' On that well-remembered day of the charge, Mr W and his comrades were not on the firing line, but were occupying a reserve pos because of the terrific ordeal they had undergone the day bfr. Aft the battle the Bat waited on the Emmettsburg Rd until the exhausted AP attempted to follow Lee's retreat into northern VA. Many amusing as well as tragic incidents of the battle 3/4s of a century ago and of the anniv R were recalled by Mr W. He was surprised and amused by the many requests for his autograph made by tourists in G. He was also asked to pose for photographs svrl times and declared that he had been asked innumerable questions, the principle one being 'How old are you?' This question, he added, was asked of almost every Vet, both U and C, at fqt intervals.

"Mr W spent part of the time staying at the encamp and the remainder at the Hotel G. He attended all of the festivities, including the programs on Jul 3 when Pres Roosevelt dedicated the Peace Memorial on Oak Hill. The Vets were seated in special stands near the Pres, and Mr W declared that he could see the Pres very well and that he 'made a very nice speech.' He described the unveiling of the monument and the lighting of the 'eternal light' by 2 Vets, 1 fm each army, as 'a very spectacular affair.'

Military Units Parade

"Parades of various military org, including units of regular army, the PA NG, the AL, and other groups, featured the celeb. Mr W especially enjoyed the stirring music by the US Army and Marine bands. R Day was commemorated Fri Jul 1, the first day of the battle, and Vets Day Jul 2. Independence Day was designated as US Army Day with many spectacular displays of the might of American armed forces. In addition to enjoying all of the festivities, Mr W also serv as a guide to Mr L, who had never visited the battlefield. An apt answer to an inquiry regarding the effect of his trip upon him was given by Mr W when he related an anecdote regarding the trip home by train. 'When we were getting off the train in Eliz,' the aged Vet said, 'I said to Mr L that I felt so well that I expected to see him at the 100th anniv R. But, of course, we all realize that the 75th was the final meeting of the boys in B&G. The majority of us are well over ae 90, but most of us were in pretty fair shape, considering everything.'"

CHICKAMAUGA

<u>THU SEP 15, 1938</u> - Recall Battle Of Chickamauga Rites Starting Tomorrow to Mark Anniv

"Along the Chickamauga, on the foggy Sun mrng of Sep 16, 1863, gray and blue-clad men fought desperately with long slim bayonets and clubbed rifles. On the mrng of that same day this yr, tomorrow, their desc, now a united people, begin a 10 day celeb to honor the men who fought desperately ovr the same ground 75 yrs bfr. On Sep 21, Pres Roosevelt himself will join the celeb by speaking and reviewing a military contingent. Again, as at G earlier in the yr, Vets of the B&G will join hands in a last battlefield R while men of the regular army re-enact the battle in which many of them fought. A pageant and historical spectacle, 'Drums of Dixie,' in which 2,000 are taking part, will recall each ngt the events commemorated and fireworks will harmlessly suggest the more deadly art of '63.

"The 10 day celeb will commemorate not only 'The Great Battle of the W,' but 5 occasions in all: the 100th anniv of peace with the Cherokee Nation; the 100th anniv of Chattanooga; the 75th anniv of the 3 closely connected battles of the Chattanooga campaign of '63, Chickamauga, Lookout Mountain, and Missionary Ridge. Congress, the State of TN, the City of

Chattanooga, and Hamilton Co all united in providing facilities for the commemoration. Besides the participation of Pres Roosevelt, Govs Gordon Browning of TN, Bibb Graves of AL, and Ed Rivers of GA will take part, and many prominent men and women fm all parts of the S are to act as hosts.

"More than 5,000 troops, Fed and NG, fm the 3 states in the conjunction of which the Chattanooga campaign was fought, will take part in the re-enactment of the battles, and in reviews and other military events. Regattas, horse shows, an air show, a mummers' parade, and other varied events will fill each day's program fm the opening of the celeb with the Cotton Ball, tomorrow ngt, to the solemn memorial and patriotic rally which close the proceedings on Sun Sep 25. A half million people are expected to attend.

"Atmosphere of the Old S is to be recreated at the opening ball, during which girls of the New S, garbed in ruffles and hoop-skirts, will make their curtsies to the King and Queen of the ball, whose identity, in accordance with custom, will not be revealed until the ngt of the affair. Eagerly sought already are the 'wooden nickels' which have been issued as souvenirs of the celeb, similar to paper money, but printed on thin wooden veneer strips. A gala carnival atmosphere has taken possession of Chattanooga. All in khaki now, sol of 1938 will march on peaceful missions ovr the ground so bitterly contested 75 yrs ago by the B&G." NEA Service, Chattanooga, TN, Sep 15.

(P): Famous Battle's Anniv To Be Marked - Now a gala celeb, but once a series of furious battles btwn U and C armies locked in conflict around Chickamauga, TN. The painting reproduced abv is an artist's conception of the battle of Chickamauga, which 75 yrs ago (Sep 19-20, 1863) shook the country.

"'Uncle' Mark Trash, 111, venerable Negro who lives in a 2-room log cabin in Chickamauga Park is looking forward to a R with his twin bro, for yrs a Bapt missionary in Africa. He is returning to Chattanooga for the anniv of the CW battle fought here. Both saw the battle. 'We were ae 43 then,' 'Uncle' Mark adds. Chatanooga, TN, Tue Sep 20, 1938.

INDEX

ABBETT Leon 25
ABBOTT Rev 1 William T Rev 1
ABEL Amy L 28
ACKERMAN George 1 JJ 1 Philip 1 Philip Jr 1
ACKLEY Edwin 1 George 1 George F 1 Mabel 1 Olive 1 Robert 1 Wilbur 1
ADAMS Charles C 1 Hugh White 1 J E Jr 1 James B 1 201 James B Mr & Mrs 201 Jeremiah Eligh 1 201 202 Samuel H 1 Sue 201 William Mrs 1 William H Mrs 201
AERZT Joseph 2
AHEARN Mrs 174
AIKEN/ATKEN E B Mrs 47 48
AIKEN William G Mrs 76
AIKMAN Robert Rev Dr 42
AKER David Mrs 129
ALBERTSON Mrs 14
ALBRIGHT Augusta 58
ALEXANDER John T Gen 163 Capt 216
ALGER Russell A 103
ALJOE (?) Robert J Mrs 21
ALLEN David S 2 G A Mrs 168 James Warner 2 John C 2 59 Margaret 158 William O 2 William Mrs 33
ALSTON Capt J 34
ALWARD Joseph 131 Mary 131
AMES Alonso H 188 Maria 188
ANDERSON Charles M Rev 161 Edward 235 George 181 Hans 3 235 236 240 John 181 John 181 John Mrs 38 Liddy 181
ANDRE Maj 121

ANGUS Catherine Ann 107 James 107 108 James Winans 108 Mary Brower 107 108
ANTHONY Joseph 3 Joseph Jr 3
APGAR Abraham 3 Charles F 3 John B 3 Lillian 3 Minnie 3
APPLEGATE Adrian S 188 Florence 178 T B Capt 162
APPLEGET Thomas B 3
ARMSTRONG Isabelle 170 William C 170 William C 170
ARNOLD J P Mrs 172
ARRIGHI Antonio A 3 Charles 3 Garry 3 George 3 Howard 3 Roswell 3
ASCHENBACH Fred W Mrs 122
ASH George W 4 Julia 147
ASHE Samuel 4
ASHLEY Robert 67
ASHTON James Yard 4 213
ASTFALK Charlotte 12 Leonard 12 Nathaniel Jr Mrs 12
ATGAR Charles Mrs 140
ATKEN/AIKEN E B Mrs 47 48
ATKINS Alfred 6
AUSTIN Harry 4 Henry C 4 Perry 5 Rev Mr 44
AVENS Capt Henry 134
AVERBECK Fred 188
AVERY Frank E 5 George B James 30
AYRES Ann Marie 24 William B 5
BACCUS George Q Rev 60
BACKERT Joseph A 193
BACON Smith 5
BADEY John 5 Vet 5

BAHR Augustus A Mrs 33
BAILEY J H Rev 184 Viola 185
W H Rev 184
BAIRD Matthew Mrs 119 W J Capt 254
BAKER David 5 Elizabeth 5 George 5 Harry C 5 Lucretia 5 Mary 42 Miss 59 Phineas M 5 18 Ralph 5 Ralph Priestly 5 Ralph P Jr 5 Ralph Priestly Cleveland Mrs 5 William Mrs 166
BALDWIN Alfred A 6 Daniel W 6 E 6 George P 176 Edward 6 Edward 6 Elizabeth 6 Elvira 6 Horace 6 John M 6 Lester 6 Walter 6 William R 6
"BALDY" 136
BALL Elizabeth 208
BANKS Gen 119 184
BARISIC Sonya 249
BARNES H S 188
BARRY William F Gen 208
BARTLETT Charles M Mrs 170
BARTON Clara 168 223 224 D W Mrs 180
BAUER Joseph 188
BAUMAN Barbara 170 Elizabeth 75 170 George 170 Julius 6 Peter 170 Philip 170
BAVOKEL John V 202
BAXTER Benjamin Mrs 23 Israel P 7
BEACH William H Mrs 12
BEAR George 170 Martha E 170
BEATTY Cornelius 136
BECK Bertha C 208
BECKER Frederick G 7 Ida 7 Joseph 7
BEDELL K O Lt 150 Susan Mrs 62 Susan 173
BEDFORD J A Mrs 87
BEDLE Joseph D 186

BEEBY Herbert U Mrs 59
BEECHLER Joseph 188
BEGLEY J H Mrs 139
BELLIS William Mrs 154
BELT D M 7
BENJAMIN John W 4
BENNET Capt 7
BENNETT Aaron Capt 51 Elizabeth A 7 Emma Large 7 Ester Jean 25 John 7 John B 8 John B Shimcall Mrs 8 Isaac E 7
BENNITT I E Mrs 8
BENSON Ethel 182 William 182
BENTLEY C L 188 253
BERGEN Thomas 8
BERGQUIST John 8 John P F 8
BERNARD Mate 57
BERRIMAN Bertha 208
BERRY Earl S 170 Mary A 170 Matilda 8 Rufus W 170 Sarah M 81 Stewart F 170 T Halsey 8
BILBEE W H 188
BILLINGS William Mrs 154 152
BILLINS Sophie 176
BINGHAM Capt 7
BIRD Chetwood Mrs 82
BISHOP Francis A v 188 212 213 Miles Mrs 95 Mrs 213 William (?) 179
BLAINE James G 131
BLANCKE Arline 151 E R Mrs 151 Raymond Jr 151
BLATT Charles 8 Charles 8
BLISS Frank H Sr 8 Frank H Jr 9 William 9
BLOODGOOD Benjamin C 9 Harriett 9
BLOOMER Dennis P 9 John L 202
BLOOMFIELD Capt 160
BLORE John C 188
BODWELL Annie Harvey 9

James L 9 James L 60 James L Capt 150 Jane Flatt 9 Laura 60 William J 9
BOGART Henry C 126 Ida 17 Robert C Mrs 120
BOGERT John/D W 10 30
BOICE Cornelius 125
BOMFORD James 47
BONNELL/BUNNELL Albert 11 Albert F 11 Carrie 10 Edward C 10 George C 11 18 J Nelson 11 Joel 10/11 Mabel 11 Roswell B/V 11 15 Roswell B Mrs 15 William P 11 18
BONNETT D Blake 11 Charles P 11 Louis B 11 Margaret Augusta 11 M B Mrs 12
BOOTH John Wilkes 24
BOPP Elizabeth 12 Leonard 12 Leonard 12 Leonard Jr 12 Lily 12 Simon 12
BORDEN Rachel Stout 77
BOTHMANN Theodore C Mrs 128
BOUCHER J W 189
BOYER Alvah O Mrs 80
BOUGHTON Stephen E 12 103
BOWMAN Andrew 187 John 189
BOWME Mary 15
BOYD Barbara 174 J C Mrs 174
BOYLE Hugh C Mrs 171 W Cooper 12
BRADLEY W E Mr & Mrs 56 W Earl Mrs 56
BRADY Agnes 13 Hugh 13 Hugh 13 James 13 John 13 Nicholas Mrs 95 Terence 13 Thomas 13
BRAGG Emma 180 200 Fannie 200 John 200
BRAGGA Camillo 13 Fanny 13 William 13
BRAKELY Lillian 49

BRANDT Heinrich 14 Mary (?) 1 Squire 14
BRANSFIELD Ellen 51
BRANSON Harper 14 William W 14
BRANT Gertrude M 125 Joseph 14 Louise 126 Malana Russell 125 William 125 William Mrs 125 William Capt 126
BRAUNE Charles F 14
BRECKINRIDGE William Campbell Preston 14
BREEN Michael 14
BRENNER Jacob Mrs 138
BREWSTER James N S Mrs 139
BRIANT Caroline 64 Emma L 24 John A Mr & Mrs 24 Samuel 64 Sarah 64
BRIGGS Lewis W 15
BRINK Beatrice 107
BRINLEY David Mrs 61
BRISBANE Arthur 59
BRITTEN Bennett 15
BRITTIN David S 15 Frank 15 John 15
BROGAW Miss 22
BROKAW James O 22
BRONSON Bruce 174 D F Mrs 174 Donald 174 Helen Adams 201 Keith 174
BRONSTETTER Christopher 15 Henry 15 John 15 William 15
BROSNAN John 104
BROW Benjamin 189
BROWER Mary 107 108 Robert 189
BROWN Charles Mrs 32 Dr 220 E G 52 118 George 16 Henry O Col 19 J T 189 John 15 John A 16 Peter 16 Robert 16 Teresa 16
BROWNELL W M Mrs 158
BROWNING Gordon 265

Hoover Mr & Mrs 121
BRUBAKER Hattie 189 223
BRUEN Clarence 109
BRUGGY Ida 37
BRUNDAGE Ralph Mrs 19
BRUNT Harvey 16 Matilda 178
BRYANT George L 16 Robert 16
___ Rindell Mrs 16
BRYSON W F 189
BUCHANAN William 189
BUCHBEE William A 17
BUCKBEE William A 16
William A Jr 16
BUCKINGHAM Gen 231
BUDD Thomas B 110 155
BULL Archibald F 17 Archibald H 17 170 Benjamin 17 Ernest 171 Evelyn Van Deventer 171 James 17 James H 17 James Henry 17 Mary Kane 17 Mary Looker 17 Sitting 141 VET 17 171 William D 17
BUNKERHOEF John 17
BUNN David J 17 18 Elizabeth 18 Ellis 17 Isaac 17 18 Margaret 18 Matthias 17 18
BUNNELL George C 18 William P 18 (See Bonnell)
BUNTING Capt 26
BURGESS Esther 112
BURNETT Sarah 135
BURNS John Mrs 13
BURNSIDE Ambrose E Maj Gen 85 122 151
BURROWS Charles 189
BURT A W Mrs 198
BUSH W J 190
BUTLER Benjamin F Gen 86 Gen 166 183 225 John T 18 Robert 261
BUTTERWORTH John F Rev 109

BUZBY J E Mrs 45
BYER Bertha 52

CAIN Araminta 186
CALENDER J Clark Rev 106
CALVARY Paul 183
CAMERON Mrs 82
CAMPBELL Albert B 240
CANNON Joseph 190 199 Joseph 190 Joseph E Mr & Mrs 190 Joseph E Jr 190 J C Mr & Mrs 190 Robert 190
CANIFF Georgiana 34
CARBERRY Frank Mrs 66
CARKHUFF Harriet 18 Ida 18 J W Mrs 51 Jacob S 18 John W 18 Lorenzo W 18 Philip A 18 Philip E 18
CARKHUFFS Maud 105
CARLTON Charles E Mrs 96 Helen M 19 ___ Newcomb Mrs 19 William J 19
CARMAN E A 19 Emma D 19 Florence I 19 Henry C 19 James L 19 James L Jr 19
CARPENTER Sallie Frances 74
CARR Keifer Mrs 28
CARROLL Charles Mrs 61 Joseph 19 May E 19 Paul 19 Paul Jr 19 Rev Fr 180 Robert 19 Robert 19
CARTER Albert 48 Albert Mrs 47 Bert 135 Capt O M 105
CARY Charles 20 Johnson W 20
CASNER Alfred B 190 Charles Mr & Mrs 190 Frederick 190 Henry Mr & Mrs 190 Mary Hague 190 William H 190
CASTIAUX Joseph Mrs 135
CASTIOUX J C Mrs 135
CAYLEY Murray A Rev 52
CHAMPION John 182

CHAPIN Lillian M 119
CHAPMAN Mary 148
CHASE Alexander 210 Clara 122
CHATTIN Charles F 20
CHEEK William H Rev 184
CHESSEMAN David August 20
CHUBB Henry C 20 Ida G 20 Walter M 20
CLADEK Capt 10 Col 15 Col John J 25 Emma 62 George B Mr & Mrs 62
CLARK Arthur B 21 Arthur B Mrs 52 Arthur B Mrs 52 Charles Homer/C 21 Cornelius Hyer 21 __ Crane Mrs 22 Deaconess 141 Eliza Norton Haskell 22 James 21 John M Mrs 12 Linda 107 Mrs 12 Mary 21   Mary Elizabeth Stevenson 21 Mary J 21 Mortimer A 21 Paul Haskell 22 Sarah Joy 22 Sarah Mather Smith 21 Theron B 21 William 22 William Jackson Rev 22
CLARKE Frances 47 Newman 47
CLARY Elizabeth 107
CLAYPOOL John M Gen 191 253 257 259 James M Gen 251
CLAYTON Asher M 22 Laura 22 Maurice 22
CLEM Elizabeth 22 John 22 John Lincoln 22
CLEVELAND ___ Brogaw Mrs 22 Edmund 22 Joseph 22 Miss 5 Morris M Mrs 113 Robert 5
CLIFFORD Charles J 23 Henrietta F 23 Marietta Huntsman 23
COATES John 23
COBB Eben B Rev Dr 8 13 33 48 53 60 102 149
COCKER William J E Mrs 37
CODDINGTON Catherine 96

Mary 141
CODY William M "Buffalo Bill" 75 102 184
COE Charles H Mrs 82
COEYMAN Martha J Hughes 23 William 23 William John 23
COLE Edmund Lewis/R 23 Frank O 191 Frank O 137 Frederick G Jr 174
COLES W H C Mrs 52
COLLIER J W P Rev 183
COLLINS Fergus 24 Grace A 53
COLYER Joseph Jr 24
COMPTON Alvah 24 Ann Marie Ayers 24 C K Mrs 125 Emma L Bryant 24 Jacob 24 Nathan V 24 Oliver 24
CONANT Caroline Melvin 171
CONAWA Wingate/ Wright B 25
CONGER Caroline 25 George 25 Jeremiah 25 J H 191 William 25
CONKLIN Mary E 120
CONNETT Isaac S v 191 214
CONNOLLY James 26 Thomas 26
CONNORS Patrick 26
CONOLLY John Mrs 12
CONRAD Dora 27 Edward 26 27 Fannie 26 27 Frederick 27 Harry Mrs 120 Joseph Mrs 22 Louis 26 27 Louise C Menge Mrs 26 27 Sue 195
CONROY Thomas J Rev 51
CONYARD Jasper 182
COODER Charles L Rev 99 149 162
COOK Alford B 27 Asa H Capt iii Clarence J 27 Clarence W 27 Edward 27 John 28 R Mrs 1
COOLEY J B 52
COOPER Elizabeth 147 George W 28 John W 28 191 260

Samuel H Mrs 50
CORBIN Abel Mrs 167 William Mrs 166 William H 168
CORSON William A 191
CORY Emma C 28 Enos W 28 Frederick N 28 H L 28 William 28
COSGROVE John Mrs 62
COSTER Alfred 182 Mary Louise 182 Rev & Mrs Peter C 182 183 William Benjamin Griffin 182
COULTER Harry C 76
COULTRAS Thomas I Rev 16
COURTNEY H E 191
COVERT C Mrs 156 Miss 69
COWIE George H 28 George W 28 Thomas A 28
COX Andrew 29 Albert 29 George Mrs 78 W H Mrs 145
COYLE Charles Joseph 29
CRAMER Oscar C Mrs 23
CRANE Alfred T 143 Ann 34 Augustus B 68 Benjamin P 29 David T Mrs 59 Edward D 30 Edward S 30 Eunice 68 Isaac 30 Jennie 29 John B 29 Louis B Rev 61 M B Moore Mrs 48 Martin Mrs 59 Mary Wade 29 Miss 21 Stephen S 191 T A 21 William 29 William Francis 10 30
CRAWN Joseph Mrs 77
CRIST Mary A 127 Walter Mrs 85
CROSBY M B 192
CROSS Benjamin F 30 Mary L Avery 30 Richard 30
CROUTHERS Anna J 149
CROWELL Augustus 30 Theodore 30
CUDDEBACK David 249
CULLEN Edward Mrs 46
CULVER Arthur 30 Augustus P

30 31 Bertram M 30 George 31 Jonathan 31 Jonathan 30 Stephen 31
CUMMINGS Alexander M 31 A E 31 Catherine A 141 Fred A 31 Joseph 31 Susie 31 William 31
CURRIDEN Benjamin 31
CURTIS Arthur R 31 Gen 98
CUSTER Gen 141 230
CYESTER Louis 192

DAHLGREN Col 119
DALLAS Jessie 32 Lindsay 32 Mary 32 William 31
DALRYMPLE Benjamin Mrs 44
DANA Carlisle 11 Laura H 11 Lucia S 11 R K Mrs 11 R Bingham 11 Robert S 192 Sylvester 192
DANFORTH C R Mrs 104
DANNEBERGER Anthony 32 Charles F 32 John J 32 Joseph 32
DARASKA Jessie Ecker vii viii John R viii
DARLING Hattie 36
DAUBNER Frank 32 George 32 John 32 55 73 127 136 Joseph 32 Leonard 32
DAUGHERTY James H Mrs 38
DAVENPORT Adaline H 171 Daisy A 171 Frederick St John 171 George B 171 William 171 William T 171 William Mrs 166
DAVIS Abbler Mrs 30 Alice M Higgins 171 Andrew 32 97 Annie L 7 Catherine 171 172 Charles R 179 Chas P Mrs 174 David Williams 171 Elizabeth H 184 Esther 179 Ethel 121 F A Mr & Mrs 121 Frederick H Mrs 190 Garrison 7 J Stanley 179 John T Mrs 179 John R 33 Joseph 172

Joseph 29 186 Mr 103 Margaret
171 172 Moses 192 Orill Edith
179 Philip 172 Pierpont V Mrs
114 R Jane 171 Richard Harding
236 Sarah 172 Thomas 33 Walter
E 33 William E 171
DAY Allen H 33 Daniel C 33
Vincent 33 William H 33
DEBO Charles Allison 172 Fred S
172 Joanna Green 172
DECASTRO Susan 15
DECKER Alfred 35 Amos A 33
Ann Crane 34 Arthur 34 Charles
34 Charles S 34 Edwin T 34
Elizabeth 34 Frank C 34 George
35 George William 34 Georgiana
Caniff 34 Harry A 33 Henry 34
Henry C 34 Isaac 35 J Albert 34
James H 35 John 34 35 Loriena 35
Richard 35 152 Richard 35
William 35
DEHART John Mrs 176
DEMILLER Anne 111
DEMINATUS Grace Ronnell 11
DEMOGUGNE John Mrs 15
DENNISON Caroline 106 Fannie
G 106 Robert 106
DENTON Anthony W 35 Charles
C Sr 35 Charles C Jr 35 Julia 35
Lydia 35 Nathan F 35
DE PEYSTER Maude 120
DEPREZ John 36
DEROUCHER John Mrs 17
DERREVERE Matthias 36
DERROM Col 93
DEVINE Edward M 36
DEVLAN Charles F 36
DEVOE William B 28
DEWESS H E Mrs 156
DEWEY Adm 43
DEWOLFF Mary 34
DEY George 192

DICESNOLA Louis Palma 36
DICKIE Robert B 36
DIETRICH John 36
DIGAN Mrs 18
DIMLER Chistina 172 David
172 David 172 William 172
DINKINS James 192 253
DISTON R E Mrs 28
DIX Gen 139
DIXON Alfred 37 Alexander 37
G Arthur 37 John J 37 Robert 37
Robert E 37 Robert Mrs 37 Sophie
151 Walter 37 Walter 37 William
A 37 William H 37
DOBBS John 38 John 38
DOBSON D Newton Rev 35
DOERRER Frederick R Mrs 123
DOHMEYER Charles B 38
DONNELL Mayra / Maria 106
DONOVAN Joseph 38 39 40
DOOLEY Charles E 38
Elizabeth 73 James J 38 John F
38 John F Mrs 38 John J 38
Michael F 38 Thomas H 38
William E 38
DORAN Joseph 40 Sarah 40
DORR Nellie 94
DOTY Alonzo 40 Charlotte 40 E
H 40 John H 40 41 Samuel 40 S
C 40
DOUBLEDAY Col Thomas 34
DOUGHERTY George H 41
Henry 41 Ray viii William E 41
DOUGLAS H Frank 41 Frank W
41 Woodruff Mrs 41
DOWD Henry Mrs 130
DOWERS George 97 George W
Mrs 96 Mr 97
DOWNEY Bernard 172 Frank
172 Kermon 172 Mary 172
Michael F 172
DRAKE Alice Van Houten 42

Arthur G 42 Carl D Mrs 1 Charles 42 Charles N 42 Charles N Jr 42 Clarence B 242 Edward K 42 78 129 Edward R 42 Elizabeth M 242 Emily 42 Eunice 42 Ezra 42 Gen J Madison 5 42 43 58 80 100 127 139 164 231 George W 242 Hannah Johnson 42 James 42 James S 42 Jonathan Baker 42 Kenneth I 242 Lewis 86 Louis L 42 Mary Baker 42 Mr 78 Ralph P 242 Robert A 42 Silas D Silas Downer 42 Theodore A 42 Victor M 249 Willis Sanford 43 236 237 238 239 240 242 243
DRAPEAU Dorothy 134 George 134 Louise 134
DRECK aka DRAKE 237
DREYER August 44 Frank 43 Frank Jr 44 Meta 44
DRUMGOOL Fr 105
DUBON Walter J 44 William 44
DUHEAU Alfred Mrs 35
DUNHAM Alfred 63 J E Mrs 62 Samuel 44
DUNN Johanna 44 J T Mrs 62 Jack 63 208 Joseph 44 Lewis A 44 Michael 44 Michael W 44 Theodore 44
DURAND James H 25
DURBAN Theodore 44
DURIE Frank Mrs 45 Samuel C 45 William Britten 45 William Britten Jr 45 William B 96
DUSHANEK John Mrs 11
DUSSENBERRY August 45 J P 45
DUTROW Adam 143 Adam L 45 George 45 Henrietta 45 Leonard 45 Milison M 45
DWIGHT H O Rev 46

Adelaide F 46 Frances Warner 46 H E 46 Mary L 46
DWYER Aloyisus F 46 Joseph F 46 Patrick 46 William J F 46 William Rev 46

EARL Marion J 174 Richard S 174
EARLE George H 257
EARLY Gen 229 230
EATON Alvin R Jr Mrs 41 Sarah E Mrs 7
ECKERSON Overseer 185
ECKERT John 46 William F 46
ECKMAN Miss 177
EDGAR John 183 Mahlon 183 Samuel 183
EDISON Thomas A 141
EDSON Alvin 47 Frances Clarke 47 Frederick C 47 John Henry 47 Mary L 47
EDWARDS Joseph 47 Joseph E 47 Robert C 47
EGAN Annie 176 J L Mrs 176
EGENOLF Peter Mrs 128
ELIOT Robert W Rev 100 Susan 74
ELLIS Arthur Mr & Mrs 47 Arthur W 48 Arthur W Jr 47 Clarice 47 Clarissa K 48 Edward B 48 George Mr & Mrs 47 George A 48 George A Jr 47 Herbert E 47 Herbert L 48 J Harold 48 Jennie M 48 M Estella 48 William 129 William A 47 William A 47 William H Mr & Mrs 47 William K 48
ELLSON John V Rev 23 84 135
ELLWOOD James 193
ELMS G 69 Henry J Mrs 69
EMMERICK Fred Mrs 76
EMMETT William Mrs 199

ENGLISH Conover Mrs 72
ENNIS George Rev Dr 48 Julia 176 Phebe 28 William 48 William Syers Mrs 48
ERICSSON John 244 245
ERNST Francis 48
ERRICKSON John Mrs 77
ERXLEBEN Blanche 242
ESDAILE Amy E 28
ESSEX Edward 48 Henry Mrs 72
ESTABROOKE Edward Manning 48 __ Moore Crane 48
ESTIL Mulford 161
EVANS Ellen Scriven x 88
EVERETT H E Mrs 167
EVERHART Lawrence Mrs 174
EWING Charles Mrs 172 Gen 172

FAGAN John B 193
FALLON Frank Mrs 143
FARAWELL John Mrs 95
FAREWELL Margaret Ann 70
FARMER Mrs 172
FARRAGUT Adm 28 62 98 142 166
FARRELL B L Mrs 92
FAULKS Emma Webster 48 Frank 49 Isaac 153 Isaac Mrs 43 N W 49 Thomas H Mrs 99 William 49
FAY Eva 49 John C 49 J Augustus Gen 49 Julius Augustus 49
FEAKES Alfred C Mrs 95
FEALDS Frank D 50
FEBREY Amos Mrs 2 Ethel 201 Harold 201 James E Mr & Mrs 201
FEE Edward 50 Frank 50 Frederick B 50 George 50 Harry 50 John 50 Thomas J 50 William R 50
FEININGER Mrs 82
FELLOWS N Warren Mrs 9
FENTON Reuben E 168
FERGUSON Joseph B Rev 167 John Rev 122
FERRIS Margaret 185
FIELD F W Mrs 60 George H 50
FINK Arthur 50 James W 50 Mary W 50 Mildred 50
FINNERTY Louis Mrs 199
FINNEY David P Mrs 67
FIRTH John M Mrs 180
FISHER Annie 53 Christian G Rev 38 H H Mr 217 Mrs 46 Spencer 57 Susan 141
FITZPATRICK John Mrs 16
FLATT Jane 9 William H 9
FLIPPER O F Rev 185
FLOOD Edward 50
FLORENCE William J 88
FLOWERS John 50
FLYNN Cornelius 51 Edward J 64 Mrs 172 Peter 51 Thomas 225 Thomas 51
FOOTE F W 51 Frederick W 147
FONDA Laura 77
FORCE Manning 83
FORD Emma 121 George B 58 Mary B 58
FORGUS William F 51
FORMAN William Mrs 20
FORSYTH Miss 101 Thomas 101
FOSSELMAN Charles H 51
FOWLER Charles B 193 201 Congressman 185
FOX Caroline Lind 51 Thomas H Mrs 105 Thomas J 51
FRANCIS Blake White 121 Blake Mrs 121 Elias 183 George A Rev 41 Leonard 183

FRANK Mrs 45
FRANKENBERGER Henry E 100
FRANKLIN Frederick H 52 James J 52 Joseph J 52 Walter 52 William Mrs 154
FRAZEE John H 52 V L Mrs 155
FRECKMAN Frederick Mrs 156
FREEMAN Edward S 52 Uel 52 143 Walter 52 William 23 52 William C 52
FRENCH Michael Mrs 105
FRICKE Annie 71 Charles W 71 Ernest 71 Frank R 71 Louis J 71 William H 71
FROMM Edward 52 John 52 Louis 52 Mary 52
FULMER Llewellyn S Rev 10
FULTON Henry Mrs 90 Jane 199

GABRIEL Cornelia W 53 Charles 53 Henry H 53 John H 53 Theodore 53
GAFFNEY Michael F 53
GALE Samuel 72
GALLAGHER Thomas 53
GARBONATI Fred 53
GARDINER Elizabeth I 54 William H 54 William H Jr 54
GARDNER Estelle 54 Lloyd 23
GARLAND Fannie 183 Preston 183
GARTHWAITE Martha 200 Samuel 54
GARTZ Frederick 54 Louise 54 William H 54
GASKILL Carrie 41
GEBHARDT Henry Mrs 38
GEERY Susan 103
GERHART E J Mrs 193 Leroy H 193
GERKE Julius 54 Reinhard 54 Robert 54
GETTYS James 252
GIBBONS William R Mrs 24
GIBBS George 21 Sarah 172
GIBSON Henry Richard 55
GIEGER John 55
GIFFORD Henry Rev 116
GILBERT Calvin 55 Fannie 94
GILDERSLEEVE Judge 162
GILL William A 172
GILLEN James P 55
GILLESPIE Blanche A 57 D A Mrs 57 James H 57
GILLICK Joseph Mrs 131
GLASER Menta C Mrs 34
GLAZEBROOK Otis A Rev DD 20 62 109 172
GLENDINNING Andrew H Mrs 89 Bruce 90 John Edmond 90 Ralph 90 Warren 90
GODFREY Clara F 164 Mabel 164 Mary E 164
GODOWN P O Mrs 158
GOFF John S 56 193
GOGGINS William T v 193 217 218
GOLDSMITH Rebecca 187
GOOD Adam 55 Emma 56 Euphemia 55 John A Mr & Mrs 56 John Hoffman 55 Mary Miller 56
GOODALL C E Rev 174 Charles F Rev 87 Fred 118
GOODRICH J A 193 John 193
GORDON Harry Mrs 37 James F 193 Joseph 174 Robert 174
GORETSKI John Mrs 95
GORHAM Charles H 56
GORRINGE Thomas Mrs 33
GOSLEE Amanda 114
GOULD Eliza 104

GRACE Joseph 56
GRAFF Emil 56 193 194 197
GRAHAM Col 122 L Y Rev
104 Lt 233 Rev Jr 122 159
GRANT Gabriel 57 Ida 82
GRANTS Mrs 7
GRAVES Bibb 265
GRAY Mary 89
GREELY Horace 78 157
GREGG John H Mrs 2
GREEN Carrie E 57 Cordelia
172 Elizabeth A Jones 57
Elizabeth Grace 67 Franklin 173
Gov 75 Harvey 57 James W 232
Joanna 172 John 57 John H 184
Josephine Hann 57 Lillian M 57
Nathaniel Gen 67 Nellie R 57
Spencer 57 Vanderbilt Mrs 142
William H 57
GREEN(E) Samuel Dana 240
241
GREENOUGH Kate 80
GREVES Selden Mrs 165
GREYSTONE Daniel 193
GRIEVES Alfred Mrs 38
GRIFFIN Alexander 194 Jacob
194
GROAT Augusta Albright 58
James Elliott 57 Mate Bernard 57
GRODEN Annie G viii Peter iv
GRODY Rosanna 95
GROENDYKE John Mrs 16
GRUBB Col E Bird 74
GULAGER Annie 151
GUNNERSON George M 194

HAGERMAN Forrest 58 Frank
58 James E 58
HAGGERTY Katherine 73
HAGUE Joseph Mrs x 88 Mary
190
HAIGES F Mrs 72

HALBERSTADT John Mrs 37
HALE George E Mrs 110
HALL Ambrose Mrs 143 Asa 58
George W 173 Mary Halsey 173
Peter 56 194
HALLAWAY Mrs 18
HALLY Frank 173 John 173
Josie 173 Margaret 173
HALSEY Charles Rev 139 Eliza
Gracie 139 Eliza Gracie King 139
HALSTEAD Miss 126
HAMER Arthur Mrs 178
HAMILTON William B Rev 61
165
HAM(M)ACKER James P 194
255 259
HAMMOND Caroline C Lang 58
Thomas B 58
HAMNER Charles S Mrs 131
HAND David P 58 Florence 5
Fred 58 Hezekiah 58 Luther T
148 Milton 58 William 58
HANDCOCK James 194
HANEY William 59
HANN Enos F 2 59
Josephine 57
HANSEL Harold Mrs 34
HARATT T M Mrs 6
HARKINS Mr & Mrs Thomas R
194 203 (See Hawkins)
HARLEY G Mrs 69
HARRIS Amanda 59 Baker 59
C C Mrs 102 Chauncey 59
Chauncey Capt 5 43 110 113 132
153 Elizabeth 59 Francis 59
George W 59 Grace E 59 J W Gen
191 194 256 Louisa 182 Luelle G
59
HARRISON Gen 38 Ida L 121
Katherine 71
HARTLING John 110
HARTUNG John 195

HARVEY Annie 9 George W 60
John 9 John H 10 60 Laura 10
HASKELL Eliza Norton 22
HASKO Joe "O E" viii
HASSON Emma 79
HATCH Durant 195 Gen _119
HATFIELD Capt / Maj 6 Capt 10
Col 14 Capt David 95 Clarence
Mrs 9 Newton Mrs 79
HATHAWAY Baylis 121 Miss 121
HAUGHWOUT William B 60
HAVER Grant Mrs 44
HAVILAND William F 119
William H 119 William H Mrs 119
HAWES W M C Rev 70
HAWKINS Charles R H 184
Frederick 184 Harold Montague 184 Ralph F 184 Mr & Mrs Thomas R 194 203
HAWLEY Paul R 259 260
HAYMER Madeline 182
HAYWARD William H Mrs 69
HAZARD Abigail 60 L K 60 Margaret 60 Margaret A Kellogg 60 Sallie 60 Thomas T 60 Thomas Tilley 60
HEADLEY Mary F 177 (See Poysher)
HEADY Charles L 61
HEARD J B Rev 56 152
HECKMAN Col 232 233
HECTOR Emil 61 George 61
HEDGES James E 13
HEDEL Theabold G Mrs 151
HEEGE Alfred 61 Jacob 61 Lester 61
HEFTI Ellen 107 Lillian 107
HEG James D 86
HELLER Ida F 160 Joseph 160
HENDERSON Archibald 61

Thomas B 62
HENDRY A Mrs 102
HENNESSY James 62 Patrick 62
HENRY Alexander 62 Edna 87 Ellen 173 Ellen Florence 87 Ellen Hopkins 62 Henry 173 James 62 John 62 John William 87 Lewis 62 Lucian 173 Lucy 83 Minnie Mrs 87 William 62 William 62 173
HERLICH Grace 47
HERMES Albert 63 Charles 63 Elizabeth R 62 Michael 62
HERRICK George Washington 63
HERRMANN John A Mrs 24
HERTER Lucy 52
HETFIELD D B 195 David Capt 80 David Maj 44
HEYER Irma 63 William D 63 William G Rev 63
HICKS Jason 94 John Mrs 176 Julia 94
HIGGINS A E 63 Adelia L Littlefield 173 Alice M 171 Anna N 64 David 173 David S 173 Francis H 63 Frank H 63 G Barton 64 George 171 J Wallace 173 J Wallace Jr 173 James 173 James Ward 173 John F 64 Margaret 64 Margaret Searing 173 Mary L 64 Spencer Littlefield 173 Timothy 64 Timothy E 64 Timothy E 64 William 171
HIGGINSON Caroline Briant 64 Ida W 65 Mary E 64 Michael W 64 William H 64
HILL Charles Edward 65 Charles E Mrs 65 W Harry 49 James Mrs 26 27
HILLER Charles M 65 Frederick 65
HIMES Henrietta N 112

HINCHMAN Capt 89
HOBART VP 164
HOBSON Belle 10
HOCK H T Mrs 145 Miss 145
HOCKENBURY Charles Mrs 26 27
HODGE Helen 65 Lawson 65 William 65
HODGINS George 174 George 174 Mary 174
HOFFMAN Catherine 65 George Mrs 19 Jacob 65 John T 65 Virginia 65
HOGAN John J Mrs 32
HOLDORF Ernest Mrs 117
HOLLAND Capt 12
HOLMES Benjamin P 66 Oliver Wendell 16 Roxanna iii
HOLSTE Charles Mrs 175
HOLT Charles H 195 242 James 91 James Mrs 91 Thomas 91
HOOKER Gen 122 162
HOOTON Samuel B 66
HOPKINS Charles F 195 Ellen 62 136
HOPPAUGH William Rev 62
HOPSON Harriet J 162
HORTON A M Mrs 83
HOUFMAN William Mrs 159
HOUSTON James 66 James 66 James Mrs 80 Reba E 66 Robert G 66 Sam Gen 206 Samuel Sr 66 Virginia 56 W C Mr & Mrs 56 Warren G 66 Wilbur D 66 William Mrs 56
HOWARD Co Clerk 99 Lt 67 234 235 William Mrs 95
HOWE E E Mrs 63 Mr 217
HOWELL B C 67 B C Jr 67 Henry C 195 W R V 67
HOYT Chester J Rev 181
HUBARD Lyttleton E Rev 120

HUBBARD Elizabeth Grace Green 67 J Frank(lin) Capt 67 125 133
HUFTEN Charles Mrs 153 Elsie 180 George 180
HUGG Harvey 67 William H 67
HUGHES Benjamin W 68 195 Benjamin W 195 Franklin Roosevelt 68 George Isaac 68 Hugh 68 Martha J 23 Mary Gertrude 68 R W 69 William H 68
HULL Charles F 69
HULSIZER Sidney 208
HUNTER Gen 128 146
HUNTSMAN Marietta 22
HURST Bishop John F 2 Rev Dr John F 201
HURT Benjamin F 69 Edward 69 Frederick 69 Herbert 69 Jeanette 69
HUTCHINSON Charles Mrs 136 ___Covert Mrs 69 Fitz 69 Frederick L Mrs 77 John S 69
HYDE B F 174 Dorsey W Mrs 141 Harlow 174 Harlow Jr 174 Loretta E 174

INGLISS James Jr 195 Rev Dr 101
INSLEE Isaac 70
IOVINO Dean viii
IRONS George Giberson 70 Longstreet 70 Lydia Jeffrey 70
IRVING Gertrude Heady 61
IVANS Mary McClain 70 Theodore Alonzo 70

JACKSON George W 70 Henry L 184 John S v 195 218 219 Thomas H 70
JACOBS L Mrs 119

279

JAMIESON A L Mrs 58
JAQUES James T Mrs 14
JARVIS Altha C 71 Grace E 71 Katherine Harrison 71 John Richardson 71 Mary 160 Walter G Rev 51 Walter M 71 William E 71
JEFFERSON Joe 88
JEFFREY Lydia 70
JEFFRIES Lloyd Mrs 57
JENKINS James Capt 29 149 Lorenzo Mrs 3 Mrs 21
JENNISON Lynn E 176
JOHNSON Carrie L 89 Col 226 Cordelia D Townley 174 Emma A 174 Hannah 42 Harris L 175 Harry 181 Isaac 195 Mary Maxwell 135 Robert E Capt 110 Samuel 201 Sarah Wooley 115
JOHNSTON Jane Seigmund 196
JONES Charles D 195 Elizabeth A 57 Ernst 71 F V L Mrs 140 Herbert Mrs 166 James Mrs 26 27 195 Obadiah F 195 Patrick Henry 71 W B Mrs 81 Woodruff 72
JORDON Richard 185
JOSEPH Mrs 77
JOY Sarah 21
JOYCE Bridget 72 Delia 72 Martin 72 Michael 72 Michael A Jr 72 Nora 72 Patrick 72
JUDD Benjamin F 196 Frederick 196

KANE A C Mrs 170 Mary 17 Milton Mrs 186
KAUFMANN Cornelia 135 Frederick Mrs 135
KEAN John 53 Senator 185
KEECH Finley Rev 112

KEEFER Edward S Mrs 87
KEELER William F 240 249
KEENE Tom 88
KEILER Valentine 72
KEIMIG Charles 72 Charles M B 72 Fred W 72 H Alfred 73 Peter 72
KEIPER Allan M 72 Daniel 72 Howard L 72 Lillie J 72 Rene D 72
KELBER John 73
KELLER George Mrs 81 Tamaseen L 94
KELLOGG Julia 131 Margaret A 60
KELLY Anna 73 Bridget C 73 Francis 73 James 73 John 73 Joseph 73 174 Joseph Mrs 174 176 Martin 73 Mary 73 Mrs 73 Patrick 73 William 73
KEMBLE C S Rev 1
KEMP H M Rev 184
KEMPEL Mrs 7
KEMPSHALT Rev Dr 164
KENDALL Florence Helen Messmore 175
KENNEDY Jennie 196 223 M J Mrs 91 Michael Mrs 81 Peter 73
KENNELLY Albert L 74 Maurice V 73 Ralph V 74
KENT Mary Emily 100
KENYON H H Mrs 180
KERGUELAN Henrietta de 192
KERR Frederick 74 John 74 John B 74 John T Rev 80 101 135 Joseph 74 Henry C Capt 23 Wilson 74
KESSINGER Robert Mrs 15
KESSLER M Mrs 63
KETCHUM George Mrs 140
KEYES E D Gen 139
KHUN Albert M Mrs 181

KIBBE Frank W 74 Irvin 74 Isaac Pease 74 Isaac St J 74 Louis G 74 O A 224 Preston 74 Sallie Frances Carpenter 74 William J 74
KIDD John Capt 123 John 153 Miss 123
KIGGINS Isaac C 13 Willard A Mrs 171
KING Adelaide Lavender York 74 Charles 74 75 139 Charles H 75 Eliza Gracie 139 Elizabeth 176 Isaac Mrs 37 151 Robert Mrs 152 Rufus 75 170 Rufus 74 Rufus III 75 Susan 74 Eliot 74 William Gracie 75
KINGSBURY Janet 111
KINKEL Albert Mrs 134
KIP Walter Mrs 134
KIRKMAN Helen 192 Randolph Mendell 199 Warren V Mrs 199
KITTELL Lillie 140
KIYLER Eugene 12 Lilly Mrs 12
KLEINHANS Councilman 170
KLOSKY Ruth 57
KNAPF Frederick C Rev 48
KNOBEL Caspar 196
KOLLACK Sheppard viii Sheppard Capt vii
KORNMEYER George Mrs 73
KRAUS Art viii
KULL Ernest Mrs 58
KUNE Margaret 53
KUNZ George Mrs 119
KYLES Col 183
KYLISCH Frank Mrs 166
KYTE Charles 75 George 75

LACOMBE Elizabeth 76 Louis 76
LA FULEY Edward 76
LAING Barry 76 Noah B 76

LAMBERT Albert 76
LAKE Rebecca 130
LAMB Jeremiah 185
LAMBOT Jules C 76 Victor 76 William 76
LAMOREAUX Clara 86
LA MOTTE Arthur 175 Edgar E 175 Ellen 175 Joseph 175 Nelson 175 Walter 175 Walter 175 Wilbur 175
LAMPHEAR H L Mrs 63
LANCE John W 77 Laura Fonda 77
LANE Clifford 77 E Clarkson 77 Elizabeth 199 Henry B 77 John W 77 Thomas 77 William 77
LANG Caroline C 58 Noah S 196 Wallace Mrs 90
LANGDON Gertrude 167
LANGFORD W S Rev Dr 172
LAPOINT Franklin 34 Julia 34
LAREN Catherine J 155
LARGE Emma 7 Isaac S 7
LARNED W F Mrs 167
LAROSA Andrew Ottison 77 Frank W 77
LARRISON Jennie 27
LAURIE James W Rev 89
LAVERE Linton Thorn 143 Pauline 143
LAW George A Rev 57 98 178
LAWRENCE Alice 77 Benjamin v 77 219 Benjamin L 77 219 Frank M 261 264 John A Mrs x 88 Joseph 77 Rachel Stout Borden 77 W P Rev 184 W P Rev 184 Ward Mrs 182 William Borden 77
LEADENHAM William Mrs 138
LEATHERBURY William 78
LECOUR Arthur Mrs 122
LEDLEY Ellesworth 78 Frank M 78 John M 78 Mrs 78

LEE B A Col 25 Harry Rene 196
William 79
LEECH H B 26
LEHLEITER Louise 10
LEIGH Frances E 184
LEMON William 232 233
LENOX A G 196
LEONARD Charles 143 Charles
H 196 Sarah 148
LEONHARD Jacob 79 Jacob Jr
79 Lillian 79
LESTER Daniel K 79 241
Edward 241 Gray B 241 John 241
LEVERIDGE Walter H Mrs 5
LEVI Charles A 79 George Mrs
62 George H 79 Joseph B 79
Richard 79 Roscoe C 79
LEVINE Joseph F Mrs 51
LEVY J H Mrs 34
LEWIS Anderson 185 Bon 183
Capt 8 13 80 103 122 132 J R
Mrs 46 W S 79
LILLY Thomas 197
LIND Caroline 51
LINDEMAR G Mrs 1
LINDSEY Nathaniel W 197
LITTELL Isaac M 24
LITTLE Chester 79 E P Rev 178
James 79 Rutherford 79 Thomas
A 80
LITTLEFIELD Adelia L 173
LLOYD George K 12 George
Kilpatrick 80 Georgia 80 James
80 Nellie Smith 80 Oliver 80
Samuel 80 Thomas 80 William
80
LOBDELL Annie 154
LOCKWOOD Charles 56 197
LOGUE Daniel C 197 239 240
LONG David 80 Emma 80 John
W 80 Phoebe N 173 Quinton J 60
Robert C 80 Stephen M 81 Walter

M 80
LONGHORST Fannie 81 George
81 Gustavus 81 Gustavus 81 Jacob
81 Lulu 81
LONEY Frederick Mrs 87
LONGSTREET Gen 175 Isaac
M 93 James Mrs 175 Mary A 93
LOOKER Mary 17
LOOP Martin E 197 256
LORING Charles B 81 Charles Jr
81 Julia 81
LOTT Anna 62 Anna V 173
LOTZ Jacob 197
LOUIS Viola 107
LOUNSBURY Virginia 143
LOVELAND Delmar Mrs 129
Herbert Mrs 2
LOVELL Charles F 81 John L 81
Sarah M Berry 81 William J 81
LOW Frederick 16 Mrs 16
LOWDEN Joseph D 82
LUCAS Fielding 197
LUCKHURST Elizabeth 176
James B 176 James H 176 Julia
Ennis 176 William J 176
LUDEY Emma T 176 Francis C
176
LUFBURROW Bertha 113
LUKENS George Mrs 110
LUM William B 82
LUNGER Guile R 82 Jacob S 82
James B Mrs 82 Stanley J 82
LUSHEAR Alfred 82 Anna 82
Clarence 82
LUSTER Albert 82 Edward 82
Frank 82 George 82 Robert Crane
82 Theodore 82
LUTZ John A 82 John B Capt 82
John B 82 148
LYDECKER A J 198
LYNCH Edgar 83 J J Mrs 62
John A Mrs 12 Joseph 83

282

Richard 83 William Mrs 92
LYNN Mildred 53
LYNNBROOK Jennie Stansfield 176
LYON Mary J 9
LYONS John B 83 John Mrs 176 Murtagh 83

MACDANIEL (?) James A 178
MACDONALD Archibald W 114 Terrence 198 W E Mrs 142
MACGREGOR Alexander 83 James 83 Jane 83 Lucy Henry 83
MACKENZIE John H 119 John M 119 John Mrs 118
MACKEY Mary 84 Joseph H 84 William H 84 William Henry 84
MACQUAIDE Samuel H 84 Thomas G 84
MADER Ethel 87 Katherine 87
MAGIE William J 24
MAGUIRE Mrs 62
MAHER Patrick 84
MAINS Edith 79
MAISE Walter Mrs 154
MAJORAU Peter C 211
MAKEPEACE George Washington iii Hannah Smith iii Norman G iii
MANAHAN James C Mr & Mrs 90
MANDEVILLE Charles A 84 Charles W 84 Frank 85
MANNING Harriet 223 Harry J Mrs 49
MANNON Asa L 85 Edward P 85 Elizabeth 85 Mary A 85 Nicholas 85
MANSKE William Mrs 156
MANSON George 198
MANVEL Cyrus 85 Frederick 85 118 Herbert E 85

118 John 85 Mary Moore 85
MARCUM "Aunt Julia" 198
MARCY William L 101
MARINUS L H 198
MARR Edward Jr 107
MARSH Bryant Mrs 21 Caroline 176 Charles 176 Charles Mrs 152 Charles T Mrs 41 Harry R 85 Harry W 85 J J 30 Jonas E 13 Joseph 85 Martha 151 Martha L 176 William J 85
MARSHALL Anna 86 Charles 86 Clifford Mrs 12 Robert 86 Samuel 86 William 86
MARTIN Adrian Mrs 34 Amos 86 Andrew 87 Balthanser 86 87 Charles 87 Conrad 87 Edward L 87 Frederick 86 George 87 George B 176 George E Mrs 14 Grant 236 Harry Stone 86 Isabelle M 176 Jacob 87 John 87 John W 198 Joseph 87 Joseph W Capt 26 148 Joseph William 86 Louis 86 Keziah P 131 Lucy 87 Luther 176 Luther Mrs 5 Manton 86 Marie 86 87 May 87 Mr 31 86 109 Raymond 87 Veronica 87 Vet 5 31 Walter N Mrs 155 William 86 William J 87 William B Mrs 83
MASKEVICH Benedict Mrs 76
MASSIE William 198 256
MATSON Luke 87 98 Morris M 87
MATTOX William 88 William R 88
MAUER Gen 83
MAXFIELD Charles Evans ix 88 Charles William ix 88 Edwin Rogers ix 88 Ellen Scriven Evans ix 88 Howard Hoyt ix 88 John F 88 John Gillen ix 88 John Guion

ix 88 Joseph B ix 88 Mary Elizabeth ix 88
MAY Ann 89 Charles A 89 Eliza Jane Thompson 89 Frederick T 89 Frederick Thompson 88 George F 89 John A 89 Mary 89 Mary Gray 89 Richard C 89 Thomas M 89
MAYHAM T C Rev 64 150
MAYS Alice Stell 90 Edmond 89 Estella 89
McCANDLESS Albert 199 David 90 219 220 David 199 George 199 Harriet 74 John 90 199 Mary Place 90 Robert v 90 190 198 199 219 220 221 Robert Mrs 199 William 199
McCANN Daniel 91 James 91 James 91 John 91 Mary 91
McCARNAN Sarah 168
McCARTNEY P J Mrs 38
McCLAIN Mary 70
McCLAREN Eugene 14 Ida M 14 Kenneth W 14
McCLELLAN Gen 126
McCLINTOCK Ferdinand 91
McCLURE George Mrs 20
McCONNELL David Mrs 98
MCCOOK Gen 163
McCORMICK John 91 Margaret 91 Thomas 91 Thomas F 91 William 91
McCOTTER Douglass Grant 91
McCOY Sylvia 3 W H 199
McCREA John E 91
McCREEDY George B/D 92 George D 92 Jane 92 Louise 92 Patricia 92
McCUDDEN Andrew 9 James 91
McCUSTER M A Mrs 38
McDEDE Anthony 92 Anthony 92 Anson 92 Mary W 92
McDERMOTT Patrick 92

McDONALD Dennis 92 James E 92 John Rev 92 John F 92 Julia 92 Julia C 92
McDOWELL Josephine Timanus 176 Pauline 176 William O 176
McELROY Sarah 16
McFEATTERS Dale 249
McFEE Lillian 37
McGARRY Michael Mrs 151
McGLYNN Frank 92 John 92 John J 92 Mary 180 Nellie 92
McGRATH Edward J 92 John 92 William 92 William 92
McGUIRE James Mrs 95
McKENZIE Col 230 James H 199 242 243 James S 93
McKEON Christopher 93 Julia 93 Raymond 93
McKIERNAN John 93
McKISSICK J Rion 4
McLAUGHLIN R Mrs 61
McLEAN John J Mrs 33 Louis Mrs 171
McLEOD Catherine 177 John V 177 Neil Sr 177 Neil 177
McMICKLE Levi B Rev 60
McNAIR Thomas Mrs 170
McVICKER Bessie 93 Charles P 93 John L 93 Louis E 93 Louis J 93 Mary 93 Mary A Longstreet 93
MEACHEM Enoch Rev 60
MEAD Arthur E 94 Benjamin C 94 Clara L 94 Joseph T 93 Tamaseen L Keller 94
MEADE Gen 136 231
MEEKER Ellis R 94 Fannie Gilbert 94 John J 94 Jonathan M 94 Jonathan Magie 99 Jonathan M Rev 94 Julia Hicks 94 Mary B 99 S Merchant 94 Theodore F 94 William H 94 William H Capt 152

MELICK William R 199
MENDELL Lillie B 199 Mary F
Randolph 199 W W 199
MENGE Adolphe 27 Charles 27
John 27 Louise C 27 Lydia E 27
Mary 27 William McKinley 27
MENNET Overton H 200 251
253 254 257 259
MERGENS Edward Mrs 22
MERRILL F G Rev 28
MERRICK Albert 95 George 95
Louis 95
MERRITT Gen 105
MERSHON Mary 29
MERWEDE Sadie 152
MESCH Elizabeth 165
MESSIG Mrs 76
MESSING Louis Mrs 169
MESSMORE Florence Helen 175
Isaac 175
MEYER Jacob 95
MIDDLEDORF Peter Mrs 15
MIDDLETON John Mrs 29
MIER Carl Mrs 34
MILBURN Sarah 179
MILDER Watson Mrs 42
MILES Gen Nelson A 141
MILLER Arnold 96 Assalon 224
Catherine 98 Catherine
Coddington 96 Charles 95
Edward 96 Evelyn 182 Fred 95
Frederick 95 George 95 Gottlieb
95 Henry 96 Jacob 95 James 96
John 95 96 John Lewis 96 Joseph
95 Lewis 96 Louis 95 Louis Mrs
166 Mary 56 Mary E 200 223 224
Max Mr & Mrs 190 Smith 96
William 96 William H 45 96
William H Jr 96
MILLS Cecil R 97 Ella Louise 97
Emory James 97 Marion 97
Robert 97 Washington "Washy"

v 210 221 222
MINARD Duane 8 Sarah T 8
MINGUS Barbara 97
George W 97 98 Harriet L 97 98
Henry H 32 97 98 Martha M 97 98
William H 97 98
MISKA Catherine Miller 98
Herman O P 98 Peter Mrs 44
MITCHELL Annie A 180 200
C S Mr & Mrs 200 Charles L 180
200 Emma Bragg 180 200 James
98 John 180 John B 200
Marguerite 200 Mary 98 180 Mary
E 200 Robert M 98 Walter 98
William 98 William J 180
MOFFETT Elmore Drake 99
MOLYNEAUX T Stuart Rev 82
MONEYHAM William 99
MONOHAN James Mrs 17
MOONEY F C Rev 18 George A
Mrs 43 J A Mrs 96
MOORE Charles Mrs 118 208
261 Gov 197 Charles H 118
George W 99 Isabelle Mrs 16 J E
Mrs 42 John E 99 Joseph Mrs 98
Martha G 53 Mary 85 Miss 48 P
W Mrs 67 Robert W 99 Samuel L
Sr 66 Samuel L 85 Samuel S 15 38
William H 18
MORGAN Brockholst Rev 112
127 Charles Mrs 52
MORGENSEN Fam 48
MORHART Adam Mrs 72
Frederick Mrs 15
MORLEY Henry Mrs 154
MORRIS Louis 160 Mary
Elizabeth 160 "Ninna" 185
"Shadow" 185 Thomas "Uncle
Jeff" Jefferson 185
MORRISON Ella D 99 James H
99 John Mrs 125
MORSE Amos Capt 99 Mabel I

M 99 Mary B Meeker 99
William Mulford 99 William M
Mrs 94
MORSS S B Mrs 104
MORTON Hosea Quimby 200
MOTT H W Mrs 168
MOUNT Gilbert Mr & Mrs 101
Miss 101
MRAVLAG Cordelia B Stimers
245 246 Victor 245
MUECK Emil 100 Margaret 100
Otto 100 Otto F 100
MUIR Frederick 100 Louise
Lehleiter 100 William Frederick
100 William W 100 Philip 100
MULFORD Emma 80 Howard 46
J L 224 Percy Mrs 85 Robert A
80 Warren 46 William 10
MULHEARN Frank Mrs 73
MULLIGAN James Capt 11
MUNN Francis W 100 Mary
Emily Kent 100
MUNSON Lt 231
MURPHY Bernard 201 Bernard
101 Bridget 201 223 Francis 201
James 101 James B 101 John 101
Lillian 101 Thomas 101
MURRAY Annie 101 __Forsyth
Mrs 101 Nicholas Rev Dr 10
Samuel 101 Samuel 101 William
101
MUTCHIE Capt 159
MYER Charles L 101__Mount
Mrs 101 Peter B 101
MYERS John D Mrs 187

NAEBOR Andrew 102 Arthur
102 Daniel 102 Frank 102 James
102 John 102 Joseph 102
NAYLOR John H "Buck" 102
NEAL Edward 102 John 102
William T 102

NEALON James 174 John J 174
NEEFUS David 102 David 102 H
W 102 James 102 William H Mrs
145
NEFF L F Mrs 176
NEGLEY William 201
NEILL Anna 102 Edward K 102
Edwin W 102 John 102 Thomas J
102
NELSON Georgianna 126 Lillia
106 Oley 201 204
NESBITT David 199 John David
199
NEVELING John W G Rev 146
NEVINS Cmdr M 149
NEVIUS Henry N 103
NEWBURY E S E Capt 168 201
NEWCOMB Helen M 19 Thomas
19
NEWELL William A 78
NEWLIN Alfred E 201
NEWSOME John Mrs 153 John
H Mrs 105
NEWTON Isaac N 240
NICHOLS Arthur L 103 Samuel
12 103
NIGHTENGALE Florence 223
NOE Noah S 103
NORMAN Richard A Mrs 85
NORRIS Benjamin H Mrs 42
Hampton Mrs 43
NORTH Joseph W 119
NORTON Adams 201 Henry L 2
123 201 207 Henry L Mrs 1
Herbert 207 Lincoln 201 John T
58 Ralph 201

OAKES Thomas Mrs x 88
OAKLEY Bronson K 202 John B
Mr & Mrs 202 Joseph Mrs 18
O'BRIEN Burke Gen 202 250
Charles Mrs 35

O'CONNELL Timothy 173
O'CONNOR James Mrs 162
O'DONNELL C Mrs 38 Cardinal 172 Charles Rev 172 Hugh Rev 172
OESE Victor 103
OGDEN James C 103 John 103
O'HEARN Michael Mrs 7
O'KEEFE Daniel 103 Emily 22
OLDEN Charles S 70
OLINGER Frederick Mrs 159
OLIPHANT Estelle 173 Thomas 172
OLIVER C R Mrs 159 Ella W 104 Emma 7 Joseph Brown 104
O'NEILL Benjamin Mrs 101 Rev Fr 180
OPIE David B 104 Eliza Gould 104 Isaac Vorhees 104
ORD Gen 86
O'ROURKE Col 105
OSGOOD Clifford Mrs 121
O'SULLIVAN Daniel 105 Dennis L 105 James 105 Patrick 105 Petronilla 105 William D 105
OSWALD Edwin H Mrs 3
OTIS Elwell Stephen 105
OW Alexander 105 Mattie E 105

PABST Grace 123 Lillian 123 William Mrs 123
PACKARD Algernon Sidney 107 Catherine Ann Angus 107 108 D N Mr & Mrs 107 David 107 Ebenezer J iii Edwin J 107 Elizabeth Clary 107 Emma 107 Fannie G Denison 106 107 Frank B 107 Hosea iii Hosea S iii Ida 107 Mary Elizabeth 107 Joseph Clary 106 107 108 Joseph White 107 108 Leslie F 107 Margaret C 107 Marie C 107 Nathaniel

Rawson 107 R W Mr & Mrs 107 Robert 106 Robert W Jr 107 Roxanna Holmes iii William C 107
PADIANS Thomas Rev 51
PAIGE R H 210
PALMER A J Rev v 202 224 225
PANGBORN Edward 108 William 29
PARCIS E N Mrs 83
PARKER Amy T 108 185 J H Mrs 63 James A 108 185 Joel 186
PARKIN Paul G 109
PARSONS Charles B 202 George 166 James K 257
PARTRIDGE M C Mrs 170
PARVIN B O Rev 148
PATTENCOON Warren Chapl 106
PATTERSON (?) Florence 179
PAUL James Robert 203 253 254 256
PAYTON Thomas 109
PEEPLES Thomas Winston 109
PEER Jacob Mrs 145
PENDER William F Mrs 95
PENDLETON Anna L 109 Arthur T 109 Arthur T Mrs 140 Edmunt 140 James L 109 Sallie Ann Pendleton 109 Samuel Heisler 109
PENNINGTON James O 110
PENNY Annie Elizabeth 140
PERRINE Bertha 90 Ida 180
PERRY Cmdr 170 E L Mrs 2 James H Col 160
PERTY Emma 105
PETERSON Thomas L Mrs 129
PFISTER Jacques Mrs 144
PHARES E W Mrs 150
PHILLIPS Elizabeth Buford 177 James A 177 William R 203 261

PICKENS Alfred H Mrs 23
PIERCE Elizabeth 85
PIERSON Ann 110 Charles W 110 David Capt 10 Henry W 110 Joseph 110
PINGRY John H Rev Dr DD 175
PITCAIRN John M 110 John M 7
PITMAN Anne de Miller 111 J R 111 John 111 John R 111 John T 111 Joseph Livingston 111
PLACE Mary 90
PLEASANTON Gen 139
PLUM Flora 111 Frank H 111 George Jr 111 George 3RD 111 George M 111 143 Oscar Mrs 148 Roger Nelson 111
POCKMAN Rev Dr 96
POLLARD Robert M 194 203
PONTIN Elmer 112 Frederick H 112 Frederick Henry 112 Frederick G 112 Henry B 112 Herbert L 112 Mary J 112
POOL Augustus G 17
PORAPP Albert 112 William 112 William 112
PORTER E A Mrs 142 John W 203
POST William Mr & Mrs 106 107
POTTER Catherine 112 Erastus E 112 Esther Burgess 112 Henrietta N Himes 112 Henry Landon 113 Julia 112 Stephen Hazard 112 William Mrs 146
POWELL Elizabeth 113 Stephen A 113 Stephen H 113 William H 113
POYSHER Jonah P 177 Mary F Headley 177 VETS 177
PRESCHER Albert Mrs 71
PRICE Daniel 113 260 George W 113 Sydney 114 Thomas H 80

PRIESTLY Ralph 5
PRINK Jacob 114
PROTT Frederick Mrs 169
PROUT Amanda Goslee 114 Curtis 114 Elizabeth Page 114 Eloise Willett 114 Henry B 114 Henry Goslee 114 John W 115 Timothy 114 William 114
PROVOST W W 115
PUGH Alexander L 115 Harry W 115 Sarah Wooley Johnson 115 Washington S 115
PUTERBAUCH Mary 82
PUTNAM Benjamin Parker 115 James H 115
PYLE Eliza 203 223

QUIEN Louis 118
QUILTY James Mrs 91
QUIMBY E A Rev 107 180
QUINN Mary M 180 Stephen J 180

RAMSEY R S 203 253
RANDOLPH George W F 116 Hannah 43 Mary F 199 Mary T 155 William H Sr 116 William H 116
RANKIN William H 50
RATH Charles 203
RAU Gertrude E 89
RAWLINS John A Gen 163
REA Frank 116 James 116 Richard 116 Robert 116
READING John 116
RECK Ernest Mrs 127
REDDY Daniel F 116
REED L T Mrs 46 John Mrs 29
REESE Charles D 116 Franklin E 116 Samuel Widdows 116 Sherman E 116
REEVE Mr 52

REGAN George 117 John 117
Thomas 117
REGETHAL Ernest Mrs 176
REID Ann 117 H M 117 Hugh
117 John 117
REISS George J Mrs 72
REITCHMYER James H 118
RENZI 230
REYNOLDS Capt 103 F J 203
Forman J 118 George 244 245
RHABANUS Rev Fr 63
RHODES Ann Schardien 118
George H 118 Georgia 118
Nathan C 119
RICE John S 250
RICHARDS Alfred H 119
Rebecca 173 Wallace 119
RICHTERS Frederick J 120 G
Frederick 120 J Charles 120
Percy W 120
RICKETTS George Robert Ashe
120 John K 120 Laura Virginia
Ring 120 Maud de Peyster 120
Philip B 120
RIEFENSTAHL William F 120
RIEHL Charles G 177 Eckman
177 John S 177
RIKER Abram Sr 120 David Jr
120
RINDELL Anthony C 120
Charles R 120 John G 120 Mary E
Conklin 120 Miss 16 Robert 16
RINEHART O C Mrs 156
RING Laura Virginia 120
RITTER Augustus N 179 J Peter
Capt 90 James H P 179 Marion
179 Marjorie 179 Mary 179
Ralph F 179 Rosamond B 179
Virginia 179
RIVERS Ed 265
ROARKE John Mrs 79
ROBERTS Edward 121 Edward

L 121 Emma Van Wart 121
James 121 James L 121 Percy 121
Perry 121 Thomas 121 William
121 William H Mr & Mrs 121
William H Jr 121
ROBINSON Benjamin D 203
Dennis 177 Eliza E 177 George
177 Hathaway 121 Henry F 121
Ichabod 173 James E 178 John
B/V 177 John Benjamin 186
Julius A 122 Kate M 9 Marie
87 Mary Halsey 173 Oscar 177
Preston 173 Raymond Mrs 92
Sadie 178 William 177
ROBSON James Joseph 122
ROBUS Irene 20
ROCKETT Thomas P 122
ROE William H Mrs 112
ROGERS Arthur 122 Charles E
122 Peter F 122 William Mrs 73
William Y 122
ROLL Jonathan S 123 Joseph H
123
ROLLINSON Mary Guion ix 88
ROOLVINK Catherine 123
Elizabeth 123 Gerard 123
Godfrey 123 John 123 Louise
123 Mary 123
ROPES George H 123 202
RORAY Louis 203
ROSE Charles J 203 253 Frank B
123 H R Rev 33
ROSS James 123 John 124
Samuel 34 William H 124
ROUSCH John 124
ROWE Hannah 178 Matthew
178
ROWLAND Charles 124 John R
124
ROXFORD H H Mrs 34
RUBECK William 178
RUDRAUFF Albert 124 John 124

John H 124 Julia 124 Mary
Matilda 124
RUGG Calvin H 124
RUHE C H William 204
RUNYON Carroll T 125 E O
Mrs 94 Enos 125 Francis 125
Nelson 125 Theodore 125
Theodore I 125 Wilhelmina Trow
125 William N 125
RUSH Jacob 204 260
RUSHTON Harry 9
RUSS Charles Edwin Mrs 162
Harriet 162 Stanley 162
RUSSELL Gen 229 Gordon M
Rev 163 Maj 126 Rose 210 223
224 Washington 204 Washington
R 125 William G 125
RUSSUM Thomas F Mrs 22
RUTHERFORD Peter 204
RYAN Mayor 88
RYBERG John Wesley 126
RYDER Alanson 126 Henry G
126 Margaret 126
RYERSON Abraham 204

SADLER Wilbur F 193
SAGE Edmund 126 VET 126
SANBORN Alex 178 George H v
126 178 Halstead 126 Joseph
Warren 127 Mr 225 Ross H 178
Sarah A 178
SANDS William Mrs 76
SANFORD Delia 127 J Horace
127 Joseph A 127 Mary Elizabeth
127 William A 127
SARISTE Louis J Capt 153
SAUER Allan F 85 Harry C 85
Leonard 127 William A Mrs 85
SAXER Paul Mrs 37
SAYERS George A 186
SCHAIBLE Adam 127 Charles
127 Christian 127 Jacob 127 Mary

127 Michael 127 William 127
SCHARDIEN Anna 118 Harold
119 John 119 John A 118
SCHATZMAN A G Rev 28
SCHECKLER Howard T 35
SCHENCK Ferdinand 211
SCHETZER Lawrence Mr & Mrs
133 Lawrence Mrs 132 William
133
SCHLEIMER Abraham Mrs 83
SCHLICHTER Charles H 128
Frederick 127
SCHMIDT Charles H 128 Fred
Mrs 121 Frederick Jr Mr & Mrs
121 Henry Mrs 26 27 Katherine
128
SCHNEIDER Adolphe G 128
August 128 H A 128
SCHOLL Frances 3
SCHOLLEY Bobbie Cmdr 248
SCHRAYER Daniel 128
SCHREIBER William Mrs 122
SCHUBLE George F Mrs 51
SCHUMANN Madeline 61
SCHURZ Carl Maj Gen 128
SCHUYLER Pieterse 180
SCHWARZ Herman E 128
SCHWINDINGER George 76
SCOTT George H 129 Henry C
129 James M Mrs 74 John W
129 Reuben E 129 Winfield Gen
5 89 206
SCRIMSHAW Mabel 47
SEABRING Ann 178 Philip 178
SEAMAN Phebe 162
SEARING Margaret 173
SEARNS George 172
SEBRING Catherine 178 James
A MacDaniel 178 John S 129
William Sr 178
SEDGWICK Gen 228
SEELY Anne 178 Edith Van

Hook 178 Fred C 178 Fred L 178
James P 178 Uriah 178 Uriah 178
William Hopping 178 204
William H Jr 178
SEIGEL Franz Gen 119 Maj Gen 128
SEVERS Charles Henry 129
SEWARD George H 204
SEXTON E B Mrs 131
SEYMOUR Laura 138 Thomas H 129
SHAFFER George A 129 130 John 129 130 John 130
SHAILER Maj 93
SHARKEY Bernard Mrs 64
SHARP Christian L "Uncle Chris" 204
SHAY Sarah 161
SHEBBEARD George R 130
SHEEDY Clara 199
SHEELY W C 251
SHEERAN William Mrs 19
SHEPPARD Jacob W 110
SHERIDAN Gen 123 146 229 230 PM 15 Phil 202 William Mrs 51
SHIMCALL Miss 8 R C Rev Dr 8
SHOEMAKER H L Mrs 121
SHOTWELL Abram R Mrs 111 Lydia 164 Robert 111
SHUMWAY Capt 229 230
SICKES Daniel Gen 104 119
SICKLES Daniel Gen 104 Gen 167 D E Maj Gen 208
SIESS Henry Mrs 71
SIGEL Gen 146
SILKWORTH John Mrs 166
SIMS Winfield Scott 130
SIMMONDS Newton M Rev 130 S Bartlett 130
SIMMONS Gertrude 118 John H 186
SIMONS Sampson S 205
SIMPSON C W Mrs 156
SINCLAIR J T Mrs 67
SLATER Adele 143
SLAVIN Joseph J 131 Hugh H Sr 130 Hugh H Jr 131 Vincent DeP 131
SLEEPER Henry Hale Rev Dr 133 172
SMITH Andrew Jackson 186 Anna 133 Annie R 133 Caruth 187 Charles Mrs 17 Clarence 179 Cornelia C 28 David 80 Douglas 174 Elias Darby 131 Elijah K 131 Frank A Rev 15 Frank K 131 Frank Wesley Mrs 174 Rev 15 George iii George F 132 Gilbert 132 133 Hannah iii Helen H 131 Herbert S S 131 Hilda W 131 Howard W 131 James Jr 113 Joel Brewster 133 John Capt 107 John J 131 Jules K 131 Julia Kellogg 131 Kezia P Martin 131 Louise 133 Mamie C Mrs 9 Martha 110 Mary 133 Michael 133 Michael Sir 64 Nellie 80 Ogden 131 R B Rev 183 Riohard 174 Richard Mrs 181 Sarah Mather 21 Sarah Milburn 179 Spencer 205 Thomas 133 Thomas H 110 W Percy 131 Walter O 131 William Bishop 179 William J 179 William H 133 William M 110 Zacheus 133
SNOW Clark v 205 226 227 Nathan C 133
SNOWDEN Howard Mrs 49
SNYDER Anna 133 Harold 133 William Mrs 73 Winfield Scott 133
SOFIELD Wilson E Mrs 94
SOLDEN Jonathan 205

291

SOMMER Charles Richard 134
SOPER A Mrs 31
SORENSON Ida 16
SORTOR Charles Mrs 7
SOVEREIGN G E Mrs 156
SPANGER John 2
SPARGO John H Mrs 12
SPARKS George Mrs 5
SPARKES Elizabeth 176
SPAULDING Charlotte King 134 E W134 Isaac 134 Isaac David 134 Jacob 134 John 134
SPENCER Capt 154
SPENCES Sarah 28
SPICER Charles 135 Frederick 135 Harriet F 135 Harry 135 Isaac 135 William 135 William S 135
SPINK Capt 183
SPRINGER George Mrs 34
SQUIER A W 135 John Winans 135 Mary Maxwell Johnson 135 Sarah Burnett 135 Theodore A 135 227 Theodore Eugene v 135 227
STAMETS Cyrus 205
STANFORD Theodore F Mrs 59
STANLEY Explorer 114
STANTON Sec 168
STARK J S Rev 184
STEEDMAN Gen 162
STEELE W A 205
STEELMAN Mathias Mrs 77
STEIN Anthony 136
STELL Alice 90
STEPHENS Richard 124 205
STEVENS L Mrs 150
STEVENSON Mary Elizabeth 21
STEWARD H 42 Rev Dr 184
STILES A W Mrs 92 James C Sr Mrs 135 James E Mrs 150
STILL Charles R 136 187
STIMERS Alban Crocker 205 240 241 245 246 247 248 Cordelia B 245 Mr 246
STINE Bernard L 136 Helen 136 James P 136 Peter 136 William E 136
STINSON George B 205
STOCKTON Martha 133
STODDER Louis N Capt 205 234 235 240 241
STOLL Charles Mrs 115
STONE G Dwight v 110 136 137 207 227 228 229 230 231 Raymond Mrs 139
STOUT Charles Mrs 148 E Mr & Mrs 56 Elijah Mrs 56 Katherine 56 Roy Mrs 58
STRADIVARIUS Antonius 211
STRAHAN William Mrs 172
STRATEMEYER Kidd 123 M H Mrs 153 Maurice H Mr & Mrs 123
STRAUSS Daniel 138 David 138 Edward 138 Lewis 138
STREEP William Mrs 61
STRICKFUSS Adelaide 178
STRINGHAM Emma 158
STRUCK Charles 138 George 33 Henry 33 138 Joseph 138 Joseph Mrs 33 William G 138
STRYKER E E Mrs 67 William S 138
STUCHELL W T Rev 60 95
STUDER A C 138 A G Maj 138 August H 138 Elizabeth 138 J A Rev 138 William 138
SULLIVAN George C Mrs 105 James T Mrs 131
SURRATT Mrs 24
SUYDAM Charles Crooke 139 Eliza Gracie 139 Eliza Gracie Halsey 139 Emily Halsey 139

SWAIN Robert 139
SWANN M J Mrs 152
SWEENY Albert R 179 Elmer E 179 Florence Patterson 179 Harold J Rev 119 179 John Thomas 179 Stella A 179 Thomas 179
SWEET George H 206
SWIFT Allan Rev 161
SYERS William Mrs 48
SYMONDS George Mrs 143
SYNEAR Elizabeth 148
SYRON Abigail 140 Matthew V 140 Nathaniel 140

TAIT Maj 162
TALIAFERRO Annie Elizabeth Penny 140 Clarence Harcourt 140 Edmund Pendleton 140 Elizabeth Octavia 140 Felix Taylor 140 Felix Taylor 140 Samuel Penny 140
TANTUM Laura 140 John R 140 Joseph K 140
TAPPEN Harry Mrs 49
TAYLOR Frank 140 George W Col 19 Johnson 206 Martha 53 Thomas 187 243 W H Rev 184 William K/H 140
TAYNOR N Mrs 31
TENCH Arthur W 206
TEN EYCK Mary 66
TERRILL Edward Mrs 60 S C Mrs 33 Susan Fisher 141 William E 141
TERRY Gen 86 George W Mrs 126
TERSTEGEN Matilda 54
THAMES Travis B Rev 49 101 147
THAYER Alice 99
THOMAS Catherine A 141 Cornelia F 107 George W 141 James Provost Mrs 47 W F Mr & Mrs 106 107 W W 195 William Mrs 106
THOMPSON Abram 210 Edward "Uncle Ed" 210 Eliza Jane 89 Frank 142 Henry B 163 Hugh Smith __ 142 Jacob 142 James 142 John 211 John D 142 Joseph 142 Mary 95 142 Sally Ann Ward 142 Walter Mrs 133 William 142 William 142
THONAN Levi E 142
THORN Albert 142 Catherine B 143 Edwin 142 Fred Mrs 143 Isaac 143 Linton Roscoe 143 Louis 143 Thompson 143 Virginia Lounsbury 143
THORNTON Edith M 143 Louis N 143 Marion H 143 Samuel P 143 W Hildreth 143 William H 143
TIER Carol 144 Edward 128 Ethel 144 Frank P T 144 James Edward 144 Walter E 144
TILDEN Thomas W 145
TILLEY William 60
TILLOU Edward L 202 207
TIMANUS Caroline Marsh 176 Henry 176 Josephine 76
TIMBROOK Ellen Sanford Walker 145 Lydia 145 Madison 145 Marion 145 Richard 145 Samuel A 145
TINGLEY Isaac S Lt 150 Katherine Wescott 179 Philo B 179
TINSMAN George W 145
TODD Gov 134 Henry H Capt v 127 146 231 L W 207
TOMLINSON Paul G Mrs 114 Rev Dr 6 44 48 81 177

TOMPKINS Charles 77 Mrs 77
TOOKER Joanna 179 John K
146 Nathan C 146 Sam 180 Sam
146
TOWN Samuel P 146
TOWNLEY Charles L 180
Clifford Mrs 71 Cordelia D 174
Dewitt 146 Edward G 58
Elizabeth Cooper 147 Ester 146
George R 146 George R Mrs 69
H C Rev 173 J Hervie 174 John
Magie 147 Jonathan 147 Jonathan
Capt 164 Maria 146 Margaret A
173 Margaret Adeline 180 Mary
E 180 Richard 147 Robert W 180
Sarah W Walker 180 Theodore
146 William E 180 William E
180
TOWNSEND S W Rev 26
TOWSON Emory S Mrs 67
TRAFTIN John Mrs 47
TRAFTON John E 147 John T
48
TRAHON Vet 147 William H
147
TRAINOR Thomas 147
TRAPP Lawrence 147
TRASH "Uncle" Mark 265 Rev
265
TRAUMAN Hattie 54
TREADWELL Edna 182
TREMBLEY Ellen F 147 John
148
TRIMBLE Arthur Nelson 148
Arthur Nelson Mrs 49 Margaret
148 May Irene 148 Thomas R 148
Thomas R Jr 148 William H 148
TRIMER Harvey G 148
TROW Wilhelmina 125
TROWBRIDGE Frank Mrs 33
TRUEX Col 60
TRUIT J P Mrs 164

TRUSCOTT Peter 249
TRUSSLER George J 148 Justus
D 148
TUCKER Charles C 148 Evelyn
34 Freeman 148 Gertrude 34
Nathan C 148 Stephen Mrs 34
Theodore M 149 ___ Wilson 148
TUFTS John M Mrs 149 Philip E
149
TULLY Walter S 137 207
TUNISON Edward Mrs 79
Frederick L 149 Samuel 149
William Sr 149 William Jr 149
TURNER Edward A 187
Elizabeth 87 Henry 150 James
Randolph 150 John T 150 Joseph
87 Louis F 150 Marguerite G 150
May 87 Nathaniel 187 William
Franklin 150

UMBER George Mrs 95
UPTON Gen 229 Mary C 207
223
URMSTON Alpheus G 150
Daniel Garthwaite 150 Frank 150
Fred W 150 J J 150 John 150
Joseph W 150 Louise 150
Thomas 150

VAIL Joseph 229
VALENTINE J W Mrs 180
VAN ARSDALE F D Mrs 89
Frank D Jr 89 Frederick T 89
VAN CLINE Rosa E 186
VAN DEVENTER Evelyn 171
VAN FLEET Annie 151 Gulager
151 Hart Irving 151 Hart S 151 J
Oscar 151 James Oscar 151
VAN HART John Mrs 176
VAN HAUSEN Frederick Mrs
124
VAN HOOK Edith 178

VAN HORN D Rev 200
VAN HOUTEN Alice 42
VAN KIRK Peter 207
VAN PELT Catherine Ann 152
Charlotte E 152 David H 151 152
Isaac Mrs 37 Jeremiah 152
Jeremiah 152 John A 176 John
H 151 John H 151 152 John W 35
152
VAN RAALTE A C Rev 155
VAN WART Emma 121 Isaac
121
VANDENBURG Arthur H 251
VANDERHORST J F Rev 183
VANDERVEER George H Mrs
179 Lois 179
VANDERWATER Joseph Mrs
113
VANSANT Leo Mrs 179 Roger
179
VAREY Edwin 88
VASSAR Thomas Rev Dr xi 88
VERMU(E)LE Charles Mrs 42
43
VERSTIG Richard A Mrs 128
VICK J O Rev 184
VINCENT Anthony H 152
VOLK Charles P 152 Frank 152
Franziska 152 Margaret 152 Peter
152 Philip 152 William 152
VOLLMER Charles G 152
Edward F 152 Frederick P 152
Franziska Volk 152 Henry J 152
John M 152 Louis 152 Louisa
152
VON BRANDIS Frederick 180
Herman M 180 Marie 180
Philipine 180
VON KUMMER Henry 180
Frederick H 180 Marie Von
Brandis 180 Udo 180 VET 180
VORHEES Anna L 162

VOSSELLER James 99
VOUGHT George S Mr & Mrs
107
VREELAND Eva 170

W S Rev 71
WADDLES Mary 14
WADE Mary 29
WAGNER Louis 153
WAGSTAFF James C Mrs 141
WAHL Frank C 153
WALKER Adeline M 180
Charles 180 Ellen Sanford 145
Gen 113 Sarah W 180 Solomon
Mrs 183 Thomas E 153
WALLACE Martha E 170 Mary
Nellie 170 Turner 170
WALLER Julia 197
WALPOLE Robert 154 Samuel
154
WALTER F E Mrs 72
WARD Florence 154 Frank 154
James 154 John 154 Marcus 26
Sally Ann 142 W B Mrs 176
William H Mrs 170
WARDELL Sarah B 135
WARNER Frances 46 Jefferson T
154 Mary E Mitchell 180 Silas C
180
WARNOCK Charles 155 James
A 155 James Alexander 154
Mary J 155
WARREN Charles Mrs 155
WASHINGTON Caruth Smith
187 George 135 185 Gertrude
185 W N 207
WATERBURY Charles S 155
WATERMAN Charles 99 George
99 William 99
WATERS Catherine J Laren 155
Israel B 155 Robert Mrs 32
WATSON Aldwyn 155 Catherine

155 George A Mrs 30 George W
155 John F 155 Mary M 207
223 Thomas 155 William H 155
WEAVER John W 155 John W
155 Peter V 155
WEBB E A Mrs 25
WEBBER John J N 240
WEBER Charles 156 Frank 156
Frederick 156 George Mrs 57
Henry M 156 John P 156 Mary
156
WEBSTER Emma 49
WEDDELL William 207
WEEDEN Gilbert Mrs 161
WEEKS Everett A Mrs 139
WEINGART Oscar Mrs 101
WELCH Edward Mrs 95
Edward S Mrs 96 J E Mrs 162
WELCOME Fred Mrs 95
WELDEN Frank E 156
William H 156 William H Jr 156
WELSH John Mrs 38
WENKE Charles Mrs 44
WENKIE George H 29
WELLS W H "Bill" 156
WERTHERS Frederick Capt 153
WERTS George T 25
WESCOTT James P 178
Katherine 179 S E 207
WESTBROOK Zerah S 156
WESTERVELT Elsie 166
William 157
WESTLAKE Sylvanus F 157
WESTON Edward Payson 157
WHEELER John Richard 157
Thomas Theodore Mrs 135
WHEELWRIGHT G/C Edward
158 George 158 Louis 158
WHELAN Capt John 19 72 92
Capt John H 92 Isaac P Rev 180
John 180 John W 180 Joseph 180
Mary McGlynn 180 Mrs 92

William J 15 38 180
WHITAKER William Force Rev
DD 10 28
WHITE Nicholas Van Sant 158
WHITEHEAD Donald L 167 K
W Mrs 167
WHITING William Mrs 3
WHITMAN S B Mrs 129 Walt
223
WHITNEY Eben 158 Emma
Stringham 158 James M 222 John
J 158 Miss 222 Samuel L 158
William H 158
WHITTENACK Mrs 20
WIGGONS Albert D 216
WILBOURNE John Mrs 151
WILDING Rev Dr 19 101
WILDMAN Ira R 193 207 253
WILEY James T 15
WILKE Frederick 159
Henry 159 Henry 159 Otto E 159
WILKINS Alfred 159 Arthur 159
Arthur S Mrs 17 Delair 159
Everett R 159 Isaac 159
WILKINSON Albert 159 Frank
A 159
WILLARD Edward Carey Mrs
163
WILLETT Eloise 114
WILLIAMS Aaron Mrs 112
Adolphe 159 Alberta 129 130
Anna 112 Anna L Vorhees 162
Charles 159 Charles J 211
Charles T 159 Clifford 162
Daniel 160 David T 159 Eliza
Norton Haskell 22 Frank Mrs 129
Fred 162 Frederick 159 G Henry
162 George Tracey Mrs 22
George W 160 Harry W 160
James 207 209 James 161 James
H 180 Jarvis W v 160 231 232
John (Alberta) Mrs 130 John H

161 L D 160 Joseph 161 Joseph S
162 Lillie 162 Luther 161 Mabel
162 Mary Elizabeth Morris 160
Mary Jarvis 160 Nellie 161 Percy
159 Phebe Seaman 162 Ray F 159
Sadie M 180 Seaman 162 Susan
Jane 180 Whited 161 William 161
William 162 William H 161 162
WILLIAMSON Angus McIntosh
117 Ann 117 Harriet J Hopson
162 Peter S 162 Stanley 162
WILLSEY Andrew J 163
WILLSIE Etta J 163 Henry 163
Henry E 163
WILSON A J 170 A McD Mrs
191 Allan 164 Edith 163 Frederick
163 George Mrs 90 140 Herbert
163 J A 170 J W Mrs 143 James
A 163 James Capt 38 39 148
James Harrison 163 John F 164
John Warren 164 Mary Mrs 151
Matthew 164 Vet 163 Virginia 90
WILTKAMP Linus Mrs 133
WINANS Aaron 164 Amie 164
Elias Crane 164 Edward P 164
Frederick Shotwell 164 Lydia
Shotwell 164 Nathan 164
WINGERT Henry W 158 232
233
WINGROVE Charles 207
WINSLOW Jacob 208 261
WINTERS William 164
WITTEMAN Adam 181 Anna M
181 Frederick 181 Henrietta
Elizabeth 181
WODEY Augustus F 165
WOLF George 165 208
Georgette 165 Marguerite 165
WOLTERS Charles Henry 165
Elizabeth Mesch 165 Henry 65
Jacob 165 Julius 165
WOOD Bertha C Beck 208

Charles 187 Charles J Rev 168
Henry 187 Henry C 181 Lorenzo
D 208 Sarah M Anderson 181
William 187
WOODARD Walton 165
WOODHOUSE John Henry 165
WOODRING Harry H 256 257
WOODRUFF A Edward 5 9 18
25 26 28 30 53 54 63 90 95 115
157 166 188 189 191 195 196 197
198 199 201 204 205 208 Amos
166 Amos 166 Belcher 29 C C
Rev 42 115 Enos 41 Henry C 166
James Mrs 17 James W Col 101
Noah Ogden 208 261 262 263 264
Ogden 101 Rachael 166 Valentine
166 W J Mrs 145
WOODEN A Mrs 84
WOODWORTH Harry G 40
WORDEN John Lorimer 235 237
240 241
WORMAN Harvey Mrs 74
WORTS Henry Nelson 166
William E 166
WRAIGHT Anna S 146
WREDER J P Mrs 136
WRIGHT Albert 166 Charles F
166 Charles F Jr 166 Edgar 9
Edgar B Mrs 9 George S 41
Harold B Capt 166 James 166
Mary 166 Mrs 40 Wilbur 166
William H Mrs 19 William P 167
Winifred 9
WRIGHTSTONE G D 209
WYMS James N 167

YESS E E Mrs 152
YOUNG Eli 118 Charles D Mrs
171 Ferdinand 207 209
YOUNGKINS Egbert Mrs 151
YOUNGLOVE Gertrude
Langdon 167 Herbert B 167 John

167 168 201 <u>John</u> Col 168
YORK Adelaide Lavender 74

ZBICK Jim 4 213
ZBINDEN Harry Mrs 34
ZEISS Melissa A 181 William N 181
ZIMMERMAN Albert 169 E 6 Frank 168 H A Mrs 6 Harry 168 <u>Henry</u> 168 Henry 169 Jacob 168 Louis 169 Mary 6 Otto 169 Otto Mrs 87 Sarah 6 Sarah McCarnan 168 William Sr 169 <u>William</u> 168 169
ZINGLER George Mrs 44
ZOOK <u>John M</u> 169

and her mn would be on the same page.

INDEX GUIDE

Last names are listed alphabetically, as are 1st names in a grouping. Members of the military are underlined. Ranks and titles are not usually used, except for a VET's CO, and religious leaders. The most famous leaders of the time, such as Lincoln, Grant and Lee were not extracted, nor names of military leaders when mentioned in a campaign, such as the Burnside Expedition. If a person's 1st name is not given, Mr, Mrs, etc, is used. If a w is mentioned with the 1st name of her h, Mrs is used. Otherwise, Mrs or Miss is not used with a female 1st name. When the mn of a w is given, or the name strongly indicated it is a mn, she appears under both names. A m dau is listed under her m name, since that

ABOUT THE AUTHOR

HARRY GEORGE WOODWORTH

I was born in Brockton, MA, 59 years ago. About 15 years ago I became curious about my Woodworth and Packard heritage. In 1989 I gave myself a Christmas gift by finding my g-g-grandfather Packard in "History of Bridgewater," with his lineage numbered back to my original 1638 Packard immigrant, who settled only a matter of miles from where I grew up. My Woodworth research finally led me to publish Woodworth genealogies and to my original 1630's Woodworth immigrant. Much of this research was in Canada, since I found out I had 5 generations in Nova Scotia.

I was also originally curious about my "recent" known Irish, Danish and Lithuanian immigrants, of which research added German and Swedish. My family legend of Indian ancestry, now known not to be in my direct Woodworth and Packard lines, led to investigating the wives. They have not revealed First American ancestry yet, but have revealed Mayflower and Royal ancestry. All has led me to membership in many genealogical organizations and Historical Societies.

I became a member of the Plymouth Co. (MA) Genealogists, Inc. of which I wrote and co-authored articles, and have submitted enough material to the newsletter to have my own occasional section, "Harry's Corner." I was accepted into the Society of Mayflower Descendants after rigorous investigation requiring primary proof. I am a member of, and have written for, the Packard & Allied Family Association, the Kings Co. (Nova Scotia) Historical Society, the Burlington Co. (NJ) HS, the Ancient & Honorable Artillery Company of MA, by right of descent, the Balzekas Museum of Lithuanian Culture, the Old Colony (MA) HS, life member, and the New England Historic Genealogical Society. This is the first book I have authored, and the first of a planned series.

I have worked for the Federal government for nearly 38 years, the last 23 with the National Weather Service, currently as a forecaster with the Mount Holly, NJ, warning and forecast office, one duty of which is the Tsunami Focal Point. I investigate the possibility of East Coast tsunamis and tsunami-like waves and submit the material to the experts for analysis. A Special Edition of East Coast tsunamis and tsunami-like waves was published in September 2002, in the International Tsunami Journal, and much of my original work, on the Mt. Holly web site as well, was used, with credit given to me, and reference to the web site. Two earthquakes induced events in the NYC and Philadelphia area were recognized as official tsunamis.

Genealogical research trying to uncover those elusive ancestors proved valuable when trying to uncover those elusive East Coast tsunamis!

www.ingramcontent.com/pod-product-compliance
Lightning Source LLC
Chambersburg PA
CBHW060943230426
43665CB00015B/2043